# Sharing Best Practices in Sport Marketing:

## The Sport Marketing Association's Inaugural Book of Papers

### Edited and Selected from the Inaugural Conference, November, 2003

**Brenda G. Pitts, Editor**
Vice President for Academic Affairs
Sport Marketing Association, 2003-2006
Professor, Director, Sport Management Masters Program
Georgia State University

Fitness Information Technology
*A Division of the International
Center for Performance Excellence*

West Virginia University

Library of Congress Card Catalog Number: 2004110849

ISBN: 1885693524

Cover design: 40 West Studios
Copyeditor: Geoff Fuller
Proofreader: Julie Burrell
Production Editor: Geoffrey C. Fuller
Typeset by 40 West Studios
Printed by Data Reproductions
Printed in the United States of America

10 9 8 7 6 5 4 3 2 1

Fitness Information Technology
262 Coliseum, WVU-PE
P.O. Box 6116
Morgantown, WV 26506-6116

800.477.4348 (toll free)
304.293.6888 (phone)
304.293.6658 (fax)
Email: fit@fitinfotech.com
Web Site: www.fitinfotech.com

# Table of Contents

# A WORD FROM THE
## ASSOCIATION

# Sport Marketing President

It is with tremendous pleasure that I share the enclosed contents drawn from more than eighty research presentations delivered at the Inaugural Sport Marketing Association Conference hosted by the University of Florida, November 13-15, 2003. This project is one of several SMA Scholarship Initiatives intended to provide SMA membership with mediums for generating as well as showcasing scholarship significant to achieving the Association's mission, which is a commitment to sharing best practices in sport marketing.

As revealed within the following pages, SMA member scholarly presentations included in the Inaugural Conference agenda addressed a plethora of contemporary issues resulting in unique, sport-related challenges for marketing managers. Scholarly products on subject matter such as corporate sponsorship, sport consumer behavior, sport product branding, and infusing technology into the promotion and sales process—all of critical importance to those in pursuit of the "best sport marketing practice"—were delivered and included in this publication.

In closing, it is critically important to acknowledge the magnificent efforts of all contributing authors, Dr. Brenda Pitts, Editor and SMA Vice President for Academic Affairs, and Dr. Gregg Bennett, 2003 SMA Conference Chair.

Richard Irwin

# Sharing Best Practices in Sport Marketing: Contemporary Sport Marketing Research

**BRENDA G. PITTS**

As an academic area of study, sport marketing has come a long way in a short period of time. I'll show my age here, but it wasn't that long ago (okay, it was nearly 20 years ago) that I was teaching the first sport marketing course at the University of Louisville with no sport marketing textbook—there were none! As I'm sure many of us did, I used foundational texts in marketing to develop my materials and the course. That was in 1984. As time went by and I had nearly 300 pages of handouts, a student said, "Dr. Pitts, you've got enough handouts for a book. Why don't you write one?" And I did. It took a few years, but it was finally published with co-author Dr. David Stotlar in 1996 and it gave me and many others a real textbook in sport marketing to use for teaching our classes. Since then, more textbooks have been written and published and, today, the professor teaching sport marketing has a choice of several.

Our research in sport marketing has grown in a similar manner. When many of us started conducting research in sport marketing, there were no sport marketing journals. We struggled with finding venues for sharing, disseminating, and publishing our works. We all cheered when the first journal in sport marketing, the *Sport Marketing Quarterly*, was started, just over a decade ago. During that decade, two more sport marketing journals were established (one of which ceased production just a few years ago). The journals have been a most welcome addition to the field because they have provided needed publication venues for sport marketing research, thus allowing us to take the body of knowledge to another level.

Finally, the last piece of the puzzle has been established: an academic association with the goal of furthering the study and practice of sport marketing and attempting to meet both the academic and the industry professional. Ideas for an association have been bandied about and even written about by many of us for several years (Mahony & Pitts, 1998). In the development of sport management, each of the content areas will grow through the addition of textbooks, journals, organizations and associations, scholarly books, and conferences. I believe and predict that each sport management content area, such as sport marketing, will expand in the same manner. For instance, I expect to one day see journals, associations, and conferences focused on one of the many sport marketing topical areas, such as sponsorship, pricing, competitive advantage, promotions, and advertising.

The Sport Marketing Association has been established and is the first of many to come. Initial planning for the organization occurred in October, 2002, and the inaugural conference was held in November, 2003. The conference brought together sport marketing professors, students, practitioners, and other individuals interested in sport marketing. Each year, the SMA will sponsor a conference so that we can get together to share our ideas, work, research, and business cards with academicians, scholars, students, practitioners, and other individuals interested in sport marketing.

## The Inaugural Book of Papers

This book of papers from the conference establishes yet another valuable venue for the dissemination of our work in sport marketing. It is another first for our field. SMA plans to publish the presentations from the conference each year as an extra product of the conference. Many thanks are extended to Andy Ostrow, owner of Fitness Information Technology, Inc. (FIT), the publisher of this book and the *Sport Marketing Quarterly,* for his generosity in publishing this book as part of the partnering relationship between FIT and SMA.

## The Papers in this Inaugural Edition

This book provides a needed additional venue for the dissemination of sport marketing research. The papers in this inaugural edition are a welcome addition to the development of the body of knowledge in sport marketing. The papers are divided into sections with similar topical content. In the first section, the authors André Richelieu, Daryl Wirakartakusumah, and Soonhwan Lee provide relevant information on building brand in relation to professional sports team properties. In the second section, authors Steven McClung, Robin Hardin, Michael J. Mondello, Larry G. Neale, Arno Scharl, and Jamie Murphy provide important and interesting information concerning the internet and sports. In the third section, Vassilis Dalakas, Gregory Rose, James Zarick, James Grant, Kathryn Dobie, John Fortunato, Angela Dunnam, and myself provide contemporary research involving the ever-present and multibillion dollar sport sponsorship industry. The topics include negotiation, diverse markets, fan identification, and value. Finally, in the last section, research on consumer behavior in the sport business industry is brought to us by several authors who present such topics as sports consumers with disabilities, attitude theory, member retention, culture, and consumer satisfaction. Those authors include Larry Allen, Gary Robb, Edward Hamilton, Dan Drane, Dan Funk, Mark Pritchard, Doris Lu, Brenda Pitts, Melissa Morgan, Jane Summers, Larry Neale, Troy Georgiu, Sharon Purchase, James Zhang, Dale Pease, Dennis Smith, Kenneth Wall, Christopher Saffici, Lori Pennington-Gray, and Daniel Connaughton.

# In Appreciation

Finally, I want to say thank you to a few individuals whose help with this project was very important. First, I want to thank Andy Ostrow at FIT. Andy and FIT have been instrumental in helping develop the general field of sport management and the specific topical area of sport marketing. FIT publishes the *Sport Management Library,* which has produced several textbooks that were the first of their kind. FIT also publishes the *Sport Marketing Quarterly,* one of the most important journals in sport marketing today. And finally, Andy's willingness to sponsor the Sport Marketing Association conference, conference materials, and this book is significant and appreciated by everyone. Second, I want to thank my graduate assistant, Stephen Rosner, for his hard work in helping me with records and materials for the conference abstracts and for the book. He spent many hours managing the databases for me. And, as he plans to go on from Georgia State University to obtain a doctorate in sport management and become a professor, I wish him all the best. Lastly, I want to thank the reviewers. Their hard work in reviewing for the conference helped make the program an incredible one.

Now, enjoy the book.

Dr. Brenda G. Pitts

### Reference Cited

Mahony, D. F., & Pitts, B. G. (1998). Research outlets in sport marketing: The need for increased specialization. *Journal of Sport Management, 12,* 259-272.

# PART I
# BUILDING BRAND:
# SPORT MARKETING EXPANSION STRATEGIES

# CHAPTER 1

# A New Brand World for Sports Teams

ANDRE RICHELIEU

Manchester United, Real Madrid, the New York Yankees, the Dallas Cowboys, and the Chicago Bulls. These professional sports teams, among others, have established themselves throughout the years as a reference in their respective sports, going beyond local recognition to gaining, in some instances, worldwide popularity. In fact, we could argue that these teams can no longer be considered as mere sports teams; they are also brands in their own right (Bobby, 2002; Shannon, 1999).

> **Manchester United, Real Madrid, the New York Yankees, the Dallas Cowboys, and the Chicago Bulls: We could argue that these teams can no longer be considered as mere sports teams; they are also brands in their own right.**

In this regard, the purpose of our research is to study how a professional sports team can position itself as a brand and leverage its brand equity. But why should a professional sports team try to become a brand in the first place?

In this paper, which is the result of our investigations of professional sports teams in Europe and in North America, we shall try to identify the main factors a sports team can exploit in order to become a brand and reinforce its brand image in the eyes of fans. These factors shall be referred to as *catalyst factors*. Furthermore, we shall identify the main obstacles encountered in the establishment of a team as a brand. These shall be called *constraining factors*. Also, moderating variables will be presented. But more important, we shall propose a framework for building the brand equity of a sports team. In other words, we will introduce the process through which a sports team can build and leverage its brand.

The conceptualization of how a team can develop its brand could have both theoretical and practical applications. First, theoretical studies on the topic are still relatively limited (Desbordes, 2000). Second, professional teams are in need of some guidelines in the context of sports merging with the entertainment and communications industries (*Sport Business Group*, 2002a). Third, brand is now

> **Truly, teams have had the potential to become brands heretofore, but it is only recently that sports teams seem to have started to capitalize on the opportunity.**

part of the vocabulary and strategic mindset of sports teams' managers, at least of the most visionary ones, as we shall see. Truly, teams have had the potential to become brands heretofore, but it is only recently that sports teams seem to have started to capitalize on the opportunity.

With this idea in mind, we will start by introducing the notion of brand. Second, we will answer the question of why a sports team should become a brand. Third, we will present how a sports team can become a brand and which variables can help or hinder the development of brand equity by professional sports teams. We will end our presentation with a recap of the key points. The paper will follow the structure of a hockey game.

## The Pre-Game Show: What Is a Brand?

A brand is "a name, a word, a sign, a symbol, a drawing, or a combination of these, which aims at identifying the goods and services of a company and differentiates them from the competitors" (Kotler, Filiatrault & Turner, 2000, p. 478). Truly, a brand has both marketing and accounting value for a company, but here, we will specifically focus on the former.

> **Successful brands are able to quickly establish a strong emotional and personal relationship with the customer, and thus, potentially trigger trust and loyalty toward the brand**

A brand is a differentiating asset for a company (Kapferer, 2001). Through its brand, a firm creates and manages customers' expectations. As such, brand image and brand quality are intertwined and instrumental in developing a successful brand (Cateora & Graham, 2001). Successful brands are able to quickly establish a strong emotional and personal relationship with the customer, and thus, potentially trigger trust and loyalty toward the brand (De Chernatony, 2001) (Figure 1). For this reason, companies that own strong brands are trying to focus the customer's attention on their brand image.

Figure 1 **What Is a Brand?**

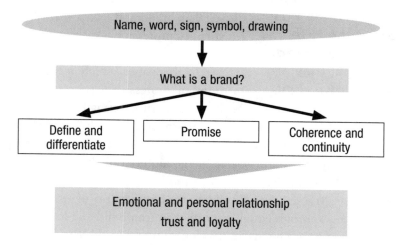

As Bedbury & Fenichell (2002) underline it, a company needs to have a brand that evokes trust from the customers and will inspire, rather than just inform, through advertising and marketing. The brand should create an environment that supports the fulfillment of customer expectations, in the message and in the product (Haynes, Lackman & Guskey, 1999). A brand is a promise a company makes to its customers, and this promise is built on the coherence and continuity of the brand's products (Kapferer, 2001). For instance, no matter where I drink a Coca-Cola, it should have the same great taste (coherence). Furthermore, the Coca-Cola that I drink today is as good as the one I had yesterday and as good as the one I will drink tomorrow (continuity).

According to Fanning (1999), there are two golden rules of successful brands:
i) continuous innovation; and ii) telling the story of a company's brands. Continuous innovation is done in order to take into account the taste of customers and also to stay ahead of the competition by anticipating change. Telling the story of a company's brands means underlying the core values of the brands and adapting them according to changes in public taste. Well-managed brands are continually telling stories about themselves. Combining branding and innovation can help boost a brand, like Apple did with the introduction of the iMac desktop computer. This initiative helped revive the Apple brand and sell six million desktop computers in four years (Mazur, 2002).

Some authors have developed the notion of *concept brands*, which offer visions, attitudes, convictions, motivations, and not necessarily intrinsic quality or improvements (Rijkenberg, 2002). Rather than defining a market segment and then trying to satisfy the particular needs of that segment, concept brands arise from emerging social and cultural trends. Richard Branson, the founder of Virgin, likes to say that what he sells is "a way of life" in order to justify the array of activities his company is involved with (Rijkenberg, 2002; Travis & Branson, 2000).

> **A brand is a promise a company makes to its customers, and this promise is built on the coherence and continuity of the brand's products. No matter where I drink a Coca-Cola, it should have the same great taste (coherence). Furthermore, the Coca-Cola that I drink today is as good as the one I had yesterday and as good as the one I will drink tomorrow (continuity).**

> **Well-managed brands are continually telling stories about themselves. Telling the story of a company's brands means underlying the core values of the brands and adapting them according to changes in public taste.**

## The Official Face-Off: Why Is My Team a Brand?

Companies have been using branding to develop a strong and enduring relationship with customers since the pre-industrial age (Kotler, Filiatrault & Turner, 2000). A relatively recent trend has seen the emergence of brand strategy as a tool for professional sports teams, so that they could nurture the relationship they have with their fans and leverage their brand asset (Cavanagh, 2001; King, 1999; Passikoff, 2000; *Sport Business Group,* 2002a).

In fact, with the exception of movie stars and singers, teams generate a stronger emotional response from their fans than in any other industry (*Future Brand,* 2002). Unfortunately, this potential emotional attachment is still underexploited by sports teams. It is only since the mid-1990s that sports teams have started working on leveraging their brand equity, and still relatively few teams seem proactive in this regard. As an executive from Manchester United stated:

> Everything is in the brand... We must think in terms of products in order to develop the company. The brand is the team, its logo, the red shirt, the players, the story; it is everything related to Manchester United. It is a precious asset in developing the business (*France 2 Télévision,* 2002).

As a matter of fact, becoming a brand can enable a sports team to position itself against other teams and entertainment offers in the market (Figure 2). This is becoming increasingly important, because sports teams are battling for the entertainment money of customers against other leisure alternatives, such as festivals, movies, restaurants, camping, traveling, etc. So why should the customers spend their time and money on a sports team?

This brings us to the next point: Beyond the value the team represents to the customers, a strong brand can help the team capitalize on the emotional attachment with the fans, in order to instil trust and trigger fan loyalty. In return, this trust and loyalty can help the sports team generate additional revenues through the sale of a variety of goods and services, within and beyond the sports arena (Gustafson, 2001; Figure 2). Indeed strong brands in sports are able to make the customers live the brand at different moments of their daily life: They live their sports team and the respective brand, just like customers who wear Levi's and not another brand of jeans, and others who drink Coca-Cola and not Pepsi (or vice versa).

> **Strong brands in sports are able to make the customers live the brand at different moments of their daily life: They live their sports team and the respective brand, just like customers who wear Levi's and not another brand of jeans, and others who drink Coca-Cola and not Pepsi (or vice versa).**

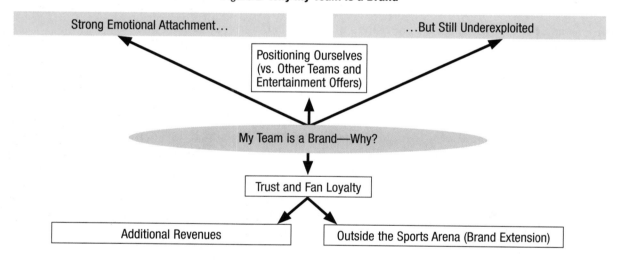

Figure 2 **Why My Team Is a Brand**

For instance, the Glasgow Celtic soccer club (2003) initially started with traditional products, such as replicas, training kits, and gifts. It has now gone into fashion wear, even branded pies and sausages. The Celtic has three stores in Ireland and makes more money from merchandise than from TV rights and sponsorship combined (Worsley, 2001).

Another example of building brand equity through brand extension is the Girondins de Bordeaux soccer team in France. The Girondins de Bordeaux (2003) soccer team has five different brands: the game brand (Adidas Collection), a sportswear brand sold in superstores (Club Collection), a leisure brand (Girondins Sport Collection), an upscale brand (Scapulaire Collection), and a brand that has products associated with their Portuguese star, Pauleta (Pauleta Collection).

### Battling Along the Boards: How My Team Can Become a Brand

In Figure 3, we propose a framework for building the brand equity of professional sports teams. This framework is a result of our investigations of professional sports teams, based on a review of the literature and interviews with sports managers in Europe and in North America[1], to see how these teams are working to build their brand equity. There are three steps that lead to brand equity: i) defining the identity of the sports team; ii) positioning the sports team in the market; and iii) developing a brand strategy. We shall elaborate on each of these components.

Figure 3  **A Framework for Building Sports Teams' Brand Equity**

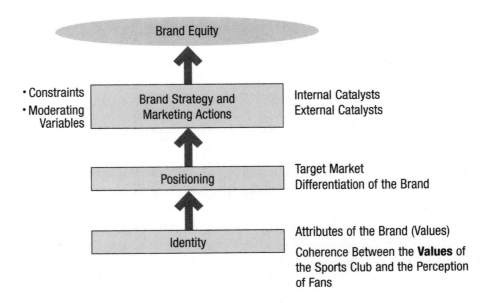

## Defining the Identity of the Sports Team

There are two main elements included in the identity of the sports team: the attributes of the team and the value the team represents to its fans.

First, the attributes refer to the values of the team and what the team stands for. In other words, what does the team want to be associated with and recognized for: simplicity, reliability, ambition, innovation, modernity, conviviality, solidarity, fighting spirit, etc.? These values give a strong meaning to the team, while providing a direction to the brand. The values of a team are the starting point in defining a long-term brand strategy for the sports team (Kashani, 1995).

In this regard, the history of a team and its presence in the community can be an asset. Top sports brands have been located in their respective cities for an extended period of time, which helps establish the brand over time (*Future Brand*, 2002). As a result, the team becomes part of the social, economic, and cultural landscape of the city, even the region it is in: Juventus of Turin, Newcastle United, the Toronto Maple Leafs, and the Boston Celtic are examples. Thus, the team is able to trigger emotional value and psychological proximity with its fans (Kapferer, 2001). We mentioned earlier that telling the story helps emphasize the values of a company in the eyes of the customers (Mazur, 2002). This applies also to professional sports teams.

Second, once the values of the team are defined, it is important to see what they mean to the fans. Indeed, the values of the team must be translated into a clear message, one that underlines the benefits of the brand for the customers, in order to trigger the buying decision. This is referred to as the *value proposition* (Kashani, 1995) or *value creation*. The benefits can be tangible, as in a cell phone, for

[1] Montréal Alouettes, Ottawa Senators, Toronto Maple Leafs, Vancouver Canucks; Girondins de Bordeaux, Lille Olympique Sporting Club, Olympique de Marseille, RC Lens: We deliberately didn't want to limit the examples given in this paper to these teams.

instance, which is compact, portable, reliable, and provides autonomy, offers email and other applications at a reasonable cost. But in the case of a sports team, the benefits are mostly intangible or emotional. And because the benefits are emotional, it is even more important to nurture the flame by replenishing the *emotional bank account*. This will help maintain the sense of belonging of the fans to the team, as well as the trust and loyalty of the fans toward the brand. You do exactly the opposite with repeated fire sales and mismanagement, which affect the trust of the fans and dilute the brand.

Moreover, without compatibility between the vision of the managers and the perception of the fans in relation to the values of the team and the value proposition, there is an incoherence that hinders any further development of the brand by the team (Figure 3). Thus, it is important for teams to ensure that what they believe they stand for is understood in the same way by their fans. That is why teams that we interviewed tend to do surveys at the end of the season, but also throughout the season in order to measure the image of the team in their community.

## Positioning the Sports Team

The positioning of the sports team relates to two elements: the selection of market segment(s) and the differentiation of the brand on the market.

First, defining the market segment(s) means that the sports team will identify the customers that are supposedly the most sensitive to the value proposition of the team. These customers represent the target market for the future development of the brand (Kashani, 1995). In the case of a sports team, these potential customers include

1. The fans that go see the games and follow the team's performance very closely;

2. Those (die hard) customers who take their passion of the team beyond the playing field and are willing to buy Manchester United ketchup (Bobby, 2002) or Toronto Maple Leafs (2003) B-B-Q sauce, take a driving lesson with Olympique Lyonnais Conduite (Le Monde, 2002) or drink the Racing Club de Lens milk (L'Équipe, 2000);

3. Those who relate to the team outside of the sports arena because the team's brand has been represented by a popular singer or actor. A case in point is the New York Yankees, whose variety of colorful hats and models have been promoted following a concert given by a rap singer who wore a red Yankees cap that night. Now, New Era, the official supplier of major league baseball's game caps, produces New York Yankees hats in an array of colors in order to fulfill the demand of young consumers who relate to the rap singers as much as they do with the team. And in fact, Yankees hats can be found worldwide;

4. Those who follow the team from a distance and are willing to show their association with the team in a more subtle way. That's why some sports teams, especially in Europe, have introduced lines of casual and everyday products, from jean shirts to dress shirts and ties, where the logo of the team is visible but elegant. We made reference to the Girondins de Bordeaux (2003) and the Glasgow Celtic (2003) earlier, but the Real Madrid (2003), and both Major League Baseball (2003) and National Hockey League (2003) clubs are also good examples.

Second, the differentiation of the brand on the market means that the sports team tries to underline how its brand is unique and why the customers should buy it, instead of another brand, either from a rival sports team or from a company outside of the sports arena. If the team is able to show and sell the uniqueness of its brand, it can provide the team with a powerful position on the market. Strong brands are indeed able to generate trust and loyalty from their customers and reinforce the emotional and personal relationship with their fans (De Chernatony, 2001; Kapferer, 2001; see Figure 1). Hence, these customers are less willing to be tempted to buy another brand.

We should mention that both the identity and the positioning of the sports team contribute to the strategic construction of the brand, which provides the foundations for the brand strategy of the team (Kashani, 1995; Figure 3).

A case in point is the French soccer team, Lille Olympique Sporting Club (LOSC). Following a market research, the team identified four key values the fans wanted the club to promote: fighting spirit, solidarity, conviviality, and modernity, which are displayed on the LOSC website (2003) (Figure 4). Both the fighting spirit and solidarity are considered to be acquired by the team and refer to the playing field. Indeed, LOSC is looking for players who are hard-workers (fighting spirit) and team players (solidarity). The LOSC management deliberately refuses to hire good players that are known for not espousing these two values.

Moreover, conviviality refers to the interaction between the team and its fans, and the involvement of the players in their community. The management believes it has some work to do in this regard, even though some initiatives have already been launched. For example, LOSC sponsors youth soccer teams in the Lille region, which play with a LOSC badge on their jersey. This can potentially trigger the sense of belonging to the team among young customers who can become LOSC fans, if they are not already, and remain fans for years to come.

Finally, modernity relates to the construction of a new soccer stadium in downtown Lille. In fact, the team plays in an old and relatively small stadium (Grimonprez-Jooris, 23,000 seats). According to the research performed by the team, the fans expressed the wish of having a facility that will better reflect the image and the ambition of a modern French soccer team (LOSC, 2003). But it takes both the new stadium and the right management to build or strengthen the team's brand equity (Todd, 2003).

Figure 4 **Strategic Construction of the Brand: The LOSC Example**

| Fighting Spirit (Acquired) | | Solidarity (Acquired) |
| Conviviality (To be strengtherned) | | Modernity (To acquire) |

## Developing a Brand Strategy

Once the identity and the positioning are clearly determined, the sports team can move forward with its brand strategy, working on catalyst factors, while dealing with constraints and moderating variables (Figure 3 and Table 1). We intend to highlight some key variables that can help a team build and reinforce its brand equity and some that can prevent it from doing so.

Table 1 **Catalyst Factors, Constraints, and Moderating Variables**

| Catalyst Factors | Constraints and Moderating Variables |
|---|---|
| Internal catalyst factors | Constraints |
| **"FANS BONDING WITH THE TEAM"**<br><br>• Entertainment experience for the fans<br>• Team's involvement in its community<br>• Physical facilities<br><br>**MARKETING ACTIONS**<br><br>• On-field jerseys<br>• Sale of team's merchandise<br>• Players' management<br>• Promotional campaigns<br>• Commercial partnerships<br>• Customer relationship marketing programs (CRM) | **FASHION**<br><br>• Trend phenomenon<br>**DECREASE IN LOYALTY**<br><br>• Decrease in customer loyalty toward brands<br>• Less and less loyalty from the players toward their team<br>**LIFE CYCLE OF SPORTS LEAGUES**<br><br>• Maturity or decline phase of professional sports leagues<br>**GENERAL ENTERTAINMENT OFFERING**<br><br>• Competition from other entertainment alternatives |
| External catalyst factors | Moderating variables |
| **MARKET SIZE**<br><br>• Access to a large fan base and lucrative TV deals<br>**Industry changes**<br><br>• Merger of sports with the entertainment and communications industries<br>**TECHNOLOGICAL ADVANCES**<br><br>• Development of new means of communications | **LEGAL FRAMEWORK**<br><br>• Centralization in managing the league's brands<br>• Legal status of the team<br>**Finances**<br><br>• Resources of the team<br>**ON-FIELD PERFORMANCE**<br><br>• Winning! |

*Internal catalyst factors.* We define catalyst factors as variables that can help a professional sports team leverage its brand. Catalyst factors can be seen as a set of tools a team might use in order to establish itself as a brand and reinforce its brand image. Internal factors are usually under the control of or belong to the sports team. We will focus on two categories of internal catalysts: *fans bonding with the team and marketing actions.*

*Fans bonding with the team.* Inspired by the work of Underwood, Bond, and Baer (2001), this category emphasizes the experience the sports team provides to its fans. We structured this category around three variables: i) the entertainment experience, ii) the team's involvement in its community, and iii) the physical facilities of the sports team.

• Entertainment experience for the fans: Sharing the experience with other fans helps stimulate, increase, and nurture the sense of belonging of the fans to the team, and contributes to leveraging the sports team's brand (Underwood, Bond & Baer, 2001). A team can improve the group experience and leverage its brand by exploiting its entertainment appeal, such as at the Stade Vélodrome in Marseille. Going to a game becomes a unique experience, an event you enjoy yourself and with other fans, whose experience can influence your own experience (Desbordes, 2000). As the vice president marketing of the Montréal Alouettes football club said, "We create and sell emotions to the fans."

For example, rituals enhance the ambience of a game and help promote the game as an event. The more attractive the ritual, the more it can potentially enhance the brand. Examples include the Anaheim

Angels' (2003) Rally Monkey and the slogans fans from rival teams exchange in the bleachers at European soccer matches. In this instance, fans are both consumers and actors; being part of the event is a must from the standpoint of social actualization of the fans (Keyes, 1998).

As the vice president marketing of the Montréal Alouettes football club said, "We create and sell emotions to the fans."

The concept of entertainment could even take the form of alternate competitions, such as the *Premier 1 GP* (2003), where competing cars represent European soccer teams (Anderlecht, Benfica, Chelsea, Feyenoord, Leeds, Olympique Lyonnais, and Valencia). Such an initiative could help a team capitalize on synergies that exist between soccer and auto racing, soccer fans generally being auto-racing fans as well.

- The team's involvement in its community: When players participate in sports clinics, visit hospitals, sign autographs in a shopping mall, and tour the region in the team's caravan, they show some willingness to be part of the community. This increases the sympathy fans have for the players of their team, which can reinforce the identification of the fans to the team, their sense of belonging, and help the team go beyond its sports club status. To a certain extent, the sports team becomes a brand with a kind of social conscience:

> At a cost of more than $100,000 per season, Théodore [Montréal Canadiens' goaltender] rented a loge for three years... then donated its use to the Montréal Canadiens Children's Foundation. Every home game, four or five children are entertained here, treated to hockey and refreshments and delightfully spoiled with souvenirs to celebrate their night. (Stubbs, 2003, p. C1)

- Physical facilities: The stadium can become a mythical place over time, which creates a special ambience and helps trigger a unique attachment of the fans to the team. Wrigley Field in Chicago and Fenway Park in Boston are good examples (Clancy & Kelly, 2001). But a new stadium can also be associated with modernity and a refreshment of the brand, as the example of LOSC shows (Figure 4).

The stadium can become a mythical place over time, which creates a special ambience and helps trigger a unique attachment of the fans to the team. Wrigley Field in Chicago and Fenway Park in Boston are good examples.

Furthermore, a team can improve the group experience and leverage its brand by exploiting its entertainment appeal. For example, the Dallas Cowboys football team owns a golf course and has turned their stadium into a theme park. This shows the fans what the Dallas Cowboys product is all about: entertainment (King, 1999).

*Marketing actions.* This category encompasses six variables a team can trigger in order to leverage its brand: i) on-field jerseys, ii) sale of team's merchandise, iii) players' management, iv) promotional campaigns, v) commercial partnerships and vi) customer relationship management programs (CRM).

A team can improve the group experience and leverage its brand by exploiting its entertainment appeal. For example, the Dallas Cowboys football team owns a golf course and has turned their stadium into a theme park. This shows the fans what the Dallas Cowboys product is all about: entertainment.

- On-field jerseys: The attractiveness of the logos and colors worn by players is worth considering, as well as the brand of the jersey (Adidas, Nike, Puma, Umbro, etc.). Truly, the playing jersey or uniform is the most exposed product of the team. It is the team's trademark, and an excellent way to catch the attention of potential customers and leverage the team's brand beyond the hardcore fans. This is why more teams are redesigning their team jerseys with new colors (Edmonton Oilers, Colorado Avalanche, New York Islanders) or a modernized logo (Arsenal, Toronto Blue Jays).

In some cases, nostalgia favors the sale of replicas of older uniforms, which represents a stream of revenues for teams which face mounting pressures on income (Cavanagh, 2001), but also for companies such as Mitchell & Ness (*Major League Baseball*, 2003) or Toffs (2003). Furthermore, in 2003-2004, the National Hockey League (NHL) teams will wear white jerseys on the road and dark jerseys at home, as it used to be until the 1960s, in order to increase the sale of jerseys around the league.

• Sale of team's merchandise: Teams try to leverage the emotional attachment to their brand through licensing and merchandising, among others (*Future Brand,* 2002). A rationale for the licensor to license a product "is linked to brand extension and the enhancement of brand image and goodwill at a consumer level [almost] without having to develop, produce, or market a new product" (*Sport Business Group,* 2002a, p. 10). The success of merchandising can even be increased when pop stars or actors wear team gear, or when it is inserted in a movie (Heim, 2000).

Merchandise sales in Canada and the United States accounted for $3 billion in 2001. They represent 18% of the global sales for sports licensed products (*Sport Business Group,* 2002a). And the potential is high in North America and in the rest of the World, especially among teenagers who are avid consumers of licensed products (Parmar, 2002), but also among women. Said the vice president of marketing for the Ottawa Senators hockey club: "Some women are more enthusiastic than men in supporting their team."

> **Merchandise sales in Canada and the United States accounted for $3 billion in 2001. They represent 18% of the global sales for sports licensed products.**

However, merchandising goes beyond selling jerseys, caps, and bobbleheads: "In several sports, licensed [video] games are now generating more revenues than traditional forms of sponsorship and are catching up with the mega sums being paid for sports broadcasting rights" (Sport Business Group, 2002a, p. 15).

We could say that the sale of team's merchandise has a dual role: On the one hand, it definitely helps build brand equity for the team among customers; on the other hand, as the team increases its brand equity, fans buy more licensed merchandise (Bobby, 2002; Cavanagh, 2001).

• Players' management: Acquiring a star player can have a strong popular impact, draw support and enhance the brand (Bobby, 2002). In Europe, soccer teams started pursuing Asian players prior to the 2002 World Cup, in order to promote the sport and their team in a huge and fertile Asian market. In 2000, the AS Roma soccer club signed the Japanese star Nakata, and now more teams are willing to follow suit.

The same could be said, to some extent, of local players. Having on its roster a local player that has a certain reputation and has established himself on the field can help draw fan support and generate loyalty to the team. These players are also more inclined to be recognized by the community and become involved locally. For instance, French Canadian players are very important to the Montréal Canadiens hockey team, which now can count on José Théodore as their number one goaltender. Ever since he won two prestigious trophies in 2001-2002, Théodore appears in several commercials on television and has become a central figure in the Montréal Canadiens (2003) marketing campaign. This brings us to the next variable: promotional campaigns.

• Promotional campaigns: First, advertising campaigns can potentially leverage the brand by enhancing what makes its value. In the case of the Seattle Mariners baseball team, the ads underline the efforts players put in to win, despite having lost two of their superstars two years in a row: Ken Griffey Jr. and Alex Rodriguez (Buckman, 2000).

Second, we should consider the tours professional sports teams go on when promoting the sport and their team. For instance, in the summer of 2003, FC Barcelona will meet Juventus of Turin and Manchester United during exhibition games in the United States. The tour is part of an agreement with the National Football League (NFL) in order to promote and leverage the FC Barcelona brand (*Football 365*, 2002).

• Commercial partnerships: Two examples are the agreements between Manchester United and the New York Yankees on one hand, and AS Roma and the New York Yankees on the other. Under these agreements, teams promote one another, sell products from the partner's franchise in its team stores, broadcast each other's games and share information on player fitness, health and training. Teams that share similar brand equity could benefit from reinforcing each other, especially when they are not part of the same sport (*Team talk*, 2001).

Moreover, sports teams can create 'subsidiaries' abroad in order to strengthen their image and become a brand of reference in potentially lucrative markets. For instance, Ajax Amsterdam launched a new franchised soccer team in South Africa in 1999: the Ajax Cape Town (Browne, 1999). Newcastle United acquired a team called Hong Kong United, in order to compete against the commercial hegemony of Manchester United in Asia (*Sport Business Group*, 2002b).

Also, agreement with distributors should be considered. The Lille Olympique Sporting Club (LOSC, soccer) has an agreement with Auchan supermarkets, which sells LOSC merchandise across France. For the LOSC, this agreement is part of a marketing strategy in order to leverage its brand and position itself as a reference in France, and eventually in Europe (*La Voix du Nord*, 2001).

• Customer relationship management programs (CRM): CRM encompasses sales force automation, contact management, telemarketing, lead generation, advertising campaign management, and customer service (Waltner, 2000). First, teams collect detailed information about their fans' demographics and psychographics when fans apply for a loyalty team card or when a team conducts a standard survey. The San Francisco Giants were pioneers in this area in the nineties. Nowadays, teams from smaller (Ottawa Senators, hockey) and bigger (San Diego Padres, baseball) markets use this system. Second, sports teams can analyze the information and better market to their customers; they get the fans out to the game and buy their products. This enables teams to offer variable ticket pricing, depending on who is playing against the local team. The Toronto Raptors (2003) and the Vancouver Canucks (2003) have adopted this approach. Third, CRM helps sports teams generate sponsoring revenues in other areas. For example, the Nashville Predators hockey club found out that their fans' favorite participant sport is golf. This inspired the team to attract a local golf course to sponsor a direct mail initiative offering a free round of golf (Waltner, 2000). However, it should be pointed out that CRM programs can be very expensive to manage, and they provide information on the current fans, not on the potential ones. This is why the Ottawa Senators are actually revisiting their loyalty program.

*External catalyst factors.* External factors are environmental elements or factors that are not under the immediate control of the sports team. There are three categories of external catalysts: i) market size, ii) industry changes and iii) technological advances.

*Market size.* We will focus on the influence the fan base and TV deals have on the ability of a team to leverage its brand.

• Access to a large fan base and lucrative TV deals: Stronger media markets generally produce stronger brands and franchises (*Future Brand,* 2002). These franchises have indeed access to a larger fan base, lucrative TV deals and higher potential income from stadium operations. Following this reasoning too closely, though, small market teams could be condemned to anonymity, which is a very deterministic view. Indeed, the Green Bay Packers football team has managed to create brand value through a unique ownership structure, a winning record and quality merchandising (*Future Brand,* 2002). And the identification to the Green Bay Packers goes beyond North America, as Packers merchandise is popular in Europe, Asia, and South America.

At the same time, it is true that smaller market teams can feel cut off. But poor management seems to be more responsible for the problems encountered than market size, as the expected dissolution of the FC Malines soccer team in Belgium illustrates. Malines, now in a state of bankruptcy, was once the winner of a European Cup in the nineteen eighties (*Le Soir,* 2002).

*Industry changes.* Some connections are appearing among three industries: sports, entertainment, and communications.

• Merger of sports with the entertainment and communications industries: An increasing number of sports teams are now owned by communications and entertainment companies (Toronto Blue Jays, Paris Saint-Germain, etc.). Although convergence has been withheld by some companies, firms still try to take advantage of new synergies in order to leverage their brand (*Sport Business Group,* 2002a). Professional sports teams offer content to those who own the pipeline (TV, Internet, radio, etc.) or add content to those who already own some content. At the same time, teams should realize that they now compete with a number of entertainment offerings to attract customers and get the latter to spend their discretionary revenue.

For professional sports teams, this merger between three industries is an opportunity to exhibit the attributes of the brand and showcase them to a larger audience. An example is the exclusive contract the Réseau des Sports (RDS) has signed with the Montréal Canadiens hockey team for the 2002-2003 season. RDS is partly owned by one of Bell Canada Enterprise's (BCE) subsidiaries, Bell Globemedia Interactive; and BCE owns the arena where the Canadiens play their home games.

*Technological advances.* These advances bring new means of communication, such as the Internet.

• Development of new means of communication: The development of new means of communication opens new frontiers for professional sports teams. The Internet could bring a substantial increase in advertising revenues and electronic commerce with the sale of licensed products (Desbordes, 2000). A website can strengthen the relationship between a team and its fans, and create a larger community on a global level (*Inc.,* 2000). Unfortunately, the potential of the Internet still seems underexploited. A team website does not always provide the fans with real info, focusing instead on promotional material and merchandise. As a result of this, sports teams may be losing

**The development of new means of communication opens new frontiers for professional sports teams. Unfortunately, the potential of the Internet still seems underexploited. A team website does not always provide the fans with real info, focusing instead on promotional material and merchandise.**

hits and ultimately money, because if fans do not visit the site, advertisers will have no reason to advertise there (Dunleavy, 2000). Ideally, teams should move from a site that only provides information to one that can help build a virtual community with the fans, beyond their local market. Most of the professional teams seem to be in this transition phase.

*The constraining factors (constraints).* Constraining factors are variables that can stop or prevent a team from leveraging its brand. Constraining factors can be seen as obstacles in a team's pursuit to establish its brand. We have identified four categories of constraints: i) fashion, ii) decline in loyalty, iii) life cycle of sports leagues, and iv) the general entertainment offering.

*Fashion.* Customers do not always know why they buy what they buy, which can dilute the brand in the long run.

- Trend phenomenon: Though it can appear to be positive at the beginning, a fashion trend is very short lived (Kotler, Filiatrault & Turner, 2000). Once the trend is gone, what was once considered cool could become dull, especially when the success comes too fast and the team is unable to sustain its success on the field over time. As such, sports teams can become victims of their own success and should be careful in exploiting a fashion trend among customers, especially teenagers whose loyalty is extremely volatile (Parmar, 2002). Brands can be misused and recuperated by gangs, as is the case with some American sports teams (Los Angeles, Detroit).

*Decline in loyalty.* Players, but also fans, are showing signs of decreasing loyalty toward sports clubs. And generally speaking, there is a decline in customer loyalty toward brands.

- Decrease in customer loyalty toward brands: Customers seem to have less and less loyalty toward brands, moving from one product to the other very quickly and very often (Kotler, Filiatrault & Turner, 2000). At the same time, if a brand is not clearly established, people will buy it for the price or not at all (Clancy & Kelly, 2001). In the world of professional sports, fans seem to start taking their distance from both management and players (Burton & Howard, 1999), as fans grow tired of greedy battles between team owners and players' unions (Daley, 2003). This will become a challenge for professional teams, which try to build their brand and leverage it by exploiting the emotional attachment of fans, at a time when the emotional attachment of fans seems to be eroding.

> **It becomes difficult for the fans to associate with players that can be traded at any time or develop a committed relationship with a team that does not even keep its nucleus of players from one year to another. Less attachment means less loyalty, which in turn makes it more challenging for teams to leverage their brand.**

- Less and less loyalty from the players toward their team: Players are becoming less and less loyal to a team, because of the free agent phenomenon and skyrocketing salaries, but also because team owners freely trade players. The latter phenomenon is often expressed before the trading deadline when teams are making a late roster move for the post-season. It becomes difficult for the fans to associate with players that can be traded at any time or develop a committed relationship with a team that does not even keep its nucleus of players from one year to another. Less attachment means less loyalty, which in turn makes it more challenging for teams to leverage their brand (see Figure 1 and Figure 2). Fans want authentic players and authentic brands (Davis, 2002, p. 21): "credibility, integrity and honesty sell just as well as—if not better than—celebrity endorsements." That is a reason why professional sports teams try to get closer to their fans: through community involvement by the players as we mentioned earlier, but also, in some instances, by giving nicknames to their players (Vancouver Canucks, 2003).

*Life cycle of sports leagues.* We refer here to the maturity or decline phase of sports leagues.

• Maturity or decline phase of professional sports leagues: This is especially true in North America and transpires in the attendance and TV ratings steady decrease over the last few years: Since the 1994 strike, the attendance at Major League Baseball games has dropped steadily. In 2002 alone, the decrease was 6.3% (Godin, 2003). But in several European countries, TV rights dropped significantly as well in 2002, reducing the expected revenues of the teams and forcing the latter to get rid of pricey veterans, such as in the German Bundesliga. That's why professional sports leagues aim at increasing their visibility and expanding overseas. Major league baseball, for one, had regular games scheduled in Japan in March, 2003, and plans to play some games in Europe in 2004. And the NBA is now drafting Asian players, which increases the notoriety of the league as a whole and of some teams in the region.

*General entertainment offering.* As underlined earlier, a sports team must sometimes fight hard for the entertainment money of the customers.

• Competition from other entertainment alternatives: Because sports teams compete against other entertainment offers in a respective city, fans could be turned away by a lack of victories and chronic mismanagement. In such an environment, a sports team needs to position itself on the market and highlight the value it brings to the customers (see Figure 3). Otherwise, people will spend their entertainment dollars on activities that do not involve professional sports teams. This holds especially true in cities where customers have the choice among a wide variety of entertainment options (arts, sports, restaurants, etc.). Professional sports teams cannot take for granted the emotional attachment of the fans; it needs to be nurtured in time. As the vice president marketing of the Montréal Alouettes football team said, "You cannot betray the emotion of your fans. Otherwise, you alienate them, they go somewhere else, and they may never come back."

> **Professional sports teams cannot take for granted the emotional attachment of the fans; it needs to be nurtured in time. As the vice president marketing of the Montréal Alouettes football team said, "You cannot betray the emotion of your fans. Otherwise, you alienate them, they go somewhere else, and they may never come back."**

*"Moderating" variables.* Finally, we have identified three categories of moderating variables, aside from the other variables. They can help a team build and reinforce its brand equity, as much as they can hurt the team's brand equity or restrain its expansion: legal framework, finances, and on-field performance of the sports team. We refer to them as moderating variables because of i) the relative lack of control teams have on these variables and ii) the impact on brand equity that is both generally difficult to assess for sports teams and ambivalent.

*Legal framework.* We shall look at the mode of operation of the league and at the legal status of the team within the league.

• Centralization in managing the league's brands: For most North American professional sports teams, the league governing body oversees the marketing and protection of individual trademarks and products. Each officially licensed product bears the logo of the league, as a seal of approval.

One of the benefits of a centralized approach to licensing and merchandising is the preservation of the quality and uniformity of official merchandise around the world. This applies to the introduction of new jerseys: For instance, the Ottawa Senators' (2003) third jersey was approved by the league and before the beginning of the season, the team knows during which games the jersey will be worn.

Moreover, with this centralized approach, the revenues from merchandising are shared among the teams, which helps smaller market teams. This centralization provides homogeneity and strengthens the overall quality of the league in itself (Mullin, Hardy, & Sutton, 2000).

However, centralization in managing the league's brand handcuffs teams in their initiatives. For example, in the National Hockey League (NHL), teams can exploit their brand within a 75-mile radius of their local market. Outside of this area, the NHL controls the marketing initiatives and teams must associate with companies that are authorized NHL sponsors for any promotional campaign. As one vice president marketing of a Canadian hockey club told us,

> The NHL does not necessarily see the specificities of the markets. As a result, teams are not able to leverage the brand as they could. We believe we would benefit more if we had more control over merchandising, for instance. The team could build more loyalty and leverage the brand better.

For the vice president marketing of the Toronto Maple Leafs hockey club, "The geographical limits imposed on us by the league are a constraint. The same applies to the equal sharing of revenues among the 30 teams. Toronto could become the Real Madrid of hockey if we had more flexibility."

In Europe, trademarks are held and marketed by individual teams, and no single body oversees trademark portfolios. Consequently, if this gives more room to manoeuvre for sports teams, there is a risk of inconsistencies in registration and enforcement of the teams' brands (*Sport Business Group*, 2002a).

• Legal status of the team: In North America, professional sports teams are franchises. In other words, business people acquire the right to exploit a team and its brand from the league, but the team remains the property of the league. The advantage of this system is a more coherent image of the league and of the teams' brands (Tourret, 1992/1993). At the same time, franchises can be contracted or moved to another city for business purposes, which can alienate fans and threaten the integrity of both the sport and the league. The balance between business and ethics is sometimes difficult to find within this system.

In Europe, professional sports teams are increasingly being managed as companies, as showcased in England. In France, to better compete with teams from major European championships (England, Germany, Italy, and Spain), first division soccer teams are putting more pressure on the league to change the legal framework in relation with television rights, stadium lease, financing of the team, etc, which should give them more flexibility to leverage their brand equity (*Le Monde*, 2002).

*Finances.* The financial state of a team is important in enabling a club develop its brand equity. However, it is not enough.

• Resources of the team: Resources, especially financial ones, can tremendously help a team in establishing its brand. The New York Yankees are probably the most convincing example in North America, whereas Real Madrid is a good case in point in Europe. At the same time, the Oakland Athletics baseball club show that it is also how you spend your money that matters (*Future Brand*, 2002). And what about the Racing Club Lens soccer team, which has managed to preserve its well-known family spirit in a city of 300,000 people, while taking into account the demands of modern soccer?

Its budget is the equivalent of US$50 million, and 10% comes from the sale of licensed merchandise. The team also sells its milk in a region where the attachment to the region and to the soccer team runs deep in the heart of the fans (*L'Équipe*, 2000).

*On-field performance.* This category has different facets. It encompasses both winning and a winning tradition.

• Winning: People like to associate themselves with winners. A team that is competitive can help leverage its brand, especially in the case of teams that are younger or those that do not yet have a Stanley Cup or a World Series under the belt. They need to build a fan base and loyalty to the team: "The best sales tool any team has is a winning record… But teams can't always be winners" (Waltner, 2000, p. 113).

But there is more to it than winning: The style of play or the fight for survival of the team can trigger an attachment toward the club and its brand. The team becomes the underdog the fans like to follow. In 2002, the Montréal Expos and the Minnesota Twins generated some sympathy, which went crescendo in the case of the Twins, as the team qualified for the playoffs. Minnesota Twins merchandise became strongly visible even on the website of Major League Baseball (2003), which is an irony considering the league planned to contract the team prior to the start of the 2002 season.

In fact, we could say that the ideal would be to build enough of a strong brand to protect the team from the contingencies of on-field performances, at least in the short term. As a manager of Lille Olympique Sporting Club said during our interviews,

> One or two bad seasons can be forgiven, but more than that, it can alter the loyalty of the fans toward the team, harm the fan support and damage the brand image of the club. And if you relegate in Second Division, that could well be the point of no return, as fans throw the towel.

In the same vein, if you dilute the product with repeated fire sales, the message you send to the fan is that your product is not worth being bought. If the owners do not believe in their team, it becomes very difficult to ask the fans to associate themselves with the team and develop any emotional attachment and loyalty toward it. If there is little or no trust in a brand, the brand equity is very weak, as we showed in Figure 1.

## The Three Stars: From a Local to an International Brand

By exploiting the strong emotional relationship they have with their fans, which is quasi-unique to the sports industry, professional sports teams can build their brand equity in order to position themselves as brands in the market. With this idea in mind, we have developed a three-stage framework, i) starting with the identity of the team, ii) then building its positioning, before iii) developing and implementing a brand strategy.

In the discussion around brand strategy, we have looked at catalyst factors a team can exploit, while managing the various constraints and the moderating variables it may have to deal with. A certain emphasis has been put on marketing strategies and merchandising. However, we should note that a brand strategy goes beyond selling caps, jerseys, and memorabilia. Often do we see teams that start

> **An established brand can move the fans along the emotional continuum in order to increase their loyalty to the team. It is able to expand its customer base beyond its market of origin, at a regional, national, and even, in some cases, at the international level.**

working on their brand equity focus exclusively on merchandising; this approach is very limitative, as are its potential benefits. A brand strategy includes merchandising, but is not limited to the latter.

As the managers of the Vancouver Canucks hockey club mentioned to us, "We are looking to build a community brand that appeals to customers beyond our home market." Indeed, every solid brand is a community brand, in the sense that it binds together a pool of customers who share the values of the brand, live the brand and take possession of it. An established brand can move the fans along the emotional continuum in order to increase their loyalty to the team. It is able to expand its customer base beyond its market of origin, at a regional, national, and even, in some cases, at the international level (Figure 5). A global brand can be a mass international brand, such as Coca-Cola, IBM, or General Motors; they appeal to the mass market across countries. But a global brand can also be a niche brand that appeals to a very specific market segment across different countries, such as IKEA. Among international sports brands, some could be continental brands, starting to emerge as true international brands (Newcastle United), whereas others could be seen as true global brands (Real Madrid).

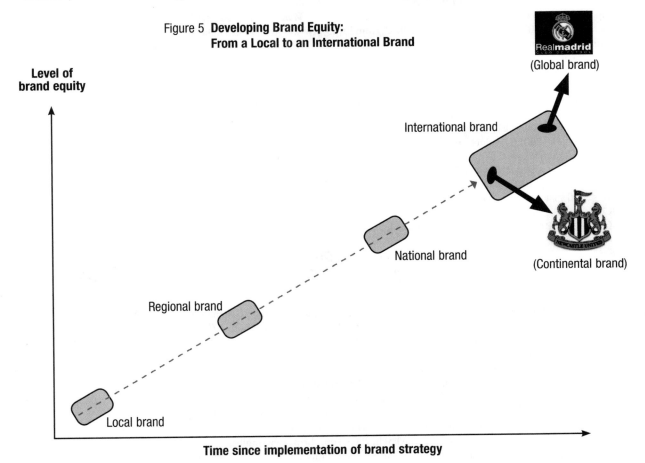

Figure 5 **Developing Brand Equity: From a Local to an International Brand**

If not every team can become a mass international brand, such as Manchester United or the New York Yankees, every sports team has the potential for building some brand equity. Even if the resources are limited, it is possible to conceive that a sports team could follow a niche strategy to expand its brand across markets, reaching to foreign customers based on its values (identity) and a shrewd positioning. Examples exist: soccer teams in Belgium and Switzerland have started to consider this issue, taking marketing more seriously in order to become commercially viable (*The McKinsey Quarterly*, 2000), even tough they may still appear to be exceptions. This may change if indeed, professional sports teams start working to build their brand equity and become brands on their own.

*Anaheim Angels.* (2003). Retrieved March, 2003, from http://anaheim.angels.mlb.com.

Bedbury, S., & Fenichell, S. (2002). *A new brand world.* London: Viking.

Bobby, D. (2002, April). Can a sports club be a brand? *Sport Business International.* Retrieved August, 2002, from http://www.wolff-olins.com/sportsclub.htm.

Browne, K. (1999). The branding of soccer. *Finance Week,* (January 29), 26.

Buckman, R. (2000). Pro sports teams appeal to fans in irreverent local ad campaigns. *Wall Street Journal,* (May 11), B16.

Burton, R., & Howard, D. (1999). Professional sports leagues: Marketing mix mayhem. *Marketing Management, 8*(1), 36-46.

Cateora, P. R., & Graham, J. L. (2001). *International marketing,* (11th ed.). Homewood, IL: Irwin.

Cavanagh, R. (2001). Clubs hope to score with global branding. *Marketing Week,* (September 13), 22.

Clancy, K. J., & Kelly, L. (2001). Stemming a slide: A lesson from the Red Sox. *Brandweek, 42*(14), 17.

Daley, K. (2003). Root, root, root but not too loud. *The Gazette,* (March 30), p. C8.

Davis, S. M. (2002). Bran authenticity: It's the real thing. *Brandweek,* (January 28), 21.

De Chernatony, L. (2001). A model for strategically building brands. *Brand Management, 9*(1), 32-44.

Desbordes, M. (2000). *Gestion du sport.* Paris: Vigot.

Dunleavy, B. P. (2000). Bottom of the Net. *The Village Voice, 45*(30), 182.

Fanning, J. (1999). Tell me a story: The future of branding. *Irish Marketing Review, 12*(2), 3-15.

*Football 365.* (2002). Retrieved December, 2002, from http://www.football365.fr/italie/story_75351.shtml.

*France 2 Télévision.* (2002, May). Le foot business. Émission *Complément d'enquête.* [Broadcast in May 2002 from Paris, France].

*Future Brand.* (2002). Winning isn't everything. It's how you build the brand that counts. Retrieved in September, 2002, from http://futurebrand.com.

*Girondins de Bordeaux.* (2003). Retrieved in March, 2003, from http://www.girondins.com.

*Glasgow Celtic.* (2003). Retrieved in March, 2003, from http://superstore.celticfc.net.

Godin, M. A. (2003). El ultimo turno? *La Presse,* (March 30), p. D1.

Gustafson, R. (2001). Product brands look set to gain new advantage. *Marketing,* (April 5), 20.

Haynes, A., Lackman, C., & Guskey, A. (1999). Comprehensive brand presentation: Ensuring consistent brand image. *The Journal of Product and Brand Management, 8*(4), 286-298.

Heim, S. J. (2000). Winning combo. *Brandweek, 41*(37), 70-72.

*Inc.* (2000). Face to face: For the fans. *22*(13), 45.

Kapferer, J. N. (2001). Is there really no hope for local brands? *Brand Management, 9*(3), 163-170.

Kashani, K. (1995). Comment créer une marque puissante? *Les Échos.* Retrieved in February, 2003, from http://www.lesechos.fr.

Keyes, C. L. M. (1998). Social well-being. *Social Psychology Quarterly, 61*(2), 121-140.

Kick-starting soccer. (2000). *The McKinsey Quarterly.* (4). Retrieved in August, 2002, from http://www.mckinseyquarterly.com/category_archive.asp?L2=16&L3=20.

King, P. (1999). Out of site. *Sports Illustrated, 91*(16), 96-100.

Kotler, P., Filiatrault, P., & Turner, R. E. (2000). *Le management du marketing.* Boucherville: Gaëtan Morin éditeur.

*L'Équipe.* (2000). Retrieved December, 2002, from http://www.lequipe.fr/Football/Lens_Modernite.html.

*La Voix du Nord.* (2001). Retrieved December, 2002, from http://www.lavoixdunord.com/vdn/journal/plus/sport/foot/losc/0817mag2.shtml.

*Le Monde.* (2002). L'Olympique Lyonnais veut être côté à tout prix. (December 11). Retrieved December, 2002, from http://www.lemonde.fr/article/0,5987,3242--301431-,00.html.

Le Soir. (2002), C'est la fin pour le FC Malines, placé en liquidation. (December 9). Retrieved in December, 2002, from http://doc.lesoir.be/scripts/$cshtml.exe?TO_PAGE=lesoir/recherche/recherche:LANG=Francais.

*Lille Olympique Sporting Club.* (2003). Retrieved in March, 2003, from http://www.losc.fr.

*Major League Baseball.* (2003). Retrieved in March, 2003, from http://www.mlb.com.

Mazur, L. (2002). Innovation and branding make a powerful mix. *Marketing,* (March 28), 16.

*Montréal Alouettes.* (2003). Retrieved in March, 2003, from http://slam.canoe.ca/Alouettes/.

*Montréal Canadiens.* (2003). Retrieved in March, 2003, from http://www.canadiens.com.

Mullin, B. J., Hardy, S., & Sutton, W. A. (2000). *Sport marketing,* 2nd ed., Champaign (Illinois): Human Kinetics.

*National Hockey League.* (2003). Retrieved in March, 2003, from http://www.nhl.com.

*Newcastle United.* (2003). Retrieved in March, 2003, from http://www.nufc.co.uk.

*Ottawa Senators.* (2003). Retrieved in March, 2003, from http://www.ottawasenators.com/profiles/mlakar.aro.

Parmar, A. (2002). Global youth united. *Marketing News,* (October 28), 1, 49.

Passikoff, R. (2000). N.Y. Yankees aside, winning isn't only key to fan loyalty. *Brandweek, 41*(43), 32.

*Premier 1 Grand Prix.* (2003). Retrieved in March, 2003, from http://www.premier1grandprix.com.

*Real Madrid.* (2003). Retrieved in March, 2003, from http://www.realmadrid.com.

Rijkenberg, J. (2002). *Concepting: Creating successful brands in a communication-oriented era.* Henley-on-Thames: World Advertising Research Centre.

Shannon, J. (1999). Battle of world football brands. *Marketing Week,* (September 9), 22.

*Sport Business Group.* (2002a). Maximising revenue from licensing and merchandising. Retrieved in August, 2002, from http://www.sportbusiness.com/static/reports_intros/index.adp.

*Sport Business Group.* (2002b). News. Retrieved in August, 2002, from http://www.sportbusiness.com.

Stubbs, D. (2003). A magical suite for children. *The Gazette,* (March 29), p. C1, C8. Retrieved in August, 2002, from http://www.sportbusiness.com/static/reports_intros/index.adp.

*Team talk.* (2001). Roma near United/Yankees link-up. Retrieved in August, 2002, from http://www.teamtalk.com

Todd, J. (2003). It's hard not to be a little excited about Expos. *The Gazette,* p. C1, C7.

*Toffs.* (2003). Retrieved in March, 2003, from http://www.toffs.com.

*Toronto Maple Leafs.* (2003). Retrieved in March, 2003, from http://www.mapleleafs.com.

*Toronto Raptors.* (2003). Retrieved in March, 2003, from http://www.nba.com/raptors.

Tourret, P. (1992/1993). Le marketing des sports américains: Le rôle essentiel des Major Leagues. *Revue Française du Marketing,* (138), 41-48.

Travis, D., & Branson, R. (2000). *Emotional branding: How successful brands gain the irrational edge.* Roseville, CA: Prima Venture.

Underwood, R., Bond, E., & Baer, R. (2001). Building service brands via social identity: Lessons from the sports marketplace. *Journal of Marketing Theory & Practice,* (Winter), 1-13.

*Vancouver Canucks.* (2003). Retrieved in March, 2003, from http://www.canucks.com.

Waltner, C. (2000). CRM: The new game in town for professional sports. *Informationweek,* (August 28), 112-116.

Worsley, J. (2001). Brand loyalty vs venue loyalty. *Leisure & Hospitality,* (October 18), Retrieved in August, 2002, from http://henleycenter.com/press/cut_20011022154033657.phtml.

# CHAPTER 2

# Behind More Luxury Suites in New NFL Stadiums: Increasing Potential Nonshared Revenue for NFL Franchises

DARYL WIRAKARTAKUSUMAH
SOONHWAN LEE

The United States is currently in the middle of a sports construction boom. Many sport franchises across the four major professional sport leagues are either receiving new sport facilities, costing at least $200 million each, or getting major stadium renovations (Greenberg, 2000; Noll & Zimbalist, 1997). In the National Football League (NFL) alone, 14 franchises have been given new stadiums to play in since 1995, including seven since 2000. These numbers do not include the major stadium renovations in Jacksonville, Oakland, Chicago, and Green Bay. Table 1 lists the seven new NFL stadiums since 2000 along with their estimated construction costs.

Among the four major professional sport leagues, the NFL has the most comprehensive revenue sharing system. The NFL distributes its total national television revenue and sales revenue from its licensing company-NFL Properties-equally among all the teams in their league (Kolias, 2001; Mullick, 1996; Tygart, 2000). In addition, revenue from ticket sales is also shared in the NFL, where after deducting 15% of gross ticket revenue from stadium and game expenses, the home team receives 60%, while the remaining 40% is distributed to the visiting team (Kolias, 2001; Mullick, 1996).

> In exchange for a higher price than general admission seating, club seats offer patrons various amenities such as wider seats, expanded menus with personalized delivery, preferred parking, and private restrooms.

Following the new trends in stadium development and team relocations in 1995, revenue sharing in the NFL was expanded to include several new sources of revenue such as club seats, personal seat licenses (PSLs), and relocation fees (Reese & Nagel, 2001). In exchange for a higher price than general admission seating, club seats offer patrons various amenities such as wider seats, expanded menus with personalized delivery, preferred parking, and private restrooms (Gotthelf, 1998a; Rafool, 1998). PSLs, on the other hand, provide advance revenue and give patrons the right to selected seats for an extended period of time over any event taking place in the stadium (McCarthy & Irwin, 1998; Mullick, 1996; Reese & Nagel, 2001). Unlike club seats and PSLs, relocation fees are a new revenue source that is not directly related to stadium seating. In fact, relocation fees are actually paid to reimburse moving expenses and provide advance-operating income for franchises that are relocating to new cities (Reese & Nagel, 2001).

Table 1  **Estimated Stadium Construction Costs for New NFL Stadiums**

| Team name | Stadium name | Year opened | Estimated stadium construction costs ($-millions) |
|---|---|---|---|
| Cincinnati Bengals | Paul Brown Stadium | 2000 | $455 |
| Denver Broncos | Invesco Field at Mile High | 2001 | $401 |
| Pittsburgh Steelers | Heinz Field | 2001 | $281 |
| Seattle Seahawks | Seahawks Stadium | 2002 | $430 |
| Detroit Lions | Ford Field | 2003 | $325 |
| New England Patriots | Gillette Stadium | 2003 | $397 |
| Philadelphia Eagles | Lincoln Financial Field | 2003 | $500 |

Note: From "NFL 2002: Franchise History and Values Stadium Data," by M. J. Duberstein and C. Strunk, September 2002. Retrieved April 12, 2003 from www.nflpa.org/PDFs/Shared/Updated%20_Franchise_Value_&_Stadium_Data.pdf.

Apart from all the shared revenue sources mentioned above, there is also a significant amount of revenue that is not included in the NFL revenue-sharing agreement. These nonshared revenue sources include revenues from luxury suites, concessions, advertising, naming rights, signage, and parking (Chapin, 2000; McCarthy & Irwin, 1998; Reese & Nagel, 2001; Rosentraub & Swindell, 2002; Tygart, 2000). Since luxury suites are considered to be the primary moneymaker among these nonshared revenue sources, several scholars have considered it as the second most important revenue stream for sport franchises behind television revenues (Chapin, 2000; Rafool, 1998).

One of the most important things with nonshared revenue is that NFL teams can use it to work around the salary cap. Even though the salary cap was designed to limit the amount of money each team may spend annually on players, the cap does permit owners to use nonshared revenue to stretch the cap by amortizing signing bonuses across the length of the contract (McCarthy & Irwin, 1998; Mullick,

1996; Reese & Nagel, 2001; Rosentraub & Swindell, 2002; Tygart, 2000). By offering multiyear contracts and prorating up-front signing bonuses over the duration of the contracts, teams with higher nonshared revenues are able to attract and sign more quality players without violating the salary cap guidelines (Reese & Nagel, 2001; Rosentraub & Swindell, 2002). Nonetheless, even if these funds were not used to pay signing bonuses, these nonshared revenues will at least increase the personal profits for team owners (Rosentraub & Swindell, 2002).

Based on the benefits mentioned above, it seems quite obvious why many NFL franchises have been requesting new stadiums or major renovations for their current stadiums to increase this nonshared source of revenue. Figure 1 illustrates the effect cycle of new stadiums as described by Gotthelf (1998b), Rafool (1998), and Tygart (2000). The new stadium will initially allow the franchise to increase their nonshared revenues, which in turn will allow the team to spend more on players. With better players, the team's chances of winning more games should improve, which usually attracts more fans to attend games. Since more attendance means more revenue generated, the effect cycle continues.

Figure 1 **Effect cycle of new stadiums.**

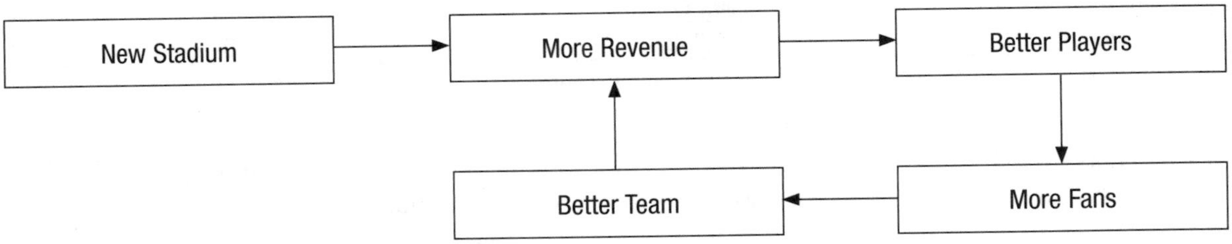


Although many studies have indicated the importance of having more luxury suites in stadiums to improve a franchise's competitiveness on and off the field, none of them have tried to compare the total potential ticket revenue (TR) with the total potential luxury suites revenues (LSR) of previous and new stadiums. Only by comparing these potential revenues can a clear conclusion be made of how significant luxury suites are in generating additional revenue. Therefore, the purpose of this study was to determine how significant luxury suites are in generating additional revenue by means of calculating the percentage of increased LSR within the increased TR of seven NFL franchises that have received a new stadium since 2000 (see Table 1).

**Although many studies have indicated the importance of having more luxury suites in stadiums to improve a franchise's competitiveness on and off the field, none of them have tried to compare the total potential ticket revenue (TR) with the total potential luxury suites revenues (LSR) of previous and new stadiums.**

For the purpose of this study, it is important to note here that the potential revenue figures will be used instead of the actual revenue figures in performing the comparisons. There are two reasons for this approach. First, actual revenue figures of private organizations, such as the NFL, are rarely shared for public consumption. Even if it were available, in most cases, gaining access to the actual detailed revenue figures would involve a significant amount of money beyond the expense limit for this study. Second, since the focus of this study is on the facility aspect, rather than the marketing or finance aspect, it seems only reasonable that the revenue figures to be used for this study should reflect on what potential can the facility offer, not on the success of marketing or financing it.

# Calculating the Numbers

In order to properly compare the TR with the LSR of the seven NFL franchise subjects of this study, several preliminary items must be identified and calculated. The first set of items to be identified is the seating capacity (SC) and the number of luxury suites (LS) of both the previous and new stadiums. Table 2 shows the explicit numbers for these items.

Table 2 **Stadium Capacity and Luxury Suites of Previous and New NFL Stadiums**

| Team name | Stadium capacity | | Luxury suites | |
|---|---|---|---|---|
| | Previous stadium | New stadium | Previous stadium | New stadium |
| Cincinnati Bengals | 59,754 | 65,535 | 20 | 114 |
| Denver Broncos | 76,098 | 76,125 | 60 | 110 |
| Pittsburgh Steelers | 59,600 | 65,000 | 115 | 127 |
| Seattle Seahawks | 72,500 | 67,000 | 0 | 82 |
| Detroit Lions | 80,311 | 65,000 | 102 | 125 |
| New England Patriots | 60,292 | 68,000 | 42 | 80 |
| Philadelphia Eagles | 65,352 | 66,000 | 89 | 163 |

Note. Information provided above was compiled from various sources.

Next, as shown in Table 3, are the average ticket prices (ATP) and luxury suites prices (LSP) of the seven NFL franchise subjects for 2002. Due to limited information of exact seat pricing, a weighed average ticket price is used instead. Furthermore, following the format provided from gathered information, LSP is expressed in a range of prices.

Table 3 **Average Ticket Prices and Luxury Suites Prices of New NFL Stadiums**

| Team name | Average ticket prices ($/game) | Luxury suites prices | |
|---|---|---|---|
| | | Minimum ($/ssn) | Maximum ($/ssn) |
| Cincinnati Bengals | 47.31 | 48,000.00 | 140,000.00 |
| Denver Broncos | 52.50 | 85,000.00 | 105,000.00 |
| Pittsburgh Steelers | 49.83 | 44,000.00 | 120,000.00 |
| Seattle Seahawks | 43.28 | 50,000.00 | 150,000.00 |
| Detroit Lions | 50.23 | 70,000.00 | 250,000.00 |
| New England Patriots | 76.19 | 33,000.00 | 125,000.00 |
| Philadelphia Eagles | 46.19 | 95,000.00 | 150,000.00 |

Note. Average ticket prices were 2002 figures taken from Team Marketing Report. Luxury suites prices were 2002 figures taken from Sports Business Journal—By The Numbers 2003: The Authoritative Annual Research Guide and Fact Book.

Once these figures are recognized, several preliminary calculations can take place. The first preliminary calculation is performed to discover the differences between the total potential nonluxury suites (NLSR) of previous and new stadiums for the seven NFL franchise subjects. Since ATP figures in Table 3 are listed per game and each NFL team will, at least, play eight home games in a season, NLSRs are initially calculated using the following general formula:

$$NLSR_{new/prev} = SC_{new/prev} * ATP * 8 * (.60) \qquad (1)$$

where the values of SC and ATP are taken from Table 2 and 3, respectively. The .60 figure in Equation 1 comes from the fact that only 60% of other home ticket revenues besides luxury suites are shared to the home team according to the NFL revenue share agreement. After all NLSRs are calculated for both previous and new stadiums, the differences between them are then calculated using the following formula:

$$(NLSR = NLSR_{new} - NLSR_{prev} \qquad (2)$$

The results of these calculations are shown in Table 4.

The next calculation is performed to discover the differences between LSRs of previous and new stadiums for the seven NFL franchise subjects. Since LSPs are presented in Table 3 as price ranges, the calculations are made separately for minimum and maximum LSRs. LSRs are initially calculated using the following general formula:

$$LSR_{new/prev\ min/max} = LS_{new/prev} * LSP_{min/max} \qquad (3)$$

where the values of LS and LSP are taken from Table 2 and 3, respectively. After all LSRs are calculated for both previous and new stadiums, the differences between each price range are then calculated using the following formula:

$$(LSR_{min/max} = LSR_{new\ min/max} - LSR_{prev\ min/max} \qquad (4)$$

The results for minimum and maximum LSRs are presented in Table 5 and 6, respectively.

Table 4  **Total Potential Nonluxury Suites Ticket Revenues of Previous and New NFL Stadiums**

| Team name | Total potential ticket revenues | | Differences ($) |
| --- | --- | --- | --- |
| | Prev. stadium ($/ssn) | New stadium ($/ssn) | |
| Cincinnati Bengals | 13,569,416.35 | 14,882,212.08 | 1,312,795.73 |
| Denver Broncos | 19,176,696.00 | 19,183,500.00 | 6,804.00 |
| Pittsburgh Steelers | 14,255,366.40 | 15,546,960.00 | 1,291,593.60 |
| Seattle Seahawks | 15,061,440.00 | 13,918,848.00 | (1,142,592.00) |
| Detroit Lions | 19,363,303.34 | 15,671,760.00 | (3,691,543.34) |
| New England Patriots | 22,049,507.90 | 24,868,416.00 | 2,818,908.10 |
| Philadelphia Eagles | 14,489,322.62 | 14,632,992.00 | 143,669.38 |

Note. prev. = previous; ssn = season.

Table 5  **Minimum Total Potential Luxury Suites Revenues of Previous and New NFL Stadiums**

| Team name | Minimum total potential ticket revenues | | Min. differences ($) |
| --- | --- | --- | --- |
| | Prev. stadium ($/ssn) | New stadium ($/ssn) | |
| Cincinnati Bengals | 960,000.00 | 5,472,000.00 | 4,512,000.00 |
| Denver Broncos | 5,100,000.00 | 9,350,000.00 | 4,250,000.00 |
| Pittsburgh Steelers | 5,060,000.00 | 5,588,000.00 | 528,000.00 |
| Seattle Seahawks | 0.00 | 4,100,000.00 | 4,100,000.00 |
| Detroit Lions | 7,140,000.00 | 8,750,000.00 | 1,610,000.00 |
| New England Patriots | 1,386,000.00 | 2,640,000.00 | 1,254,000.00 |
| Philadelphia Eagles | 8,455,000.00 | 15,485,000.00 | 7,030,000.00 |

Note. prev. = previous; ssn = season; min. = minimum.

Table 6  **Maximum Total Potential Luxury Suites Revenues of Previous and New NFL Stadiums**

| Team name | Maximum total potential ticket revenues | | Max. differences ($) |
| --- | --- | --- | --- |
| | Prev. stadium ($/ssn) | New stadium ($/ssn) | |
| Cincinnati Bengals | 2,800,000.00 | 15,960,000.00 | 13,160,000.00 |
| Denver Broncos | 6,300,000.00 | 11,550,000.00 | 5,250,000.00 |
| Pittsburgh Steelers | 13,800,000.00 | 15,240,000.00 | 1,440,000.00 |
| Seattle Seahawks | 0.00 | 12,300,000.00 | 12,300,000.00 |
| Detroit Lions | 25,500,000.00 | 31,250,000.00 | 5,750,000.00 |
| New England Patriots | 5,250,000.00 | 10,000,000.00 | 4,750,000.00 |
| Philadelphia Eagles | 13,350,000.00 | 24,450,000.00 | 11,100,000.00 |

Note. prev. = previous; ssn = season; max. = maximum.

The last calculation to perform is to actually discover the percentage of increased LSR within the increased TR for the seven NFL franchise subjects. The increased TR itself is calculated using the following formula:

$$(TR_{min/max} = (NLSR + (LSR_{min/max} \quad (5)$$

where the values of (NLSR and LSRmin/max are taken from Table 4, 5, and 6, respectively. Thus, using the common percentage formula of

$$\% (LSR_{min/max} = (LSR_{min/max} /(TR_{min/max} * 100\% \quad (6)$$

the percentage of potential increased LSR from the potential increased TR for the seven NFL franchise subjects can be determined. The minimum and maximum results of these final calculations are shown in Table 7 and 8, respectively.

**Table 7  Minimum Percentages of Potential Increased Luxury Suites Revenues from Potential Increased Ticket Revenues for the New NFL Stadiums**

| Team name | $\Delta LSR_{min}$ ($) | $\Delta TR_{min}$ ($) | $\Delta LSR_{min}$ (%) |
|---|---|---|---|
| Cincinnati Bengals | 4,512,000.00 | 5,824,795.73 | 77.46 |
| Denver Broncos | 4,250,000.00 | 4,256,804.00 | 99.84 |
| Pittsburgh Steelers | 528,000.00 | 1,819,593.60 | 29.02 |
| Seattle Seahawks | 4,100,000.00 | 2,957,408.00 | 138.63 |
| Detroit Lions | 1,610,000.00 | (2,081,543.34) | -77.35 |
| New England Patriots | 1,254,000.00 | 4,072,908.10 | 30.79 |
| Philadelphia Eagles | 7,030,000.00 | 7,173,669.38 | 98.00 |

Note. $\Delta LSR_{min}$ = Minimum total potential increased luxury suites revenues; $\Delta TR_{min}$ = Minimum total potential ticket revenues; $\Delta LSR_{min}$ = Minimum percentage of potential increased luxury suites revenues from potential increased ticket revenues.

**Table 8  Maximum Percentages of Potential Increased Luxury Suites Revenues from Potential Increased Ticket Revenues for the New NFL Stadiums**

| Team name | $\Delta LSR_{max}$ ($) | $\Delta TR_{max}$ ($) | $\Delta LSR_{max}$ (%) |
|---|---|---|---|
| Cincinnati Bengals | 13,160,000.00 | 14,472,795.73 | 90.93 |
| Denver Broncos | 5,250,000.00 | 5,256,804.00 | 99.87 |
| Pittsburgh Steelers | 1,440,000.00 | 2,731,593.60 | 52.72 |
| Seattle Seahawks | 12,300,000.00 | 11,157,408.00 | 110.24 |
| Detroit Lions | 5,750,000.00 | 2,058,456.66 | 279.34 |
| New England Patriots | 4,750,000.00 | 7,568,908.10 | 62.76 |
| Philadelphia Eagles | 11,100,000.00 | 11,243,669.38 | 98.72 |

Note. $\Delta LSR_{max}$ = Maximum total potential increased luxury suites revenues; $\Delta TR_{max}$ = Maximum total potential ticket revenues; $\Delta LSR_{max}$ = Maximum percentage of potential increased luxury suites revenues from potential increased ticket revenues.

## Discussion and Conclusion

The first comparison made between new NFL stadiums that were opened since 2000 and the previous stadiums owned by the same NFL franchises was on the total potential NLSRs. New England seemed to be the leading team in this area by increasing their NLSRs about $2.8 million, followed by Cincinnati and Pittsburgh, which both increased about $1.3 million. Two interesting figures, however, appeared for Detroit and Seattle, where their NLSRs actually dropped since they moved to their new stadium. A partial reason for the move to still take place, despite suffering from the potential revenue drop, is shown by the next comparison.

Total potential LSRs of previous and new NFL stadiums were the second items to be compared. Cincinnati seemed to have the highest potential of increasing their LSRs by about $13 million, followed by Seattle and Philadelphia, which increased their maximum potential to about $12 million and $11 million, respectively. On the minimum side of potential LSRs,

**Two interesting figures appeared for Detroit and Seattle, where their NLSRs actually dropped since they moved to their new stadium.**

Philadelphia had the highest minimum potential by about $7 million, followed by Cincinnati, Denver, and Seattle all around $4 million.

Stepping back a little to the Detroit and Seattle case mentioned earlier, by comparing the NLSRs and LSRs of both franchises, a better understanding can now be realized. Seattle's case is more obvious, since their minimum potential LSR alone of around $4 million is higher than their potential deficit NLSR of around $1 million. Another reason to support Seattle's persistence in moving to their new stadium relates to the fact that their previous stadium-Husky Stadium, owned by University of Washington-was only for temporary use while their new stadium was under construction. By not using their own stadium, many other revenue sources such as concessions and parking could be lost, not to mention additional costs like rental fees.

Detroit's case is a little more complex than Seattle's. From Detroit's maximum potential LSR of around $5.7 million, the move would be justifiable, since their potential deficit NLSR is only around $3.7 million. Based on their minimum potential LSR of around $1.6 million, however, Detroit will still be running a potential deficit of around $2.1 million. Due to this matter, several additional arguments have to be stated to support Detroit's decision to move to their new stadium. Brockinton (2002) perhaps shared one of the most significant arguments by stating that Detroit's deal with their previous stadium, Silverdome, did not favor the franchise. Under the terms of the deal between the franchise and the stadium owners, Detroit would not receive any stadium-based revenue outside ticket sales. This means Detroit would not receive revenues from concessions, in-stadium advertising, merchandise sales, club seats, and most importantly, luxury suites. With this argument in mind, Detroit's move to their new stadium appears justifiable.

The last comparison made on the minimum and maximum percentages of potential increased LSRs from potential increased ticket revenues for the new NFL stadiums was the main focus of this study. From the minimum standpoint, Seattle apparently had the highest potential LSR percentage by about 139%, which indicates that part of Seattle's minimum potential increased LSR has substituted a deficit in its potential NLSR. Denver, Philadelphia, and Cincinnati also showed a significant role in their potential increased LSRs with contributions of 75%-100% towards their potential increased ticket revenues, respectively. As discussed earlier, since Detroit's minimum potential LSR is lower than its deficit in potential NLSR, it appears quite obvious why Detroit's minimum percentage of potential increased LSR from potential increased ticket revenues turned up in a negative figure.

> Denver, Philadelphia, and Cincinnati also showed a significant role in their potential increased LSRs with contributions of 75%-100% towards their potential increased ticket revenues, respectively.

> From the maximum standpoint, Detroit apparently had the upper hand among the seven franchises by reaching percentage of around 279%.

From the maximum standpoint, Detroit apparently had the upper hand among the seven franchises by reaching percentage of around 279%. As pointed out earlier, this figure indicates that part of Detroit's maximum potential increased LSR has substituted a deficit in its potential NLSR. As with the minimum figures, Seattle once again proved how significant the role of their potential increased LSRs with a contribution of about 110% towards their potential increased ticket revenues. The rest of the franchises all showed the same results as their potential increased LSRs percentages ranged from 53% to 100%.

In conclusion, increasing potential ticket revenue in the NFL by adding more luxury suites has proven to be significant. It becomes even more significant considering that luxury suites are nonshared revenue sources in the NFL. By increasing nonshared revenues, NFL franchises have a better chance in attracting and signing better players, which gives them a better chance of winning more games. As pointed out earlier, winning more games leads to more fans, which in turn leads to more revenue.

For future studies, several different approaches could be suggested. First, use the same calculation approach but with more detailed data; with more detailed data, the potential projections will consequently be more accurate. Second, extend the scope of the study to include stadium renovations; comparisons can then be made between new stadiums and stadium renovations. Lastly, the scope of study could include all new NFL stadiums since 1995; by involving more franchises, the results of the study should become more reliable.

> **By increasing nonshared revenues, NFL franchises have a better chance in attracting and signing better players, which gives them a better chance of winning more games. Winning more games leads to more fans, which in turn leads to more revenue.**

# References

Brockinton, L. (2002, September 2). Lion's will get far more revenue mileage out of this year's model. *Sports Business Journal.* Retrieved April 12, 2003, from http://www.sportsbusinessjournal.com/article.cms?articleId=24461&s=1.

Chapin, T. (2000). The political economy of sports facility location: An end-of-the-century review and assessment. *Marquette Sports Law Journal, 10*(2), 361-382.

Gotthelf, J. (1998a, April 27). Mixing old-time ballpark feel with luxury pays off: Designers find fan comfort, money making perks not mutually exclusive with today's facilities. *Sports Business Journal.* Retrieved April 12, 2003, from http://www.sportsbusinessjournal.com/article.cms?articleId=20363&s=1.

Gotthelf, J. (1998b, April 27). Owners expect public to ante up to get, keep pro teams. *Sports Business Journal.* Retrieved April 12, 2003, from http://www.sportsbusinessjournal.com/article.cms?articleId=20362&s=1.

Greenberg, M. J. (2000). Stadium financing and franchise relocation act of 1999. *Marquette Sports Law Journal, 10*(2), 383-399.

Kolias, S. J. (2001). Offensive interference: How communities have harnessed market forces to retain NFL franchises, eliminating the need for H.R. 3817's proposed antitrust exemption. *Sports Lawyers Journal, 8*(1), 43-65.

McCarthy, L. M., & Irwin, R. (1998). Permanent seat licenses (PSLs) as an emerging source of revenue production. *Sport Marketing Quarterly, 7*(3), 41-46.

Mullick, S. J. (1996). Browns to Baltimore: Franchise free agency and the new economics of the NFL. *Marquette Sports Law Journal, 7*(1), 1-37.

Noll, R. G. & Zimbalist, A. (1997). Are new stadiums worth the cost? *Brookings Review, 15*(3), 35-39. Retrieved April 12, 2003, from http://www.breadnotcircuses.org/brooking.html.

Rafool, M. (1998, March 27). Playing the stadium game: Financing professional sports facilities in the '90s. Paper presented at the National Conference of State Legislatures. Retrieved April 12, 2003, from http://www.ncsl.org/programs/fiscal/lfp106.htm.

Reese, J. T., & Nagel, M. S. (2001). The relationship between revenues and winning in the national football league. *International Journal of Sport Management, 2,* 125-133.

Rosentraub, M. S., & Swindell, D. (2002). Negotiating games: Cities, sports, and the winner's curse. *Journal of Sport Management, 16,* 18-35.

Tygart, T. T. (2000). Antitrust's impact on the National Football League and team relocation. *Sports Lawyers Journal, 7*(1), 30-57.

# PART II
# SPORT MARKETING AND THE INTERNET

# CHAPTER 3

# Marketing on the Web: Collegiate Athletic Sites

STEVEN MCCLUNG
ROBIN HARDIN
MICHAEL J. MONDELLO

## Abstract

This study examines 'official' collegiate athletic Internet websites. Specifically, the research looks to examine the strategies that NCAA institutions use to market themselves and generate revenue through the university-sanctioned site. The research also examines what interactive strategies the sites employ to gather and hold audiences on the sites and the perceived function(s) of the site by the sports information directors of the institutions. The results indicate the sites are seen primarily as a means to distribute information, but there may be potential to use the site as a marketing and revenue-generation tool. Strategies used for revenue generation include ticket and merchandise sales, and strategies for marketing included interactive user features. The potential of the sites as marketing and revenue generation tools has not been fully developed though.

Sixty-six percent of adults have Internet access, and they spend an average of seven to eight hours online each week (Harris, 2002). This burgeoning new medium has multiple applications for many users, from information and entertainment to banking, financial transactions, and shopping. One source of entertainment on the World Wide Web is sports-related sites. Specifically, sport sites are popular because of the uses the Web provides for sports fans. Sports websites can provide a means of disseminating information that traditional media cannot. A website provides a multitude of functions for the sports fan, including data storage, interactivity, immediacy, worldwide accessibility for esoteric sports, and serves as both an individual and mass medium at the same time (Kahle & Meeske, 1999). The neighborhood bar has also been moved to the Web as chat rooms provide a place for fans to interact with one another and exchange opinions about their favorite sports teams.

# Introduction

> **The neighborhood bar has been moved to the Web as chat rooms provide a place for fans to interact with one another and exchange opinions about their favorite sports teams.**

Traditional media have been good to collegiate sports programs in terms of providing exposure and revenue. Television has been the leader in exposure and revenue generation for the National Collegiate Athletic Association (NCAA) in both football and basketball. The four Bowl Championship Series football games combined to reach a record television audience of 127 million viewers in 2001 with the average attendance for those games at more than 77,000. Overall attendance for all bowl games increased 7.6% from 2000 to 2001 to nearly 1.3 million (About the BCS, 2002). The NCAA Division I men's basketball tournament televised by CBS is a huge revenue source for NCAA and its member institutions. CBS recently paid the NCAA $6 billion for the rights to broadcast the men's basketball tournament and retail sales of collegiate merchandise topped $2.7 billion in 1999 (NCAA, 1995).

This revenue stream does not include the revenues individual institutions garner from their radio and television networks. Most Division I institutions have developed radio and television agreements and some are financially extensive. Notre Dame, for example, has an exclusive television contract with NBC. Many schools have established statewide or regional radio and television networks that include enough affiliates to cover an entire state. Tennessee has nearly 100 radio stations that broadcast its football games (Ford & Painter, 2002).

> **Television and radio are currently the leaders in media revenues and exposure for collegiate athletic programs. But the Web has the potential to do so as well and is making progress in those areas.**

Television and radio are currently the leaders in media revenues and exposure for collegiate athletic programs. But the Web has the potential to do so as well and is making progress in those areas.

Rogers (1995) suggested adoption of innovation comes in stages and innovations have an S-shaped adoption rate. Earlier adopters are those who start using the innovation and slowly pull the curve upward. As more people begin adoption, a take-off period starts the upward swing of the curve and this is eventually followed by a leveling off period of late adopters who help form the top of the S-shaped curve. The adoption of the Web by Division I collegiate programs has fully filled Rogers adoption curve as all of these programs have a Web presence.

These programs have adopted the Web in general, but they have yet to adopt all of the programs, technology, and marketing strategies that are available via the Web. Many of these sites have yet to fully utilize the technology that can make these sites serve purposes other than simply providing an outlet for information. In other words, there are subadoption curves of the Web that are not fully developed, but some collegiate programs are making inroads into the new medium both in terms of technology and as a revenue stream.

> **Many of these sites have yet to fully utilize the technology that can make these sites serve purposes other than simply providing an outlet for information.**

Georgia Tech is using specific Web technology for the sale and renewal of season football tickets (Liberman, 2001). Major league baseball's San Francisco Giants are allowing fans to resell their tickets online. A season ticket holder may not be able to attend a particular game, but can post tickets on the website of the Giants for someone else to buy. The Giants are not directly making any money in this transaction, but this enhances the attendance at games. Subsequently, this in turn creates more consumers for souvenirs and concessions sold at the stadium, which in turn can increase potential revenue for

> **It is the adoption of these specific Web technologies that will allow these sites to better market the programs and generate revenue.**

the Giants organization (Liberman, 2001). It is the adoption of these specific Web technologies that will allow these sites to better market the programs and generate revenue.

Sports-related sites are also beginning to develop business models to maximize revenue generation through their websites. These sites are generally content-based sites that provide news, information, and statistics to fans. Three different economic models have emerged and sports-related sites are either adopting one of the three models or using hybrid models based on the original three (Caskey & Delpy, 1999).

The advertising-sponsorship model is characterized by banner advertising that appears on the website. The sites make money by measuring *cost per thousand* or the click through method. Cost per thousand is the same concept as in traditional media's use of the term (What does it cost to reach 1,000 viewers or readers?). The click-through method is based on the number of times an advertisement is clicked on thus taking a Web surfer to another website (Caskey & Delpy, 1999).

The second model applied to the sports segment is the subscription model. Many fan-based sites are utilizing this strategy to charge for certain premium material that cannot be accessed elsewhere; some information on the website cannot be accessed without a subscription. A log-in screen appears when a user tries to access the information. A subscription allows the user to enter a user name and password to access the information. There is also the online commerce model that allows sports marketers to sell merchandise and tickets online (Caskey & Delpy, 1999).

> **Sports websites can increase cost efficiency by distributing information in a way that is less expensive than fax or mail.**

Researchers have identified key functions of the Web for sports business. Sports websites can increase cost efficiency by distributing information in a way that is less expensive than fax or mail. Performance improvement in fan communication, market penetration, and product transformation can also be considered primary functions of the sports business on the Web (Duncan & Campbell, 1999).

Sports-oriented sites are also employing strategies that enhance user functions appropriate for this business. Improving customer service, improving advertising, creating distribution channels, handling communications more efficiently, and providing low cost entertainment are all seen as important user functions of successful sports-related sites on the Internet (Duncan & Campbell, 1999).

Some media economists argue the value of Internet sites isn't always measured in dollars and cents. The value of a site can be measured in other ways. Information goods have value to suppliers, users, and society that range far beyond the simple exchange value that is often the focus of short-term fiscal policy (Bates, 1988). So it could be argued that the value of these sites can be measured in ways other than monetary.

> **Some media economists argue the value of Internet sites isn't always measured in dollars and cents.**

Still, many of these sites are commercial interests and fan-based sites. Each NCAA Division I-A and I-AA institution has a site that is considered an official site of the institution. The sports information director is generally the manager of the site in terms of content, function, and ultimately, value. This research examines these sites and their role(s) and value as part of the marketing and media operation of the institution as perceived by the sports information directors.

# Research Questions

This study particularly addresses the following research questions:

1. What marketing strategies appear on the athletic department main page?

2. What revenue generation strategies appear on the athletic department main page?

3. What interactive user features are available on the website?

4. What function do sports information directors perceive the website serving?

# Methodology

The data for this research was collected in two phases. The first part consisted of a content analysis of Division I-A collegiate athletic department websites, and the second part was a survey of collegiate sports information directors at Division I-A and Division I-AA schools. For the purposes of this study, classification of institution is being defined as the classification of the football program. A list was obtained from the NCAA that identified the schools in each classification.

In order to obtain the URL of the official athletic site, the researchers began at the institution's main page, and navigated the site until the official athletics page was reached. In other words, the search for the official sports page began at the institution's *.edu* site and continued until the official athletic department page was found.

That list was then entered into the HTTrack software program. This program automatically visits and downloads the content of listed websites. Only the main page was collected because a Web surfer evaluates a site based on the initial assessment of the main page, so it is likely that the biggest impact of a website is derived from the its main page. This acts as the entry point to a site and serves much like a newspaper's front page. Information available and accessible from the main page is important because if expectations by the visitor are not met, they are likely to leave the site (Chan-Olmsted & Park, 2000). It was believed these athletic programs would want to showcase any advanced Internet features on those pages that patrons visit first. Similarly, it was believed that these athletic programs would showcase, or at least identify, important content on the main page. In addition, it was considered important to examine as many different sites as possible, in order to get the full picture of this rapidly evolving medium. Thus, the decision to collect data from all sites, but at only at the top level, that being the main page.

The second part of the data collection was the survey of sports information directors at institutions participating in either Division I-A or Division I-AA. The survey was placed online and sports information directors were emailed to request their participation in the survey. Email addresses were gathered from the website of the College Sports Information Directors Association and the National Directory of Collegiate Athletics. The period of data collection lasted approximately six weeks and had a response rate of 37%.

# Results

The results of the content analyses of Division I-A websites revealed the revenue generation and marketing strategies of the websites (see Table 1). Nearly 94% ($N = 108$) of the sites had at least one link to ticket information. This link may or may not have led the user to a sublevel where tickets could be purchased directly. The link may have provided only information about how to purchase tickets or

Table 1 **Marketing Strategies on Main Pages of Division I-A Institutions**

|  | N* | Percent** |
|---|---|---|
| Word Official on Page | 86 | 74.8 |
| Link to Ticket Information | 108 | 93.9 |
| Link to Donor Information | 102 | 88.7 |
| Link to Merchandise | 91 | 79.1 |
| Athletic Department Logo or Icon | 104 | 90.4 |
| University Logo or Icon | 11 | 9.6 |
| Conference Logo or Icon | 39 | 33.9 |
| NCAA Logo or Icon | 13 | 11.3 |

\* Appears at Least Once on Main Page
\*\* 115 Total I-A Institutions

Table 2 **Interactive User Features on Main Page**

|  | N* | Percent** |
|---|---|---|
| Email Update | 52 | 45.2 |
| Free Email | 44 | 38.3 |
| Send Electronic Postcard | 33 | 28.7 |
| Make Start Page | 16 | 13.9 |
| Graphic Downloads | 19 | 16.5 |
| Chat | 23 | 20.0 |
| Surveys or Polls | 51 | 44.3 |

\* Appears at Least Once on Page

\*\* 115 Total I-A Institutions

seating diagrams of athletic facilities. Eighty-eight percent ($N$ = 102) had links to donor information, and 79.1 ($N$ = 91) had links to merchandise. Another source of revenue can be derived from advertising on the site. Eighty-seven percent ($N$ = 100) had some sort of advertising on the site, with the number of advertisements ranging from 1 to 11, with a mean of 3.8 advertisements per site. The results of the survey did reveal that I-A sites are more likely to have advertising than I-AA sites with a chi-square value of 4.841 with p = .028.

The sites did, however, want to ensure that user was aware of the site on which he or she was surfing, and to brand the site as such. The word official appeared on 74.8% ($N$ = 86) of the sites, and the athletic department logo or icon was on 90.4% ($N$ = 104) of the sites. The sites clearly wanted to distinguish themselves from the university, conference, or NCAA. Fewer than 10% ($N$ = 11) of the sites had a university logo or icon, and NCAA logos or icons only appeared on 11.3% ($N$ = 13) of the sites. Conference affiliation was a most prominent of these three, but logos or icons still only appeared on 33.9% ($N$ = 39) of the sites.

Another marketing technique was examined on the Division I-A sites. This was interactive user features used to attract and retain audiences (see Table 2). The most prevalent of these interactive features was the ability to get email updates about the athletic department and the website, with 45.2% (*N* = 52) of the sites having this feature. The use of surveys or polls was popular as well, with 44.3% (*N* = 51) of the sites having at least one on the page. These were unscientific surveys that would ask questions such as whom the player of the game was or what the final score of an athletic contest would be. Free email was also used on 38.3% (*N* = 44) of the sites. This consists of somebody having an email account through the site. An example would be a fan of Marshall University, who might have an email address johndoe@herd.com. No other interactive user feature was used on more than 30% of the sites.

Two indices were created from the survey questions to determine if the websites were geared more toward providing information or for generating revenue. Three questions were developed for each index. The means of three questions for the purpose of the site as an information source were all above 5.5, and the means for the three questions for the purpose of the site as revenue generation were all below 4 (see Table 3). Two distinct factors loaded in a factor analysis, which revealed that the questions were measuring the same dimensions. Therefore, it appears the primary purpose of the sites was to provide information. The means for three questions were then collapsed to create two indices. A paired-sample *t*-test was then conducted on the two indices and revealed a combined mean of 18.14 for informational purposes and 10.36 for revenue-generation purposes. A *t*-value of 14.175 revealed a significant difference in the two means at the $p$ = .000 level.

Therefore, the purpose of the sites is seen as a way to provide information to fans, the media and the public. But some sports information directors apparently believe the *potential* for revenue generation is there. Eighty-five percent (*N* = 71) of the survey respondents believe the website has the potential to be a source of revenue. The survey encompassed both Division I-A and I-AA sports information directors. Just more than 50% (*N* = 42) of the respondents said the site allows the user to buy tickets online, and 63.9% (*N* = 53) of the sites allows for the purchase of merchandise.

Table 3 **Mean Rating of Purpose of Web Site**

| Purpose of Web Site | Mean* |
|---|---|
| To Provide Information for Fans | 6.48 |
| To Provide Information for Media | 5.61 |
| To Provide Information to the General Public | 6.05 |
| To Sell University-Related Merchandise | 3.29 |
| For Fund Raising | 3.31 |
| To Provide an Outlet to Sell Tickets | 3.76 |

*1=least important, 7=most important

There were no statistical differences in the perceived purposes of the site as an information source between Division I-A and I-AA sports information directors, but there was a difference in the perceived ability for revenue generation on the sites between the two groups (see Table 4).

An independent samples t-test revealed no difference in the informational index means of 18.18 for I-AA and 18.10 for I-A. But there was a difference in the revenue-generation indexes of 9.16 for I-AA and 11.72 for I-A ($t = -2.889$, $p = .005$). A comparison of each component that comprise the indices revealed significant differences in two of those components. Differences lie within the purpose of the site to sell merchandise ($t = -2.983$, $p = .004$) and to sell tickets ($t = -2.424$, $p = .018$).

Both I-A and I-AA sports information directors believe the website has the potential to be a source of revenue but a chi-square revealed I-A sports information directors feel more strongly this. A chi-square value of 5.178 with $p = .023$, indicates the differences. The ability to purchase merchandise is also significantly more available on I-A sites than I-AA, as a chi-square value of 10.553 with $p = .001$ shows. There is no difference in the ability to purchase tickets as revealed by a chi-square value of 3.520 with $p = .061$.

> Just more than 50% (*N* = 42) of the respondents said the site allows the user to buy tickets online, and 63.9% (*N* = 53) of the sites allow for the purchase of merchandise.

Table 4  **Means and t-test of Purposes of Web Site Based on Classification**

| Purpose | Classification | N | Mean* | t-value | Sig. |
|---|---|---|---|---|---|
| To Provide Information for Fans | Division I-AA | 44 | 6.45 | -.280 | .780 |
|  | Division I-A | 39 | 6.51 |  |  |
| To Provide Information for Media | Division I-AA | 44 | 5.57 | -.323 | .747 |
|  | Division I-A | 39 | 5.67 |  |  |
| To Provide Information for General Public | Division I-AA | 44 | 6.16 | .887 | .378 |
|  | Division I-A | 39 | 5.92 |  |  |
| To Sell University Related Merchandise | Division I-AA | 44 | 2.75 | -2.983 | .004 |
|  | Division I-A | 39 | 3.90 |  |  |
| For Fund Raising | Division I-AA | 44 | 3.09 | -1.358 | .178 |
|  | Division I-A | 39 | 3.56 |  |  |
| To Provide an Outlet to Sell Tickets | Division I-AA | 44 | 3.32 | -2.424 | .018 |
|  | Division I-A | 39 | 4.26 |  |  |
| Informational** | Division I-AA | 44 | 18.18 | .137 | .892 |
|  | Division I-A | 39 | 18.10 |  |  |
| Revenue Generation*** | Division I-AA | 44 | 9.16 | -2.889 | .005 |
|  | Division I-A | 39 | 11.72 |  |  |

\* 1 = least important, 7 = most important

\*\* Combined Means of To Provide Information for Fans, Media, General Public

\*\*\* Combined Means of Sell University Related Merchandise, Fund Raising, Outlet to Sell Tickets

$p \leq .05$

# Conclusions

Fewer than half of NCAA Division I-A institutions operate in the black (Fulks, 2000). However, that doesn't mean that their media operations lose money. Many colleges have extensive sports radio and television networks that bring in funds to the program. Most Division I-A programs generate media dollars from local television and from national television coverage through their conference affiliations. Most colleges have some radio presence and many of the Division I-A schools have extensive radio networks.

**The demographics of Web users and sports fans overlap, and this gives sports marketers an ideal medium to reach their target audience.**

Traditional electronic media are a valued revenue stream for many of these programs. The Internet is making money from sports-related sites. The three business models are generating revenue from users. It can be said that the ability to profit from sports on the Web is there, but it can also be said that NCAA websites are not quite there yet.

The importance of the Web as a marketing tool has been recognized (Delphy & Bossetti, 1998). The demographics of Web users and sports fans overlap, and this gives sports marketers an ideal medium to reach their target audience.

One of the reasons that these sites may not be generating enough revenue to keep the site operations in the black is the perception of value and use by the sports information office and by the athletic department in general. Clearly, most college athletic programs perceive the site as an information distribution vehicle, but beyond that, no clearly defined goals of the sites are apparent. Division I-A sports information directors believe that the sites have the potential for revenue generation and think they should be used that way. Division I-AA schools do not see marketing as such an important use of the site.

**Clearly, most college athletic programs perceive the site as an information distribution vehicle, but beyond that, no clearly defined goals of the sites are apparent.**

**The sites tend to rely largely on the advertising/banner model that is common for many Internet sites. Content subscription and the commerce models are proving to be very successful for sports on the Web, but these sites don't seem to have moved very far in either of those directions.**

Perhaps the reason for the disparity of opinion, or the lack of clearly defined goals for these sites, comes from the marketing model approach these sites take. There are three distinct marketing models for sports sites on the Web, but these sites don't seem to firmly grasp one particular model. Rather, these sites are a loosely constructed hybrid of two or more of these models. The sites tend to rely largely on the advertising/banner model that is common for many Internet sites. Content subscription and the commerce models are proving to be very successful for sports on the Web, but these sites don't seem to have moved very far in either of those directions.

It was stated earlier that the diffusion curve for NCAA sports sites on the Internet has been nearly fully developed; most all Division I sports departments do have a site on the Web. But the problem of making money probably is a subcurve of the original diffusion of Internet presence. Part of the problem may be the perception of value and use of the sites by the athletic department, and the communication of those uses to the fans. Many of these sites aren't designed to make money; the strategies and models used by people who do make money on sports websites apparently are not as widely used on the NCAA sites.

As subdiffusion curves develop, maybe these sites will become profitable and begin to become an integral part of NCAA electronic media. Both the sites' and the athletic departments' focus on these tools seem to be developing. Perhaps the curve for profitability is just beginning to take an upward swing. Athletic organizations do need to recognize the Web's potential as a marketing and revenue-generation tool and take advantage of this communication technology. The full potential of the use of the Web by collegiate athletic departments has not been fully explored.

## References

About the BCS (2002, May 4). espn.com. Retrieved May 4, 2002, from http://www.espn.go.com.

Bates, B. J. (1998). Information as an economic good: Sources of individual and social value. In V. Mosco and J. Wasko (Eds.), *The Political Economy of Information* (pp. 76-94). Madison, WI: University of Wisconsin Press.

Caskey, R., & Delpy, L. (1999). An examination of sport web sites and the opinion toward the use and viability of the web as a profitable sports marketing tool. *Sport Marketing Quarterly, 8*(2), 13-24.

Chan-Olmsted, S. M., & Park, J. S. (2000). From on-air to online world: Examining the content and structures of broadcast TV stations' Web sites. *Journalism and Mass Communication Quarterly, 77*(2), 321-339.

Delphy, L., & Bosette, H. (1998). Sport management marketing via the World Wide Web. *Sport Marketing Quarterly, 7*(1), 21-27.

Duncan, M., & Campbell, R. (1999). Internet users: How to reach them and how to integrate the Internet into the marketing strategy of sport businesses. *Sport Marketing Quarterly, 8*(2), 35-41.

Ford, H., & Painter J. (2002). 2002 Volunteers football: Tennessee. Knoxville, TN: Department of Athletics.

Fulks, D. (2000). Revenues and expenses of division I and II intercollegiate athletic programs: Financial trends and relationships 1999. Retrieved September 27, 2002, from http://www.ncaa.org.

Hardie, M. E. (1998). Cyber Superbowl satisfies. *The Forrester Brief, 1*(2), 1.

Kahle, L., & Meeske, C. (1999). Sports marketing and the internet: It's a whole new ballgame. *Sport Marketing Quarterly, 8*(2), 9-13.

Liberman, N. (2001) Giants, Georgia Tech tout potential gains from selling tickets online. *Street and Smiths Sports Business Journal, 3*(50), 17.

NCAA (1995, November 18). *NCAA Reaches Agreement Rights with CBS Sports.* Retrieved March 1, 1999, from http://www.ncaa.org.

Rogers, E. (1995) (4th ed.). New York: The Free Press.

Stork, P., Neufeld, E., Johnson, M., Zeff, R., Cohen, E, DeBow, Y., and Spinelli, M. (1997). 1998 online advertising report. New York: Jupiter Communications, Inc.

Taylor, H. (2002, April 17). Internet penetration at 66% of adults. Retrieved April 17, 2002, from http://www.harrisinteractive.com

# CHAPTER 4

# Sport Marketing on Fortune Global 500 Web Sites

LARRY G. NEALE
ARNO SCHARL
JAMIE MURPHY

## Abstract

This research investigates how the world's leading companies, the Fortune Global 500, use sports-related terms and phrases on their Web site. An automated process mirrored leading transnational corporations' Web presence and then searched their sites. Analysis of about four gigabytes of Web-based text revealed regional and industry differences in how the world's largest corporations use sports terms on their sites.

## Introduction

**Researchers continue to study corporate sponsorship, but few study how corporate Web sites complement corporate sports sponsorships.**

Increased noise in print and broadcast media along with an increased interest in sports worldwide has pushed corporate sponsorship higher in recent years (Shank, 2002; Terrian, 2002). There has been a corresponding increase in the use of the World Wide Web (WWW) as a medium for internal and external corporate communication (Leichty & Esrock, 2001). In Australia, corporate sport sponsorship doubled from 1996 to 2000, reaching A$700 million. This figure omits an additional A$700 million from the 2000 Sydney Olympics (Lloyd, 2000).

> **These country and industry differences among Global 500 Web sites provide insights into online sports marketing and a basis for future research.**

Researchers continue to study corporate sponsorship, but few study how corporate Web sites complement corporate sports sponsorships. This snapshot of how corporate Web sites reflect sports and sports sponsorship drew upon automated Web tools to mirror the Web site content of the world's largest companies for sports-related terms. After grouping the terms into meaningful associations, the analysis compared usage of these associations. These country and industry differences among Global 500 Web sites provide insights into online sports marketing and a basis for future research of online sports marketing and leading businesses.

## Literature Review

### Corporate Sports Sponsorship, from the Modern Olympics to 2003

Corporate sports sponsorship dates at least to the inaugural modern Olympic Games, Athens in 1896, where companies bought advertising space in the official Olympic program (Sandler & Shani, 1993). Coca-Cola was the first corporation to buy official Olympic sampling rights, at St. Moritz' 1928 Winter Games (Stotlar, 1993). Sponsorship slumbered until the International Olympic Committee (IOC) and the city of Montreal lost money on the 1976 Summer Games. This US$30 million deficit spurred the IOC to focus on sponsorship.

> **Sponsorship slumbered until the International Olympic Committee (IOC) and the city of Montreal lost money on the 1976 Summer Games. This US$30 million deficit spurred the IOC to focus on sponsorship.**

Two factors hindered corporate sponsorship for the next summer games though, a US-led boycott and Moscow's communist environment. Sponsorship soared four years later, helping the Los Angeles Summer Olympics earn a US$225 million profit (Shaheeh, 1999; Stotlar, 1993).

Today, athletes across myriad sports benefit from this increased corporate sponsorship. In May 2003, 18-year-old American high school basketball player LeBron James signed a seven-year Nike deal approaching US$90 million. This falls short, though, of Nike paying US$100 million to golfer Tiger Woods. Tennis player Venus Williams has the highest women's sports sponsorship deal, US$40 million with footwear and apparel maker Reebok (Teather, 2003).

> **At least one study shows a temporary boost in a company's stock price immediately after announcing stadium naming rights.**

### Corporate Sponsorship Objectives

At least one study shows a temporary boost in a company's stock price immediately after announcing stadium naming rights (Clark, Cornwell, & Pruitt, 2002). This short-term benefit illustrates why sports research differs on the perceived benefits of corporate sponsorship (Pope, 1998). Some researchers argue that sponsorships should increase sales (Abratt, Clayton, & Pitt, 1987), while others argue for enhancing a company's image, product or brand (Armstrong, 1988; Javalgi, Traylor, Gross, & Lampman, 1994). Table 1 summarizes four objectives of corporate sponsorship campaigns.

Table 1  **Objectives of Corporate Sponsorship Campaigns**

| Corporate Objectives | Marketing Objectives | Media Objectives | Personal Objectives |
|---|---|---|---|
| **Public Awareness** | Business Relations | Generate Visibility | Management Interest |
| **Corporate Image** | Reach Target Market | Generate Publicity | |
| **Public Perception** | Brand Positioning | Enhance Ad Campaign | |
| **Community Involvement** | Increase Sales | Avoid Clutter | |
| **Financial Relations** | Sampling | Target Specificity | |
| **Client Entertainment** | | | |
| **Government Relations** | | | |
| **Employee Relations** | | | |
| **Compete with other Companies** | | | |
| **Shareholder Wealth** | | | |

Source: (Pope, 1998)

Unlike cinema or music, examples of competing entertainment, international sports such as soccer and golf have standards and etiquette that transcend cultural, religious, and linguistic barriers. Athletes from a record 199 nations competed at the Sydney 2000 Olympics, with even more expected in Athens in 2004.

> **Unlike cinema or music, international sports such as soccer and golf have standards and etiquette that transcend cultural, religious, and linguistic barriers.**

## Modern Sports Marketing

Shank (2002, p.2) defines sports marketing as applying marketing principles to products through association with sport. Estimates on the global value of sports marketing depend upon the variables included, such as sponsorships and revenue. He estimates world sports marketing at approximately US$350 billion in 2002. Thanks to the Internet, sports marketing takes an increasingly global perspective (Mullin, Hardy, & Sutton, 2000; Pope, Forrest, & Murphy, 1996; Summers, 2003).

> **[The NBA] invited online fans, regardless of their country, to select the All-Star team. This multilingual initiative helps explain why one third of www.nba.com's traffic during the All-Star selection originated outside the U.S.**

The Internet gives sports teams, leagues, fans, and consumers a two-way communication platform, independent of time or location. For example, the US-based National Basketball Association (NBA) invited online fans, regardless of their country, to select the All-Star team. In addition to English, the NBA provided French, Spanish and Italian versions of the Web site. This multilingual initiative helps explain why one third of www. nba.com's traffic during the All-Star selection originated outside the U.S. (Mullin et al., 2000).

While one expects large sports organizations such as the NBA or National Football League (www.nfl.com) to establish Web sites, there seems to be no research investigating how major corporations incorporate sports into their Web sites.

> **There seems to be no research investigating how major corporations incorporate sports into their Web sites.**

# Methodology

To investigate the importance of sports marketing to major corporations, this research mirrored and processed the Web sites of the world's leading companies, the Fortune Global 500. Researchers have used Fortune magazine's rankings of top companies to study disciplines such as business ethics (Morf, Schumacher, & Vitell, 1999; Reicher, Webb, & Thomas, 200; Weaver, Treviño, & Cochran, 1999), health care (Montenegro-Tores, Engelhardt, Thamer, & Anderson, 2001), human resources (Baker, DeTienne, & Smart, 1998; Lee & Blaszczynski, 1999), quality management (Baker et al., 1998; Lawler III, Mohrman, & Ledford Jr., 1992), and international business (Gabba, Pan, & Ungson, 2002).

Researchers are also analyzing Internet use by Fortune-ranked companies. Studies have investigated Web sites from perspectives including content (Perry & Bodkin, 2000), marketing (Palmer & Griffith, 1998), global usage patterns (McManis, Ryker, & Cox, 2001), customer relationship management (Romano Jr., 2002-3), and email use (Leichty & Esrock, 2001).

## Gathering Web Content

Since the 1700s and across myriad media, scholars have used content analysis techniques to draw inferences about a medium's subject matter (Krippendorf, 1980). They have applied this technique to Web sites in general (McMillan, 2000; Scharl, 2000) and sports Web sites in particular (Pope et al., 1996). Web sites reflect industry trends and competitive strategies, but methodological problems hinder content analysis of Web sites (McMillan, 2000) and textual data (Rourke, Anderson, Garrison, & Archer, 2001).

Two common techniques rely upon automated tools (Scharl, 2000) or humans (McMillan, 2000) to code a Web site's content. Both methods should be integrated with external success measures such as hits, visits, or performance indicators gathered via questionnaires (Scharl, 2000). Human coding, common on Fortune Web site studies (Leichty & Esrock, 2001; McManis et al., 2001; Palmer & Griffith, 1998; Perry & Bodkin, 2000), is time consuming, suffers from reliability issues and usually analyzes just the home page rather than many pages (McMillan, 2000). Automated analysis, which this study uses, quickly and reliably processes sites but faces technical obstacles depending upon the algorithm used and each site's HTML and other coding (Thelwall, 2002).

Due to changes in the list since its date of publication, mergers for example, this April 2003 study began with 493 of the Fortune Global 500 companies. A robot started at the home page and then followed the site's hierarchical structure until amassing 10 megabytes of data, including visible (raw text including headings, menus, and link descriptions) and invisible text (embedded markup tags, scripting elements, and so forth). This study disregards information found in hierarchical levels beyond the 10-megabyte limit, which fall short of reflecting common use. This limit helps compare systems of heterogeneous size and manage storage space.

> A robot started at the home page and then followed a site's hierarchical structure until amassing 10 megabytes of data, including visible and invisible text.

Similar to respondents failing to reply to an online or mail survey, 77 sites failed to reply to the mirroring process for several reasons (e.g., little textual information, sites not accessible, and difficult to parse for technical reasons). Over two out of five (43%) of the remaining 416 sites represented US companies. Most other companies had their headquarters in Europe (31%) or Asia (24%). The most predominant industry in these 416 sites was finance and insurance (24%), followed by resources (9%) and food/beverage/tobacco (8%). The mirroring process yielded almost four gigabytes of textual Web data, representing more than 9000 documents and about two million words.

## Analyzing Web-Based Corpora

Corpora are collections of recorded content used as a basis for the descriptive analysis of a language. Approaches to analyzing Web-based corpora stem from corpus linguistics, discourse analysis, computer science, Web engineering, and socioeconomic survey analysis (Lebart, Salem, & Berry, 1998). Previous research has gathered and analyzed the structure and content of large samples of Web information systems (Bauer & Scharl, 2000; Scharl, 2000; Scharl & Bauer, 1999; Thelwall, 2002). The Web-monitoring technology underlying this research investigates and visualizes regularities in this data. The analysis applies and extends methods from corpus linguistics and textual statistics (Biber, Conrad, & Reppen, 1998; McEnery & Wilson, 1996).

A sample as culturally heterogeneous as the Fortune Global 500 necessitates identifying the language(s) used. Several techniques tackle this issue, usually based on trigrams and common short words (Hull & Grefenstette, 1996). Trigrams compare a document's frequency of three-letter sequences with a particular language's distribution of these same three-letter sequences. Similarly, common short words such as determiners, conjunctions, and prepositions help divine a language. Both methods produce similar results for chunks of text larger than ten words (Grefenstette, 1995), so this research used short words' computationally lighter technique.

The algorithm classified multilingual sites—i.e., localized versions of the same content—and multilingual content within each document. The 416 sites' use of English content dwarfed content in four other West European languages. English was 11 times more prevalent than French, 16 times more common than German, and used 33 times more often than Spanish or Italian. After detecting the document languages, statistical tests of term frequency distributions analyzed regional differences among corporations.

## Sport Marketing Terms

Given the international focus of this study, the preliminary list of sports stemmed from those recognized and listed by the International Olympic Committee (www.olympic.org). Due to the preponderance of US companies in the Global 500 and English content in the remaining Web sites, popular US sports, general sports terms and popular sports in English-speaking countries-cricket and rugby for example-augmented the list of Olympic sports.

# Results

## Corporate Reflections of Sport

The initial analysis of the 416 sites revealed difficulty interpreting some terms. Golf and marathon, for example, showed up as a Volkswagen car model and an oil company. Terms such as health, swimming, climbing or running also had several meanings. After eliminating terms such as these, *sport* or *sports* was the most popular term, appearing on seven out of ten sites (70%).

*Sport* or *sports* was the most popular, appearing on seven out of ten sites (70%).

The terms Olympic or Olympics appeared on one out of three sites (33%) but only 1% of the sites (five corporations) included the term Paralympics.

The terms Olympic or Olympics appeared on one out of three sites (33%) but only 1% of the sites (five corporations) included the term Paralympics. Selecting the most popular sport proved difficult due to different countries use of the terms football and soccer. Football was on 29% of the sites compared to soccer at 21%. Fishing (24%), baseball (21%) and basketball (20%), closely followed in popularity.

Just 11 corporate sites included the term *sports marketing*. The Massachusetts Mutual Life Insurance Company (www.massmutual.com) led all Global 500 corporations in using the term sports marketing on their site, followed by Hyundai Motor, Hyundai, Anheuser Bush, McDonalds, Samsung Electronics, United Parcel Service, Pepsi Cola, News Corporation, and Bank of America.

The results of a one way ANOVA test showed significant industry differences [$F(27, 388) = 2.915$, $p < .0001$] in the use of the terms sport or sports but no industry differences [$F(27, 388) = 0.453$, $p = .992$] using Olympic or Olympics. Of those industries with at least five corporations, the automotive sector led in using the terms sport(s) and the retail sector included Olympic(s) most often on their sites.

### Corporate Reflections of Sports Marketing

To investigate sports marketing rather than the use of sports terms, the final analysis deleted retail companies that might sell sports products, such as Wal-Mart or Kmart, as well as other companies. Marriott featured recreational mountain biking and golfing, while Berkshire Hathaway promoted a work environment better than golfing or fishing. The analysis also ignored companies with less than ten percent English content, and eight companies not based in Europe, North America, or Asia. Of the remaining 292 companies, over half (54%) were North American, 32% in Europe and 14% in Asia. One out of five (23%) companies was in finance and insurance, followed by companies in food/beverage/tobacco (10%) and resources (9%).

Due to difficultly interpreting the use of terms and low use of some terms, the final analysis combined terms such as soccer, football, and rugby or canoeing, kayaking, and rowing. The final analysis also ignored terms that failed to appear on at least ten Web sites. Table two shows the regional distribution of various sports marketing terms. As North American companies made up over half the sample and about one out seven companies was Asian, the results should reflect this distribution-given no regional differences in sports. This was not the case.

The terms *skating* (ice skating and figure skating), *baseball, basketball, paddling* (canoeing, rowing and kayaking), *extreme sports* (bmx and skateboarding), *equestrian, hockey, softball, volleyball, skiing, stock cars* (Nascar and Winston Cup) and *golfing* (golfing, PGA, LPGA) showed a North American bias. *Windsurfing, boxing, mountain biking, tennis, Formula One,* and *cricket,* though, had proportionally more European presence. Finally, the Asian sites had a proportionally greater use of the terms *chess, SCUBA, badminton, boxing, football* (rugby league, rugby union and soccer), *martial arts* (karate, judo and taekwondo), *fishing,* and *cricket.*

# Conclusions

As discussed earlier, there are limits to automated analysis of Web sites (Thelwall, 2002). Still this study investigated over 400 top corporations' use of sports-related terms on their Web sites. Sport is important to these leading companies; seven out of ten mentioned sports on their sites. As just one in three sites mentioned the Olympics, this may suggest that some companies sponsor the Olympics but fail to promote their sponsorship through their Web sites. These results may also suggest rich sponsorship opportunities for the International Olympic Committee.

# Table 2 **Regional Distribution of Sports Marketing Terms**

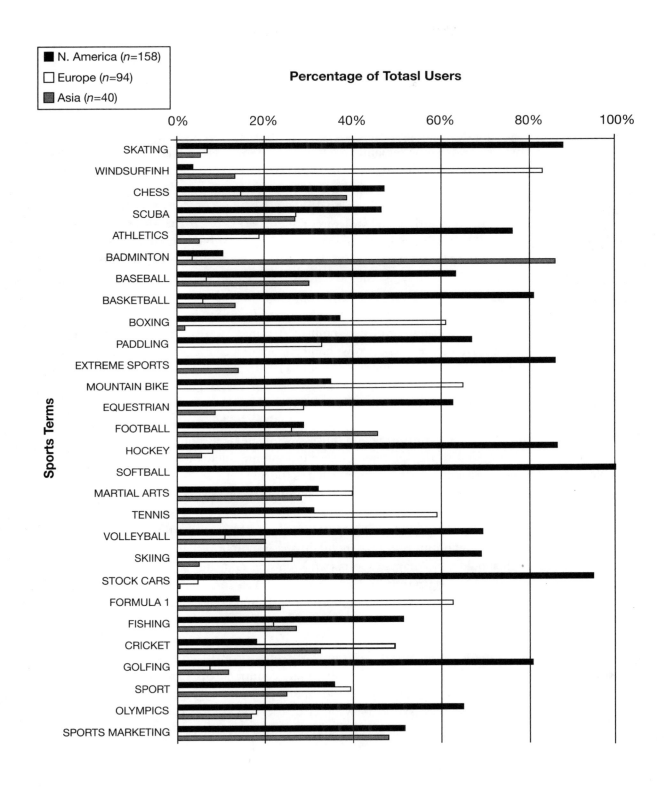

The findings also showed geographic and industry differences in the use of sports marketing terms. These results help sports marketers investigate opportunities or compare against current initiatives. For example, softball seems an untapped market outside of North America and windsurfing represents a North American opportunity.

## Future Research

While simple descriptive representations outline the relative importance of topics by economic sectors, they fail to reflect complex or dynamic semantic relationships. Future research should apply alternative visualization techniques such as dendograms and plots based on correspondence analysis (Hair, Anderson, Tatham, & Black, 1998) to address this shortcoming. Web analysts usually encode multidimensional data comprising so many variables that orthogonal structures fail to suffice (Lebart et al., 1998). Subdividing a problem or computationally reducing the dimensionality often yields results that convey more information and are faster and easier to interpret.

Helping uncover structural traits, correspondence analysis identifies low-dimensional subspaces that approximate the original distribution of data points. A principal axes method based on linear algebra, correspondence analysis represents the rows and columns of a contingency table in a joint plot known as a perceptual map (Hair et al., 1998; Lebart et al., 1998). The resulting table is a powerful, two-dimensional representation for comparing text categories such as Web genres, organizational Web information systems, and individual documents (Scharl, 2000).

Future research would also benefit from longitudinal studies of changes in Fortune Global 500 Web sites' use of sports terms. The mirroring and processing of site data should coincide with events such as the Soccer World Cup or the Olympic Games to examine fluctuations during major global championships. For studies using specific US terms such as the Super Bowl, Southeastern Conference (SEC), or NCAA, the *Fortune* 1000 contains twice the number of corporations and only those based in the US.

Comparing the popularity of corporate web sites that include a large proportion of sporting terms versus those that contain a low proportion may highlight the importance that corporations place on sports. Future research should also compare sports rich Web sites and sites poor in the use of sports terms by studying consumer beliefs and attitudes to corporate Web sites, specifically factors such as awareness, trustworthiness, aesthetic appeal, community interest, and entertainment. Does the use of sports terms enhance a Web site?

Future research should also investigate corporate Web sites use of sports stars. A preliminary list of sports stars is the Laureus World Sports Awards (www.laureus.com). This annual event honors the world's best sportsmen and women across disciplines and countries. Six Laureus categories could

serve as a beginning: World Sportsman of the Year; World Sportswoman of the Year; World Newcomer of the Year, World Comeback of the Year; World Sportsperson of the Year with a Disability; and World Alternative Sportsperson of the Year. Again, US sports stars should augment this list, perhaps with Harris Interactive's (www.harrisinteractive.com) annual poll of popular US sports stars.

# References

Abratt, R. Clayton, B., & Pitt, L. (1987). Corporate Objectives in Sports Sponsorship. *International Journal of Advertising, 6,* 351-362.

Armstrong, C. (1988). Sports sponsorship: A case study approach to measuring its effectiveness. *European Research,* May, 99-103.

Baker, W. H., DeTienne, K., & Smart, K. L. (1998). How Fortune 500 companies are using electronic résumé management systems. *Business Communication Quarterly, 61*(3), 8-19.

Bauer, C., & Scharl, A. (2000). Quantitative evaluation of Web site content and structure. *Internet Research: Networking Applications and Policy, 10*(1), 31-43.

Biber, D., Conrad, S., & Reppen, R. (1998). *Corpus linguistics: Investigating language structure and use.* Cambridge, MA: Cambridge University Press.

Clark, J. M., Cornwell, T. B., & Pruitt, S., W. (2002). Corporate stadium sponsorships, signalling theory, agency conflicts and shareholder wealth. *Journal of Advertising Research, 42*(6), 16-32.

Gabba, V., Pan, Y., & Ungson, G. R. (2002). Timing of entry in international market: An empirical study of U.S. Fortune 500 firms in China. *Journal of International Business Studies, 33*(1), 39-55.

Grefenstette, G. (1995). *Comparing two language identification schemes.* Paper presented at the 3rd International Conference on Statistical Analysis of Textual Data, Rome, Italy.

Hair, J. F., Anderson, R. E., Tatham, R. L., & Black, W. C. (1998). *Multivariate data analysis.* Upper Saddle River N.J.: Prentice Hall.

Hull, D. A., & Grefenstette, G. (1996). *Querying across languages: A dictionary-based approach to multilingual information retrieval.* Paper presented at the 19th Annual International ACM SIGIR Conference on Research and Development in Information Retrieval, Zurich, Switzerland.

Javalgi, R. G., Traylor, M. B., Gross, A. C., & Lampman, E. (1994). Awareness of sponsorship and corporate image: An empirical investigation. *Journal of Advertising, XXIII*(4), 47-58.

Krippendorf, K. (1980). *Content analysis: An introduction to its methodology.* Beverly Hills: Sage.

Lawler III, E. E., Mohrman, S., & Ledford Jr., G. E. (1992). The Fortune 1000 and total quality. *The Journal for Quality and Participation, 15*(5), 6-10.

Lebart, L., Salem, A., & Berry, L. (1998). *Exploring textual data* (Vol. 4). Dordrecht: Kluwer Academic Publishers.

Lee, D.W., & Blaszczynski, C. (1999). Perspectives of "Fortune 500" executives on the competency requirements for accounting graduates. *Journal of Education for Business, 75*(November/December), 104-107.

Leichty, G., & Esrock, S. (2001). Change and response on the corporate Web site. *American Communication Journal, 5*(1).

Lloyd, S. (2000). The games are over: Let the sponsorship begin. *Business Review Weekly* (10 November).

McEnery, T., & Wilson, A. (1996). *Corpus linguistics.* Edinburgh: Edinburgh University Press.

McManis, B. L., Ryker, R., & Cox, K. C. (2001). An examination of Web usage in a global context. *Industrial Management and Data Systems, 101*(8/9), 470-478.

McMillan, S. J. (2000). The microscope and the moving target: The challenge of applying content analysis to the World Wide Web. *Journalism and Mass Communication Quarterly, 77*(1), 80-98.

Montenegro-Tores, F., Engelhardt, T., Thamer, M., & Anderson, G. (2001). Are Fortune 100 companies responsive to chronically ill workers? *Health Affairs, 20*(4), 209-219.

Morf, D. A., Schumacher, M. G., & Vitell, S. J. (1999). A survey of ethics officers in large organizations. *Journal of Business Ethics, 20*(3), 265-271.

Mullin, B. J., Hardy, S., & Sutton, W. A. (2000). *Sport marketing 2nd ed.* Champaign, IL: Human Kinetics.

Palmer, J. W., & Griffith, D. A. (1998). An emerging model of Web site design for marketing. *Communications of the ACM, 41*(3), 44-51.

Perry, M., & Bodkin, C. (2000). Content analysis of Fortune 100 company Web sites. *Corporate Communications: An International Journal, 5*(2), 87-96.

Pope, N. (1998). *Overview of Current Sponsorship Thought.* Retrieved May 26, 2003, from http://pandora.nla.gov.au/nph-arch/O1998-Mar-12//http://www.cad.gu.edu.au/cjsm/pope21.htm.

Pope, N., Forrest, E. J., & Murphy, J. (1996). *Sports marketing on the Internet.* Paper presented at the Australia New Zealand Marketing Academy, Auckland, New Zealand.

Reicher, A. K., Webb, M. S., & Thomas, E. G. (200). Corporate support for ethical and environmental policies: A financial management perspective. *Journal of Business Ethics, 25*(1), 53-64.

Romano Jr., N. C. (2002-3). Customer Relationship Management for the Web-access challenged: Inaccessibility of Fortune 250 business Web sites. *International Journal of Electronic Commerce, 7*(2), 61-117.

Rourke, L., Anderson, T., Garrison, D. R., & Archer, W. (2001). Methodological issues in the content analysis of computer conference transcripts. *International Journal of Artificial Intelligence in Education, 12*(1), 8-22.

Sandler, D. M., & Shani, D. (1993). Sponsorship and the Olympic games: The consumer perspective. *Sport Marketing Quarterly, 2*(3), 38-43.

Scharl, A. (2000). *Evolutionary Web development.* London: Springer.

Scharl, A., & Bauer, C. (1999). *Explorative analysis and evaluation of commercial Web information systems.* Paper presented at the 20th International Conference on Information Systems (ICIS-99), Charlotte, USA.

Shaheeh, N. (1999). *The Olympics supermarket: Money is the chief player.* Retrieved May 27, 2003, from http://www.islamon-line.net/iol-english/dowalia/money-30-Sep-2000/money1.asp.

Shank, M. D. (2002). *Sports marketing: A strategic perspective.* Upper Saddle River, NJ: Prentice Hall.

Stotlar, D. (1993). Sponsorship and the Olympic Winter Games. *Sport Marketing Quarterly, 2*(1), 35-43.

Summers, J. (2003). Sport marketing. In J. R. McColl-Kennedy (Ed.), *Services marketing: A managerial approach.* Milton QLD: John Wiley.

Teather, D. (2003). *Sponsor passes £55m to school basketball star before his first game.* Retrieved May 27, 2003, from http://www.guardian.co.uk/international/story/0,3604,962553,00.html.

Terrian, J. (2002). Career paths in sports marketing and corporate sponsorships today. Retrieved June 22, 2003, from Marquette University Web site at http://classwork.busadm.mu.edu/classwork/Terrian/.

Thelwall, M. (2002). Methodologies for crawler based Web surveys. *Internet Research: Electronic Networking Applications and Policy, 12*(2), 124-138.

Weaver, G. R., Treviño, L. K., & Cochran, P. L. (1999). Corporate ethics practices in the mid-1990's: An empirical study of the Fortune 1000. *Journal of Business Ethics, 18*(3), 283-294.

# PART III
# SPONSORSHIP AND SPORT MARKETING

# CHAPTER 5

# The Impact of Fan Identification on Customer Response to Sponsorships

**VASSILIS DALAKAS**
**GREGORY M. ROSE**

## Abstract

This study of baseball fans found that fans who highly identified with a team had more favorable responses to the team's sponsors. Moreover, other factors that also influence consumer response to sponsorships, like perceived fit between the sponsors and the team, perceived sincerity of the sponsors, and perceived status of the sponsored property, were also influenced by team identification. Compared to moderate and low-identification fans, highly identified fans perceived a stronger fit between the sponsors and the team, perceived the sponsors as more sincere, perceived the team as having higher status, and had more positive beliefs about sponsorship in general. Overall, identification had a significant effect on consumer response to sponsorships, both directly and indirectly. These effects are consistent with marketing theory and have significant managerial implications.

## Introduction

Sponsorship is defined as "a cash and/or in-kind fee paid to a property (typically in sports, arts, entertainment, or causes) in return for access to the exploitable commercial potential associated with the property" (Ukman, 1996, p.1). Corporations have been increasingly using sponsorship as a marketing communications tool in order to reach their target consumers and build brand equity (Cornwell, Roy, & Steinard, 2001; Javalgi, Traylor, Gross, & Lampman, 1994).

**Approximately two thirds of sponsorship spending involves sports properties (events or organizations).**

Approximately two thirds of sponsorship spending involves sports properties (events or organizations). In order to realize the magnitude of sponsorship in sports, one may consider the following examples: the 2000 Olympic Games in Sydney generated $550 million from the International Olympic Committee's 11 worldwide sponsors as well as an additional $315 million from local sponsors (Landler, 2000); sponsoring a NASCAR racing team can cost as much as $17 million (Knight, 2002); and 22 of the 25 college football bowl games in 2001-2002 had a title sponsor. Substantial amounts are also spent on sponsorships of festivals, tours, arts, and causes (IEG Sponsorship Report, 2000). Corporate involvement through sponsorship and advertising is big business in American sports, both on-site and during broadcasts of sporting events. As an example, consider the 2002 telecast of the NCAA basketball tournament on American broadcast network CBS. The Final Four games saw Microsoft's "Agile Move," Cingular's "At the Half" half-time show, Pontiac's "Sky Cam," Mountain Dew's "Bird's Vision" camera angles, and the Chevrolet "Players of the Game."

> **The 2000 Olympic Games in Sydney generated $550 million from the International Olympic Committee's 11 worldwide sponsors as well as an additional $315 million from local sponsors; sponsoring a NASCAR racing team can cost as much as $17 million; and 22 of the 25 college football bowl games in 2001-2002 had a title sponsor.**

As sponsorship continues to grow as a marketing communications tool, it becomes more important to understand how sponsorships influence consumer attitudes and behavior. Recognizing an initial lack of academic research in the area of consumer response to sponsorship, scholars have called for further research on this topic (e.g., Cornwell & Maignan, 1998; Meenaghan, 1999). As a result, more systematic effort to investigate and understand this phenomenon has emerged the past few years, generating more rigorous studies investigating consumer response to sponsorships (e.g., Johar & Pham, 1999; Madrigal, 2000; Madrigal, 2001; Speed & Thompson, 2000). Indicative of the increasing attention to sponsorship by academic researchers is the fact that, in 2001, two advertising/marketing journals (*Journal of Advertising Research* and *Psychology & Marketing*) dedicated special issues to articles dealing with sponsorship.

Our study builds on previous research and advances our understanding of consumer response to sponsorship by concentrating on the effect of fan identification, both directly and indirectly, on consumer response to sponsorship. Research has shown that several factors may influence how favorably consumers respond to sponsors (Speed & Thompson, 2000). We examine the effect of fan identification on these factors to assess its overall impact on how consumers respond to corporate sponsorships.

## Theoretical Background

### Consumer Response to Sponsorship

Speed and Thompson (2000) provided a comprehensive model of consumer response to sponsorship that supplied an excellent foundation for all future research in this area. They found that a consumer's previous attitude toward a sponsor, the perceived fit between a sponsor and a sponsored event, and the perceived sincerity of the sponsor all influenced the likelihood of the consumer noticing the sponsor (interest), the favorability of the consumer's perceptions of the sponsor (favor), and the likelihood of the consumer purchasing from the sponsor (use). When consumers already like a company that becomes a sponsor, when they feel that the sponsorship "makes sense" in terms of who sponsors what, and when they feel a sponsor is genuinely interested in supporting a specific organization or event rather than simply capitalizing on the commercial benefits of the organization's popularity, they tend to respond more favorably to the sponsor.

Additional variables were also significant for response to sponsorships: liking the sponsored event influenced intention to use the sponsor's products, status of the sponsored event influenced interest in the sponsor and favor for the sponsor, and perceived ubiquity of the sponsor (how many different events it sponsors) had a negative impact on interest in and use of the sponsor.

In addition to the variables tested by Speed and Thompson, we also considered consumers' knowledge about use of sponsorship as a marketing tool. Friestad and Wright's (1994) work on persuasion knowledge suggests that consumer response to marketing persuasion tactics may be influenced by the consumers' level of understanding of such tactics. Therefore, people's beliefs about different forms of persuasion and what marketers try to accomplish through each form should affect the way people respond to persuasion attempts. Given that sponsorships, as a marketing communications tool, are another type of persuasion attempt used by companies, consumers' beliefs and understanding of sponsorships should be examined when looking at consumer response to sponsorships (Meenaghan, 2001). For example, proponents of sponsorship point to how, without the support from sponsors, many events would not be possible. Consumers who are aware of this connection and care about these events are likely to respond quite positively to sponsors. In fact, in some cases, such positive response to sponsors may reach levels of true gratitude toward the sponsors on the part of the consumers (Crimmins & Horn, 1996).

> **When consumers feel a sponsor is genuinely interested in supporting a specific organization or event rather than simply capitalizing on the commercial benefits of the organization's popularity, they tend to respond more favorably to the sponsor.**

> **Proponents of sponsorship point to how, without the support from sponsors, many events would not be possible. In fact, in some cases, such positive response may reach levels of true gratitude toward the sponsors on the part of the consumers.**

### Social Identity-Team Identification

Speed and Thompson's study (2000) examined the effect of *personal liking* for an event on responses to event sponsors. In our study, we used *fan identification,* a stronger form of liking. Using identification is more representative of the strong relationships that fans form with organizations, especially within the context of sports, where the majority of sponsorships take place.

When an individual falls into and belongs to a social category (such as fan of a sport team), "it provides a definition of who one is in terms of the defining characteristics of the category-a self-definition that is part of the self concept" (Hogg, Terry, & White, 1995, p. 259). As a result of developing this type of social identity, the social category one belongs to provides emotional and value significance to the individual (Hogg & Abrams, 1990).

Identification with a sports team can involve defining one's identity in terms of one's attachment to a sports team; the sports team essentially becomes part of one's self identity (Belk, 1988; Kelley & Tepper, 1998; Madrigal, 2000). Consequently, a strong affiliation with a sports team can influence many aspects of a fan's behavior. Sports marketers credit passionate fans for keeping the sports industry alive and prosperous (King, 2002). Team identification has an effect on the amount of time, money, and effort that a fan invests in a sports team (Fisher & Wakefield, 1998; Wann & Branscombe, 1993). Specifically, identification influences game attendance (Fisher & Wakefield, 1998) and the amount one spends on licensed

> **A strong affiliation with a sports team can influence many aspects of a fan's behavior. Sports marketers credit passionate fans for keeping the sports industry alive and prosperous.**

merchandise (Fisher & Wakefield, 1998; Wann & Branscombe, 1993). Dalakas, Kropp, Shoham, and Florenthal (1997) found that highly identified fans both in the United States and Australia had positive attitudes towards their team's sponsors. Additionally, similar results were found with fans in Greece and South Korea (Dalakas & Kropp, 2002). Moreover, studies of American college football fans revealed that highly identified fans held more favorable attitudes towards team sponsors and were more inclined to purchase from the team's sponsors (Madrigal, 2000).

A strong social identity motivates members of a group to use intergroup comparisons that favor the in-group (Hogg & Abrams, 1990). Therefore, team identification also affects people's perceptions and evaluations of themselves, other people, events, and situations. Research on team identification has documented that strong affiliation with a sports team can influence many aspects of a fan's behavior. For example, high identification has been found to a) lead to higher levels of arousal during a sports contest (Branscombe & Wann, 1992), b) cause a strong positive bias for other fans of the same team (Wann & Dolan, 1994a), c) lead to biased attributions for and evaluations of the team's performance and ability for future accomplishments (Dietz-Uhler & Murrell, 1999; Wann & Dolan, 1994b; Wann & Schrader, 2000), d) correlate highly with a willingness to cheat in order to assist the team (Wann, Hunter, Ryan, & Wrigh, 2001), e) lead to higher likelihood to *bask in the reflected glory* (BIRG) of the team's victories and lower likelihood to *cut off reflected failure* (CORF) after team losses (Wann & Branscombe, 1990), and f) cause higher fan aggression (Wann, 1993; Wann, Carlson, & Schrader, 1999).

> **Heider's classic work on Balance Theory provides a basic conceptual foundation for explaining this tendency of highly identified fans to see whatever is associated with their team in a positive light.**

Heider's classic work on Balance Theory (Heider, 1958) provides a basic conceptual foundation for explaining this tendency of highly identified fans to see whatever is associated with their team in a positive light. Balance Theory suggests that if people have a strong positive (or negative) attitude towards a 'unit' (person, object, organization, brand, issue, etc.), they will need to have a similarly positive (or negative) attitude towards anything that is associated with that 'unit'. Inconsistency is likely to cause imbalance and dissonance, thereby motivating individuals to change their attitudes in a way that restores balance. For example, if one feels very positively about protecting the environment, one would be more likely to have similarly positive feelings toward companies that have an active environmental agenda. Not liking such companies would be inconsistent with one's support for environmental causes. The stronger one's attitude is toward an entity, the stronger the expected effect of associating that entity with something else. In many respects, Balance Theory is at the very essence of any type of sponsorship association (Crimmins & Horn, 1996); a company may reach its target consumers by forming an association with a property that these consumers care about. Consumers' lack of strong positive feelings for the property makes the association one of little significance and value to the consumers, who, consequently, are likely to be indifferent toward the sponsor.

## Hypotheses

In extending the sponsorship model by Speed and Thompson (2000), we propose that strong team identification can lead to strong positive responses toward the sponsors in two ways. Strong allegiance to a team should make a fan feel positive toward the sponsor directly, through the premises of Balance Theory: When a consumer feels very positively towards his or her favorite team and sponsors become associated with that team, the consumer should also develop positive feelings toward the team's sponsors.

Strong identification can also lead to a positive response to sponsorship indirectly by coloring the fan's perceptions of other factors that may influence response to sponsorship like, for example, perceived sincerity of the sponsor, perceived fit between the sponsor and the sponsored team, and perceived status of sponsored event (all variables that were found by Speed and Thompson to affect response to sponsorship). Moreover, because highly identified fans are more involved with a team and more likely to know and understand about sponsorships and their benefits, identification should also influence beliefs about sponsorship in general. Given that perceived ubiquity of sponsor does not entail valence, it is not considered a factor that will be influenced by one's identification with the sponsored property. Overall, the following hypotheses are proposed:

H1: Highly identified fans will be more aware of their team's sponsors than moderate and low-identification fans.

H2: Highly identified fans will have higher levels of a) interest, b) favor, and c) use for the sponsors than moderate and low-identification fans.

H3: Highly identified fans will perceive the fit between their team and the sponsors as stronger than moderate and low-identification fans.

H4: Highly identified fans will perceive the sponsors of their team as more sincere than moderate and low-identification fans.

H5: Highly identified fans will perceive the status of their team (sponsored property) as higher than moderate and low-identification fans.

H6: Highly identified fans will have more positive beliefs about sponsorship in general than moderate and low-identification fans.

# Methodology

### General Procedure and Sample

Data were collected from a convenience sample (of students and non-students) just outside the metropolitan area of a large city in the southeastern United States. Given that our study pertained to the baseball team of the city, we intentionally avoided collecting data on-site at the team's baseball games because it would have possibly led to a sample skewed in identification with the baseball team. Consequently, we expected more variance in level of identification with the baseball team within our selected sample.

Marketing students in upper-division courses were used as data collectors; they were asked to approach students on a college campus (at dormitories, classes, or student center) of a private college in the region. Also, the surveyors approached people outside the campus, at their places of employment (primarily offices and stores in the area). The study participants either completed the survey at the time it was given to them or, in the case of many of the people off-campus, at their own convenience, and then gave it to the surveyors a week later when they returned to collect completed surveys. All participants, students and non-students, were volunteers who received no compensation or extra credit for their participation.

Of the 250 surveys distributed, complete data were obtained from 197 for a response rate of 78.8%. There was a relatively balanced representation of men and women in the sample, with men comprising 53.8% of the sample. Approximately 65% of the sample was college students. The mix of students and non-students provided a more balanced sample, addressing some of the concerns that have been raised for using solely student samples (e.g., Wells, 1993). Moreover, including students in this study was appropriate given that many people in this age group usually tend to be active followers of sports and are, consequently, a meaningful group to study when the context of the research is sport-related (Dalakas & Kropp, 2002; Lardinoit & Quester, 2001). T-tests on all of the variables of the survey indicated that there were no differences between students and non-students.

## Constructs and Measures

The major league baseball team of the metropolitan area served as the *sponsored property*. For *sponsors*, we used two of the team's actual sponsors: one that was well-known as a sponsor (a soft drink company) and one with low to moderate level of awareness as a sponsor (an auto parts provider).[1] We used two sponsors to increase our ability to generalize our conclusions; we used sponsors with different levels of awareness to ensure that our findings would result from the variables of interest rather than the respondents' relative familiarity with (or lack thereof) a company.

The measures used in the study were primarily from the model by Speed and Thompson (2000); we selected items with the highest factor loadings from the original study.

Perceived fit between sponsor and the property was measured with four items, seven-point Likert agree/disagree statements, where 1 corresponded to *strongly disagree* and 7 corresponded to *strongly agree*. The items were "(Name of sponsor) and (name of baseball team) fit together well," "(Name of sponsor) and (name of baseball team) stand for similar things," "It makes sense to me that (name of sponsor) sponsors (name of baseball team)," and "The image of (name of sponsor) and (name of baseball team) are similar."

The perceived sincerity of the sponsor was measured with two items, seven-point Likert agree/disagree statements, where 1 corresponded to strongly disagree and 7 corresponded to strongly agree: "(Name of sponsor) would probably support the (name of baseball team) even if the (name of baseball team) were not doing well" and "(Name of sponsor) is likely to have the best interests of the (name of baseball team) at heart."

The perceived ubiquity of the sponsor was also measured with two items, seven-point Likert agree/disagree statements, where 1 corresponded to strongly disagree and 7 corresponded to strongly agree: "(Name of sponsor) sponsors many different sports or teams" and "It is very common to see (name of sponsor) sponsoring sporting events or sports teams."

Previous attitude towards the sponsor was measured with two items: "How do you feel about (name of sponsor)?" (7-point scale: dislike it/like it) and "What is your opinion of (name of sponsor)?" (7-point scale: unfavorable/favorable). Status of event (sports team) was measured with one item: "The (name of baseball team) are important where I live."

Instead of personal liking, we used *team identification*, which encompasses a stronger sense of personal liking. Identification was measured with a modified version of the Sport Spectator Identification Scale (Wann & Branscombe, 1993). Previous studies have established this scale as a reliable measure (Dalakas & Kropp, 2002; Madrigal, 2000; Wann & Branscombe, 1993). Ten items were used. Sample items included "It is important to me that the (name of baseball team) win," "I see myself as a big fan of the (name of baseball team)," "I want to attend the (name of baseball team) games," "I always display the (name of baseball team) name or logo on my clothing at my house or at my work." Using identification rather than simply *liking* provided a broader measure of one's association with a sponsored property, which should be able to capture a more meaningful effect of such association.

In order to generate items for general beliefs about sponsorship we conducted informal interviews with college students, asking them to list what positive and negative thoughts they had about sports sponsorships in general. Based on people's comments, we generated three items for positive beliefs and three items for negative beliefs to include in the questionnaire. All items were measured with a seven-

[1] Prior to designing the questionnaire, informal interviews were conducted with people in the area to identify level of awareness with the different sponsors of the team.

point Likert scale (strongly disagree/strongly agree). The items for beliefs about sponsorship were "Sponsorships are useful for sports," "Sponsorships are necessary for sports," "Consumers benefit from sport sponsorships," "There are too many sponsorships in sports today" (reverse-coded), "Sponsorships are commercializing sports" (reverse-coded), and "Sponsorships are just gimmicks to make you buy" (reverse-coded).

Similar to Speed and Thompson (2000), we used the following items for the dependent measures of consumer response to the sponsors: a) *interest* ("Sponsorship will make me more likely to notice the sponsor's name on other occasions" and "Sponsorship will make me more likely to pay attention to the sponsor's advertising"), b) *favor* ("Sponsorship will improve my perception of the sponsor" and "Sponsorship makes me more favorable toward sponsor"), and c) use ("Sponsorship will make me more likely to use the sponsor's brand" and "I would be more likely to buy from the sponsor"). The measures of interest, favor, and use were also consistent with what have been defined as key organizational objectives for the use of sponsorship as a communications tool: increasing awareness and improving corporate and brand image, which would lead, consequently, to increase in sales (Cornwell & Maignan, 1998; Cornwell et al., 2001; Madrigal, 2000).

## Correlations and Reliability

The correlations for the two items measuring attitude toward a sponsor were .77 (sponsor A; auto parts provider) and .86 (sponsor B; soft drink company). The items for the perceived sincerity of a sponsor had a correlation of .45 (sponsor A) and .44 (sponsor B), whereas the correlations for the items measuring the perceived ubiquity of a sponsor had a correlation of .62 (sponsor A) and .61 (sponsor B). The four items measuring the perceived fit between the sponsor and the property had a reliability of .80 (sponsor A) and .82 (sponsor B), while the six items measuring beliefs about sponsorship had a reliability of .71, and the Sport Spectator Identification Scale (Wann & Branscombe, 1993) had a reliability of .94.

**The findings confirmed that participants were highly aware of the soft drink company being a sponsor and less aware that the auto parts provider was a sponsor.**

The correlations for the dependent variables were as follows: interest (.57 for sponsor A and .71 for sponsor B), favor (.66 for sponsor A and .62 for sponsor B), and use (.92 for sponsor A and .88 for sponsor B).

The findings confirmed that participants were highly aware of the soft drink company being a sponsor and less aware that the auto parts provider was a sponsor. The mean for awareness of the soft drink company as a sponsor was 3.26 ($SD$ = .97), whereas awareness for the auto parts store as a sponsor was 1.85 ($SD$ = 1.02). Awareness was measured by a four-point scale, ranging from 1 ("had no idea it was a sponsor") to 4 ("definitely knew it was a sponsor").

# Results

An index was developed from the questions of the Identification Scale. Participants' responses to all scale questions were averaged into a summary measure for team identification. Participants were then divided into three groups of similar size (low, moderate, and high identification) based on the summary score of each person on the 7-point identification scale. Participants with a score of 4.10 and higher were classified as highly identified fans, those with a score between 2.50 and 4.09 as moderate fans, and those with a score of 2.49 and below as low-identification fans. Seventy two percent of the respondents indicated that the baseball team used for the study was their favorite baseball team and 44% of the respondents indicated that the team was their favorite team in all sports.

One-way ANOVA tests were conducted for the three levels of team identification in regard to each of the dependent measures. Tukey's Honestly Significant Difference tests were used to assess group differences. Table 1 summarizes the results for the items that examined team identification's direct effect on response to sponsors.

Table 1 **Effect of Team Identification on Response to Sponsors**

| | High-ID fans (H) | Moderate-ID fans (M) | Low-ID fans (L) |
|---|---|---|---|
| **Awareness of sponsor A (auto parts)** | 2.44 M, L | 1.63 H | 1.48 H |
| **Awareness of sponsor B (soft drink)** | 3.62 | 3.25 L | 2.84 H |
| **Interest in sponsor A** | 4.20 M, L | 3.37 H, L | 2.42 H, M |
| **Interest in sponsor B** | 4.39 M, L | 3.67 H, L | 3.00 H, M |
| **Favor toward sponsor A** | 4.10 M, L | 3.31 H, L | 2.58 H, M |
| **Favor toward sponsor B** | 4.52 M, L | 3.80 H, L | 3.05 H, M |
| **Intent to purchase from sponsor A** | 3.86 M, L | 2.91 H, L | 2.25 H, M |
| **Intent to purchase from sponsor B** | 4.02 M, L | 3.26 H, L | 2.54 H, M |

Note: Awareness was measured on a 1-4 scale where 1 corresponded to "had no idea it is a sponsor" and 4 corresponded to "definitely knew it is a sponsor." All other variables were measured through seven-point scales where high numbers indicated more positive responses (e.g., higher interest).

Letters after each score indicate Tukey's Honestly Significant differences (.05 or lower) among groups. For example, indicating M, L next to the mean of high-identification fans states that this was a significant difference from the moderate- and low-identification fans.

Table 2 **Effect of Team Identification on Perceptions and Beliefs About Sponsorship**

| | High-ID fans (H) | Moderate-ID fans (M) | Low-ID fans (L) |
|---|---|---|---|
| **Perceived fit between sponsor A (auto parts) and baseball team** | 4.10 M, L | 3.48 H | 3.17 H |
| **Perceived fit between sponsor B (soft drink) and baseball team** | 4.99 L | 4.76 | 4.13 H |
| **Perceived sincerity of sponsor A** | 3.83 M, L | 3.23 H | 2.87 H |
| **Perceived sincerity of sponsor B** | 4.64 M, L | 4.05 H | 3.85 H |
| **Perceived status of sponsored property** | 5.53 M, L | 3.47 H, L | 1.63 H, M |
| **Beliefs about sponsorship** | 4.51 M, L | 3.64 H | 3.72 H |

Note: Variables were measured through seven-point scales where high numbers indicated more positive responses (e.g., stronger perceived fit).

Letters after each score indicate Tukey's Honestly Significant differences (.05 or lower) among groups. For example, indicating M, L next to the mean of high-identification fans states that this was a significant difference from the moderate- and low-identification fans.

Table 2 summarizes the results on team identification's impact on perceptions about the sponsorship. Previous research (Speed & Thompson, 2000) found that the perceived fit between sponsor and property, the perceived sincerity of the sponsor, and the perceived status of the property all influence consumer response to sponsors. Our study also found significant correlations ($p < .01$) between each of these variables and response to sponsorship, ranging from .4 to .6. Therefore, identification's impact on perceptions did have an indirect effect on response to sponsors. Although identification influences people's beliefs about sponsorship in general, the beliefs *per se* were not found to be highly correlated with response to sponsors.

Overall, the findings confirmed the hypotheses in regard to both sponsor A and sponsor B. In all cases, highly identified fans had more positive responses to sponsors (directly and indirectly) than low-identification fans. All differences were statistically significant at .05 level. Also, in all but two cases (awareness of soft drink company as a sponsor and perceived fit between team and soft drink company), highly identified fans had more positive responses (statistically significant) to sponsors (directly and indirectly) than moderate fans.

Specifically, in regard to sponsor A, the auto parts shop, high-identification fans were more aware of the sponsorship than moderate and low-identification fans (supporting H1), were more likely to notice the sponsor (supporting H2a), feel favorable toward the sponsor (supporting H2b), and use the sponsor's products (supporting H2c) than either moderate or low-identification fans. Moreover, high-identification fans perceived a stronger fit between the auto parts shop and the team than moderate and low-identification fans (supporting H3) and perceived the sponsor as more sincere than moderate or low-identification fans did (supporting H4).

> In all cases, highly identified fans had more positive responses to sponsors (directly and indirectly) than low-identification fans. Also, in all but two cases, highly identified fans had more positive responses (statistically significant) to sponsors (directly and indirectly) than moderate fans.

> In regard to the auto parts shop, high-identification fans were more aware of the sponsorship than moderate and low-identification fans, were more likely to notice the sponsor, feel favorable toward the sponsor, and use the sponsor's products than either moderate or low-identification fans.

The findings were consistent for sponsor B, the soft drink company. However, in two cases (e.g., awareness of company as a sponsor and perceived fit between team and the sponsor), perceptions of high-identification fans were significantly different only from the low-identification fans and not from the moderate ones. Overall, H1, H2, H3, and H4 were all supported, suggesting a consistent pattern for the effects of identification for both the sponsor with high overall awareness and the sponsor with lower overall awareness.

In regard to perceived status of the baseball team (sponsored property), highly identified fans perceived the team as having higher status than moderate and low-identification fans. Similarly, regarding general beliefs about sponsorship, highly identified fans again had more positive beliefs than the other fans. The differences in both cases were statistically significant, providing support for both H5 and H6.

# Discussion and Managerial Implications

As predicted, team identification created a more positive response to sponsors and made fans/consumers more likely to patronize the companies that sponsor their favorite team. This is consistent with the basic premise of Balance Theory and shows a strong tendency of sponsor *favoritism* that highly identified fans exhibit.

Our study provided additional insight on why strong team identification may create positive responses to sponsorship. Team identification influenced perceived fit between sponsor and sponsored property as well as perceived sincerity of the sponsor, and perceived status of the sponsored property, all factors that have been found to influence consumer response to sponsorships (Speed & Thompson, 2000). While high-identification fans are likely to notice, favor, and use their team's sponsors directly, they also, indirectly, tend to perceive other factors associated with the sponsors in a more positive light, therefore, increasing the overall impact of the sponsorship. Consequently, team identification seems to trigger a *halo effect* that makes fans/consumers more receptive to sponsors and sponsorships in multiple levels. It is interesting to note that team identification, which is largely of an affective nature, affects perceptions of a more cognitive nature, like perceived fit between sponsor and property. This finding also reinforces and supports previous research in this area.

> **Team identification seems to trigger a *halo effect* that makes fans/consumers more receptive to sponsors and sponsorships in multiple levels. It is interesting to note that team identification, which is largely of an affective nature, affects perceptions of a more cognitive nature, like perceived fit between sponsor and property.**

It is important to note that identification is stronger and broader than mere liking for a property; a consumer may like a property but not necessarily be passionate about it, whereas a consumer's passion about a property is bound to also include liking for the property. The distinction between fair-weather fans (who *like* a team) and die-hard fans (who *identify* with a team) illustrates the difference between liking and identification.

The implications of our findings are clear: Companies interested in using sponsorship as a marketing communications tool should seek and identify properties with highly identified, passionate fans that fit the profile of the company's target market; such commitment is bound to elicit favorable responses to their sponsorships, translating into creating awareness and building brand equity among the target market. Sponsors should consider-independent of the nature of the property-the level of commitment the property's fans have toward the property.

This becomes especially relevant for some organizations or teams that may be in smaller markets and, thus, may not appear at first sight to be very appealing to big potential sponsors. The example of the Green Bay Packers in the National Football League provides a great illustration of an attractive 'small' team to sponsor because of its fans' identification. From 1989 to 1998, the Packers filled 97.4 percent of the seats at their 80 home games, despite playing in the league's smallest market and coldest weather (Thomas, 1999). In fact, overall, teams in smaller cities and markets tend to generate more fan support and a more loyal fan base than teams in bigger cities and markets (Thomas, 1999).

> **Companies should seek and identify properties with highly identified, passionate fans that fit the profile of the company's target market; such commitment is bound to elicit favorable responses to their sponsorships, translating into creating awareness and building brand equity among the target market.**

This insight is important, given the tendency of many sponsors to pursue high-profile prestigious events (like the Olympics or the soccer World Cup) in hopes of a positive consumer response to such sponsorship. Sponsorship of such properties is usually very expensive. For example, Hyundai paid an estimated $35 million to be the sole automotive "official partner" for the 2002 World Cup (Treece, 2002), and affiliation with the Olympics is worth at least $40 million (Miyazaki & Morgan, 2001). However, such expensive sponsorships may not necessarily yield meaningful results unless fans have a strong degree of identification with these properties. Moreover, our findings indicated that highly identified fans are likely to perceive their favorite event, team, or organization as one with higher status, which in turn, also helps the sponsors. This can be particularly relevant for small or medium-size companies that can only pursue sponsorship opportunities with smaller-scale properties.

We should note that, although strong fan identification is relatively common within sports, it is not limited to sports. Consumers may be strongly identified with non-sports properties and organizations, like the university they attended or a symphony or museum, especially at a local level (Bhattacharya, Rao, & Glynn, 1995). Such identified consumers would want to support these properties and, subsequently, the sponsors that associate with them.

> **Hyundai paid an estimated $35 million to be the sole automotive "official partner" for the 2002 World Cup. However, such expensive sponsorships may not necessarily yield meaningful results unless fans have a strong degree of identification with these properties.**

From the standpoint of a property, strong fan identification may be beneficial in many ways. Naturally, highly committed fans will spend more money on the property by purchasing tickets, licensed merchandise, and similar activities. The benefits, however, do not end there. Properties with highly identified fans can leverage this commitment in their sponsorship proposals and their pursuit of sponsors. A property with highly identified fans should be extremely attractive to potential sponsors given that a loyal and identified fan base can provide a sponsor with a successful sponsorship investment. Managers of properties should consciously encourage and develop strong fan identification. Creating programs that reinforce such identification, such as active fan clubs, can yield meaningful results. This issue is particularly relevant for American professional sports, where frequent relocation of sports teams and increasing ticket prices may have alienated many fans (Burton & Howard, 1999). Not surprisingly, such movements make it difficult to establish a strongly identified fan base and, in that respect, should make sponsors carefully consider the value of sponsoring these properties.

## Limitations and Future Research

We should note that our study provided insight regarding attitudes and intentions toward sponsors but not actual behavior. Future research should investigate further the extent to which these positive attitudes do indeed translate into purchases from the sponsor. This question becomes extremely relevant in terms of how fan identification would influence brand preferences when competing brands (a sponsor and a non-sponsor) may vary in price or other important characteristics. Future research should also examine how identification with one property may elicit *negative* responses toward sponsors of rival properties. This is a natural extension of Balance Theory (liking a property means disliking the property's rivals and, consequently, disliking the rivals' sponsors) that raises interesting questions for future research efforts.

Although sports sponsorship is a large and growing phenomenon, future research should also examine the effects of fan identification in contexts outside sports. Finally, future research efforts should investigate the magnitude of the effects of fan identification on sponsorship within a crosscultural context. Given that sports fans around the world are legendary for how identified they can become with their favorite teams, crosscultural research could further our understanding of this area.

# References

Belk, R. (1988). Possessions and the extended self. *Journal of Consumer Research, 15* (September), 139-168.

Bhattacharya, B., Rao, H., & Glynn, M. A. (1995). Understanding the bond of identification: An investigation of its correlates among art museum members. *Journal of Marketing, 59*(4), 46-57.

Branscombe, N. R., & Wann, D. L. (1992). Physiological arousal and reactions to outgroup members during competitions that implicate an important social identity. *Aggressive Behavior, 18,* 85-93.

Burton, R, & Howard, D. (1999). Professional sports leagues: Marketing mix mayhem. *Marketing Management,* 37-46.

Cornwell, T. B., & Maignan, I. (1998). An international review of sponsorship research. *Journal of Advertising, 27*(1), 1-21.

Cornwell, T. B., Roy, D. P., & Steinard, E. A., II. (2001). Exploring managers' perceptions of the impact of sponsorship on brand equity. *Journal of Advertising, 30*(2), 41-51.

Crimmins, J., & Horn, M. (1996). Sponsorship: from management ego trip to marketing success. *Journal of Advertising Research, 36*(4), 11-21.

Dalakas, V., & Kropp, F. (2002). Attitudes toward purchasing from sponsors: A cross-cultural perspective. *Journal of Euromarketing, 12*(1), 19-39.

Dalakas, V., Kropp, F., Shoham, A., & Florenthal, B. (1997). Special sports identities: A cross-cultural comparison of the commercial implications of team identification. In *Proceedings of the Sixth Symposium of Cross-Cultural Consumer and Business Studies* (pp. 275-279). Provo, UT: Brigham Young University.

Dietz-Uhler, B., & Murrell, A. (1999). Examining fan reaction to game outcomes: A longitudinal study of social identity. *Journal of Sport Behavior, 22*(1), 15-27.

Fisher, R. J., & Wakefield, K. (1998). Factors leading to group identification: A field study of winners and losers. *Psychology and Marketing, 15*(January), 23-40.

Friestad, M., & Wright, P. (1994). The persuasion knowledge model: How people cope with persuasion attempts. *Journal of Consumer Research, 16*(December), 354-360.

Heider, F. (1958). *The Psychology of Interpersonal Relations.* New York: Wiley.

Hogg, M. A., & Abrams, D. (1990). *Social identifications: A social psychology of intergroup relations and group processes.* London: Routledge.

Hogg, M. A., Terry, E. J., & White, K. M. (1995). A tale of two theories: A critical comparison of identity theory with social identity theory. *Social Psychology Quarterly, 58*(4), 255-269.

IEG Sponsorship Report. (2000). Survey: Led by internet sponsors, corporate interest surged in 2000. *19*(19), 1, 4-5.

Javalgi, R. G., Taylor, M. B., Gross, A. C., & Lampman, E. (1994). Awareness of sponsorship and corporate image: An empirical investigation. *Journal of Advertising, 23*(December), 47-58.

Johar, G. V., & Pham, M. T. (1999). Relatedness, prominence, and constructive sponsor identification. *Journal of Marketing Research, 36*(3), 299-312.

Kelley, S., & Tepper, K. (1998). Sports fanatics: An in-depth look at wildcat mania. Paper presented at the Advertising and Consumer Psychology Conference. Portland, Oregon.

King, B. (2002). Passion that can't be counted puts billion of dollars in play. *Sports Business Journal,* (March 11), 25-26.

Knight, D. (2002). Sponsoring of auto racing teams is serious business. *Knight Ridder Tribune Business News,* (May 19), 1.

Landler, M. (2000, September 29). Fighting marketing pirates: Olympics sponsors guard their investments. *The New York Times,* pp. C1.

Lardinoit, T., & Quester, P. G. (2001). Attitudinal effects of combined sponsorship and sponsor's prominence on basketball in Europe. *Journal of Advertising Research, 41*(1), 48-58.

Madrigal, R. (2000). The influence of social alliances with sports teams on intentions to purchase corporate sponsors' products. *Journal of Advertising, 29*(4), 13-24.

Madrigal, R. (2001). Social identity effects in a belief-attitude-intentions hierarchy: implications for corporate sponsorship. *Psychology and Marketing, 18*(2), 145-165.

Meenaghan, T. (1999). Commercial sponsorship: The development of understanding. *International Journal of Sports Marketing and Sponsorship, 1*(1), 19-31.

Meenaghan, T. (2001). Sponsorship and advertising: A comparison of consumer perceptions. *Psychology and Marketing, 18*(2), 191-215.

Miyazaki, A. D., & Morgan, A. G. (2001). Assessing market value of event sponsorship: Corporate Olympic sponsorships. *Journal of Advertising Research, 41*(1), 9-15.

Speed, R., & Thompson, P. (2000). Determinants of sports sponsorship response. *Journal of the Academy of Marketing Science, 28*(2), 226-238.

Thomas, G. S. (1999). NFL's best fans back the pack. *Sports Business Journal, 1*(40), 1, 16-18.

Treece, J. B. (2002). Even in Japan, Hyundai takes World Cup honors. *Automotive News,* (April 29), 3, 31.

Ukman, L. (1996). *IEG'S complete guide to sponsorship: Everything you need to know about sports, arts, event, entertainment and cause marketing.* Chicago, IL: IEG, Inc.

Wann, D. L. (1993). Aggression of highly identified spectators as a function of their need to maintain a positive social identity. *Journal of Sport and Social Issues, 17,* 134-143.

Wann, D. L., & Branscombe, N. R. (1990). Die-hard and fair-weather fans: effects of identification on BIRGing and CORFing tendencies. *Journal of Sport and Social Issues, 14*(August), 103-117.

Wann, D. L., & Branscombe, N. R. (1993). Sports fans: Measuring degree of identification with their team. *International Journal of Sport Psychology, 24,* 1-17.

Wann, D. L., & Dolan, T. (1994a). Influence of spectators' identification on evaluation of the past, present, and future performance of a sports team. *Perceptual and Motor Skills, 78,* 547-553.

Wann, D. L., & Dolan, T. (1994b). Spectators' evaluations of rival and fellow fans. *The Psychological Record, 44,* 351-359.

Wann, D. L., & Schrader, M. P. (2000). Controllability and stability in the self-serving attributions of sport spectators. *Journal of Social Psychology, 140*(2), 160-168.

Wann, D. L., Carlson, J. D., & Schrader, M. P. (1999). The impact of team identification on the hostile and instrumental verbal aggression of sport spectators. *Journal of Social Behavior & Personality, 14*(2), 279-286.

Wann, D. L., Hunter, J. L., Ryan, J. A., & Wrigh, L.A. (2001). The relationship between team identification and willingness of sport fans to consider illegally assisting their team. *Social Behavior and Personality, 29*(6), 531-526.

Wells, W. D. (1993). Discovery oriented consumer research. *Journal of Consumer Research, 19*(March), 489-504.

# CHAPTER 6

# Total Sponsorship Value and Achieving Sponsorship Objectives: The Case of Selected Running Road Races in the United States

JAMES ZARICK
JAMES GRANT
KATHRYN DOBIE

## Abstract

Organizers and directors of sporting events are finding it harder than ever to attract sponsors in an economic environment that has led to cutbacks at all corporate levels. While some corporate sponsors may continue to contribute at some level due to a desire to be considered a *good neighbor*, most no longer feel that they have that luxury. In order to be considered a potential part of a company's promotional strategy, the attainment of corporate objectives must be considered.

The purpose of this study was to determine if a significant relationship existed among various elements of a running road race and the attainment of corporate objectives. If such a correlative relationship exists, the information has implications for event organizers and directors as they compete for corporate sponsorships. It also has implications for sponsoring organizations as they choose between sponsorship opportunities.

Results of the study indicated that merely promoting the event through various print, radio, and/or TV advertising is not sufficient for sponsoring organizations to attain their promotional objectives. The identity of sponsors must be promoted as well as the event itself. Event size as measured by the number of participants had a significant effect. This may be due to the shear magnitude of the events as much as anything. But it does show mutually benefit of sponsor-event relationships: the greater the sponsorship, the more able the event director is to increase efforts to attract greater numbers of participants, and the larger the event, the more exposure for the sponsoring organization.

> The purpose of this study was to determine if a significant relationship existed among various elements of a running road race and the attainment of corporate objectives.

# Introduction

Athletic events were initially viewed as a matter of personal and/or national pride and achievement. Athletes competed for the right to be called champion. Today, many sports competitions have become big business. The focus has moved from the playing field to the bottom line. Owners, organizers, and athletes want to know how they can make money. Ticket sales and concessions represent only part of the potential income to be gained from sporting events. Professional and amateur athletes and organizations turn to outside sources of revenue for additional financial support. These outside sources of support include broadcast rights, advertising, online sites, licensed apparel, and sponsorships (Genzale 1998).

> **Sponsorship objectives vary as widely as the companies that engage in sports sponsorship activities. Some of the more common objectives are improved company and product awareness, increased sales, better community relations, entertainment for clients, or even a favorite interest of a top executive.**

Sports organizations have become an excellent medium for the transmission of corporate messages. Sponsorship has become an important communication medium over the past 30 years (Armstrong, 1988; Gardner & Shuman, 1986; Pope & Voges, 1994). In 1997, expenditures for sports sponsorships were in excess of $3.2 billion (Genzale, 1998). It is expected that this figure will continue to grow as long as the stated objectives of the sponsors are achieved.

Sponsorship objectives vary as widely as the companies that engage in sports sponsorship activities. Some of the more common objectives are improved company and product awareness, increased sales, better community relations, entertainment for clients, or even a favorite interest of a top executive (Pope 1997). Though the objectives may vary, the goals are not as diverse. Essentially, the sponsor must be able to measure the effectiveness of the sponsorship for achieving the objective.

> **Currently, the research that has focused on assessing the effectiveness of corporate sponsorships in achieving company objectives has been inconsistent. The objective of the current research is to question how a corporation measure whether their marketing objectives have been met through the use of sports sponsorships.**

Currently, the research that has focused on assessing the effectiveness of corporate sponsorships in achieving company objectives has been inconsistent. Komoroski and Biemond reported a lack of standard practice or policy (1996) and Pope (1997) noted the lack of research to validate the effectiveness of sports sponsorships at the academic level. The objective of the current research is to question how a corporation measure whether their marketing objectives have been met through the use of sports sponsorships. Without a method of documenting sponsorship results, it will become harder for sports directors at all levels to promote sponsorship investment by business organizations.

# Previous Research

Literature regarding the sponsorship of sports and sports events can be divided into three related areas: corporate objectives and motivation, implementation, and evaluation. For ease of review, the survey of previous research will be presented in like manner.

## Objectives and Motivation

The desire to achieve particular objects is the underlying motivation for a company to engage in sponsorship activities. Companies have used event sponsorship as a vehicle to promote image and to attract additional business (DelPrete, 1996). In fact, the majority of companies who engage in sponsorship activities do so to promote their image (Ludwig & Karabestsos, 1999). In a related vein, some companies use sponsorship activities as a philanthropic outreach (Wilson, 1997; Kuzma, Shanklin, & McCally, 1993).

The 1993 study by Kuzma, Shanklin, and McCally sought to establish an importance ranking of corporate sponsorship objectives. The top three objectives were to increase awareness of the company, improve company image, and demonstrate community responsibility. Increasing sales was ranked ninth out of ten. The importance of creating awareness of the company and promoting the corporate image illustrates the importance of a close match between the athlete/event to be sponsored and the popularity and image of the athlete/event (Kuzma et al., 1993). A recent study (Ludwig & Karabetsos, 1999) confirmed the importance that corporate sponsors assign to the objectives of increasing public awareness and company/product image.

> **The importance of creating awareness of the company and promoting the corporate image illustrates the importance of a close match between the athlete/event to be sponsored and the popularity and image of the athlete/event.**

Pope (1997) recognized that image objectives did not give a complete picture of the underlying business rationale for engaging in sponsorship activities. A survey of the literature produced a range of objectives that included marketing and media objectives in addition to the previously recognized social or community responsibility objectives. (See Table 1.)

Table 1 **Corporate Objectives for Sponsorship Activities**

| Image | Marketing | Media | Other |
|---|---|---|---|
| public awareness | business relations | generate visibility | mgmt. interest |
| corporate image | reach target market | generate publicity | |
| public perception | brand positioning | enhance ad campaign | |
| community involvement | increase sales sampling | avoid clutter | |
| financial relations | | target specificity | |
| client entertainment | | | |
| government relations | | | |
| employee relations | | | |
| compete with other companies | | | |
| Pope, 1997 | | | |

In many cases, there may be multiple objectives (Mullin, Hardy & Sutton, 1993). When multiple objectives are present, the interaction may make it difficult to assess the achievement of any of them (Arthur, Scott, Woods, & Baker, 1998).

Sport sponsorship is most effective when regarded as an integral part of an integrated promotion mix (Sleight, 1991; Parker, 1991; Arthur, Scott, Woods, & Booker, 1998). However the multiplicity of sponsors' names and logos has a tendency to diminish the sponsor's impact in creating awareness and enhancing their image (Greenwald & Fernandez-Balboa, 1998).

## Evaluation

Studies show that fewer than 25% of major-event sponsors know how to make the most effective use of the sponsorship opportunity (Heffler, 1994). Major impediments to measuring effectiveness are that there are few clear-cut winners or losers in advertising (Phillips & Moutinho, 1998), and the effects on the consumer are difficult to measure (McCarville, Flood, & Froats, 1998). In fact, only 50% (Gross, Traylor, & Schuman, 1987; Kuzma, 1990) to 70% (Cunningham & Taylor, 1995) of corporations evaluate their sponsorship efforts.

In addition to trying to determine how sponsors assess sponsorship effectiveness, one must also wonder who measures the effectiveness (Ludwig & Karabestsos, 1999). The results of this study indicated that measures were evaluated in-house as often as by the event organizer. The importance of establishing effectiveness measures was the focus of the studies by Hansen and Scotwin (1995) and Meenaghan (1991). In a later study, corporations were asked to identify and rank the criteria that they used to evaluate their sponsorship activities (Ludwig & Karabestsos 1999). The results of this study indicated that the greater the importance the sponsoring organization placed on an objective, the more likely that the sponsor organization would have an evaluation assessment to determine if the objective had been met.

> Studies show that fewer than 25% of major-event sponsors know how to make the most effective use of the sponsorship opportunity.

> Increased pressure on marketers to provide evidence that sponsorship moneys are well spent and achieve the established objectives makes it more important to develop standardized systems of evaluation.

Increased pressure on marketers to provide evidence that sponsorship moneys are well spent and achieve the established objectives makes it more important to develop standardized systems of evaluation (Heffler, 1994; Komoroski & Biemond, 1996). White and Irwin (1996) proposed that as event and sponsorship objectives were not the same, it was more appropriate to use a generalized set of guidelines. A more recent study (Erdmann, Kennett, & Sneath, 1999) highlighted the importance of determining sponsor objectives and judging the effectiveness of the event in meeting those objectives.

## The Study

If sport sponsorships are to be validated as an effective promotional tool, a system of measures must be developed that can be used by event sponsors and sponsoring organizations alike. Previous studies that attempted to develop a standardized system of evaluation for corporate sponsorships focused on the sponsorship agreement (Komorski & Biemond, 1996). The objective of this study is to determine the effectiveness of corporate sponsorships of selected running road races in the United States.

### Sample

A convenience sample of 20 running road races was selected for this study. The races varied from one mile to 26.22 miles. The number of participants ranged from 300 to 8000. The top three sponsors of each of the races, based on the total dollar value of the sponsorship, were identified for the study. A representative from each of the sponsoring organizations was asked to complete the survey instrument. A total of 21 sponsors representing fifteen different running road races responded, a response rate of 46.6%.

## The Survey Instrument

The survey instrument was developed specifically for this study. It contains elements that are common to most running road race sponsorship agreements. Success was measured as the perception of sponsors that they had attained the specific objectives of the sponsorship.

A pilot test of the instrument was used to determine any problems that might be associated with the content of the instrument or with the data collection procedures. The final survey instrument consisted of sixteen questions. (See Appendix A.)

> The survey instrument contains elements that are common to most running road race sponsorship agreements. Success was measured as the perception of sponsors that they had attained the specific objectives of the sponsorship.

## Results

The reported value of the sponsorships ranged from $200 to $6000. The most frequently reported figures were $2500 (four sponsorships), $3000 (three sponsorships), and $6000 (three sponsorships). Spearman Rho rank order correlations were calculated to determine if there was a correlation between the total dollar value of the sponsorship and success in achieving the stated objectives, and between the total dollar value of the sponsorship and factors that might predict the success of the sponsorship. All correlations were tested at the $p < .05$ level. See Tables 2 and 3.

**Table 2** Correlation Between Total Value of the Sponsorship and Success in Achieving Objectives

| Measure | Spearman Rho Correlation Coefficient |
|---|---|
| Successful Promotion of the Company | -> 404* |
| significant at $p < .05$ | |

The calculated correlation coefficient for the relationship between total dollar value of the sponsorship and the successful achievement of stated objectives indicates a significant negative relationship.

Table 3 **Spearman Rho Correlation Coefficients for Total Sponsorship Value and Factors Expected to Contribute to the Achievement of Sponsorship Objectives**

| Factors | Spearman Rho Correlation Coefficient |
|---|---|
| **Agreement greater than one year** | **-.017** |
| Length of agreement | -.094 |
| Title sponsor | -.223 |
| Print advertising | .334 |
| Radio advertising | -.375* |
| TV advertising | -.436* |
| Live TV coverage | -.214 |
| Signage on race course | -.144 |
| Name on t-shirt | -.458* |
| Name on entry form | .260 |
| Number of runners | .404* |
| significant at $p < .05$ | |

## Appendix A: **Road Race Sponsorship Questionnaire**

Directions: Please answer each of the following questions about the race sponsorship with which your company was (is) involved.

1. Is your sponsorship agreement with this race for more than a year?

        Yes_____        No_____

2. For what length of time is your sponsorship agreement with this race? _____

3. Did your company's contribution make your company the title sponsor of this race?

        (Example: The Chevrolet 10K)

        Yes _____        No_____

4. Was this race advertised in print? (Example: newspaper, magazine, newsletter...)

        Yes_____        No_____

5. Was this race advertised on the radio?

        Yes _____        No_____

6. Was this race advertised on TV?

        Yes _____        No_____

7. Was there live TV coverage of the race?

        Yes _____        No_____

8. Was signage on the race course a part of your sponsorship agreement for this race?

        Yes _____        No_____

9. Did your company's name appear on the race T-shirt?

        Yes _____        No_____

10. Did your company's name appear on the race entry form?

        Yes _____        No_____

11. How many runners were there in this race? _____

12. What percentage of those runners were male and what percentage were female?

        Male_____        Female_____

13. Which gender were you targeting with this sponsorship?

        Male_____        Female_____        Both_____

14. Do you consider this sponsorship to have been a successful promotional endeavor for your company?

        Yes _____        No_____

15. How would you rate the success of this sponsorship as compared to other promotional endeavors in which your company has engaged?

        More successful_____        Less Successful_____        Equally successful_____

16. What is the estimated total worth of your company's contribution of product, services, and cash to the sponsorship of this race?

        $_____

Name of the race_____

Name of the race sponsor_____

Name of the contact person_____

Phone # of the contact person_____

The correlation coefficients were calculated for the relationships between the total dollar value of the sponsorships and the factors that would be expected to contribute to meeting the sponsorship objectives. Four of the fourteen factors tested had a statistically significant relationship with the total dollar value of the sponsorship. The total number of runners entered in the race had a positive relationship with total dollar value of sponsorship. Radio advertising, television advertising, and the presence of the sponsor's name on the t-shirt had a significant negative relationship with the total dollar value of the sponsorship.

## Discussion

Based on the results of this study, a statistically significant negative relationship was found to exist between the dollar value of the sponsorship and the success of the sponsorship. This suggests that it is not the amount of dollar value that is involved but rather other factors that determine the success of the sponsorship effort in achieving organizational objectives. The responsibility for not achieving organizational objectives may lie with the establishment of goals that for one reason or another are not realistic. It may also lie with the lack of a clear plan of execution by either the sponsor or the event organizer. The responsibility for tying sponsorship to an integrated corporate communications effort and/or to the overall communication plan for the event lies with the sponsor and the event organizer.

**Based on the results of this study, a statistically significant negative relationship was found to exist between the dollar value of the sponsorship and the success of the sponsorship. This suggests that it is not the amount of dollar value that is involved but rather other factors that determine the success of the sponsorship effort in achieving organizational objectives.**

Significant relationships were found to exist between the total dollar value of the sponsorships and radio advertising, television advertising, the sponsor's name appearing on the race t-shirt, the number of runners in the race and the percentage of runners who were male or female.

There was a negative relationship between the total dollar value of the sponsorship and the likelihood that the event would be advertised on radio/TV. Considering the character of the majority of running road races, local and/or regional, and the limited budget for advertising, there was probably little electronic media advertising. What there was would generally advertise the event as opposed to advertising the sponsors.

The negative relationship between the logo of the sponsor on the race t-shirt and the total dollar value of the sponsorship might well be explained by such factors as logo placement and size, the number of runners wearing the t-shirt, and the frequency that it is worn following the event. Since the effectiveness of this type of exposure is long-term, and the questionnaire was administered using a short-term perspective, it is likely that the statistical results are spurious.

Race participation had a significant positive relationship to the total dollar value of the sponsorship. This implies that the greater the sponsorship value, the more runners were attracted to the race. However, it is more likely that the greater number of potential runners, the more likely that the sponsor would be willing to contribute a greater dollar value. This could be because the race would receive greater media coverage and a greater number of racers, it would be more likely that the sponsor's name would be recognized, or another sponsor motivation.

# Managerial Implications

The results of the study suggest many issues that event organizers and sponsoring organizations must consider. The first issue relates to the objectives of the sponsoring organization. Organizational objectives must be clear, measurable, and attainable. Sponsorship should be only one element of an integrated promotional strategy designed to accomplish the established organizational objectives. The event director must understand what efforts will be necessary in order to support the organizational objectives of the sponsor. If it is not within the scope of the event organizer's capabilities to support the stated objectives of the sponsor, this must be articulated up front. It is important that sponsors and organizers agree on the identification of the sponsor's objectives, how they are to be measured, and the organizer's responsibilities regarding the attainment of sponsor objectives. Unless both parties have a clear understanding of the responsibilities of each, misunderstandings and unmet objectives will be commonplace.

> **Sponsorship should be only one element of an integrated promotional strategy designed to accomplish the established organizational objectives.**

Visibility is a primary concern of corporate sponsors. To support visibility requirements, event sponsors must be prepared to include the name/logo or other identification of the sponsors in all promotion for the event. This includes recognition of the provision of in-kind resources such as t-shirts, beverages, etc. The forecast number of participants is a factor in the level of exposure that a sponsor can expect. Sponsors should be provided with accurate forecasts of the number of participants including a history of the participation levels at past events.

Event directors have the responsibility for understanding what resources they expect from sponsors. Just as importantly, they are responsible for understanding what resources they are capable of providing. There should be a record of the activities and results so that contributing sponsors can make decisions regarding objectives and support levels in an informed manner. It is imperative that sponsor and organizers communicate expectations and responsibilities. These concerns should be embedded in the terms of the contract between the two parties so that there is less likelihood of misunderstandings and disagreement. Until both parties take responsibility for the planning and execution of the necessary activities, the probability that sponsor objectives will be accomplished is diminished.

> **It is important that sponsors and organizers agree on the identification of the sponsor's objectives, how they are to be measured, and the organizer's responsibilities regarding the attainment of sponsor objectives. Unless both parties have a clear understanding of the responsibilities of each, misunderstandings and unmet objectives will be commonplace.**

# Recommendations for Future Research

This is an exploratory study, the results of which are not generalizable to the total population. However, the principles of this research are applicable to all event organizers/directors as they develop their strategies to attract sponsor support. It is important that further research in these areas be conducted in order to provide a foundation for strategy formation by sponsors and event organizers/directors.

> **The principles of this research are applicable to all event organizers/directors as they develop their strategies to attract sponsor support.**

The first issue that must be defined is the determination of the goals and objectives that are reasonably attainable by sponsoring organizations. The goals and objectives must be quantifiable and measurable. Researchers can assist in defining appropriate measures for specific objectives. This will assist in the design of promotion efforts by event organizers to maximize the probability that sponsor's objectives will be met.

A second issue for researchers to examine is whether differences exits between sponsor's goals and objectives in different sports, and on the geographical coverage of an event, e.g., national vs. local. This type of study using international comparisons is also needed. Comparison studies would shed some insight into the strategies that are most appropriate for events having different characteristics.

# References

Armstrong, C. (1988). Sports sponsorship: A case study approach to measuring its effectiveness. *European Research,* May, 97-103.

Arthur, D., Scott, D., Woods, T., & Booker, R. (1998). Sport sponsorship: A process model for the effective implementation and management of sport sponsorship programmes. *Sport Marketing Quarterly, 7*(4), 49-60.

Cunningham, M. H., & Taylor, S. F. (1995). Event marketing: State of the industry and research agenda. *Festival Management and Event Tourism, 2*(3/4), 122-137.

DelPrete, D. (1996). Good sponsors know how to set their goals. *Marketing News, 30*(2), 35.

Erdmann, J. W., Kennett, P. A., & Sneath, J.Z. (1999). The sponsorship audit: A collegiate athletics case study. In J. W. Wilson (Ed.). *Marketing for the Millennium* pp. 256-261. Proceedings of the Atlantic marketing Association. Annapolis, MD: Atlantic Marketing Association.

Gardner, M., & Shuman, P. (1986). Sponsorship: An important component of the promotions mix. *Journal of Advertising, 16*(1), 11-17.

Genzale, J. (1998). Dynamic U.S. sports industry finds a new voice. *Street and Smith's Sports Business Journal, 1*(1), 57

Greenwald, L., & Fernandez-Balboa, J. M. (1998). Trends in the sport marketing industry and in the demographics of the United States: Their effect on the strategic role of grassroots sport sponsorship in corporate America. *Sport Marketing Quarterly, 7*(4), 35-47.

Gross, A. C., Traylor, M. B., & Shuman, P. J. (1987). Corporate sponsorship of art and sports events in North America. Conference proceedings from the General Sessions of the Marketing Research Congress, Montreux, Switzerland, pp. 535-561.

Hansen, F., & Scotwin, L. (1995). An experimental inquiry into sponsoring: What effects can be measured? *Marketing and Research Today, August, 23*(3), pp. 173-182.

Heffler, M. (1994). Making sure sponsorships meet all the parameters. *BrandWeek, 35*(20), 16.

Komorski, L., & Biemond, H. (1996) Sponsorship accountability: Designing and utilizing an evaluation system. *Sport Marketing Quarterly. 5*(2), 35-39.

Kuzma, J. R. (1990). An investigation into the role of event's marketing in corporate strategy. Order Number 9101326, University Microfilms International, Michigan.

Kuzma, J. R., Shanklin, W. L., McCally, J. F., Jr. (1993). Number one principle for sporting events seeking corporate sponsors: Meet benefactor's objectives. *Sport Marketing Quarterly, 2*(3), 27-33.

Ludwig, S., & Karabestsos, J. D. (1999). Objectives and evaluation processes utilized by sponsors of the 1996 Olympic Games. *Sport Marketing Quarterly, 8*(3), 11-19.

McCarville, R. E., Flood, C. M., & Froats, T. A. (1998). The effectiveness of selected promotions on spectator's assessments of a nonprofit sporting event sponsor. *Journal of Sport Management, 1*(12), 51-62.

Meenaghan, T. (1991). The role of sponsorship in the marketing communications mix. *International Journal of Advertising, 10*(1), 35-47.

Mullin, B. J., Hardy, S., & Sutton, W. A. (1993). *Sport marketing.* Champaign, IL: Human Kinetics.

Parker, K. (1991). Sponsorship: The research contribution. *European Journal of Marketing, 25*(11), 22-300.

Phillips, P. A., & Moutinho, L. (1998). The marketing planning index: A tool for measuring strategic marketing effectiveness. *Journal of Travel and Tourism Marketing, 7*(3), 41-57.

Pope N. (1997). Subject outline-1, 1997, Week *. FF13M02 Special Topic in Marketing, Australia: Griffith University. Retrieved December 12, 1997, from http://www.cad.gu.edu.au/market/cyber-journal_of_sport_marketing/vol1-no1pope2.html.

Pope, N. K., & Voges, K. E. (1994), Sponsorship evaluation: Does it match the motive and mechanism. *Sport Marketing Quarterly, 3*(4), 37-45.

Sleight, S. (1991). *Sponsorship: What it is and how to use it.* Maidenhead, Berkshire, England: McGraw Hill.

White, A. B., & Irwin, R. L. (1996). Assessing a corporate partner program: A key to success. *Sport Marketing Quarterly, 5*(2), 21-28.

# CHAPTER 7

# Banking on the Pink Dollar: Sponsorship Awareness and the Gay Games

BRENDA G. PITTS

## Abstract

Since 1982, the Gay Games have been staged every four years; the most recent one was Gay Games VI in Sydney, Australia, in November, 2002. It is an international event that attracts participation and spectators from over 100 countries. Sponsorship dollars have increased steadily and significantly at each Gay Games, from zero dollars in 1982 to $10 million in 2002. Sponsorship has come from both mainstream companies and gay and lesbian companies. At a time when lesbian and gay people are not yet fully accepted, appreciated, or understood in many countries, why would companies choose to use the Gay Games as a sponsorship venue, risking backlash from homophobic markets? Therefore, an objective of this study was to explore corporate sponsorship and the Gay Games. To date, three studies have been conducted on sponsorship and the Gay Games. This paper provides an overview of those studies and their results, an overview of the gay and lesbian sports market, and strategies marketers can use to reach the gay and lesbian sports market.

> **Why would companies choose to use the Gay Games as a sponsorship venue, risking backlash from homophobic markets?**

## Sponsorship and the Sport Industry

Although there is not one definitive study on total sponsorship activity in any single country or globally, some reports and predictions offer that sponsorship promotional activity between 1996 and 2000 range from US $5.4 billion to US $11.6 billion (Amis, McDaniel, & Slack,1999; International Events Group, 1998; Lough & Irwin, 1999). Sport sponsorship is undoubtedly partially, if not significantly, responsible for the growth in sport business. It has been partially responsible for the horizontal expansion of the sport industry, as outlined by indicators of growth in Pitts and Stotlar (2002), particularly the sport performance industry segment as theorized by the Pitts, Fielding, and Miller Sport Industry Segmentation Model (1994), and other leading scholars in sport marketing: Brooks (1994),

> **Sponsorship is business-brand recognition, capitalism, and profit.**

Mullin, Hardy, and Sutton (2001), and Shilbury, Quick, and Westerbeek (1998). Indeed, sport sponsorship itself is an already large and constantly growing sport business industry segment.

Sponsorship is business-brand recognition, capitalism, and profit. The sports event is nothing more than a vehicle for a corporate sponsor to build brand. The primary goal of companies utilizing sponsorships is to create exposure for the brand name and to develop associations (Aaker & Joachimsthaler, 2000; see Endnote 1). Moreover, sponsorship is one of many promotional tools that have the potential to contribute to brand building. "Sponsorship entails the commercial association of a brand with a property such as a sporting event, a team, a cause, the arts, a cultural attraction, or entertainment" (Aaker & Joachimsthaler, 2000, p. 202).

Expenditures on sport sponsorship are justified because the sponsoring companies believe brand recognition and loyalty can be achieved and can affect market share (Aaker & Joachimsthaler, 2000; Pitts, 1998). Research results support this belief. In assessing stadium advertising, Stotlar & Johnson (1989) found that between 62 and 77% of attendees noticed the advertising. At an LPGA tournament, it was found that 98% of those attending (451 subjects) noticed the advertising (Cuneen & Hannan, 1993). In that study, results also showed that sponsors that had products or services on site were recognized in greater frequencies than those who did not. Findings from a study on signage at a sports event showed that 59% of those surveyed noticed sponsor or brand logos and that 54% had a more favorable attitude toward sponsors involved with the event (Friedman, 1990). And in a study of spectators' perceived image of a corporation and its products due to sponsoring a sports event, Turco (1994) reported that the results indicated that sponsorship companies can enhance consumers' image of the company as a result of sports event sponsorship.

> **Sponsorship is especially effective as a marketing tool in reaching consumer populations that tend to be marginalized by society. These populations respond with a greater notice and appreciation of the company's willingness to sponsor their events.**

Sponsorship, as a brand-building tool, is also used to reach new or emerging markets. It is especially effective as a marketing tool in reaching consumer populations that tend to be marginalized by society (Tharp, 2001). These populations respond with a greater notice and appreciation of the company's willingness to sponsor their events. Further, gay and lesbian consumers "prefer to buy from companies that have a visible presence in the Gay community" (Tharp, 2001, p. 233).

## Sponsorship, Brand Awareness, and the Gay and Lesbian Market

Reports of estimates of the spending power of the gay and lesbian market have caught the attention of the corporate world, even though some of those reports are accused of being inflated. With headlines such as "$514 billion spending power," "20 million consumers," and the "Dream Market," many companies have taken notice and now deliberately target the lesbian and gay market (Curiel, 1991; Johnson, 1993; Miller, 1990; Yankelovich, 1994). Additionally, it is reported

> **Studies show that gay and lesbian people spend disproportionately on luxury and premium products**

widely that lesbian and gay people are more willing than non-gay/lesbian people to spend money, and studies show that gay and lesbian people spend disproportionately on luxury and premium products, such as travel, vacations, phone services, books, recorded music, alcoholic beverages, theater, clothing catalogues, and greeting cards (Button, 1993; Davis, 1993; Elliot, 1993a; Elliott, 1993b; Fugate, 1993; Johnson, 1993; Miller, 1990, 1992; Penaloza, 1996; Summer, 1992; Tharp, 2001; Warren, 1990). Moreover, lesbian and gay consumers have been found to be younger, more brand and fashion conscious, and more brand loyal than their heterosexual counterparts (Badgett, 1997; Cronin, 1993; "Gays Celebrate. . . ," 1994; Miller, 1990; Webster, 1994).

**Moreover, lesbian and gay consumers have been found to be younger, more brand and fashion conscious, and more brand loyal than their heterosexual counterparts**

**Eighty-nine percent of gay and lesbian consumers actively seek out goods and services that target the lesbian and gay market.**

Additionally, the literature reveals that lesbian and gay people seem to notice, be more aware, can more correctly identify, and will aggressively support the companies who are sponsors of lesbian and gay events (Baker, 1997; Kates, 1998; Lukenbill, 1995; Penaloza, 1996). A study by Simmons Market Research Bureau (1996) found that 89% of gay and lesbian consumers actively seek out goods and services that target the lesbian and gay market. Among suggestions on targeting the gay and lesbian market are the following: hire openly lesbian and gay employees; include sexual orientation in the company's antidiscrimination policies; offer partner benefits; donate to gay and lesbian charities and organizations; provide gay- and lesbian-friendly service; and sponsor lesbian and gay events. This should be considered as more companies study whether or not to target the gay and lesbian market. Moreover, further research involving the lesbian and gay market's brand recognition and brand loyalty will be key to the company's decision-making process.

## Sponsorship and the Gay Games

Recent research reveals that there is a growing gay and lesbian sports industry and estimated to be approximately $180 million to $15 billion in size and involves an estimated 11 to 13 million lesbian and gay sports people and over 15,000 sports events in the US (Pitts, 1997; 1999; Pitts & Ayers, 2001; Simmons Market Research Bureau, 1996). One event that will probably change those numbers is the Gay Games. The Gay Games is a multisport and cultural festival held every four years since 1982. A study of visitor spending and economic scale of Gay Games V, held in Amsterdam in 1998, revealed it to be just over $350 million (Pitts & Ayers, 2001). Some of this is attributable to sponsor spending. Additionally, sponsor involvement and spending at the Gay Games has grown significantly (see Table 1).

There were only a few local companies involved as sponsors for Gay Games I in 1982. That number increased to 80 for Gay Games V in 1998. Such an increase is the result of many factors. However, the increase alone indicates the attractiveness of the event to corporations as a highly viable vehicle for reaching the lesbian and gay market. Some reasons include the following. First, the Gay Games is a very large event, attracting several thousand sports participants and spectators as well as cultural event participants and visitors. Some reports state the visitors reached a million in 1994 and 1998. The Gay Games is now referred to as an international mega event and placed among the ranks of the largest multisports events in the world. For example, although the Gay Games does not rival the

**The Gay Games is now referred to as an international mega event and placed among the ranks of the largest multisports events in the world.**

Table 1 **Gay Games Facts**

| Gay Games: | I | II | III | IV | V | VI |
|---|---|---|---|---|---|---|
| Year | 1982 | 1986 | 1990 | 1994 | 1998 | 2002 |
| Place | San Francisco, USA | San Francisco, USA | Vancouver, Canada | New York, USA | Amsterdam, Netherlands | Sydney, Australia |
| Participants | 1,300 | 3,482 | 7,300 | 10,864 | 14,843 | 16,000 |
| Countries | 12 | 22 | 28 | 40 | 78 | 131 |
| Sports | 16 | 17 | 31 | 31 | 31 | 30 |
| Spectators | 50,000 | 75,000 | 200,000 | 1 million | 800,000 | 300,000 |
| Workers | 600 | 1,200 | 3,000 | 7,0003,042 | 6,000 | |
| Budget | $395,000 | $885,000 | $3m | $6.5m | $10m | $16m |
| Sponsorship | in-kind | $210,000 | $350,000 | $1m | $2.7m | $10m |
| # of companies | a few | a few | 4 major | 5 major, 20 minor | 50 major, 16 grants, 14 govt | 30 major, 14 grants, 3 govt |
| Economic Impact | No data | no data | $50m | $112m | $304m | $140m |

Olympic Games in relation to media coverage or mass market appeal, it is larger in size in relation to participants-there were more sports participants in each of the three recent Gay Games-Gay Games IV in 1994, Gay Games V in 1998, and Gay Games VI in 2002-than for the Olympic Games in 1996 and 2000.

Second, spectator appeal of the Gay Games has grown. The Federation of Gay Games, the international governing body of the Gay Games, has attempted to enhance the commercial appeal of the Gay Games, first out of necessity to fund the event, and second to enhance awareness of the event and thus participation. Third, as noted earlier, reports of estimates of the spending power of the gay and lesbian market has caught the attention of the corporate world. And, perhaps more importantly, it appears that the lesbian and gay market can be highly brand loyal. Thus, the Gay Games is an excellent opportunity to reach the market.

> **There were more sports participants in each of the three recent Gay Games-Gay Games IV in 1994, Gay Games V in 1998, and Gay Games VI in 2002-than for the Olympic Games in 1996 and 2000.**

The Gay Games has increasingly become the target of the corporate world for sponsorship. In general, companies cite a number of reasons for sponsorship, such as to increase company awareness, improve company image, demonstrate community responsibility, and increase awareness of specific products (Kuzma, Shanklin, & McCally, 1993). Evidenced by the large increase in sponsoring companies between Gay Games I in 1982 and Gay Games VI in 2002, it appears that the Gay Games has become a target of choice (refer again to Table 1). For instance, there were three times the number of sponsors for Gay Games V in 1998 than for Gay Games IV in 1994. Moreover, the depth and breadth of type of company in relation to product, scope, size, as well as mainstream or gay and lesbian company, continues to escalate. As an example, Table 2 provides a list of some of the sponsor companies of Gay Games V.

**Table 2  Partial List of the Official Sponsors of Gay Games V, 1998**

| Corporate Sponsors | | |
|---|---|---|
| A2000 (Amsterdam television company) | Gay SA Newsmagazine | Randstad (large sports event organizing company; did the Atlanta Olympic Games in 1996) |
| Absolut Vodka | Gay Times | Red Bull (energy drink) |
| AccountView (business software company) | GayPlanet (web site) | Rolling Rock (beer) |
| Amsterdam RAI (congress center) | GWK (bank) | Schipolfonds (airport) |
| Amsterdams Fonds voor de Kinst | Icon (television) | Staatsloterij (lottery) |
| Avis Car Rental | Kennedy van der Laan (lawyers) | Speedo |
| Bacardi Breezer | KLM Royal Dutch Airlines | Spring Water Company |
| COC (Dutch Society for the Integration of Homosexuality) | Kodak International | Stichting Aidsfonds |
| Columbia FunMaps | KPN Telecom (phone) | Stichting Friends for Life |
| Curve Magazine | Levi Strauss & Co. | The Licensing Channel |
| Energie Noord West (Netherlands electricity/utilities company) | NZH-groep (public transportation) | ZaZare Diamonds (diamond jewelry company that created the official Gay Games gold and diamond jewelry line) |
| | Out Magazine | |
| | Puschkin Red (flavored drink) | |
| | Randon beveiliging (large sports event organizing company; did the Atlanta Olympic Games in 1996) | |

## Sponsorship Recognition and Gay Games V: The Study

This section provides the second study involving Gay Games V in 1998 in Amsterdam and a comparison of all three studies involving sponsorship and the Gay Games-Gay Games IV in 1994, Gay Games V in 1998, and Gay Games VI in 2002. The stakeholders, such as the sponsoring companies and organizations and the Federation of Gay Games, have a need for relevant information concerning sponsorship and the Gay Games (Pitts, 1999). The information could prove to be most helpful to the Federation of Gay Games in their quest to find more sponsorship and to sport marketers of companies considering the Gay Games as a sponsorship venue. Therefore, the purpose of the 1998 study was to assess sponsor company awareness of attendees at Gay Games V in Amsterdam.

## Methodology

> **The survey contained three sections-demographics, sponsor recognition, and attitudes toward sponsors.**

Two methodologies are used in measuring advertising effectiveness: direct and intermediate. Intermediate research examines consumer response to advertising. Within this, there are two methods: *recall* and *recognition*. Both measure the consumer's recognition or memory of advertising, both are measures of sponsor company awareness, and both are commonly used when studying sponsorship and sports events (Gardner & Shuman, 1987; Javalgi, Traylor, Gross, & Lampman, 1994; Kuzma, Shanklin, & McCally, 1993; Milne & McDonald, 1999). For purposes of this study, the recognition method was used. A survey instrument was designed based on previous research (Cuneen & Hannan, 1993; Pitts, 1998; Sandler & Shani, 1993; Stotlar & Johnson, 1989; Stotlar, 1993). Subjects included Gay

## Table 3 Demographics: Education, Travel to the Games, Gay Games Involvement

| Education Level Category | f | P | Travel to the Games | f | P |
|---|---|---|---|---|---|
| grade school | 3 | 1.3 | family only | 3 | 1.3 |
| some high school | 4 | 1.7 | partner only | 25 | 10.8 |
| vocational/tech school | 4 | 1.7 | friends only | 50 | 21.7 |
| high school | 10 | 4.3 | alone | 31 | 13.4 |
| some college | 22 | 9.5 | both friends & family/partner | 48 | 20.8 |
| college degree | 87 | 37.0 | organization | 45 | 19.5 |
| graduate degree | 62 | 26.8 | multiple responses | 27 | 11.7 |
| post graduate work | 32 | 13.9 | | | |
| doctoral degree | 2 | .9 | | | |

| Gay Games Involvement | female (69) | | male (155) | | Total (228) | |
|---|---|---|---|---|---|---|
| | f | P | f | P | f | P |
| athlete/sports participant | 42 | 60.8 | 100 | 64.5 | 143 | 62.7 |
| cultural/arts participant | 4 | 5.7 | 8 | 5.1 | 14 | 6.1 |
| spectator | 11 | 15.9 | 24 | 15.4 | 35 | 15.3 |
| Gay Games worker/staff | 2 | 2.8 | 4 | 2.5 | 6 | 2.6 |
| media | 1 | 1.4 | 1 | .6 | 2 | .8 |
| multiple responses | 9 | 13.0 | 18 | 11.6 | 27 | 11.8 |

## Table 3 Demographics: Gender, Age, Age by Gender

| Gender | f | P | Age | f | P |
|---|---|---|---|---|---|
| Female | 71 | 30.7 | 18-24 | 1 | 0.4 |
| Male | 156 | 67.5 | 25-34 | 70 | 30.3 |
| Other | 2 | 0.9 | 35-44 | 110 | 47.6 |
| | | | 45-54 | 37 | 16.0 |
| | | | 55-64 | 9 | 3.8 |
| | | | 65+ | 2 | 0.8 |

| Age By Gender: | Female: | | Male: | |
|---|---|---|---|---|
| | f | P | f | P |
| 18-24 | 0 | --- | 1 | 0.6 |
| 25-34 | 20 | 28.1 | 50 | 32.0 |
| 35-44 | 35 | 49.2 | 73 | 46.7 |
| 45-54 | 13 | 13.0 | 24 | 15.3 |
| 55-64 | 3 | 3.0 | 6 | 3.8 |
| 65+ | 0 | --- | 2 | 1.2 |

**Table 3** Demographics: Sexual Orientation, Household Description, Household Income

| Sexual Orientation | *f* | *P* |
|---|---|---|
| Lesbian/Gay | 218 | 94.4 |
| Bisexual | 6 | 2.6 |
| Heterosexual | 3 | 1.7 |

| Household Description | Female | | Male | | Total | |
|---|---|---|---|---|---|---|
| | *f* | *P* | *f* | *P* | *f* | *P* |
| Only adult in my household | 40 | 56.3 | 62 | 39.7 | 103 | 44.5 |
| I live with my partner | 24 | 33.8 | 63 | 40.3 | 88 | 38 |
| I live with a friend/roommate | 5 | 7 | 27 | 17.3 | 32 | 13.8 |
| Other | 1 | 1.4 | 3 | 1.9 | 4 | 1.7 |

| Household Income | *f* | *P* | Household Income | *f* | *P* |
|---|---|---|---|---|---|
| below $10,000 | 6 | 2.6 | 90,000-109,999 | 30 | 13.0 |
| 10,000-29,999 | 19 | 8.2 | 110,000-129,999 | 11 | 4.8 |
| 30,000-49,999 | 50 | 21.6 | 130,000-149,999 | 13 | 5.6 |
| 50,000-69,999 | 38 | 16.5 | 150,000-169,999 | 2 | .9 |
| 70,000-89,999 | 38 | 16.5 | 170,000+ | 18 | 7.8 |

Games V (Amsterdam, August, 1998) attendees: registered sports participants, registered cultural participants, spectators, coaches, workers, and media. Additionally, the survey contained three sections-demographics, sponsor recognition, and attitudes toward sponsors.

> **Data were analyzed within the three sections—demographics, sponsor recognition, and attitudes toward sponsors.**

Three methods of data collection were used: on-site, research assistants, and web site. On-site, the mall intercept approach was used. Research assistants were recruited and trained. The assistants sought out people in their community who attended the Games and asked them to complete a survey. Using a web site, the survey was published and survey data were collected via the web site. Statistics common to recognition research were used in analyzing the data.

# Results, Conclusions, & Discussion

## Results

Data were analyzed within the three sections-demographics, sponsor recognition, and attitudes toward sponsors. Results and discussion are presented by those three sections.

## Demographics

*Gay Games Attendee Demographics.* Demographical and lifestyle data are reported in Table 3. The findings reveal that the average attendee in this sample included 47.6% are in the 25-34 age bracket, 94.4% are lesbian or gay, and many (44.5%) live alone while almost the same percentage (38.0%) live with a partner. Household income data reported reveals that although the largest group (21.6%) fall into the $30,000-49,999 bracket, it is interesting to note that three other brackets consist of numbers close to that: 16.5% each for the $50,000-69,999 and $70,000-89,999 brackets and 13.0% for the $90,000-109,999 bracket. A large number of attendees reported a high level of education: 78.6% hold a college degree (including those with graduate degrees, post graduate work, and doctoral degrees). Of this sample, 62.7% reported that they attended the Gay Games as a registered sports participant, while 11.8% reported that they attended as spectators. Study participants could select more than one category as a response to this question.

Based on the data reported, the following conclusions are drawn when compared against previous research:

(1) All demographics are closely similar to the demographics taken in the 1994 Gay Games IV sponsorship study (Pitts, 1998). Thus, it appears the study samples are similar in most ways.

2) Some demographical information taken in each study were different types of information and, of course, cannot be compared.

(3) Although the data should not be generalized to the total worldwide lesbian and gay population because the sample is not large enough, it is interesting to note the relatively high education level compared to the United States general population (according to U.S. Census Bureau and Simmons Market Research Bureau). Worldwide education rates have not yet been attained for comparison.

> It is interesting to note the relatively high education level compared to the United States general population.

(4) The relatively high level of household income might indicate the segment of people who can afford to travel and participate in such an event. A study of visitor spending and economic scale revealed that the average attendee spent a mean of $2,514 to attend the Gay Games (Pitts & Ayers, 2001).

## Sponsor Recognition

As in most sponsorship recognition or recall research, the instrument included questions regarding both official and 'dummy' sponsors. Results are presented here in the two areas.

*Official Sponsor Recognition.* The survey contained questions regarding official corporate sponsors and some nonexistant (dummy) sponsors. The data concerning recognition of the official corporate sponsors revealed the following (see Table 4).

(1) Recognition rates of correctly identified sponsor companies ranged from 1.9% to 98.8%, with an average of 64.2%. Six are in the 90% range and over half (9 of 17) of the answers are in the 70% range and above.

(2) It is important to note that in every company category except one (12 of 13), the correct sponsor company

> In every company category except one (12 of 13), the correct sponsor company was the top selected answer.

Table 4 **Sponsor Awareness Results**

| Sponsor | f | P |
|---|---|---|
| **KLM Airlines** | 217 | 97.7 |
| **RedBull (Energy Drink)** | 143 | 97.9 |
| **Heineken** | 64 | 46.4 |
| **Rolling Rock** | 47 | 34.1 |
| **Absolut Vodka** | 65 | 49.6 |
| **Bacardi Breezer** | 24 | 18.3 |
| **Speedo** | 117 | 90.7 |
| **Avis** | 103 | 84.4 |
| **Levi Straus** | 95 | 90.5 |
| **Genre (magazine)** | 48 | 46.6 |
| **OUT** | 33 | 32.0 |
| **Curve** | 2 | 1.9 |
| **A2000 (TV)** | 82 | 98.8 |
| **NZH Groep (public transportation)** | 44 | 73.3 |
| **Schipol Fonds (airport)** | 57 | 96.6 |
| **Energie Noord West** | 41 | 85.4 |
| **SENS/Staatsloterji (lottery)** | 14 | 46.7 |

was the top selected answer. This is important for three reasons: First, this is similar to the findings of the Gay Games IV 1994 study (Pitts, 1998); second, this is different from the findings in other similar studies; and third, this is especially interesting because there were over three times as many sponsors for Gay Games V in 1998 than there were in Gay Games IV in 1994. Such an increase should bring clutter and confusion. However, it appears that even with 80 sponsors, the study participants were able to correctly identify the sponsor company in most cases.

On the other hand, such a high correct identification rate could be the result of using recognition methodology. That is, recognition methodology allows the study participant to see a list of possible companies. This list triggers the memory and, therefore, acts as a clue to the identity of the company. The sight of a company name might trigger the memory of that particular company as a sponsor, whereas recall methodology requires the study participant to name the company without the use of any possible clues.

(3) The most recognized company (98.6% answered yes and 97.7% correctly identified the company) was also the company that most supported their sponsorship with other forms of advertising. The airlines, KLM Royal Dutch Airlines, did heavy on-site signage at every sports and cultural venue, had a very large and visible booth in Friendship Village staffed with several people every day, gave away promotional merchandise every day, gave away customized (for the Gay Games) luggage tags, did direct mail before and after the dates of the Gay Games, did print advertising in several lesbian and gay print media, and each day held a drawing for free airline tickets on KLM.

(4) It is interesting to note that some of the questions that received the lowest percentage of 'yes' answers received some of the highest identification answers (see Table 5). For instance, only 30.2% answered 'yes' to the question "Is there an airport as an official sponsor?" Yet, 96.6% correctly identified Schipol Airport as the official sponsor. This might be explained by the fact that most likely every person who flew into Amsterdam flew into Schipol Airport and therefore recognized the name of the airport.

Table 5 **Percentage of "Yes" Responses Compared to Percentage of Correctly Identified Companies**

| | "Yes" responses | Gay Games sponsor correctly identified | |
|---|---|---|---|
| airlines (KLM) | 98.6 | A2000 | 98.8 |
| energy drink (Red Bull) | 68.5 | Red Bull | 97.9 |
| beer (Heineken, Rolling Rock) | 65.4 | KLM | 97.7 |
| liquor (Absolut, Bacardi Breezer) | 60.9 | Schipol | 96.6 |
| sports clothing (Speedo) | 58.6 | Speedo | 90.7 |
| rental car (Avis) | 58.3 | Levi | 90.5 |
| clothing company (Levi Straus) | 50.4 | Energie | 85.4 |
| magazine (OUT, Genre, Curve) | 50.0 | Avis | 84.4 |
| television company (A2000) | 39.7 | NZH Groep | 73.3 |
| public transportation (NZH Groep) | 30.7 | Absolut | 49.6 |
| airport (Schipol) | 30.2 | SENS | 46.7 |
| electricity (Energie Noord West) | 23.4 | Genre | 46.6 |
| lottery (SENS/Staatsloterji) | 14.8 | Heineken | 46.4 |
| | | Rolling Rock | 34.1 |
| | {Yes average: 49.9} | OUT | 32.0 |
| | | Bacardi Breezer | 18.3 |
| | | Curve | 1.9 |
| | | {correct average: 64.2} | |

Only 39.7% answered 'yes' to the question "Is there a television company as an official sponsor?" Yet, 98.8% correctly identified A2000 as the official sponsor. This was the highest correctly identified company. This might be explained by the fact that A2000 was the primary local television station/channel and did local coverage of the Games. So, the cameras were fairly visible.

Only 30.7% answered 'yes' to the question "Is there a public transportation company as an official sponsor?" Yet 73.3% correctly identified NZH Groep as the official sponsor. While the study participants obviously didn't think a public transportation company was a sponsor, they did know and recognize that Gay Games participants were receiving free public transportation and probably then recognized the name of the company in the list of offered answers.

*'Dummy' Sponsor Recognition.* As is done with most sponsor recognition or recall studies, 'dummy' sponsor questions were a part of the survey for analysis. 'Dummy' sponsor questions are mixed with other questions. Study participants are not told which questions are the 'dummy' sponsor questions. This is done, for example, to analyze ambush-marketing activity and to determine if study participants' answers to these questions are different from their answers to the official sponsor recognition questions. The results are as follows (refer to Table 6).

(1) It appears that study participants seemed to know which companies were not official sponsors of Gay Games V. Although the answers of 'No' definitely outweighed the answers of 'Yes', most study participants circled answers to try to identify a company. Additionally, although most answers were lower than most answers about the official sponsors, some were about the same level as the lowest about official sponsors.

Table 6  **Results on Questions Asked About Dummy Sponsors**

| Category | | f | P |
|---|---|---|---|
| **Bottled water company:** | Naya | 45 | 72.6 |
| **Credit card company:** | Visa | 16 | 35.6 |
| | Mastercard | 15 | 33.3 |
| **Soft drink company:** | Coca-Cola | 10 | 50 |
| | Pepsi Cola | 7 | 35 |
| **Official car company** | Ford | 6 | 50 |

(2) It is interesting to note that Naya spring water received a recognition rate of 72.6%. Although Naya was not an official sponsor of this Gay Games, Naya was an official sponsor—and a highly recognized sponsor (76.2%)—of Gay Games IV in 1994. It is possible that some study participants knew and remembered this and thought that Naya was once again a sponsor.

## Attitudes Toward Sponsors

Two primary reasons a company sponsors events are to influence consumer awareness of the company and to affect purchase behavior. That is, the sponsoring company seeks to make its company or products known to potential consumers and, through the company's show of support for the event, to influence support of the company through sales. To study the level of support of the sponsoring companies and to determine if Gay Games attendees were willing to support the sponsoring companies, two questions were included on the survey and findings are presented in Table 7.

A company's level of support for the event can be portrayed in its advertising. Some of the sponsoring companies of Gay Games V used the words "proud sponsor of the Gay Games" in their advertising. One question in the survey sought to determine if study participants recognized the company's use of these words: "Have you seen advertising that uses the words 'proud sponsor of the Gay Games?'" Over half, 58% (134), of the study participants responded yes. When asked to list those companies, 67.9% (91 of the 134) listed KLM Royal Dutch Airlines, while other companies received far fewer mentions. However, it should be noted that 12 of the 13 companies that study participants listed 2 or more times were all official sponsor companies. (The exception was Miller beer.) This could mean that study participants were able to remember those companies whose advertising contained the 'proud sponsor' words. On the other hand, because this question was placed at a point in the survey just after the list of questions about the sponsors, it might only mean that study participants were able to look above for clues on company names to write on the survey. Interestingly, however, if that had been the case, one would assume that the study participant would have listed all of the official sponsor companies from the list of questions. Because that didn't happen, it could be surmised that study participants tried to recall from memory those companies who used the words in their advertising.

**The results of the question in the study reveal that a large percentage—73.1%—of the attendees in this study are more likely to buy the products of the Gay Games sponsors.**

The purpose of the second question—"Are you more likely to buy the products of the Gay Games sponsor companies because they are sponsors of the Gay Games?"—was to attempt to determine level of brand loyalty. That is, in some respects, a company considering becoming a sponsor of the Gay Games will want to know if their efforts (expenditure of funds) have a more likely chance of resulting in a positive return on investment. Therefore, if the company could determine that consumers would be more likely to

**Table 7** **Survey Responses to Questions on Sponsor Advertising, Solicitation, and Likely Purchase of Sponsor's Products**

**(1) Survey Question:** Have you seen advertising that uses the words "proud sponsor of the Gay Games" in the ad?

| Responses | Yes | | No | | no answer | |
|---|---|---|---|---|---|---|
| | f | P | f | P | f | P |
| | 134 | 58 | 68 | 29.4 | 29 | 12.5 |

**(2) Survey Question:** List the company(ies):

| Company | f | Company | f |
|---|---|---|---|
| KLM | 91 | Police | 1 |
| Avis | 10 | Rainbow Realty | 1 |
| Durex | 9 | Adidas | 1 |
| Levi Straus | 8 | Tzabago | 1 |
| Speedo | 6 | ZaZare Diamonds | 1 |
| Kodak | 5 | GWK | 1 |
| Absolut | 4 | Nashuatec | 1 |
| Red Bull | 4 | Heineken | 1 |
| OUT | 3 | Bacardi | 1 |
| Miller Beer | 3 | Naya | 1 |
| A2000 | 2 | Planet Out | 1 |
| Rolling Rock | 2 | | |
| Randstad | 2 | | |

**(3) Survey Question:** Are you more likely to buy the products of the Gay Games sponsor companies because they are sponsors of the Gay Games?

| Responses | Yes | | No | | no answer | |
|---|---|---|---|---|---|---|
| | f | P | f | P | f | P |
| | 169 | 73.1 | 13 | 13.4 | 31 | 13.4 |

purchase their products, the company might be more likely to sponsor a particular event.

The results of the question in the study reveal that a large percentage—73.1%—of the attendees in this study are more likely to buy the products of the Gay Games sponsors. Therefore, this finding should be good news to the sponsors of Gay Games V.

Comparatively, this finding is higher than the results of other studies with a similar question (Sandler & Shani, 1993; Stotlar, 1993). On the other hand, it is lower than a similar

> Moreover, more businesses are finding it easier to ignore anti-gay and -lesbian rhetoric by people and institutions who react to a company's gay- and lesbian-friendly policies or advertising with boycotts or pressure to change.

question and finding in the sponsorship study at Gay Games IV (Pitts, 1998). That finding revealed that an incredible 92.3% of the study participants would be more likely to buy a sponsor's product. Together, the findings of both studies of attendees at Gay Games events are higher than studies at the Olympic

Games (Sandler & Shani, 1993; Stotlar, 1993). Because of the nature of the instrument and methodology, there is no followup question to attempt to determine why so many attendees have a "more likely to buy" attitude toward sponsors.

There is research that shows that lesbian and gay consumers are more brand loyal than their heterosexual counterparts (Badgett, 1997; Cronin, 1993; "Gays Celebrate. . .", 1994; Miller, 1990; Webster, 1994), and Pitts (1998) suggested that lesbian and gay people seem to be more appreciative of support and will reward it with loyalty. Additionally, research by the Simmons Market Research Bureau (1996) revealed that an estimated 89% of gay

> **There is a need for further critical examination of why attendees at the Gay Games events appear to have a high likely to buy response rate.**

and lesbian people said they would go out of their way to buy products that advertise to gay and lesbian consumers. Moreover, more businesses are finding it easier to ignore anti-gay and -lesbian rhetoric by ultra-conservative anti-gay and -lesbian people and institutions who react to a company's gay and lesbian-friendly policies or advertising with boycotts or pressure to change. Companies are choosing instead to pay much more attention to the research on the lesbian and gay market and consumer behavior (Hannaham, 1996; Kimbrough, 1997; Miller, 1994; Quinones, 1998; Reda, 1994; Research Alert, 1997; "Support Causes. . .," 1997; Wilke, 1997). Regardless, there is a need for further critical examination of why attendees at the Gay Games events appear to have a high likely to buy response rate.

## Conclusions and Recommendations

> **If the current increase in the number of sponsors continues, Gay Games organizers will most likely have to face the issue of clutter that other large sports events with large numbers of sponsors face.**

Based on the results of this study, some conclusions can be drawn and recommendations made. The conclusions drawn in the study and its results support the literature that lesbian and gay people seem to notice, be more aware, can more correctly identify, and will support the companies who are sponsors of lesbian and gay events. This is important information for companies who are considering where to put sponsorship dollars.

Similar research should be conducted at Gay Games events in the future and compared to this study. Potential studies that could be conducted include recall and recognition evaluation, as well as pre- and post-event evaluation. Further analysis could include media exposure analysis, intent to purchase, change in sales measure, and changes in company image.

If the current increase in the number of sponsors continues, Gay Games organizers will most likely have to face the issue of clutter that other large sports events with large numbers of sponsors face. That is, with a higher number of sponsors' signage, advertising, and on-site presence, attendees are bombarded with a number of logos and ads making it more likely that a particular sponsor's signs or ads will be "lost in the jungle." Indeed, the lower sponsor awareness rate in this study of the Gay Games in 1998 compared to the rate in the study of the Gay Games in 1994 might be partially attributable to the high number of sponsors as well as their increased presence during the Games. Organizers of the Gay Games in the future would be wise to study this issue.

> **To date, there are no known studies involving corporate sponsorship and the International Gay and Lesbian Football Association (soccer), the International Gay Bowling Organization, the EuroGames, the National Gay Rodeo Association, the International Gay and Lesbian Martial Arts Organization, or the North American Gay Volleyball Association.**

Table 8 **Partial Results of Sponsorship Awareness Studies at Gay Games IV in 1994, Gay Games V in 1998, and Gay Games VI in 2002**

|  | **1994 GGIV** | **1998 GGV** | **2002 GGVI** |
|---|---|---|---|
| **Sponsorship awareness level (avg)** | 73.7% | 64.2% | 68% |
| **Intent to purchase sponsor's brand** | 92.3% | 73.1% | 74% |

Research is needed in relation to corporate sponsorship and other gay and lesbian sports events. To date, there are no known studies involving corporate sponsorship and such large lesbian and gay sports events as national and international competitions staged by the International Gay and Lesbian Football Association (soccer), the International Gay Bowling Organization, the EuroGames, the National Gay Rodeo Association, the International Gay and Lesbian Martial Arts Organization, and the North American Gay Volleyball Association. These organizations host or sanction several annual events, each of which attracts several hundred participants, and some of which attract thousands. The organizations usually host an annual national or international championship tournament/contest that typically attracts between 3,000 and 12,000 participants. For instance, the annual international championship tournament of the International Gay Bowling Organization usually attracts over 6,000 participants. All of these organizations have a number of corporate sponsors. Knowledge gained from sponsorship research would be valuable to all stakeholders and to potential stakeholders.

**Those companies that have not yet considered the gay and lesbian market might consider the Gay Games as a first opportunity to reach the market.**

Additionally, the information would add to a small but growing body of literature on lesbian and gay sports. Faculty and students in sport management, sport marketing, and related fields of study such as recreation, physical education, and business could benefit from such knowledge. For instance, this information is particularly informative in lectures about corporate sponsorship and niche marketing.

For sport marketing professionals in sport sponsorship business, the information found in this study can be used in a number of ways. For instance, those who are looking to match potential sponsoring companies with a high brand loyal target market through a sporting event ought to consider the Gay Games. Those companies that have not yet considered the gay and lesbian market might consider the Gay Games as a first opportunity to reach the market. Additionally, there are numerous other lesbian and gay sports events and organizations that could be considered for sponsorship opportunities and they exist in most cities in most countries around the world. Some are local events while others are national or international. While the Gay Games offers an international opportunity with an unusually large audience every four years, the local events and organizations are year-round. Companies could consider combining sponsorship with the local organizations to develop relationship and/or cause marketing exchanges while using the Gay Games as a capstone event to reach the wider and global market. One example of a company that has done this successfully is Miller Beer (an American beer company). Miller sponsors several local, regional, and national lesbian and gay sports events in the United States year round and was a major sponsor for Gay Games IV. Therefore, it was probably no coincidence that Miller Beer was one of the most highly recognized sponsors of the Gay Games.

**Miller sponsors several local, regional, and national lesbian and gay sports events in the United States year round and was a major sponsor for Gay Games IV. Miller Beer was one of the most highly recognized sponsors of the Gay Games.**

**Table 9** **How to Reach the Gay and Lesbian Market**

| |
|---|
| • Actively engage in sponsorship of gay and lesbian sports events and organizations. |
| • Use direct marketing strategies to lesbian and gay sports fans (Example: Gay Night at the Atlanta Braves). |
| • Use explicit recognition and support of work to eliminate homophobia in sports, especially in college athletics, professional sports, and high school sports. Example: boycott and/or pressure those organizations that have policies that protect or encourage discrimination based on sexual orientation. |
| • Get involved in gay and lesbian community projects and organizations to support causes. |
| • Your company should offer domestic partner benefits. Example: An increasing number of Fortune 500 companies offer full DP benefits. |
| • Create specific marketing and advertising materials and strategies that have explicit gay and lesbian content. |
| • Conduct or obtain extensive research on the lesbian and gay market that can be used for marketing strategies. |
| • Advertise in gay and lesbian media. Examples of magazines include the Advocate, Curve, OUT, Girlfriends, Genre, POZ, Ten Percent, Southern Voice, Lesbian Connection, and Lesbian News. Examples of broadcast media include Gay Entertainment Television, Q Network, and Gay Cable Network. |
| • Create a gay and lesbian marketing director or department whose responsibility is to oversee marketing strategies for the company. This person would also act as a liaison to the lesbian and gay community. |

## Banking on the Pink Dollar: Sponsorship and the Gay Games

> **Indeed, sponsorship awareness levels at three Gay Games show patrons levels at 73.7% (Gay Games IV in 1994), 64.2% (Gay Games V in 1998), and 68% (Gay Games VI in 2002).**

In relation to sponsorship awareness, companies can be assured that their sponsorship dollars are well spent, have value, and will most likely show a return on investment. A look at the three studies on sponsorship awareness on three Gay Games reveals some interesting numbers that support the general research on the gay and lesbian market in relation to high brand loyalty. Indeed, sponsorship awareness levels at three Gay Games show patrons levels at 73.7% (Gay Games IV in 1994), 64.2% (Gay Games V in 1998), and 68% (Gay Games VI in 2002). Furthermore, when asked if they would be more likely to purchase products of sponsors, patrons' levels were 92.3%, 73.1%, and 74%, respectively (see Table 8). In other research, the motivations of sponsors were examined and compared to those sponsors of non-gay/lesbian sports events. Among the findings, the number one answer was "to increase sales" followed by "to build brand loyalty," "sponsor many gay sports events in Toronto," "give back to the community," and "improve image in the community" (Jarvis, 2002).

In addition, the earlier study on visitor spending (Pitts & Ayers, 2001) shows that people who are attending the Gay Games typically spend an average of 10 days at the destination and spend an average total of $2,514.00 (USD). Of this, some of the spending categories were $349 spent on food, $124 on entertainment, $192 on retail shopping, $111 on souvenirs, $674 on lodging, and $590 on commercial transportation. In another study exploring sports tourism and the emerging use of destination marketing with the Gay Games, it was reported that "the attraction, size, and enormity of the event" is very attractive to "national and international mainstream governing sports organizations, government departments, and tourism offices. The potential economic and cultural impact for such stakeholders as the hotel, restaurant, tourism sites and offices, and airlines industries" is enormous (Pitts & Ayers, 2000, p. 389). Hence, it would appear that the Gay Games has gained an acceptable level of attractiveness as a venue for corporate sponsorship and that companies seeking the gay and lesbian market through sports should give considerable attention to the Gay Games as a potentially successful venue.

## Reaching the Gay and Lesbian Sports Market

**Besides sponsorship of the Gay Games and other gay and lesbian sports events, what are some specific marketing strategies that companies can use to reach "the pink market"?**

Besides sponsorship of the Gay Games and other gay and lesbian sports events, what are some specific marketing strategies that companies can use to reach "the pink market"? Table 9 provides a short list of strategies. A company might use one or a combination of the strategies. As you can see, most are relationship-marketing strategies. For more in-depth strategies and discussion, it is recommended that companies seek professional help through companies that specialize in research and marketing and the gay market, such as Prime Access, Overlooked Opinions, Mulryan/Nash, WinMark, and Revendell Marketing.

## References

Aaker, D. A. & Joachimsthaler, E. (2000). *Brand leadership.* New York: The Free Press.

Amis, J., McDaniel, S., & Slack, T. (1999). Shifting the paradigm in sponsorship research. Paper presented at the 1999 conference of the North American Society for Sport Management, University of British Columbia, Vancouver, British Columbia, Canada.

Badgett, M. V. L. (1997). Beyond biased samples: Challenging the myths on the economic status of lesbians and gay men. In A. Gluckman & B. Reed (Eds.), *Homo economics: Capitalism, community, and lesbian and gay life* (pp. 66-71). New York: Routledge.

Baker, D. (1997). A history in ads: The growth of the gay and lesbian market. In A. Gluckman and B. Reed (Eds.). *Homo Economics: Capitalism, community, and lesbian and gay life.* (pp. 11-20) New York: Routledge..

Brooks, C. M. (1994). *Sports marketing: Competitive business strategies for sports.* Englewood Cliffs, NJ: Prentice Hall.

Button, K. (1990, November 9). The gay consumer. *Financial Times,* p. 10.

Cronin, A. (1993, June 27). Two viewfinders, two pictures of gay America. *New York Times,* section 4, p. 16.

Cuneen, J., & Hannan, M. J. (1993). Intermediate measures and recognition testing of sponsorship advertising at an LPGA tournament. *Sport Marketing Quarterly, 2*(1), 47-56.

Curiel, J. (1991). Gay newspapers. *Editor and Publisher Fourth Estate, 124*(3), 14-19.

Davis, R. A. (1993). Sky's the limit for tour operators. *Advertising Age, 64,* January 18, p. 36.

Elliott, S. (1993a, May 7). As the gay and lesbian market grows, a boom in catalogues that are out, loud and proud. *New York Times,* p. C-17.

Elliott, S. (1993b, June 15). When a play has a gay theme, campaigns often tell it as it is. *New York Times,* p. C-15.

Friedman, A. (1990, December). Sport marketers must work harder and smarter to score. *Athletic Business,* p. 22.

Fugate, D. L. (1993). Evaluating the U.S. male homosexual and lesbina population as a viable target market segment: A review with implication. *Journal of Consumer Marketing, 10*(4), 46-57.

Gardner, M. P., & Shuman, P. J. (1987). Sponsorship: An important component of the promotions mix. *Journal of Advertising, 16*(1), 11-17.

Gays celebrate and business tunes in. (1994, June 27). *Fortune,* 14.

Hannaham, J. (1996, November). Feeding the gay market. *OUT Magazine,* pp. 117-118, 162.

International Events Group Sponsorship Report. (1998, December 22). 1998 sponsorship spending $6.8 billion. Chicago: International Events Group.

Javalgi, R., Traylor, A. F., Gross, A. C., & Lampman, E. (1994). Awareness of sponsorship and corporate image: An empirical investigation. *Journal of Advertising, 23*(4), 47-58.

Johnson, B. (1993, January 18). The gay quandary: Advertising's most elusive, yet lucrative target market proves difficult to measure. *Advertising Age, 64*(18), p. 29.

Kates, S. M. (1998). *Twenty million new customers! Understanding gay men's consumer behavior.* New York: The Harrington Park Press.

Kimbrough, A. W. (1997, June 13). Numbers draw advertisers to tap gay market. *Atlanta Business Chronicle,* p. B15.

Kuzma, J. R., Shanklin, W. L., & McCally, J. F. (1993). Number one principle for sporting events seeking corporate sponsors: Meet benefactor's objectives. *Sport Marketing Quarterly, 5*(2), 27-32.

Lough, N. L., & Irwin, R. L. (1999). The objectives sought among sponsors of women's sport: Do they differ from general sponsorship? Paper presented at the 1999 conference of the North American Society for Sport Management, University of British Columbia, Vancouver, British Columbia, Canada.

Lukenbill, G. (1995). *Untold millions: Positioning your business for the gay and lesbian consumer revolution.* New York: HarperBusiness.

Miller, C. (1990, December 24). Gays are affluent but often overlooked market. *Marketing News,* p. 2.

Miller, C. (1992, July 20). Mainstream marketers decide time is right to target gays. *Marketing News,* p. 8.

Miller, C. (1997). Top marketers take bolder approach in targeting gays. *Marketing News, 28*(13), 1-2.

Milne, G. R., McDonald, M. A. (1999). *Sport marketing: Managing the exchange process.* Boston: Jones and Bartlett.

Mullin, B., Hardy, S. & Sutton, W. (2001). *Sport marketing.* Champaign, IL: Human Kinetics.

Penaloza, L. (1996). We're here, we're queer, and we're going shopping! A critical perspective on the accommodation of gays and lesbians in the U.S. marketplace. In D. L. Wardlow (Ed.), *Gays, Lesbians, and Consumer Behavior: Theory, Practice, and Research Issues in Marketing.* pp. 9-41. New York: Haworth Press.

Pitts, B. G. (1997). From leagues of their own to anindustry of their own: The emerging lesbian sports industry. *Women in Sport and Physical Activity Journal, 6*(2), 109-139.

Pitts, B. G. (1998). An analysis of sponsorship recall during Gay Games IV. *Sport Marketing Quarterly, 7*(4), 11-18.

Pitts, B. G. (1999). Sports tourism and niche markets: Identification and analysis of the growing lesbian and gay sports tourism industry. *Journal of Vacation Marketing, 5*(1), 31-50.

Pitts, B. G. & Ayers, K. (2001). An analysis of visitor spending and economic scale on Amsterdam from the Gay Games V, 1998. *International Journal of Sport Management, 2,* 134-151.

Pitts, B. G., Fielding, L. W., & Miller, L. K. (1994). Industry segmentation theory and the sport industry: Developing a sport industry segment model. *Sport Marketing Quarterly, 3*(1), 15-24.

Pitts, B. G. & Stotlar, D. (2002). *Fundamentals of sport marketing (2nd ed.).* Morgantown, WV: Fitness Information Technology, Inc.

Quinones, E. R. (1998). Major advertisers increase buys in gay press: Large corporate clients cite loyalty, affluence of readers, cast gay media ads as part of larger marketing strategy. *Dallas Voice.* Retrieved July 20, 2001, from http://dallasvoice.com

Reda, S. (1994, September). Marketing to gays & lesbians: The last taboo. *National Retail, 76*(9), pp. 18-21.

Research Alert. (1997). Newest gay/lesbian research: Not about head count, but consumer spending. *Research Alert, 15*(8), pp. 1-4.

Sandler, D. M., & Shani, D. (1993). Sponsorship and the Olympic Games: the consumer perspective. *Sport Marketing Quarterly, 2*(3), 38-43.

Shilbury, D., Quick, S., & Westerbeek, H. (1998). *Strategic sport marketing.* Australia: Allen & Unwin.

Simmons Market Research. (1996). The 1996 gay and lesbian market study. New York: Simmons Market Research.

Stotlar, D. K. (1993). Sponsorship and the Olympic Winter Games. *Sport Marketing Quarterly, 2*(3), 35-43.

Stotlar, D., & Johnson, D. A. (1989). Assessing the impact and effectiveness of stadium advertising on sport spectators at Division I institutions. *Journal of Sport Management, 3*(2), 90-102.

Support Causes Important to Lesbians. (1997). *About Women and Marketing, 10*(5), 12-14.

Summer, B. (1992). A niche market comes of age. *Publishers Weekly,* June 29, p. 36-41.

Tharp, M. C. (2001). *Marketing and consumer identity in multicultural America.* Thousand Oaks, CA: Sage Publications.

Turco, D. M. (1994). Event sponsorship: Effects of consumer brand loyalty and consumption. *Sport Marketing Quarterly, 3*(3), 35-37.

Warren, J. (1990). Vibrant subculture: Readers' buying power a key to a thriving gay press. *Chicago Tribune,* p. 2.

Wilke, M. (1997). Big advertisers join move to embrace gay market. *Advertising Age, 68*(31), 1-4.

Yankelovich. (1994, June 9). Gay/Lesbian/Bisexual Monitor Survey. New York: Yankelovich and Associates, cited in *New York Times,* p. D-1.

Endnotes

(1) For further discussion about brand theory, see Aaker, D. A., & Joachimsthaler, E. (2000). Brand leadership. New York: The Free Press.

# CHAPTER 8

# The Negotiation Philosophy for Corporate Sponsorship of Sports Properties

JOHN A. FORTUNATO
ANGELA DUNNAM

## Abstract

As sponsorships with sports properties become a strategy that corporations continue to implement, it is important for these corporations to negotiate an agreement that could best achieve the business objectives of (1) reaching a target audience, (2) increasing brand recall, and (3) increasing sales. In order to successfully achieve these sponsorship business objectives, there is much for a corporation to consider when entering into a sponsorship agreement with a sports property. Corporations must negotiate to control for factors that could hinder the success of a sponsorship agreement. These factors include placement in reaching a target audience, the association of the sponsoring brand with the image of the sports property, advertising clutter, ambush marketing, and protecting exclusivity in an attempt to generate an increase in sales. This essay builds on previous literature to provide a comprehensive philosophy of what corporations should consider when negotiating a sponsorship agreement with a sports property.

## Introduction

Several corporations are now utilizing sponsorships of sports properties as part of their overall strategic advertising communication plan. The sports marketing firm IEG projects corporate sponsors will spend $7.21 billion investing in sports properties in 2003 in North America, with at least 90% of that expenditure in the United States. This expenditure represents an 11.2% jump in corporate sports sponsorships from 2002 (e.g., Hiestand, 2003). The projections also claim that sports sponsorships will account for 69% of all total sponsorship dollars, a slight increase for 2003, and corporations such

Corporate sponsors will spend $7.21 billion investing in sports properties in 2003 in North America, with at least 90% of that expenditure in the United States. This expenditure represents an 11.2% jump in corporate sports sponsorships from 2002.

as PepsiCo, which ranked first in the 2002 IEG ranking of sponsor spending, investing as much as $235 million in sports sponsorships (e.g., Hiestand, 2003). Recognizing this phenomenon, scholars are proceeding to examine the impact of this advertising communication strategy. Regardless of any specific strategy, the corporate business objectives of a sponsorship agreement are the same as other advertising or marketing strategies and identified here as (1) reaching a target audience, (2) increasing brand recall, and (3) increasing sales.

In order to successfully achieve these sponsorship business objectives, there is much for a corporation to consider when entering into a sponsorship agreement with a sports property. This essay builds on previous literature to provide a comprehensive philosophy of what corporations should consider when negotiating a sponsorship agreement with a sports property. The intention is not to provide any specific strategies, but rather a philosophical approach to help achieve the sponsorship business objectives. These objectives are, however, not necessarily easily attained, and there are several critical factors that corporations must be aware of that could affect the success of a sponsorship agreement. These factors include placement for exposure to the target audience, the association of the sponsoring brand with the image of the sports property, advertising clutter, ambush marketing, and protection of exclusivity in an attempt to create an opportunity for putting the product of the corporation directly into consumers' hands and generate an increase in sales.

The key advantageous distinction for a corporation in utilizing sponsorship as a communication strategy to reach its audience is the ability to negotiate with the sports property and leverage the agreement to benefit both the sports property and the sponsoring corporation. All of these critical factors can be controlled through negotiation and an increase in investment in order to give the corporation a

Through negotiation of sponsorship agreements anything is possible—at the right price.

tremendous opportunity to achieve the sponsorship business objectives. Not considering and controlling for these factors through negotiation could jeopardize the success of the agreement. Through negotiation of sponsorship agreements anything is possible—at the right price.

## Sponsorship Principles

### What Is Sponsorship?

The benefits to the sports property are obvious upon entering into a sponsorship agreement because they add another major revenue stream. If negotiated and executed properly, the benefits of the sponsorship agreement to the corporation will be apparent and the business objectives will be achieved. The desired outcome is a successful partnership that benefits both the sponsoring company and the sports property.

A *sports property* may include anything from an entire sports league to a team, an event, or an individual player. A corporation can invest in a sports property to attain a brand association with the sports property's image, and more importantly, to utilize the eminence of the sports property to gain exposure for the corporate brand in a way that will increase sales.

If there are unlimited possibilities through negotiation, as is the thesis being presented here, sponsorship becomes difficult to define. No two sponsorship agreements are alike and the negotiated details define the difference. That is why the negotiation is critical and can indicate what is possible and how the deal can be leveraged to best benefit both the corporation and the sports property. Meenaghan (1991) does, however, offer one of the more accepted definitions of sponsorship, describing it as "an investment, in cash or in kind, in an activity, in return for access to the exploitable commercial potential associated with that activity" (p. 36). Dean (2002)

> **No two sponsorship agreements are alike and the negotiated details define the difference.**

explains that "for the payment of a fee (or other value) to the sponsee, the sponsor receives the right to associate itself with the sponsee or event" (p. 78). He adds that "by associating itself with the sponsee, the sponsoring firm/brand shares in the image of the sponsee" (p. 78).

Corporations invest in sponsorship because of the expected return on the investment. While these definitions acknowledge an investment, the desired return should be more than just brand association; the desired return should be an increase in sales. In this light, sponsorship is not different in its business objectives from any other advertising or marketing communication strategy.

Corporations can invest in a sports property through purchasing spot advertising on television or through event sponsorship. Sutherland and Galloway (1981) would probably see no difference between sponsorship and spot advertising in the overall objectives of each strategy because they claim that "advertising does not create needs; it merely reflects those needs that are already existent in society at the time" (p. 25). They say that

> products that are advertised heavily have a status conferred upon them—i.e., they are felt by customers to be 'the more popular' products. The media are assumed to carry that which is more important, more in demand, more notorious. Just as 'the ordinary person' does not appear on TV, neither does 'the ordinary product" (p. 27).

They conclude that "advertising (media prominence) functions as a significant cue to the customer in judging what is and is not acceptable and popular with others (p. 28).

McAllister (1998) distinguishes between sponsorship and spot advertising (buying a single commercial within a program). He defines sponsorship as "the funding of an entire event, group, broadcast or place by one commercial interest in exchange for large amounts and special types of promotion connected with the sponsored activity" (p. 358). McAllister (1998) also claims that

> **"Advertisers have been continually frustrated with the viewer's ability to 'zap' ads, with the fragmentation of the media audience, and with the high cost of spot advertising in different media, and they have turned to sponsorship as a corrective to these problems."**

> from the sponsors' point of view, advertisers have been continually frustrated with the viewer's ability to 'zap' ads, with the fragmentation of the media audience, and with the high cost of spot advertising in different media, and they have turned to sponsorship as a corrective to these problems. (p. 359)

Diminishing television ratings have created a need for corporations to employ different strategies to reach an audience: thus, sponsorship. The audience is not all in one location, therefore corporations need to be to in various places in order to reach all of their various demographic groups. Farrelly, Quester, and Burton (1997) point out that it is not uncommon for corporations to engage in multiple sponsorship relationships over the course of a given year. This is especially important for corporations whose products have a wide audience. Corporations such as McDonalds or Coca-Cola, which both transcend many demographic lines of income, race, gender, and geography, need to advertise and sponsor in a variety of locations to reach the different target audiences that might use their products.

Meanwhile, for corporations with a more narrow target audience, such as Mercedes Benz or Lexus, sponsorship at golf or tennis provides an opportunity to reach that desired niche.

Similar to advertising, sponsorship is often one component of a larger communication strategy. Cornwell and Maignan (1998) claim that sponsorship activities will be more effective if coordinated with other marketing communications and promotional activities. Fortunato (2001) points out that often a sponsorship agreement will include the purchase of broadcast commercial time. He says that "one of the strategies regarding potential sponsorship of the NBA was that sponsor companies also had to purchase advertising time for games televised by the NBA's broadcast partners. For example, if Gatorade wanted to be the official sports drink of the NBA and have players drinking out of green cups with the Gatorade logo on them, Gatorade also had to buy commercial time on NBA television broadcasts" (Fortunato, 2001, p. 78).

Corporations that sponsor sports properties also have a tremendous opportunity through the manner in which their brand name might be exposed to the audience on television. In addition to commercial time, sports programming offers the opportunity for a television network to generate advertising revenue within the framework of the program content itself. Unlike sports television, most other programming-prime-time dramas, movies, news magazine shows, and situation comedies-can only offer commercial time to advertisers. The sports format allows networks to sell billboards, still shots (when coming out of commercial of a company logo) with voice-overs announcing the company name and slogan against the backdrop of the live event, pre-game and halftime shows, scoreboards, starting lineups, players of the game, and halftime statistics-all serving as extra forms of advertising revenue within the context of the actual program itself.

People might change channels during commercials, but if they tune in to watch a game, it's difficult to escape the brand exposure that occurs during the game. Advertisers are moving to sponsorship to put their brand name in a position where it is virtually impossible to ignore. Because of the television exposure sponsors receive, it has become desirable to sponsor a player of the game award, tie corporate brand names to the sports event's title (i.e., Tostitos Fiesta Bowl) or half-time show (i.e., Cingular Wireless at the Half) so that announcers repeatedly name the corporation, or prominently locate signage (behind home plate for a baseball game, at mid-court for a basketball game, or on the 50-yard line of a football game).

Through negotiation, sponsorship can include any possibility: signage in the stadium, stadium naming rights, stadium give-aways, appearances with athletes, promotional events at the stadium, promotional spots in a television or radio broadcast, logos on a car or even on a person. For example, the GoldenPalace.com sponsors boxers by having the name of the company featured on the backs of boxers (e.g., McKelvey, 2003). If a game is on television, the amount of space to sell and the possible audience reached grow

> **Corporations such as McDonalds or Coca-Cola, which both transcend many demographic lines of income, race, gender, and geography, need to advertise and sponsor in a variety of locations to reach the different target audiences. Meanwhile, for corporations with a more narrow target audience, such as Mercedes Benz or Lexus, sponsorship at golf or tennis provides an opportunity to reach that desired niche.**

> **Fortunato says that "if Gatorade wanted to be the official sports drink of the NBA and have players drinking out of green cups with the Gatorade logo on them, Gatorade also had to buy commercial time on NBA television broadcasts."**

> **People might change channels during commercials, but if they tune in to watch a game, it's difficult to escape the brand exposure that occurs during the game.**

exponentially. Sponsorship is whatever the corporation and the sports property deem it can possibly be through their negotiated agreement.

## Sponsorship Objectives

The question of what companies want upon entering a sponsorship agreement is vital to examine. Thjomoe, Olson, and Bronn (2002) believe that "a logical approach to sponsorship decision making would dictate that firms should have clear targets and goals for sponsorship" (p. 6). While all sponsorship agreements are different, the objectives for the sponsoring corporations remain the same. Meenaghan (1991) describes three stages of the objectives of sponsorship, beginning with giving money to gain attention, moving to more specific goals associated with a return on the investment, and finally culminating in the third level, where the corporation assumes control over the activities of its sponsored property.

The progression of these three levels is dictated by the amount of investment and the desire and need of the sports property for that revenue. Sports properties that are desperate for the corporate revenue source might be more willing to capitulate to demands of a sponsor. For example, the annual Blue/Grey College Football All-Star game, which is normally played on Christmas Day, did not take place in 2002 because of the lack of a sponsor. If that game is played again, organizers might be willing to give a corporate sponsor whatever they desire. More-prominent sports properties that do not find it difficult to recruit sponsors might not give in to the demands of a corporate sponsor knowing that there is another corporation in that product category probably very willing to take that spot. Southwestern Airlines is the official airline of the NFL, but if the NFL was not pleased with the arrangement, the NFL could simply offer the same deal to a rival airline and probably have no trouble securing sponsorship from that product category.

Many authors indicate that brand awareness and brand image through association with a sports property are the major sponsorship objectives. Gwinner (1997) claims that sponsorship is used to increase brand awareness through exposure, increase goodwill through corporate generosity, and establish, enhance, or change brand image by linking itself with a favorable cause, sports event, or sports team. Roy and Cornwell (1999) add that corporate/brand image enhancement, breaking free from media add clutter, and increased brand awareness rank as the top three objectives.

Keller (1993) defines brand image as the "perceptions about a brand as reflected by brand associations held in memory" (p. 3). Aaker (1997) uses the term *brand personality* and defines it as "the set of human characteristics associated with a brand" (p. 347). Both of these definitions highlight that image and personality perceptions of a brand are in the mind and the actions of the audience.

Gwinner and Eaton (1999) claim that brand image transfer will occur when a corporation and a sports property are linked through sponsorship. They add that this image transfer is stronger between brands and events that have an image-based similarity: for example, corporations sponsoring college athletics through a contribution to the general scholarship fund of a university in recognition of a player of the game. Stipp and Schiavone (1996) point out that sponsorship goals assume that the target audience for the sponsorship will transfer from the sponsored property to the sponsor itself. In conducting research on celebrities, Till and Shimp (1998) state marketers "hope their target audience's positive feelings toward a chosen celebrity will transfer to the endorsed brand or will otherwise enhance the brand's standing" (p. 67). However, they caution that "activation of negative information about a celebrity can have an adverse effect-through lowered brand evaluations-on the endorsed brand with which that celebrity is associated" (p. 72). These results highlight the importance of wise selection of the sports properties to associate brands with before making a major financial investment.

Brand awareness is not an ambitious-enough business objective for a sponsoring corporation who needs consumers to purchase products. The objectives of sponsorship should include developing goodwill, fostering an image, building awareness, and increasing sales.

Brand awareness is obviously important, but it is only one step toward sales. Brand awareness is not an ambitious-enough business objective for a sponsoring corporation who needs consumers to purchase products. Cornwell and Maignan (1998) believe that the objectives of sponsorship should include developing goodwill, fostering an image, building awareness, and increasing sales. Dean (2002) claims "management objectives for sponsorship may be both economic (increased revenues and profits, increased brand awareness, increased channel member interest in the brand) and noneconomic (creation of goodwill with the community, improvement of corporate image, boosting employee morale, recruiting new employees, pure altruism)" (p. 78).

The importance of brand association and recall must be considered as well as the possible addition of audience and the potential increase in sales. Any communication strategy should attempt to accomplish three business objectives: (1) reaching a target audience, (2) increasing brand recall, and (3) increasing sales. The specific strategy employed is almost irrelevant so long as this philosophical approach to attaining objectives is considered upon negotiating a sponsorship agreement.

Any communication strategy should attempt to accomplish three business objectives: (1) reaching a target audience, (2) increasing brand recall, and (3) increasing sales. The specific strategy employed is almost irrelevant so long as this philosophical approach to attaining objectives is considered upon negotiating a sponsorship agreement.

### Sponsorship Evaluation

Knowing if objectives are achieved is difficult for corporations to ascertain. Direct association of consumer behavior with any advertising, marketing, public relations, or sponsorship strategy can never definitively be argued. Several authors point to the great difficulty in evaluating sponsorship agreements (e.g., Cornwell, 1995; Farelly, Quester, & Burton, 1997; Harvey, 2001; Hoek, 1998; Miyazaki & Morgan, 2001). Copeland, Frisby, and McCarville (1996) point out that many sponsoring corporations do not have formal evaluation procedures of their sponsorship agreements. Miyazaki and Morgan (2001) state that "methods commonly used to evaluate general advertising effectiveness on brand awareness or image do not differentiate between the value of a sponsorship per se and the value of general advertising and exposure that would accompany a similar nonsponsorship campaign" (p. 10).

Crimmins and Horn (1996) claim the most common way of quantifying the consumer impact of sponsorship is through measures of visibility. While some corporations might utilize the media exposure they receive as an evaluation measure, Speed and Thompson (2000) point out that approach will not provide direct evidence of sponsorship's effect on a targeted audience's level of brand awareness or image. Thjomoe et al. (2002) also contend that while measurement of sponsoring brand exposure "might be an appropriate method for measurement of such sponsorship goals as building brand awareness, it is clearly not appropriate for more advanced goals such as changing brand image or enhanced relationships with stakeholders/customers" (p. 13). They add that most companies "are still waiting for more effective and efficient ways to research sponsorship effects, and that this desire will probably grow as firms become more professional in their approach" (p. 14).

In studying sponsorship through stadium signage, Clark, Cornwell, and Pruitt (2002) found that these sponsorships can "significantly enhance the stock price of sponsoring companies."

Other authors have utilized the stock price of a corporation as an evaluation measure. In studying sponsorship through stadium signage, Clark, Cornwell, and Pruitt (2002) found that these sponsorships can "significantly enhance the stock price of sponsoring companies" (p. 16). Clark et al. (2002) state that "many investors clearly believe that stadium sponsorship can indeed serve as an important element in a company's overall marketing strategy" (p. 30). They add that "sponsorships are able to add direct financial value to the firm and help differentiate the brand" (p. 30). This finding is similar to the results of Miyazaki and Morgan (2001), who found evidence that the acquisition of Olympic sponsorships is seen by the investment marketplace to be a positive event (p. 13). This approach could be considered problematic because there are many variables that could go into the increase or decrease of a stock price. If success is achieved, the communication strategy could be considered one of the important variables, though.

While many scholars have examined methods that could be employed to evaluate sponsorship agreements, these studies evaluate the success of sponsorship deals after the agreement is reached. Evaluation is obviously an important component and final step of the process, but with evaluation being difficult, proactivity in the negotiation of a sponsorship deal will greatly contribute to a successful agreement for a corporation. It is more important for corporations to be clear on their business objectives upon entering

> **Many corporations are not sufficiently evaluating their sponsorship investments and many are naïve about purchasing sponsorship packages.**

into the negotiation of sponsorship deal and try to control the factors that might hinder the success of the agreement. Burton, Quester, and Farrelly (1998) point out that many corporations are not sufficiently evaluating their sponsorship investments and many are naïve about purchasing sponsorship packages. The point to consider here is that perhaps a successful sponsorship agreement can be determined before the deal is signed by negotiating elements that protect the corporation and help control the communication environment.

## The Negotiation

The primary responsibility on entering the negotiation is with the corporation as the determinant of its own success. Corporations have to believe that they have some control over the parameters of the sponsorship agreement. It is the responsibility of the corporation to learn the benefits and attributes of the sports property, to learn how the deal can be leveraged and what can be negotiated, to determine what is possible. The negotiation of what is possible is the most distinct advantage of sponsorship. Any strategy should achieve the sponsorship business objectives: (1) reaching a target audience, (2) increasing brand recall, and (3) increasing sales. These objectives are an indication of the progression and potential behavior of a consumer.

### Target Audience

Which sports property the corporation decides to sponsor is at the complete discretion of the sponsor. Corporations must know who their target audience is. Determination of the proper sports property is thus the initial critical decision. In addition to who, placement includes the timing factors involved in the agreement. The timing of the sponsorship is important in that it should coincide with the temporal selling of the product. For example, Gatorade has a distinct selling season, warm weather, and therefore sponsoring and advertising with the NBA and the NBA playoffs from April through June strongly matches the beginning of its peak selling season and re-introduces the brand to its target audience (e.g., Fortunato, 2001).

Exposure of the brand to the desired target audience has to be the initial objective of a sponsorship agreement. Achievement of the first objective of reaching the desired target audience might be the most vital to the success of the entire sponsorship agreement. Advertising and sponsorship with sports properties becomes necessary for certain corporations who need to reach a certain target audience. Wenner (1989) claims that advertising during sports programming is a good proposition because this type of programming offers the desirable-and relatively hard to reach-male audience between the ages of 18 and 49. He points out the sports programming demographic tends to be well-educated with considerable disposable income and "advertisers are willing to pay top dollar for this audience because they tend to make purchase decisions about big-ticket items such as automobiles and computers" (p. 14).

There are natural connections between corporations, sports properties, sports television, and consumers. For example, the sponsoring of sports is an incredible opportunity for sneaker or sports drink corporations to attract consumers. The advantage for the sponsor corporations is that the viewers not only see the product and their athletes sponsoring the product in commercials, they also see that athlete wearing or using their product in a real-life situation, the actual game. When Nike or Gatorade sponsors Michael Jordan, the viewer not only sees Jordan in Nike or Gatorade commercials, but then when the game resumes, Jordan is playing in his Nike sneakers or drinking Gatorade during a timeout. These products actually help these athletes perform their jobs. This opportunity is not available for many other types of products.

> When Nike or Gatorade sponsors Michael Jordan, the viewer not only sees Jordan in Nike or Gatorade commercials, but then when the game resumes, Jordan is playing in his Nike sneakers or drinking Gatorade during a timeout.

McAllister (1996) emphasizes the critical aspect of the proper exposure and argues that advertisers want to control the attention the viewer gives to the advertisement. He states, "advertisers know that that first necessary (but not sufficient) condition for persuading a potential consumer to buy a product is to force the consumer to notice the message. If the consumer does not see the ad or ignores the ad, then the advertiser's message is wasted" (p. 18). Their investment is also wasted and chance of any return on that investment becomes minimal.

## Product Brand Recall

In recognizing sponsorship as a major revenue stream, sports properties will try to attract brands from a variety of product categories. Differentiation of the brand is important, but it becomes difficult when many other corporations are in the same location and perhaps not possible if other brands from the same product category are also consistently mentioned. Being in the right location gives the opportunity for exposure to a desired target audience, but sponsoring corporations have much to consider if mere exposure can lead to brand recall.

The initial barrier to brand recall is advertising clutter. McAllister (1996) defines advertising clutter as "the amount of time devoted to nonprogram content on television, including product commercials, program promotions and public service announcements" (p. 24). The more corporations that sponsor a sports property, the more difficult it is to have consumers notice your brand from all of the others. Two glaring examples of this are in NASCAR or along the boards in hockey where many corporations are located.

Signing a sponsorship agreement to be an Official sponsor also does not eliminate the challenge of brand recall, especially from competition within a product category. McAllister (1996) claims that advertisers would like to control what other ads run near their ads, or in the case of sponsorship, what other corporations might also be associated with the event or sports property. Clearly, the corporation would most be concerned with competing brands from the same product category. For instance, if Coca-Cola was an official sponsor, it would not want Pepsi obtaining exposure in that same location.

One of the critical factors that corporations therefore need to negotiate in a sponsorship agreement is to reduce the opportunity of ambush marketing. Meenaghan (1996) defines ambush marketing as a "corporate sponsorship practice in which a company, often an event sponsor's competitor, attempts to deflect the audience's attention to itself and away from the sponsor" (p. 103). McKelvey (2003) explains that ambush marketing is when "companies create the impression of an affiliation with a sports event without 'official' sanctioning from the property itself" (p. 23). Duke (2001) defines ambush marketing as "when companies that didn't pay for event sponsorship show up at the event anyway" (p. 43). He claims that "few would deny that the unofficial presence of brands has an impact on the profile that the official sponsors receive. Indeed, sponsorship awareness surveys frequently reveal nonassociated companies as being more closely identified with an event than those who have invested millions to be there" (p. 43).

Elliot (2002) states, "when an organization tries to gain the benefits of such an association without paying out these significant sums of money, corporate angst among those who have done so is understandable" (p. 14). Even the boxers use of a logo on their backs is considered ambush marketing and could create clutter for the main advertiser whose brand name might prominently adorn the boxing ring. Sports leagues have some regulatory control over their players and enforce rules regarding players' uniform appearances. With no sanctioning league in boxing, HBO and Showtime have created measures to help protect the major sponsors by adding restrictions on body sponsorship in boxers' contracts and provisions that enable them to take a percentage of any body sponsorship revenue (e.g., McKelvey, 2003). If the desired outcome is a successful partnership and relationship between the sponsor and the sports property, Elliot (2002) points out that "ambush marketing has a negative effect on everyone involved with an event and, in the end, on sport itself" (p. 14). He claims that while it is virtually impossible to stop companies from ambush marketing, there are things that official corporate sponsors and sports properties can do to control the communication environment in which the brand name will be exposed to the audience.

One of the strategies to prevent ambush marketing and a positive benefit of a sponsorship agreement with a league is the exclusivity of a particular product category that a corporation receives. McAllister (1998) describes exclusivity as a promotional incentive for sponsors, where unlike spot advertisers or commercials, sponsors can now be the exclusive voice of an event. Exclusivity must be negotiated and paid for, but it could eliminate any competition that one corporation might receive from a rival for a sponsored event. For example, Visa has been the exclusive sponsor of horse racing's Triple Crown Challenge, which features the Kentucky Derby, Preakness Stakes, and Belmont Stakes, eliminating American Express from advertising on any of these events. McAllister (1998) focuses on the role of sponsorship in college football bowl games claiming, "by being the 'signature sponsor' of an event these corporations hope their name will be strongly tied to the event, and will receive most of the promotional benefit" (p. 363). Miyazaki and Morgan (2001) claim that "the ability to be an exclusive sponsor in one's product category presumably aids in avoiding the competitive interference that typically is experienced in other media contexts" (p. 10).

It is incumbent upon the sponsoring corporation to ensure that another brand of the same product category will not have the opportunity for exposure by the audience. The responsibility lies with the sponsoring corporation because any expectation that a sports property would turn down additional revenue from another brand is probably unrealistic. In recognizing sponsorship as a major revue source, the sports properties will make efforts to ensure the success of the agreement because they don't want to eliminate a corporate partner. Some sports properties are now making efforts to better educate corporate partners because "research indicates that some sports pro organizations fall short of educating corporate

> **Exclusivity comes at a price, but clearly one that the sponsoring corporation should invest in to try to prevent advertising clutter and ambush marketing to help achieve the sponsorship business objectives.**

clients about all of the benefits and attributes of the products they offer, particularly sponsorship programs. This leads to less than acceptable renewal rates" (IEG Sponsorship Report, April 29, 2002, p. 1). The same report claims professional sports "organizations should implement a systematic sales program that continually educates and supports corporate customers pre- and post-sale" (IEG Sponsorship Report, April 29, 2002, p. 1). Despite the efforts of the sports property to help achieve a successful partnership, it is the responsibility of the corporation to identify possible threats to the success of their sponsorship agreement. Exclusivity comes at a price, but clearly one that the sponsoring corporation should invest in to try to prevent advertising clutter and ambush marketing to help achieve the sponsorship business objectives.

## Sales

Image transfer and awareness might still not occur if advertising clutter and ambush marketing are not controlled. Through sponsorship, corporations should do more than simply build awareness. If sales are an objective, and it is strongly argued here that sales are and should be the ultimate objective, there are opportunities for the corporation to negotiate for the facilitating of movement of the brand's product. Cornwell, Roy, and Stienard (2001) point out that sponsorship can do more than simply generate awareness.

Research has indicated that an image transfer can lead to increased sales. Harvey (2001) argues that "sponsorship changes the consumer's perception of a specific sponsor-which can rub off positively on brands of that sponsor in terms of willingness to purchase those brands" (p. 64). Madrigal (2000) examined football games and pointed out that fan identification can even extend from support of a team to support of companies that sponsor and are associated with that team. He asserts that

> loyalty toward a preferred team may have beneficial consequences for corporate sponsors. Consistent with the idea of in-group favoritism, higher levels of team identification among attendees of a sporting event appear to be positively related to intentions to purchase a sponsor's products. (p. 21)

Trusdell (1997) lends support for this claim, describing one survey that found that over 70% of NASCAR fans purchase the products of NASCAR sponsors. Madrigal (2000) also claims "favorable purchase intentions are more likely to occur as identification with the team increases and when intentions are perceived as a group norm" (p. 13).

> **Ukman comments that "what sponsors need now are not more signs, but opportunities to connect with consumers."**

Some corporations can easily move from image transfer to the consumer behavior of purchase. Sponsorship is about getting the product in the hands of consumers or providing the customer with an experience that will lead to tangible rewards for the corporation. Ukman (1998) comments that "what sponsors need now are not more signs, but opportunities to connect with consumers. Value today rests exclusively with properties that deliver loyal audiences and activation vehicles that allow sponsors to create brand preference" (p. 2).

Some corporations have the ability for a point-of-purchase sale where the consumer can see the signage in the stadium and immediately purchase the product. This concept creates the idea that sponsorship is not merely signage and why sponsorship deals that provide exclusivity, such as pouring rights for beer or soda companies or signing up for credit card companies at stadiums, make tremen-

> **Often a trip to the stadium does not allow a choice for the consumer; it is either Pepsi or Coca-Cola, Budweiser or Coors, or the ability to sign up for a Visa or MasterCard.**

dous sense. Often a trip to the stadium does not allow a choice for the consumer; it is either Pepsi or Coca-Cola, Budweiser or Coors, or the ability to sign up for a Visa or MasterCard.

This immediate point of purchase is only possible for a few types of products. Many of the other corporations need the purchase to occur at a later time. Therefore, they attempt to provide the consumer with a memorable experience that the consumer will credit the brand company with and lend support through their behavior and purchase of that sponsor's products. This is why many corporations might leverage their sponsorship with a stadium give-away or perhaps requiring a ticket stub to receive a discount.

## Discussion

The communication environment for a corporate brand to reach an audience has changed. Many media options have allowed a diverse audience to spread itself all over the media spectrum. Declining television ratings have made it difficult for corporations to expose their brand products to a large number of people. Competition for attention is thus fierce. Corporations need to expose their brand when their target audience is available and then must present the brand in a fashion that will almost ensure being noticed. Sponsorship with sports properties has become a viable communication strategy in order to (1) reach a target audience, (2) increase brand recall, and (3) increase sales.

> **Negotiation becomes the key, and for the right investment, corporations can create the communication environment so that their brand has an exclusive contract that eliminates the competition from other brands of the same product category and controls for advertising clutter and ambush marketing.**

In terms of the business objectives, sponsorship is no different than commercial advertising. Sponsorship is also similar in that it is a component of a larger communication plan to build a brand and generate sales. All indications are that in the future, sponsorship will continue to be part of the strategic communication plan of many corporations. Miyazaki and Morgan (2001) claim that "with brand and corporate image playing key roles in the development and selection of marketing strategies, the use of event sponsorship likely will continue to grow" (p. 13). Parmar (2002) claims the number of dollars spent on sponsorship is expected to significantly increase, especially with the various sports properties and the diversification of the audience in attempting to reach a niche demographic. The result could be more corporate-owned events that reduce advertising clutter, attempt to control ambush marketing, and maximize exposure to the desired target audience.

With the investment in sponsorship reaching incredible dollar amounts and the difficulty of evaluating the effectiveness of these deals, it is important for corporations to be aware of the critical factors that can hinder the success of a sponsorship agreement. Being proactive and controlling the factors that could hinder success become essential. Negotiation becomes the key, and for the right investment, corporations can create the communication environment so that their brand has an exclusive

> **The primary responsibility for success is with the corporation.**

contract that eliminates the competition from other brands of the same product category and controls for advertising clutter and ambush marketing. Through an exclusive agreement that eliminates competition in a product category, possibilities to leverage the deal and facilitate getting the product into the hands of the consumer or provide an experience that will help lead to brand recall and eventual purchase become the business objectives that should attempted to be achieved.

While the specific communication strategy that is employed might change, the philosophical approach and the desire to control for certain factors to assist in the achievement of business objectives should not. The primary responsibility for success is with the corporation, but this should not be problematic as the corporation can choose the sports property it desires to associate with and the level of investment in attempting to ensure success. No two sponsorship deals are the same, and through sponsorship negotiation and the willingness to make an extra investment, anything becomes possible.

# References

Aaker, J. L. (1997). Dimensions of Brand Personality. *Journal of Marketing Research, 34*(3), 347-356.

Burton, R. Quester. P. G, & Farrelly, F. J. (1998). Organizational power games. *Marketing Management, 7*(1), 27-36.

Clark, J. M., Cornwell, T. B., & Pruitt, S. W. (2002). Corporate stadium sponsorships, signaling theory, agency conflicts, and shareholder wealth. *Journal of Advertising Research, 42*(6), 16-33.

Copeland, R., Frisby, W., & McCarville, R. Understanding the sport sponsorship from a corporate perspective. *Journal of Sport Management, 10*(1), 32-48.

Cornwell, T. B. (1995). Sponsorship-linked marketing development. *Sport Marketing Quarterly, 12*(4), 13-24.

Cornwell, T. B., & Maignan, I. (1998). An international review of sponsorship research. *Journal of Advertising, 27*(1), 1-21.

Cornwell, T.B., Roy, D.P., & Stienard, E.A. (2001). Exploring managers' perceptions of the impact of sponsorship on brand equity. *Journal of Advertising, 30*(2), 41-51.

Crimmins, J., & Horn, M. (1996). Sponsorship: From management ego trip to marketing success. *Journal of Advertising Research, 36*(4), 11-22.

Dean, D. H. (2002). Associating the corporation with a charitable event through sponsorship: Measuring the effects on corporate community relations. *Journal of Advertising, 31*(4), 77-88.

Duke, T. (2001, March). Playing to win. *Ad Age Global, 1*(7), 43-45.

Elliot, P. (2002). The loveable rogues who devalue sporting events: Brands that do not want to fork out on expensive sports sponsorship often turn to ambush marketing. *Marketing Week, 25*(26), 14.

Farrelly, F. J. Quester, P. C., & Burton, R. (1997). Integrating sports sponsorship into the corporate marketing function: An international comparative study. *International Marketing Review, 14*(3), 170-182.

Fortunato, J.A. (2001). *The ultimate assist: The relationship and broadcast strategies of the NBA and television networks.* Cresskill, NJ: Hampton Press.

Gwinner, K.P. (1997). A model of image creation and image transfer in event sponsorship. *International Marketing Review, 14*(3), 145-158.

Gwinner, K.P., & Eaton, J. (1999). Building brand image through event sponsorship: The role of image transfer. *Journal of Advertising, 28*(4), 47-58.

Harvey, B. (2001). Measuring the effects of sponsorship. *Journal of Advertising Research, 41*(1), 59-65.

Hiestand, M. (2003, January 1). No slowing down on sports sponsorships. *USA Today.* Retrieved May 21, 2003, from http://www.usatoday.com/sports/columnist/hiestand/2003-01-01-hiestand_x.htm.

Hoek, J. (1998). Sponsorship: An evaluation of management assumptions and practices. *Marketing Bulletin, 10.*

*IEG Sponsorship Report.* (2002, April 29). Consultative selling pays off in retaining NBA team sponsors, *21*(8), 1, 4-5.

Keller, K. L. (1993). Conceptualizing, measuring, and managing customer-based brand equity. *Journal of Marketing, 57*(1), 1-22.

Madrigal, R. (2000). The influence of social alliances with sports teams on intentions to purchase corporate sponsors' products. *Journal of Advertising, 29*(4), 13-24.

McAlliser, M. P. (1996). *The commercialization of American culture.* Thousand Oaks, CA: Sage.

McAllister, M. P. (1998). College bowl sponsorship and the increased commercialization of amateur sports. *Critical Studies in Mass Communication, 15*(4), 357-381.

McKelvey, S. (2003). More tales of body art and 'branding.' *Brandweek, 44*(3), 23.

Meenaghan, T. (1991). The role of sponsorship in the marketing communications mix. *International Journal of Advertising, 10*(1), 35-47.

Meenaghan, T. (1996). Ambush marketing: A threat to corporate sponsorship. *Sloan Management Review, 38*(1), 103-114.

Miyazaki, A. D., & Morgan, A. G. (2001). Assessing market value of event sponsoring: Corporate Olympic sponsorship. *Journal of Advertising Research, 41*(1), 9-15.

Parmar, A. (2002). Sponsorship. *Marketing News, 37*(1), 13.

Roy, D. P., & Cornwell, T. B. (1999). Managers' use of sponsorship in building brands: Service and product firms contrasted. *International Journal of Sports Marketing and Sponsorship, 1*(6), 345-360.

Speed, R., & Thompson, (2000). Determinants of sport sponsorship response. *Journal of the Academy of Marketing Science, 28*(2), 226-238.

Stipp, H., & Schiavone, N. P. (1996). Modeling the impact of Olympic sponsorship on corporate image. *Journal of Advertising Research 36*(4), 22-28.

Sutherland, M., & Galloway, J. (1981). Role of advertising: Persuasion or agenda-setting? *Journal of Advertising Research, 21*, 25-29.

Thjomoe, H. M., Olson, E. L., & Bronn, P. S. (2002). Decision-making processes surrounding sponsorship activities. *Journal of Advertising Research 42*(6), 6-16.

Till, B. D. & Shimp, T. A. (1998). Endorsers in advertising: The case of negative celebrity information. *Journal of Advertising, 27*(1), 67-82.

Trusdell, B. (1997, Feb). Life in the fast lane. *Sales & Marketing Management,* 66-71.

Ukman, L. (1998, November 9). Assertions. *IEG Sponsorship Report, 17*(21), 2.

Wenner, L. A. (1989). Media, sports, and society: The research agenda. In L.A.Wenner (Ed.), *Media, sports, and society* (pp. 13-48). Newbury Park: Sage.

# Part IV
# Consumer Behavior, Emerging Markets, and Sport Marketing

# CHAPTER 9

# Tapping the Market of Golfers with Disabilities

LAWRENCE ALLEN
GARY ROBB
EDWARD HAMILTON
DAN DRANE

Between 1990 and 1999 there was a 5% decrease in the number of golfers in the United States, from 27.8 million to 26.4 million, while the number of courses grew from 13,951 to 16,743, representing a 20% increase in the supply of golf courses during the same time period (National Golf Foundation, 2000). These changes also resulted in a golfer-per-course drop from 1,993 in 1990 to 1,577 in 1999. Losing 416 golfers per course amounts to $16,640 ($40 for average greens and cart fees; NGF, 2000) in lost revenue for each round of golf these individuals do not play. This figure does not represent the additional lost revenue in food, beverage, apparel, and equipment purchases. The loss of revenue over this 10-year period could have run into the hundreds of thousands of dollars per course. As a result, many courses in the United States have been placed in a financially unstable situation due to this loss of market share and overall revenues.

Many of the major golf organizations have been attempting to address the loss of players by suggesting new programs to bring more women, youth and minorities into the game. "For the Good of the Game Program," administered by the USGA; the "Growth of the Game Grant Program," sponsored by the PGA of America; and the "First Tee," sponsored by several major golf organizations, are but three examples. In addition, efforts have been made to develop better instructional programs to increase the retention rate of new players. A variety of cost-cutting and marketing strategies also have been

> Between 1990 and 1999 there was a 5% decrease in the number of golfers in the United States, from 27.8 million to 26.4 million, while the number of courses grew from 13,951 to 16,743

suggested by many of these organizations. The latest effort, called "Golf 2020," is a united effort of all the major golf organizations to work in a concerted effort to grow the game. It is too early to determine the effectiveness of this latest initiative, but previous attempts have not yielded substantial gains in new players or in the retention of existing players.

The National Alliance for Accessible Golf is a new effort that brings together, not only the major golf organizations, but also American universities, rehabilitative organizations, organizations serving individuals with disabilities, and golfers with disabilities. This organization is seeking to set up pilot programs around the United States involving all these groups and individuals on a local level, to create and document an instructional program and comprehensive golf delivery system that encourages and sustains play by golfers with disabilities. This is the most ambitious effort to date to expand the golf market to individuals with disabilities. However, as with the "Golf 2020" program, it is too early to determine its effects.

## An Untapped Market

**More often than not they use no assistive device; they merely need to be able to play the game of golf without walking sustained distances.**

Interestingly, there has not been a major effort to bring a substantial new market into the game of golf: individuals with disabilities. There are approximately 54 million disabled Americans, representing 20.6% of the total population (U.S. Department of Commerce, 1994). Of these individuals, 26 million have a disability that restricts their physical mobility (U.S. Department of Commerce, 1994). They may use crutches, walkers, wheelchairs, canes, or scooters, but more often than not they use no assistive device; they merely need to be able to play the game of golf without walking sustained distances. New technology and changes in golf policies have allowed some of these individuals to enjoy the game of golf and become regular patrons at many courses.

Recent studies have suggested that nearly 10% of the population of disabled Americans presently play the game of golf (U.S. Forest Service, 1995; National Center on Accessibility, 1994). This is compared to approximately 11.5% (NGF, 2000) of the nondisabled population in the United States that participate in golf. Even with a limiting condition, Americans with a disability are finding their way to the golf course at a rate close to nondisabled Americans. An even more striking statistic is that over 35% of Americans who are disabled and who presently do not play golf are interested in taking up the game. This is higher than the general population of nondisabled Americans (National Golf Foundation, 1999).

**An even more striking statistic is that over 35% of Americans who are disabled and who presently do not play golf are interested in taking up the game. This is higher than the general population of nondisabled Americans.**

Using the above percentages of disabled Americans playing the game of golf and those interested in playing the game of golf, and only looking at those individuals who have a disability that restricts their physical mobility, let's determine the impact of these individuals on the game of golf.

## Potential Impact

As stated above, there are approximately 26 million Americans with a disability that limits their physical mobility. Nearly 10% of these individuals, or 2.6 million, are currently playing the game. They are already counted in the figures presented by the National Golf Foundation and other sources that cite the number of golfers. Of those Americans with physical mobility disabilities not playing golf (23.4 million), 35% or 8.2 million Americans are interested in playing the game. For purposes of discussion, assume 50% of these interested individuals actually take up the game. This would represent 4.1 million disabled Americans who could be new golfers.

The most recent information from NGF states that the average green fees at a daily fee course is $28 and the average cart fee is $12 (NGF, 2000). If the 4.1 million new disabled golfers played only one round of golf per year, it would mean an additional $164,000,000 in revenue to golf courses across America. According to the NGF, the average occasional golfer plays 3.5 rounds of golf a year. Assuming this level of play, an additional $574,000,000 dollars would be captured. These

> **If the 4.1 million new disabled golfers played only one round of golf per year, it would mean an additional $164,000,000 in revenue to golf courses across America.**

figures, although substantial, do not reflect the total impact these additional golfers would make on the golf industry because, expenditures for food, beverage, instruction, equipment, and apparel are not counted in this figure.

Looking at this impact per course provides a better picture of the meaning of this new market to the individual golf course owner and operator. In 1999, there were 16,743 courses in the United States (NGF, 2000). Given the 4.1 million new golfers, this would mean an additional 245 golfers/course or a total of 1822 golfers/course. Based on the previously mentioned rounds for the average occasional golfer, an additional $34,300 in greens fees and cart fees would be realized by each course. Again, this is a very conservative figure given that nearly all golfers with disabilities do not play alone and the expenditures for other golf outing expenses are not included in this figure. Of course, not every course is going to attract golfers with disabilities and a significant number of courses charge greens fees and cart fees that are considerably higher than the average daily fee course cited by the NGF study. Therefore, those courses who do market to the population of golfers with disabilities will generate significantly more revenue than is cited in this article.

## Realizing This Potential

The potential impact cited in this study is predicated on the accuracy of the assumption regarding the number of individuals with disabilities who can actually be attracted to taking up the game on a continuous basis. The assumption of 50% catchment rate for new golfers with disabilities is achievable given their expressed interest in the game.

However, individuals with disabilities do have special concerns and needs as they relate to turning their interest into actual participation in golf. The National Center on Accessibility at Indiana University and the National Project on Accessible Golf at Clemson University conducted a study in 1995 to determine the characteristics and desires of people with disabilities who are interested in participating in the game of golf, as well as the barriers they face in pursuing the game. These characteristics, interests, and barriers to participation must be considered and addressed by golf course owners and operators if they are to realize the full involvement of individuals with disabilities into the game of golf. Responding to these interests and needs is neither costly nor difficult. However, addressing them does take time and sensitivity on the part of golf course staff and professionals. Actually, there may be savings in operational costs because of policy changes and minor course design modifications. For example, eliminating unnecessary stairs or fences will save maintenance costs for mowing and landscaping.

Eleven hundred disabled Americans, identified from a number of organizations serving disabled Americans, were randomly selected to receive the survey regarding their golf behavior. Four hundred and forty-five usable questionnaires were returned for a response rate of 40%. As stated previously, approximately 10% of these individuals stated that they presently play golf, and 35% who do not now play golf indicated that they were interested in taking up the game. Twenty-two per cent (22%) of those who do not play golf now, played before they became disabled.

> **Actually, there may be savings in operational costs because of policy changes and minor course design modifications. For example, eliminating unnecessary stairs or fences will save maintenance costs for mowing and landscaping.**

Initially, individuals who were disabled and did not currently play the game, regardless of interest level, were asked what factors would increase their interest in taking up the game of golf. Table 1 presents the six major factors that would influence their interest in becoming a golfer. Clearly, instructional services, enhancing skills and knowledge of the game, and customer-friendly staff are the keys to initiating play by individuals with disabilities. More PGA professionals need to be trained in providing instruction to potential golfers with disabilities.

A second set of questions was asked specifically of golfers who were disabled. The next three tables relate to these questions. Table 2 presents the ten primary factors that hinder one's participation in golf. Many of these factors are the same as those of nondisabled individuals. However, the ones specific to individuals with disabilities are lack of independence on the course (33%), no one to play with (26%), uncomfortable playing in front of others (21%), no one to assist me (21%), and health problems (21%). Having playing partners and achieving a sense of independence are very important factors relating to participation in golf. These circumstances can be overcome by creating a partner system at courses that match a nondisabled player with a disabled player. Many nondisabled golfers are interested in assisting others to enjoy the game.

**Table 1  Factors Influencing Participation**

| Factors influencing participation | % of Respondents |
|---|---|
| Lessons specific to the disabled | 38% |
| Know how to swing better | 32% |
| Affordability | 30% |
| Course staff know how to assist | 27% |
| Know the rules and etiquette | 26% |
| Others are sensitive to the disabled | 18% |

> **It is interesting that only 21% of the respondents said that health problems were barriers to their participation. Clearly, the physical ailment is not the primary factor limiting their play.**

Lastly, it is interesting that only 21% of the respondents said that health problems were barriers to their participation. Clearly, the physical ailment is not the primary factor limiting their play.

Table 3 presents factors that would help the golfer with disabilities play more effectively. The first two factors relate to accessibility of facilities. Even though federal accessibility guidelines have been in existence since the early 1960s, it appears that some golf facilities still have nonaccessible restrooms and clubhouses. In addition to facility accessibility, access to the course itself is a factor. In many cases, a golf cart designed specifically to accommodate the golfer with disabilities can eliminate many of the mobility problems they may face on a course. A few golfers with disabilities also suggest assistance on the course itself would help them play more effectively. A caddy or even a playing partner could again, provide this assistance.

Table 2 **Factors Hindering Participation in Golf**

| Hinders participation | % of Respondents |
|---|---|
| Affordability | 36 % |
| Lack of independence on the course | 33 % |
| No one to play with | 26 % |
| Uncomfortable playing in front of others | 21 % |
| No one to assist me | 21 % |
| Health problems | 21 % |
| Lack of time | 17 % |
| Lack of transportation | 12 % |
| Do not enjoy heat/sun | 5 % |
| No golf courses nearby | 5 % |

Table 3 **Factors Influencing Effectiveness of Play**

| Factors Influencing Effectiveness | % of Respondents |
|---|---|
| Restroom accessibility | 40% |
| Clubhouse accessibility | 31% |
| Golf carts with hand controls | 24% |
| Access to greens | 17% |
| Golf carts have swivel seats | 17% |
| Course is less hilly | 14% |
| Assistance on the course | 7% |

Table 4 **Factors Increasing Play**

| Factors Increasing Frequency of Play | % of Respondents |
|---|---|
| Affordability | 43% |
| Knowledge of swinging club better | 38% |
| Lessons specific to the disabled | 36% |
| Course staff knowing how to assist | 31% |
| Accessible facilities | 29% |
| Others are sensitive to the disabled | 29% |
| Availability of accessible cart | 24% |
| Knowledge of rules and etiquette | 5% |

Lastly, golfers with disabilities were asked what factors would increase their frequency of play. Table 4 presents these results. The factors remained quite constant with individuals with disabilities who do not currently play the game (See table 1) and those who do presently play the game. The number one factor that would increase their frequency of play is affordability (43%). Various attempts have been made at off-peak pricing and other promotional strategies, but clearly this is an issue not only with the golfer who is disabled but also with much of the golfing population. The second most frequently cited factor was knowledge of swinging the club better (38%), followed by lessons specific to disabled golfers (36%), course staff knowing how to assist a golfer with disabilities (31%), course facilities being accessible (29%), others being sensitive to the disabled (29%), availability of an accessible cart (24%) and lastly, knowledge of rules and etiquette (5%). Again, many of these factors are easily addressed by providing lessons for golfers with disabilities and by having some customer service training for the staff relating specifically to serving golfers with disabilities.

**The number one factor that would increase their frequency of play is *affordability* (43%). Various attempts have been made at off-peak pricing and other promotional strategies, but clearly this is an issue not only with the golfer who is disabled but also with much of the golfing population.**

## Conclusions

Clearly, Americans with disabilities are an untapped market for the golf industry. Although there are over 50 million disabled Americans, approximately 26 million have a disability that affects their mobility. Of these people, 10% already play the game and an additional 35% are interested in playing golf. Given that not all people interested in playing the game will ever translate this interest into participation but

> **For a period of time, golf for individuals with disabilities will continue to be a very newsworthy feature. The promotional and marketing appeal of serving golfers with disabilities will have untold benefits to individual courses as well as the game itself.**

assuming 50% do actually take up this game, this could mean additional revenues in excess of 1/2 billion dollars for the US golf industry. Not only do these new players bring significant new revenues to the game but they also bring collateral rewards to the game as well. Golf is promoted as a game for everyone. Certainly embracing individuals with disabilities supports and advances this cause. These new players also bring a tremendous network of support organizations and services and supportive friends and family who will promote and support the game. Third, for a period of time, golf for individuals with disabilities will continue to be a very newsworthy feature. The promotional and marketing appeal of serving golfers with disabilities will have untold benefits to individual courses as well as the game itself. However, even though the tangible benefits of expanding the game of golf to individuals with disabilities far outweigh the costs, still the most important reason for embracing golfers with disabilities is because it is the right thing to do.

## References

US Forest Service. (1995). *Outdoor recreation survey.* Athens, GA: USFS.

National Center on Accessibility. (1995). Survey of golfers with disabilities. Unpublished monograph. Bloomington, IN: NCA.

U.S. Department of Commerce. (1994). *Census report on population.* Washington, DC: U.S. Government Printing Office.

National Golf Foundation. (1999). Strategic Perspective on the Future of Golf. Jupiter, FL: NGF.

National Golf Foundation. (2000). *Golf participation in the US: 2000 Edition.* Jupiter, FL: NGF.

# CHAPTER 10

# Beyond Valence: The Use of Contemporary Attitude Theory to Examine the Predictive Ability of Attitudinal Measures in Professional Team Sport

DANIEL C. FUNK
MARK PRITCHARD

## Abstract

Measuring consumer attitudes continues to be a central concern for researchers and practitioners within the field of sport marketing. This study utilized contemporary attitude theory to measure nine properties of an individual's attitude and their relationship to consumer commitment in a team sport context ($N$ = 379). Structural equation modeling demonstrated the predictive validity of obtaining attitudinal measures beyond the traditional affect measure to predict commitment to a professional baseball team. These data support the multi-property view of the attitude construct and suggest that properties related to importance, personal relevance, intensity, knowledge, and direct experience provided better predictions of team commitment than affect. This study highlights the need for expanding the type of attitudinal measures used in sport marketing surveys to improve the quality and predictive validity of attitudinal information aimed at understanding sport behavior. The present study also provides a framework to integrate prior work in social psychology on attitude formation and leisure research on psychological commitment to better understand attitude formation in a team sport context.

This study highlights the need for expanding the type of attitudinal measures used in sport marketing surveys to improve the quality and predictive validity of attitudinal information aimed at understanding sport behavior.

During the last decade, scholars have recognized the need to utilize theoretical frameworks from social psychology to develop better methodologies and understanding of attitude-related research on leisure behavior (e.g., Ajzen & Driver, 1992; Bright, 1997; Bright & Manfredo, 1995; Manfredo, Yuan, & McGuire, 1992). A respondent's attitude toward a leisure activity has typically been measured in terms of valence (i.e., affective reactions toward an object or issue) based on single-item measures or aggregate scores taken from Likert-type scales (e.g. Carron, Hausenblas, Mack, 1996; Mahony & Howard, 1998; Murrell & Dietz, 1992; Turco, 1996; Virnig & McLeod, 1996). However, considerable variability remains in the extent to which valence or affect information from surveys serve as useful predictors of psychological or behavioral outcome variables (e.g., Funk, Haugtvedt, & Howard, 2000; Mahony & Moorman, 1999). Given the limitation of previous research devoted to the attitude construct in sport, the present study sought to investigate the predictive validity of attitude properties in providing additional insight beyond the traditional valence measure. The purpose of this study was to utilize contemporary attitude theory to diagnose the underlying structural properties of an individual's attitude and its relationship to commitment in the team sport context.

> **The purpose of this study was to utilize contemporary attitude theory to diagnose the underlying structural properties of an individual's attitude and its relationship to commitment in the team sport context.**

The term attitude represents a hypothetical construct referring to a general and enduring positive or negative feeling toward or evaluative response to some person, object, or issue (Petty & Cacioppo, 1986). Contemporary theorizing in attitude research suggests that valence conveys information related to the attitude's appearance in terms of affect along some positive-negative evaluative continuum (e.g., Krosnick & Petty, 1995). Although affect measures on questionnaires have proven valid and reliable (e.g., Torabi, 1988), a researcher's ability to obtain quality attitudinal information can be improved through the use of multiple measures (e.g., Krosnick & Abelson, 1992). For example, McCready, and Long (1985) demonstrated that multiple-attitude measures were better predictors of exercise adherence than a single-attitude measure. Prior work in the leisure industry has demonstrated that measurements related to various properties of an individual's involvement in a leisure activity or issue provides insight into the formation of that attitude (Bright, 1997; Bright & Manfredo, 1995; Bright, Manfredo, Fisbein, & Bath, 1993). These efforts have provided a means to diagnose the underlying structure of an individual's attitude in terms of various properties (e.g., accessibility, extremity, certainty, and personal relevance) to improve the predictive ability of attitudinal measures. For example, Bright (1997) found attitude properties beyond valence (e.g., certainty and personal relevance) achieved more accurate behavioral predictions in support of specific types of recreation management strategies. The notion that some properties are more vital implies that the level of formation determines whether the attitude is stable or unstable, consequential or inconsequential, and influential or unimportant on people's leisure choices.

Previous research in social psychology has demonstrated that attitudes supported by various properties determine the extent to which that attitude is formed (e.g., Basilli, 1996; Krosnick, Boninger, Chuang, Berent, & Carnot, 1993; Verplanken, 1991). In the literature, nine properties have received considerable attention: importance, intensity, extremity, certainty, knowledge, direct experience, personal relevance, affect (i.e., valence), and belief (e.g., Basilli, 1996; Krosnick et al., 1993; Wegener, Downing, Krosnick, & Petty, 1995). A number of studies have demonstrated that attitudes possessing such properties create an evaluative response that is persistent over time, resistant to counter persuasive attempts, biases thoughts, and consistent with behavior (Petty, Haugtvedt, & Smith, 1995). However, this research has been conducted in a piecemeal fashion examining properties separately from outcomes or consequences. A few studies by Krosnick et al. (1993) and Bassili (1996) have created interest in multivariate studies considering many properties simultaneously to understand their impact on attitudes toward specific objects and social issues. Currently, a fair amount of disagreement exist among researchers in terms of how these properties bundle together and subsequently manifest various outcomes (e.g., resistance, behavior; Abelson, 1988, Basilli, 1996; Lastovicka & Gardner, 1979, Krosnick et al., 1993; Krosnick & Petty, 1995; Verplanken, 1991).

Similar to previous work in social psychology, leisure research has generally examined attitude formation in terms of two strength-related outcomes or consequences: psychological commitment and behavioral consistency (e.g., Backman & Crompton, 1991; Havitz & Dimanche, 1997; Howard, Edington & Selin, 1988; Selin, Howard, Udd, & Cable, 1988). This work has utilized the multidimensional perspective of brand loyalty that posits loyalty as consisting of both an attitudinal and behavioral component (Crosby & Taylor, 1983; Day, 1969;

> **Currently, a fair amount of disagreement exist among researchers in terms of how these properties bundle together and subsequently manifest various outcomes.**

Dick & Basu, 1994; Jacoby & Kyner, 1973). The main focus of this line of research has been to examine the relationship between affect and commitment. However, these efforts have not addressed the relationship between psychological commitment and the level of formation among various structural properties found within an individual's attitude. Therefore, the present study integrates prior work in social psychology on attitude formation and leisure research on commitment in a team sport context. The present study selected nine attitude properties that have been well studied to explore the effectiveness and generality of attitudinal measures to predict commitment and subsequent behavior.

The current paper begins by briefly defining the attitude properties utilized for the study and how they have traditionally been measured, and then reviews examinations of their interrelations in prior research. A conceptual model is then offered and tested empirically to understand the distinct nature of each attitude property, the commonalties that may emerge among various properties and their relative influence on commitment. The potential theoretical and practical implications for this line of research are then discussed.

> **The present study integrates prior work in social psychology on attitude formation and leisure research on commitment in a team sport context.**

## Attitude Properties

### Attitude Importance

*Attitude importance* represents a person's perception of the psychological significance and value he or she attaches to a sport team (e.g., Krosnick 1988). Attitudes that individuals attach personal importance to and care deeply about are the subject of frequent conscious thought, produce stronger affective reactions, and are more extensively linked to other attitudes, beliefs, and values in memory (Krosnick, 1989). Important attitudes have been found to be more persistent and resistant, as well as less likely to change (Pratkins & Greenwald, 1989; Wood, 1982). Previous measures of attitude importance have relied on individual self-reports of how important an issue or object was to them personally (Krosnick, et al., 1993).

### Attitude Extremity

*Attitude extremity* represents the degree of favorableness or unfavorableness of an individual's evaluation of a sports team. The more extreme (i.e., polarized) an evaluation becomes, the further it deviates from neutrality regardless of valence (Judd & Johnson, 1981; Tesser, 1977). Extreme attitudes have been found to be more resistant to change (Abelson, 1995; Tesser, Martin, & Mendolia, 1995), persistent (Haugtvedt, Schumann, Schneier, & Warren, 1994), likely to produce stronger contrast effects (Brent & Granberg, 1982), and associated with less complex beliefs (Linville, 1982). Attitude extremity has typically been measured as the deviation of an individual's attitude from the mid-point on semantic differential scales and single-item rating instruments (Krosnick et al., 1993).

## Attitude Intensity

*Attitude intensity* refers to potency of feeling that an individual has toward a particular athletic team. Attitude intensity has been defined as the strength of feeling for an attitude object (Krosnick & Schuman, 1988; Schuman & Presser, 1981). Some attitude objects create strong emotional reactions while other objects produce little reactions (Krosnick & Schuman, 1988). Intense attitudes have been suggested to be more stable (Schuman & Presser, 1981) due to the implication that these attitudes have for ego-involvement. Measures of attitude intensity generally involved asking individuals how strong or intense their feelings were toward some attitude object (Krosnick et al., 1993). These measurements have relied on self-report responses to assess the intensity of feeling or emotion that the attitude object produces.

## Attitude Certainty

*Attitude certainty* refers to the confidence or conviction individuals have in their attitudes about a team. Certainty represents the degree to which individuals were confident that their attitude towards an object was correct (e.g., Budd, 1986; Gross, Holtz, & Miller, 1995). Attitude certainty has been found to be resistant to counter-persuasive information and suggested to strengthen attitude-behavior consistency by allowing individuals to have more confidence in their attitudes to make judgments about future events and guide behavior (Fazio & Zanna, 1978a). Attitude certainty has usually been assessed through self-reporting measures that ask respondents how sure they were in their opinion about an object, how easily their opinion could be changed, or how confident they were in their opinion (Krosnick et al., 1993).

## Attitude Knowledge

*Attitude knowledge* refers to the amount of attitude-relevant knowledge that accompanies an individual's attitude related to a sports team. Individuals who possess large amounts of knowledge about an attitude object are more likely to evaluate an object consistently with previous beliefs (Tesser & Leone, 1977) due to greater cognitive resources available and the extensive linkages between the attitudes and other cognitive components (e.g., Eagly & Chaiken, 1993). Attitudes based on higher levels of relevant knowledge are more likely to moderate the attitude-behavior relationship (Kallgren & Wood, 1986), less likely to change (Wood, 1982), and more likely to predict behavior (Davidson, Yantis, Norwood, & Montano, 1985) than attitudes based on little information. The amount of attitude-relevant knowledge has generally been measured by asking participants how knowledgeable they feel about an object (Krosnick et al., 1993).

## Direct Experience

*Direct experience* refers to the degree of prior experience, participation, or amount of direct contact one has had with the team or related activities. Attitudes based on direct experience are reported to have greater clarity, be held with more confidence, and remain more consistent with behavior than attitudes not based on direct experience (Doll & Ajzen, 1992; Fazio & Zanna, 1978b). Attitudes formed via direct experience have been found to be more resistant to negative information by linking the attitude object to prior beliefs and experience (Wood, 1982) and predictive of behavior (Fazio, Chen,

McDonald, & Sherman, 1982). Direct experience has been assessed with self-report measures asking individuals how involved they were in activities related to an object (Krosnick et al., 1993), or if they have committed any actions in regards to an object (Schuman & Presser, 1981).

## Personal Relevance

*Personal relevance* refers to an individual's level of involvement with a team. Some attitudes have been generally considered to be more personally relevant than other attitudes (e.g., Petty, Cacioppo, & Schumann, 1983) and have significant consequences for some aspect of an individual's life (Petty & Cacioppo, 1990). Personal relevance stems from involvement theory (e.g., Sherif, Sherif, & Nebergall, 1965) suggesting the level of involvement determines how closely one attends to information (e.g., stories), how interested one is in obtaining information, and how important information about the object is (Thomsen, Borgida, & Lavine, 1995). Relevance has generally been measured with self-reporting measures that assess the level of interest and/or attention given to information about an object (e.g., Krosnick et al., 1993).

## Affective-Cognitive Consistency

*Affective-cognitive consistency* represents the level of correspondence between an individual's feelings about a team (i.e., affect) and his or her cognitions (i.e., beliefs) about attributes of that team (e.g., I like the team but it has little chance of being competitive). This consistency reflects whether evaluative implications of one's beliefs about an attitude object were consistent with one's overall feelings toward the object (Rosenberg, 1968). Affective-cognitive consistency has been measured through the use of affective and cognitive indexes drawn from a series of semantic differential scales (Chaiken, Pomerantz, & Giner-Sorolla, 1995; Crites, Fabrigar, & Petty, 1994). The affective component has generally assessed the extent to which an attitude object creates an affective state, while the cognitive component assessed the extent to which an attitude object possesses attributes that the person perceives as favorable or unfavorable (e.g., Eagly & Chaiken, 1993). For the purpose of this study, affective-cognitive consistency was decoupled to examine each independently.

## Relation Among Properties

The general assumption among scholars is that measures of these attitude properties can, "differentiate stable and consequential attitudes from mutable and inconsequential ones" (Bassili, 1996; p. 637). However, researchers can only speculate as how these properties bundle together. A limited number of studies has explored the underlying structure of the properties with multivariate studies that examine many properties simultaneously, but has also produced ambiguous results as to their structure. Early studies have indicated that the attitude properties bundle together and reflect a few higher-order latent constructs (e.g., Abelson, 1988; Lastovicka & Gardner, 1979). However, these studies have received criticism for their use of data reduction techniques (i.e., exploratory factor analysis) without controlling for random and systematic measurement error (e.g., Cote & Buckley, 1988).

Krosnick et al., (1993) analyzed ten dimensions of an individual's attitude toward abortion and capital punishment and found moderate correlations among most of the measured properties. Bassili (1996) found a distinctive structural constitution among nine properties for individuals who held strong versus weak attitudes toward employment quotas for women and laws about pornography. Taken together, this

> **Evident in the attitude change literature is the notion that crystallized attitudes are not easily changed. Resistance to change has been suggested to be the general underlying factor contributing to consumer commitment.**

body of evidence suggests that although the properties are interrelated, they represent distinct and independent dimensions of an individual's attitude and support the widely held multiple construct view of attitude strength (e.g., Krosnick & Petty, 1995). However, to better understand the structural relations among these properties, more empirical evidence is still needed.

A great deal of empirical research has linked various attitude properties to attitude resistance in separate investigations (e.g., Krosnick & Abelson, 1992; Krosnick & Petty, 1995). Evident in the attitude change literature is the notion that crystallized attitudes are not easily changed. Resistance to change has been suggested to be the general underlying factor contributing to consumer commitment (e.g., Crosby & Taylor, 1983; Dick & Basu, 1994; Haugtvedt & Petty, 1992). Commitment represents the psychological processes critical in measuring the attitudinal component of brand loyalty (Day, 1969; Jacoby & Kyner, 1973; Pritchard, Havitz, & Howard, 1999). Iswaski & Havitz (1998) argue that an individual's psychological commitment stems from greater knowledge, certainty, affective-cognitive consistency, and personal relevance related to a leisure activity. This type of commitment is thought to reflect preference (i.e., volition) stability towards an object, brand, or issue and resistance to persuasive attempts promoting alternative choices (e.g., Crosby & Taylor, 1983; Dick & Basu, 1994; Petty & Cacioppo, 1986). Although the notion that psychological commitment leads to behavior and intent has intuitive appeal, prior studies in leisure have produce equivocal results (e.g., Backman & Crompton, 1991; Havitz & Dimanche, 1997; Parks, 1996).

The utility of adopting contemporary attitude theory is that the relationship between attitude properties and consumer commitment can be explored in a team sport context. The present study integrates previous research from social psychology and leisure to develop and test a model in order to investigate the effectiveness and predictive validity of attitudinal information in determining individual differences in commitment to an athletic team (see Figure 1). An overview of the model is presented followed by methodology utilized to test the model.

## Attitude Model

Although conceptually and empirically distinct, similarities should emerge among certain properties and reflect three general dimensions: 1) cognitive function, 2) subjective meaning, and 3) definitive position. The *cognitive function* dimension represents properties that reflect the individual's attitude within a network of associative links that are connected to cognitive elements such as team-related knowledge, direct personal experience, and one's feelings and beliefs about the team and its attributes. This bundling of properties should determine the basis for an individual's evaluation of the team from memory (i.e., cognitive function). For example, an avid fan's response to a questionnaire reflects her or his ability to evaluate the meaning of the questions based on more direct experience with the team, factual knowledge of team, and greater internal consistency between feelings and thoughts. The dimension *subjective meaning* represents properties developed from subjective perception that contribute to the meaning individuals place on the attitude toward the team. Individuals will subjectively evaluate the team and related information based on personal relevance, importance, and the intensity of the emotion created by the team. This evaluative response is based to a greater extent upon subjective dispensation in contrast to more objective processing found in the cognitive function dimension. The third and final dimension, *definitive position,* represents those properties of an individual's attitude that have a definite quality and direction without an emotional element. An individual who strongly dislikes a team will be just as certain of her or his attitude and extreme in his or her evaluation of that team than an individual who strongly likes the team. For example, an avid Boston Red Sox

> For example, an avid Boston Red Sox fan's attitude toward the Red Sox would be equally as certain and extreme as their dislike for the New York Yankees.

Figure 1 **Proposed Attitude Model for Structural Relations Among Attitude Properties and Commitment**

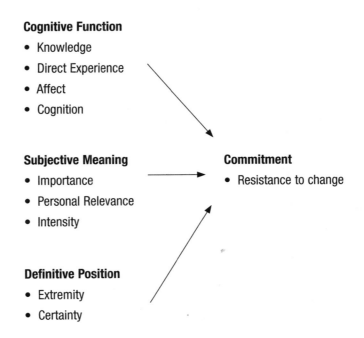

fan's attitude toward the Red Sox would be equally as certain and extreme as their dislike for the New York Yankees.

As depicted in the model, an individual's level of commitment toward the team should correspond to the level of formation among each of the nine attitude properties. This commitment should reflect a bundling of properties into cognitive, subjective, and definitive groupings. Higher levels of commitment are suggested to stem from an individual's willingness to resist changing their affiliation from the team to an alternative team. The level of commitment should in turn be indicative of reported past behavior and intent such as attending games, watching the team on TV, reading about the team in print media, and talking about the team amongst friends, family, or acquaintances.

> **Higher levels of commitment are suggested to stem from an individual's willingness to resist changing their affiliation from the team to an alternative team.**

## Methodology

A concern in the design of the present study involved the selection of an athletic team that would provide enough variability among participants to measure structural differences among the attitude properties and commitment (e.g., Schurr, Ruble, & Ellen, 1985; Shelly & Cartin, 1984; Zillman, Byant, & Sapolsky, 1989). A 60-item pretest questionnaire of five regionally located sports teams (i.e., two collegiate and three professional) was distributed to undergraduates ($N = 40$). Respondents rated their feelings related to each team on twelve different measures for each team and a composite score was calculated. The Cleveland Indians professional baseball team was selected because the variability reported was higher than the other four teams.

> **The Cleveland Indians professional baseball team was selected because the variability reported was higher than the other four teams.**

Attitude scale items were next developed and an instrument was designed and tested in order to assess the predictive validity and reliability of attitude properties and commitment items. Thirty-two attitude scale items were generated from Krosnick et al., (1993) to measure nine properties importance, extremity, intensity, certainty, knowledge, direct experience, personal relevance, affect, and belief. In line with Krosnick et al., (1993), responses to items were measured using multiple formats ranging from 3-point, 4-point, 5-point, and 7-point Likert-type scales; 100-point thermometer scale with label points of 0, 50, 100; and semantic differential scales anchored at both ends. For the purpose of this study, ten items were also developed to measure an individual's commitment to the Cleveland Indians. The ten commitment items were designed to reflect psychological commitment (e.g., Crosby & Taylor, 1983; Haugtvedt & Petty, 1992; Haugtvedt & Wegener, 1992).

**The 42-item Cleveland Indians Baseball survey was initially tested in two pilot tests (*N* = 15 and *N* = 21) and refined. The survey was then distributed to 388 undergraduates enrolled in two introductory marketing courses at a large midwestern university.**

The 42-item Cleveland Indians Baseball survey was initially tested in two pilot tests (*N* = 15 and *N* = 21) and refined. The survey was then distributed to 388 undergraduates enrolled in two introductory marketing courses at a large midwestern university. The use of a nonrandom homogenous sample was preferred because the goal of the study was theory application and not effects application (Calder, Phillips, & Tybout, 1981). Of the original sample, nine individuals were eliminated due to incomplete surveys and the final sample (*N* = 379) included 216 males' (57%) and 163 females (43%).

## Data Analysis

A confirmatory factor analysis was used to examine the psychometric properties of the scale. A covariance matrix (*N* = 379) was utilized as the input to test the attitude model. All first-order latent factors had three-scale items except affect, belief, and commitment, which had five, five, and ten respectively. The error term for each scale item was constrained to not correlate. The error term for each latent variable was left to freely correlate. Per Kline's (1998) recommendation, five fit measures (chi square divided by degree of freedom ($\chi^2/df$), root mean square error of approximation (RMSEA), comparative fit index (CFI), non-normed fit index (NNI), and standardized root means square residual (SRMR) were examined to assess whether the data fit the hypothesized measurement. The data collected from participants were analyzed using Joreskog and Sorbom's (1993) Linear Structural Relations (LISREL) VIII to test the hypothesized measurement and structural model. The measurement model specified the correspondence between 32-manifest variables, 9 correlated latent attitude properties, and 10 manifest variables representing commitment to team. The measurement model assessed the contribution of each scale item as well as incorporated how well the scale measured the concept and its reliability into the estimation of the relationship between the nine attitude properties and commitment. The structural model was tested simultaneously with the measurement model and specified that the 9 latent attitude properties were independently related to commitment (see Figure 2).

## Results

The construct means, standard deviations, and Cronbach alphas are reported in Table 1. All scores were translated to 7-point scales for this analysis. Construct means for the nine attitude properties ranged from 2.62 to 4.78 and standard deviations ranged from 1.47 to 1.95. The mean score for commitment was 3.02 (*SD* = 1.77). Cronbach alphas ranged from .78 to .96 and above the .70 benchmark

**Table 1  Attitude Properties and Commitment Means, Standard Deviations, and Internal Consistency Measures (N = 379)**

| Attitude Properties | M | SD | |
|---|---|---|---|
| Importance (IMP) | 3.32 | 1.95 | .94 |
| Personal Relevance (PER) | 2.62 | 1.47 | .82 |
| Intensity (INT) | 3.40 | 1.75 | .81 |
| Direct Experience (DXP) | 2.93 | 1.71 | .87 |
| Knowledge (KNW) | 3.07 | 1.72 | .92 |
| Affect (AFF) | 4.22 | 1.64 | .96 |
| Certainty (CER) | 4.78 | 1.67 | .78 |
| Cognitive (COG) | 4.28 | 1.58 | .95 |
| Extremity (EXT) | 3.84 | 1.65 | .83 |
| Outcome Variable | | | |
| Commitment | 3.02 | 1.77 | .92 |

Note: Mean scores and Standard Deviations were transformed to 7-point scale.

**Table 2  Correlation Matrix of Attitude Properties and Commitment from Phi Matrix (N = 379)**

| | IMP | INT | CER | DXP | EXT | KNW | PER | AFF | COG | COM |
|---|---|---|---|---|---|---|---|---|---|---|
| IMP | 1 | | | | | | | | | |
| INT | .94 | 1 | | | | | | | | |
| CER | .51 | .49 | 1 | | | | | | | |
| DXP | .88 | .85 | .46 | 1 | | | | | | |
| EXT | .54 | .52 | .28 | .49 | 1 | | | | | |
| KNW | .89 | .85 | .46 | .80 | .49 | 1 | | | | |
| PER | .93 | .90 | .49 | .84 | .51 | .85 | 1 | | | |
| AFF | .77 | .74 | .40 | .69 | .42 | .69 | .73 | 1 | | |
| COG | .71 | .69 | .37 | .64 | .39 | .65 | .68 | .56 | 1 | |
| COM | .99 | .95 | .51 | .89 | .54 | .90 | .94 | .77 | .72 | 1 |

IMP = Importance
INT = Intensity
CER = Certainty
DXP = Direct Experience
EXT = Extremity

KNW = Knowledge
PER = Personal Relevance
AFF = Affective Reaction
COG = Cognitive Emotion
COM = Commitment

**Table 3** **Individual Scale Items, Squared Multiple Correlations, and Path Coefficients for Latent Factors from Confirmatory Factor Analysis. (N = 379)**

| Attitude Property Scale Items | Factor Loadings | Path Coefficients |
|---|---|---|
| **Importance (IMP)** | | |
| How much do you personally care about the Cleveland Indians? | .89 | 1.88 |
| Compared to how you feel about other professional sports teams, how important are the Cleveland Indians to you? | .91 | 2.14 |
| I care a great deal about the Cleveland Indians. | .83 | 1.57 |
| **Personal Relevance (PER)** | | |
| How closely do you pay attention to information about the Cleveland Indians? | .76 | 1.51 |
| How interested are you in obtaining information about the Cleveland Indians? | .87 | 1.73 |
| I am very interested in information about the Cleveland Indians. | .87 | 1.84 |
| **Intensity (INT)** | | |
| Compared to how you feel about others sports teams, how strong are your feelings regarding the Cleveland Indians? | .71 | 1.47 |
| How intense is your attitude toward the Cleveland Indians? | .87 | 1.96 |
| Would you say your feelings about the Cleveland Indians are . . . | .74 | 1.39 |
| **Direct Experience (DXP)** | | |
| How often do you participate in pre-game activities related to Cleveland Indians' games? | .87 | 1.56 |
| Participated in various activities: attended, watched, listened, talked, read, etc. | .76 | 1.65 |
| How often do you participate in post-game activities related to Cleveland Indians' games? | .91 | 1.66 |
| **Knowledge (KNW)** | | |
| How much knowledge do you have about the Cleveland Indians? | .92 | 1.92 |
| If you were to list everything that you know about the Cleveland Indians, how long would the list be? | .91 | 1.52 |
| Compared to other teams, I consider myself to be an expert about the Cleveland Indians. | .87 | 1.54 |
| **Affect / Feelings  (AFF)** | | |
| Devoted - Opposed | .89 | 1.59 |
| Awful - Nice | .84 | 1.46 |
| Favorable - Unfavorable | .94 | 1.72 |
| Pleasant - Unpleasant | .92 | 1.58 |
| Excited - Bored | .88 | 1.71 |
| **Certainty (CER)** | | |
| I am convinced about my opinion of the Cleveland Indians. | .83 | 1.31 |
| How certain are you of your feelings about the Cleveland Indians. | .76 | 1.52 |
| With what degree of certainty do you hold your opinion about the Cleveland Indians. | .64 | 1.58 |

Table 3 **Continued**

| Attitude Property Scale Items | Factor Loadings | Path Coefficients |
|---|---|---|
| **Cognition / Beliefs (COG)** | | |
| Necessary - Unnecessary | .89 | 1.59 |
| Unproductive - Productive | .89 | 1.53 |
| Useless - Useful | .95 | 1.66 |
| Valuable - Worthless | .93 | 1.67 |
| Weak - Strong | .78 | 1.28 |
| **Extremity (EXT)** | | |
| Foolish - Wise | .71 | 1.32 |
| Good - Bad | .83 | 1.60 |
| Worthless - Beneficial | .81 | 1.59 |
| **Commitment** | | |
| Given the choice, I would increase the amount of time I spend following the Cleveland Indians during the baseball season. | .81 | 1.79 |
| I watched a lot of Cleveland Indians' games on TV last season. | .92 | 2.04 |
| I would watch a game featuring the Cleveland Indians baseball team regardless of which team they were playing against. | .88 | 1.79 |
| How often do you wear or display Cleveland Indians' team logo items on your clothing, at your place of work, or where you live. | .69 | 1.56 |
| I am a committed fan of the Cleveland Indians' baseball team. | .85 | 1.78 |
| Following the Cleveland Indians has a high priority among my leisure activities. | .87 | 1.87 |
| How willing are you to defend the Cleveland Indians publicly, even if it causes controversy. | .73 | 1.18 |
| During the baseball season, how closely do you follow the Cleveland Indians using various sport channels on TV, radio, local news, in the newspaper, and sport magazines. | .90 | 1.66 |
| I would be difficult for me to be a fan of the Cleveland Indians baseball team. | .93 | 1.92 |
| I would attend more Cleveland Indians' games if I had the time and money. | .85 | 1.74 |

Notes:

1. Path Coefficients are the unstandardized measurement paths for each parameter from the Lamda Matrix.

2. t-values for scale items in measurement model were significant at $p < .05$

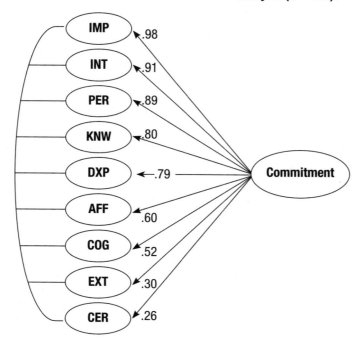

Figure 2 **Structural Relations Among Attitude Properties and Commitment From Structural Equation Modeling Analysis (*N* = 379).**

**Notes**

1. Factor Loadings represent the squared multiple correlation coefficients for manifest indicators. For example: The latent variable Commitment accounts for 98% of the variance in attitude importance.

2. Correlations were deleted from the figure for simplicity and clarity of presentation.

(Nunnally & Bernstein, 1994). The interrelationship among the attitude properties are reported in the Table 2 and ranged from *r* = .28 to *r* = .94. Although the independence of each attitude property is a concern, high correlations among the subscales were expected with distinct yet interrelated dimensions (e.g., much like the relationship between height and weight). Furthermore, all of the nine properties were more highly correlated to commitment than other attitude properties.

The results of the confirmatory factor analysis indicated the data used to test the measurement model received an acceptable fit. Examination of the parameter estimates and the accompanied t-test revealed that each manifest item was significant at *p* < .05, in the direction dictated by theory, and above *r* = .60 (Bagozzi & Yi, 1988). The individual item factor loadings ranged from *r* = .64 to *r* = .95 and the unstandardized path coefficients ranged from 1.38 to 2.14. See Table 3. The $\chi^2$ value of 2,227 divided by 770 degrees of freedom was 2.89. This measure was slightly above the 2.50 recommendation (e.g., Kline, 1998) but is sensitive to sample size. The RMSEA value of .08 and was within the acceptable range of .05 to .08 for an acceptable fit of the data (Hair et al., 1998). The NNFI and CFI measures were both .91 (e.g., Bentler, 1990). The SMRM was .08 below the .10 ceiling for acceptable fit (Kline, 1998).

The structural model estimated a series of separate, but interdependent, multiple regression equations simultaneously. Inspection of the coefficients of determination in Figure 2 revealed that commitment accounted for 98% of the variance in importance, 90% in intensity, 87% personal relevance, 80% direct experience, 79% in knowledge, 61% in affective reactions, 53% in cognitive thoughts, 38% in extremity, and 26% in certainty. A competing models strategy (e.g., Thompson & Daniel, 1996) was utilized to test whether the

**Inspection of the coefficients of determination in Figure 2 revealed that commitment accounted for 98% of the variance in importance, 90% in intensity, 87% personal relevance, 80% direct experience, 79% in knowledge, 61% in affective reactions, 53% in cognitive thoughts, 38% in extremity, and 26% in certainty.**

Table 4 **Goodness-of-Fit Measures for Specified Model and General Attitude Model**

| Goodness-of-Fit Measures | Multi-Property Model * | Single Attitude Model ** |
|---|---|---|
| **Absolute Fit Measures** | | |
| Likelihood-ratio ($\Psi^2/df$) | 2.89 | 6.07 |
| Root mean square error of approximation (RMSEA) | .07 | .12 |
| Goodness-of-fit (GFI) | .74 | .45 |
| Normed Fit Index (NFI) | .87 | .72 |
| Comparative Fit Index (CFI) | .91 | .75 |
| Parsimony Goodness-of- Fit (PGFI) | .68 | .41 |

Note:  * Iterations = 64; ** Iterations = 99

$\underline{N}$ = 379; Both Models were positive definite

hypothesized structural model achieved a better fit for the data than a general attitude model (i.e., 32-items reflecting a single commitment factor).  The two models were assessed utilizing six indices or fit measures:  chi square ($\chi^2$), Root Mean Square Error of Approximation (RMSEA), Goodness-of-Fit Index (GFI), Normed Fit Index (NFA), Incremental Fit Index (IFI), and Parsimony Goodness-of-Fit Index (PGFI).  Table 4 lists the fit indices for both models.  Inspection of the goodness-of-fit indices in Table 4 indicated that the data supported the hypothesized model better than the general attitude model.  These results suggest that the nine attitude properties are distinct and their relationship to commitment can be independently examined.

A subsequent SEM analysis was conducted to test the conceptual model proposed from Figure 1.  This model specified that importance, intensity, and personal relevance reflected a second-order latent subjective meaning factor; the properties knowledge, direct experience, and affect and belief reflected a cognitive function factor; and certainty and extremity properties reflected a definitive position second order factor.  All three of these second order latent factors were subsequently hypothesized to reflect commitment.  However, the specified conceptual model achieved a poor fit for the data and was unreliable (i.e., not positive definite).

> **These results suggest that the nine attitude properties are distinct and their relationship to commitment can be independently examined.**

## Discussion

Measuring consumer attitudes continues to be a central concern for researchers and practitioners within the field of sport marketing.  However, only recently have efforts been directed at exploring the utility and predictive validity of multiple attitudinal measures (Funk, Haugtvedt, & Howard, 2000; Gladden & Funk, 2002).  Given the importance ascribed to developing better methodologies and understanding of attitudes in other disciplines (e.g., marketing, business, psychology, leisure, etc.), it is surprising that sport researchers have largely ignored the application of contemporary attitude theory.  The present data supports the notion that an individual's attitude toward a team comprises multiple properties beyond the traditional valence measure (i.e., affect), and our understanding of spectator and fan attitudes can be enhanced with multiple measures.

Measuring consumer attitudes continues to be a central concern for researchers and practitioners within the field of sport marketing. However, only recently have efforts been directed at exploring the utility and predictive validity of multiple attitudinal measures.

In general, these data support previous multivariate studies as to the structural nature of the attitude construct (e.g., Bassili, 1996; Krosnick et al., 1993) and provide the initial framework to understand the nature and role of attitudes in sport marketing research. The scale utilized provides a diagnostic tool to investigate the underlying structure of consumer attitudes in a subset of leisure-spectator sport. As a diagnostic tool, the scale can be used to measure the relative influence of each property in relation to a specific outcome variable (e.g., purchase behavior, identification, loyalty, sponsorship involvement) and will increase the predictive validity of attitudinal research. This structural perspective could also be extended to provide sport marketers with new insight into differentiating attitude formation toward job satisfaction, organizational commitment, and other related areas that rely on utilizing attitude measures.

Based on observed relationship between importance and commitment ($R^2 = .98$) in the model, individuals who attach a great deal of psychological significance and value to their attitude toward the team would be less likely to change their affiliation with the team and subsequently more likely to engage in team-related behavior (e.g., watching, attending, purchasing; Funk, Haugtvedt & Howard, 2000). Furthermore, an individual's attitude toward a sports team that generated intense emotion ($R^2 = .90$), was more personally relevant ($R^2 = .87$), accompanied by a significant amount of relevant knowledge ($R^2 = .79$), and based on direct personal experience ($R^2 = .80$) may be indicative of commitment. These data suggest that properties beyond affect may well be the driving force behind consumer attitude and

This structural perspective could also be extended to provide sport marketers with new insight into differentiating attitude formation toward job satisfaction, organizational commitment, and other related areas that rely on utilizing attitude measures.

commitment to a team, brand or leisure activity. Although the proposed model should fit equally well in an entirely new sample of individuals, judgment as to the stability of the model should be reserved until such a procedure is employed.

These data suggest that properties beyond affect may well be the driving force behind consumer attitude and commitment to a team, brand or leisure activity.

The present data provided initial evidence for the utility of obtaining attitudinal measures beyond valence (i.e., feelings toward the team) to understand consumer loyalty and marketing-related activities. Although the predictive ability of affect ($R^2 = .61$) was noteworthy, five additional measures were more robust properties contributing to team commitment: importance ($R^2 = .98$), intensity ($R^2 = . 90$), personal relevance ($R^2 = .87$), knowledge ($R^2 = .79$) and direct experience ($R^2 = .80$). Although the observed relationship between commitment and certainty ($R^2 = .26$) and extremity ($R^2 = .32$) were significant p < .01, stronger relationships were expected (e.g., Bright, 1997; Tesser et al., 1995). These properties may have distinct conceptual and operational features that lack an emotive characteristic that contributed to an observed curvilinear U pattern for the data and may have produced a contrast effect (e.g., Brent & Granberg, 1982). Both highly committed individuals and those strongly opposed to the Indians were just as certain of their attitudes and extreme in their evaluation of the team, which represents highly formed attitudes. In contrast, moderately committed individuals were less confident and extreme, reflecting less attitude formation. These results suggest that certainty and extremity provide a means to delineate weak or non-attitudes from strong attitudes regardless of affect. However, the

> **Both highly committed individuals and those strongly opposed to the Indians were just as certain of their attitudes and extreme in their evaluation of the team, which represents highly formed attitudes. In contrast, moderately committed individuals were less confident and extreme, reflecting less attitude formation.**

use of extremity and certainty measures to predict behavior should incorporate information related to other attitude dimensions to increase predictive validity.

These data did not support the proposed model that properties cluster together and form three higher order factors related to commitment. However, inspection of the $R^2$ values indicated a grouping tendency. The subjective properties converged with higher $R^2$ values ranging from .98 to .87 for a mean of .92, the cognitive properties clustered with moderate $R^2$ values .80 to .53 for a mean of .68, while the definitive aspect properties bundled together with low $R^2$ values of .38 and .26 for a mean of .32. Subsequent testing is needed to empirically support this structure or refine the conceptual model offered.

## Direction for Future Marketing Research on Attitudes

These data provide initial evidence for the nature and influential role that properties beyond affect contribute to consumer commitment. However, future research devoted to understanding how attitudes toward a team initially form is needed. Of particular relevance is previous work in social psychology that has identified a link between social identification (Tajfel & Turner, 1979) and the attitude property importance (Boninger, Krosnick, & Berent, 1995). Within spectator sport, work by Wann and Branscombe (1990) and Branscombe and Wann (1991) has utilized group identification (i.e., team identification) to explain cognitive, emotional, and behavioral differences among sports fans. Taken together, this research suggests that the importance attached to one's self-concept that is derived from a relationship with an athletic team would be a likely avenue to investigate one possible determinant of attitude formation and commitment.

A fuller understanding may also be gained by expanding the levels of commitment by dichotomizing the internal complexity of commitment (e.g., Mahony, Madrigal, & Howard, 2000). For example, attitude measures could be compared to Pritchard et al.'s (1999) Psychological Commitment Inventory (PCI) to provide an analysis of high, mid-range, and low PCI scores. In addition, team commitment (high, moderate, and low) could be examined through multiple discriminant analysis to examine the relative contribution of each property. Dichotomizing team commitment using season ticket holders vs. single game attendees or non-consumers may also be equally instructive to further understand attitude formation.

Multivariate studies simultaneously examining various attitude properties and commitment levels in a variety of leisure settings could provide insight into whether differences exist between persons in participatory activities and spectating-based entertainment pursuits. This line of research could also include assessing attitude formation toward corporate sponsors of sporting events and properties over the length of the contract (e.g., McDaniel & Heald, 2000). Future research should also explore the extent of attitude formation and the complexity of team-related information to understand the linkage between properties and the number of concepts and categories employed (Pritchard et al., 1999).

## Limitations

There are several limitations of the current study that suggest the need for further research. First, while many well-studied attitude properties were included, accessibility was not measured due the inability to measure response latency (e.g., Fazio et al., 1982). Second, despite previous work supporting the independence of each attitude property (Basilli, 1996; Krosnick et al., 1993), the high correlations observed among some of the properties require further refinement of the scale items before subsequent use in sport marketing related research. Third, since the current study did not examine a random sample of a community's general population, respondent characteristics and sociodemographic factors may limit the findings. Fourth, acquiescence and social desirability on the part of individuals responding to attitude statements can create potential response set concerns.

## Conclusion

> This research suggests that the subjective disposition of an individual's self-concept that is derived from involvement with an athletic team would be a likely candidate to initiate an investigation into a possible determinant of attitude formation.

Overall, this study produced two main results. First, contemporary attitude theory was utilized to show the utility of multiple measure to assess consumer attitudes in sport marketing research. The predictive validity of obtaining attitudinal measures beyond the traditional affect measure to predict commitment was demonstrated. Second, the present study provided a framework to integrate prior work in social psychology on attitude formation and leisure research on psychological commitment to better understand attitude formation in a team sport context. Taken together, this research suggests that the subjective disposition of an individual's self-concept that is derived from involvement with an athletic team would be a likely candidate to initiate an investigation into a possible determinant of attitude formation.

## References

Abelson, R. P. (1988). Conviction. *American Psychologist, 43*, 267-275.

Abelson, R. P. (1995). Attitude Extremity. In R. E. Petty & J. A. Krosnick (Eds.), *Attitude Strength: Antecedents and Consequences*, (p. 25-42). Mahwah, NJ: Lawrence Erlbaum Associates.

Ajzen, I., & Driver, B. L. (1992). Application of the theory of planned behavior to leisure choice. *Journal of Leisure Research, 24*, 207-224.

Baade, R. A., & Tiehan, L. J. (1990). An analysis of major league baseball attendance: 1969-1987. *Journal of Sport and Social Issues, 14*, 14-32.

Backman, S. J., & Crompton, J. L. (1991). Using loyalty matrix to differentiate between high, spurious, latent and loyal participants in two leisure services. *Journal of Park and Recreation Administration, 9*, 1-17.

Bagozzi, R. P., & Yi, T. (1988). On the evaluation of structural equation models. *Journal of the Academy of Marketing Science, 16*, 74-94.

Bassili, J. N. (1996). Meta-judgments versus operative indexes of psychological attributes: The case of measures of attitude strength. *Journal of Personality and Social Psychology, 71*, 637-653.

Becker, M. A., & Suls, J. (1983). Take me out to the ball game: The effects of objective, social, and temporal performance information on the attendance at major league baseball games. *Journal of Sport Psychology, 5*, 302-313.

Bentler, P. M. (1985). *Theory and Implementation of EQS: A structural equations program.* Los Angeles: BMDP Statistical Software.

Bentler, P. M., & Bonett, D. G. (1980). Significance tests and goodness-of-fit in the analysis of covariance structures. *Psychological Bulletin, 88*, 588-600.

Bollen, K. A. (1989). *Structural Equations with Latent Variables.* New York: John Wiley & Sons, Inc.

Boninger, D. S., Krosnick, J. A., & Berent, M. K. (1995). The causes of attitude importance: Self-interest, social identification, and values. *Journal of Personality and Social Psychology, 68*, 61-80.

Branscombe, N. R., & Wann, D. L. (1991). The positive social and self-concept consequences of sports team identification. *Journal of Sport and Social Issues, 15*, 115-127.

Brent, E., & Granberg, D. (1982). Subjective agreement and the presidential candidates of 1976 and 1980. *Journal of Personality and Social Psychology, 42*, 560-570.

Bright, A. D. (1997). Attitude-strength and support of recreation management strategies. *Journal of Leisure Research, 29*, 369-379.

Bright, A. D., & Manfredo, M. J. (1995). The quality of attitudinal information regarding natural resource issues: The role of attitude-strength, importance, and information. *Society and Natural Resources, 8,* 399-414.

Bright, A. D., Manfredo, M. J., Fishbein, M., & Bath, A. (1993). Application of the theory of reasoned action to the National Park Service's controlled burn policy. *Journal of Leisure Research, 25,* 263-280.

Budd, R. J. (1986). Predicting cigarette use: The need to incorporate measures of salience in the Theory of Reasoned Action. *Journal of Applied Social Psychology, 16,* 633-685.

Calder, D. F., Phillips, L. W., & Tybout, A. M. (1981). Designing research for application. *Journal of Consumer Research, 8,* 197-207.

Carmines, E. G., & McIver, J. P. (1981). Analyzing models with unobserved variables: Analysis of covariance structures. In G. W. Bohrnstedt and E. F. Borgatta, (Eds.). *Social Measurement: Current Issues* (pp. 65-115). Beverly Hills, CA: Sage.

Carron, A. V., Hausenblas, H. A., & Mack, D. (1996). Social influence and exercise: A meta-analysis. *Journal of Sport & Exercise Psychology, 18,* 1-16.

Chaiken, S., Pomerantz, E. M., & Giner-Sorolla, R. (1995). Structural consistency and attitude strength. In R. E. Petty & J. A. Krosnick (Ed.). *Attitude Strength: Antecedents and Consequences* (pp. 387-412). Mahwah, NJ: Lawrence Erlbaum Associates.

Cote, J. A., & Buckley, M. R. (1987). Estimating trait, method, and error variance: Generalizing across 70 construct validation studies. *Journal of Marketing Research, 24,* 315-318.

Crites, S. L., Fabrigar, L. R., & Petty, R. E. (1994). Measuring the affective and cognitive properties of attitudes: Conceptual and methodological issues. *Personality and Social Psychology Bulletin, 20,* 619-634.

Crosby, L. A., & Taylor, J. R. (1983). Psychological commitment and its effect on post-decision evaluation and preference stability among voters. *Journal of Consumer Research, 9,* 413-431.

Davidson, A. R., Yanits, S., Norwood, M., & Montano, D. E. (1985). Amount of information about the attitude-object and attitude-behavior consistency. *Journal of Personality and Social Psychology, 45,* 997-1009.

Day, G. S. (1969). A two-dimensional concept of brand loyalty. *Journal of Advertising Research, 9*(September), 29-36.

Dick, A. S., & Basu, K. (1994). Customer Loyalty: Toward an integrated conceptual framework. *Journal of Academy of Marketing Science, 22,* 99-113.

Doll, J., & Ajzen, I. (1992). Accessibility and stability of predictors in the theory of planned behavior. *Journal of Personality and Social Psychology, 63,* 754-765.

Eagly, A. H., & Chaiken, S. (1993). *The Psychology of Attitudes.* Fort Worth, TX: Harcourt, Brace Jovanovich, Inc.

Fazio, R. H., & Zanna, M. P. (1978a). Attitudinal qualities relating to the strength of the attitude-behavior relationship. *Journal of Experimental Social Psychology, 14,* 398-408.

Fazio, R. H., & Zanna, M. P. (1978b). On the predictive validity of attitudes: The roles of direct experience and confidence. *Journal of Personality, 46,* 228-243.

Fazio, R. H., Chen, J., McDonald, E. C., & Sherman, S. J. (1982). Attitude accessibility, attitude-behavior consistency, and the strength of the object-evaluation association. *Journal of Experimental Social Psychology, 18,* 339-357.

Funk, D. C., Haugtvedt, C. P., & Howard, D. R. (2000). Contemporary attitude theory in sport: Theoretical considerations and implications. *Sport Management Review, 3,* 124-144.

Gladden, J., & Funk, D. C. (2002). Developing an understanding of brand associations in team sport: Empirical evidence from consumers of professional sport. *Journal of Sport Management, 16,* 54-81.

Gross, S. R., Holtz, R., & Miller, N. (1995). Attitude Certainty. In R. E. Petty & J. A. Krosnick (Eds.). *Attitude Strength: Antecedents and Consequences,* (p. 215-246). Mahwah, NJ: Lawrence Erlbaum Associates.

Hair, J. F., Anderson, R. E., Tatham, R. L., & Black, W. C. (1995). *Multivariate Data Analysis.* (4th ed.). Prentice Hill: NJ.

Haugtvedt, C., & Petty, R. E. (1992). Personality and persuasion: Need for cognition moderates the persistence and resistance of attitude changes. *Journal of Personality and Social Psychology, 63,* 308-319.

Haugtvedt, C., & Wegener, D. (1994). Message order effects in persuasion: An attitude strength perspective. *Journal of Consumer Research, 21,* 205-218.

Haugtvedt, C., Schumann, D., Schneier, W., & Warren, W. (1994). Advertising repetition and variation strategies: Implications for understanding attitude strength. *Journal of Consumer Research, 21,* 176-189.

Havitz, M. E., & Dimanche, F. (1997). Leisure involvement revisited: Conceptual conundrums and measurement advances. *Journal of Leisure Research, 29,* 245-278.

Howard, D. R., Edginton, C. R., & Selin, S. W. (1988). Determinants of program loyalty. *Journal of Parks and Recreation Administration, 6,* 41-51.

Iwasaki, Y, & Havitz, M. E. (1998). A path analytic model of the relationships between involvement, psychological commitment, and loyalty. *Journal of Leisure Research, 30,* 256-280.

Jacob, J. & Kyner, D. B. (1973). Brand loyalty vs. repeat purchasing behavior. *Journal of Marketing Research, 10,* 1-9.

Joreskog, K. G., & Sorborm, D. (1993). *LISREL VIII.* Chicago: Scientific Package for Statistical Software.

Judd, C. M., & Johnson, J. T. (1981). Attitudes, polarization, and diagnosticity: Exploring the effects of affect. *Journal of Personality and Social Psychology, 41,* 25-36.

Kallgren, C. A., & Wood, W. (1986). Access to attitude relevant information in memory as a determinant of attitude-behavior consistency. *Journal of Experimental Social Psychology, 22*, 328-338.

Kline, R.B. (1998). *Principles and practice of structural equation modeling.* New York: Guilford Press.

Krosnick, J. A. (1988). The role of attitude importance in social evaluation: A study of policy preferences, presidential candidate evaluations, and voting behavior. *Journal of Personality and Social Psychology, 55*, 196-210.

Krosnick, J. A. (1989). Attitude importance and attitude accessibility. *Personality and Social Psychology Bulletin, 15*, 297-308.

Krosnick, J. A., & Abelson, R. P. (1992). The case of measuring attitude strength in surveys. In J. Tanur (Ed.). *Questions About Survey Questions* (pp. 173-203). New York: Russell Sage.

Krosnick, J. A., & Petty, R. E. (1995). Attitude strength: An overview. In R. E. Petty & J. A. Krosnick (Eds.), *Attitude Strength: Antecedents and Consequences,* (pp. 1-24). Mahwah, NJ: Lawrence Erlbaum Associates.

Krosnick, J. A., & Schuman, H. (1988). Attitude intensity, importance, and certainty and susceptibility to response effects. *Journal of Personality and Social Psychology, 54*, 940-952.

Krosnick, J. A., Boninger, D. S., Chuang, Y. C., Berent, M. K., & Carnot, C. G. (1993). Attitude strength: One construct of many related constructs? *Journal of Personality and Social Psychology, 65*, 1132-1151.

Lastovicka, J. L., & Gardner, D. M. (1979). Components of involvement. In J. C. Maloney & B. Silverman (Eds.), *Attitude Research Plays for High Stakes* (pp. 53-73). Chicago: American Marketing Association.

Linville, P. W., & Jones, E. E. (1980). Polarized appraisals of out-group members. *Journal of Personality and Social Psychology, 38*, 689-703.

Mahony, D. F., & Howard, D. R. (1998). The impact of attitudes on the behavioral intentions of sport spectators. *International Sports Journal, 2*, 96-110.

Mahony, D. F., & Moorman, A. M. (1999). The impact of attitudes toward athletes on the behavioral intentions of professional football and professional basketball fans. *Sport Management Review, 2*, 43-66.

Mahony, D. F., Madrigal, R., & Howard, D. (2000). Using psychological commitment to team (PCT) scale to segment sport consumers based on loyalty. *Sport Marketing Quarterly, 9*, 15-25.

Manfredo, M. J., Yuan, S. M., & McGuire, F. A. (1992). The influence of attitude accessibility on attitude-behavior relationships: Implications for recreation research. *Journal of Leisure Research, 24*, 157-170.

McDaniel, S. R., & Heald, G. R. (2000). Young consumers' response to event sponsorship advertisements of unhealthy products: Implications of schema-triggered affect theory. *Sport Management Review, 3*, 163-184.

McReady, M. L., & Long, B. C. (1985). Locus of Control, attitudes toward physical activity, and exercise adherence. *Journal of Sport Psychology, 7*, 346-359.

Murrell, A. J., & Dietz, B. (1992). Fan support of sports teams: The effect of a common group identity. *Journal of Sport and Exercise Psychology, 14*, 28-39.

Nunnally, J. C., & Bernstein, I. H. (1994). *Psychometric theory,* (3rd ed.), New York: McGraw-Hill.

Parks, S. (1996). Relationship between involvement and attitudinal loyalty constructs in adult fitness programs. *Journal of Leisure Research, 28*, 233-250.

Petty, R. E., & Cacioppo, J. T. (1986). The elaboration likelihood model of persuasion. In L. Berkowitz (Ed.), *Advances in Experimental Social Psychology* (Vol. 19, p. 123-205). San Diego: Academic Press.

Petty, R. E., & Cacioppo, J. T. (1990). Involvement and persuasion: Tradition versus integration. *Psychological Bulletin, 107*, 367-374.

Petty, R. E., Cacioppo, J. T., & Schumann, D. W. (1983). Central and peripheral route to advertising effectiveness: The moderating role of involvement. *Journal of Consumer Research, 10*, 135-146.

Petty, R. E., Haugtvedt, C., & Smith, S. M. (1995). Elaboration as a determinant of attitude strength: Creating attitudes that are persistent, resistant, and predictive of behavior. In R. E. Petty & J. A. Krosnick (Ed.), *Attitude Strength: Antecedents and Consequences.* (pp. 93-130). Mahwah, NJ: Lawrence Erlbaum Associates.

Pratkins, A. R., & Greenwald, A. G. (1989). A sociocognitive model of attitude structure and function. In L. Berkowitz (Ed.), *Advances in Experimental Social Psychology* (Vol. 22, p. 245-285). San Diego: Academic.

Pritchard, M. P., Havitz, D. R., & Howard, D. R. (1999). Analyzing the commitment loyalty link in service contexts. *Academy of Marketing Science, 27*, 333-348.

Rosenberg, M. J. (1968). Hedonism, inauthenticity, and other goads toward expansion of a consistency theory. In R. P. Abelson, E. Aronson, W. J. McGuire, T. M. Newcomb, M. J. Rosenberg, & P. H. Tannenbaum (Eds.), *Theories of Cognitive Consistency: A Sourcebook* (p. 73-111). Chicago: Ran McNally.

Schuman, H., & Presser, S. (1981). *Questions and Answers: Experiments on Question Form, Wording, and Context in Attitude Surveys.* Orlando, FL: Academic Press.

Schurr, K. T., Ruble, V. E., & Ellen, A. S. (1985). Myers-Briggs type indicator and demographic characteristics of students attending and not attending a college basketball game. *Journal of Sport Behavior, 8*, 181-194.

Selin, S. W., Howard, D. R., Udd, E., & Cable, T. T. (1988). An analysis of consumer loyalty to municipal recreation programs. *Leisure Sciences, 10*, 217-223.

Shelly, F. M., & Cartin, K. F. (1984). The geography of baseball fan support in the United States. *North American Culture, 1*, 77-95.

Sherif, C. W., Sherif, M., & Nebergall, R. E. (1965). *Attitude and Attitude Change: The Social Judgement-Involvement Approach.* Philadelphia: Saunders.

Tajfel, H., & Turner, J. C. (1979). An integrative theory of intergroup conflict. In W. G. Austin and S. Worchel (Eds.), *The Social Psychology of Intergroup Relations.* Montery, CA: Brooks/Cole.

Tesser, A., & Leone, C. (1977). Cognitive schemas and thought as determinants of attitude change. *Journal of Experimental Social Psychology, 13,* 340-356.

Tesser, A., Martin, L., & Mendolia, M. (1995). The impact of thought on attitude extremity and attitude-behavior consistency. In R. E. Petty & J. A. Krosnick (Eds.). *Attitude Strength: Antecedents and Consequences,* (p. 73-92). Mahwah, NJ: Lawrence Erlbaum Associates.

Thompson, B., & Daniel, L. G. (1996). Factor analytic evidence for the construct validation of scores: A historical overview and some guidelines. *Educational and Psychological Measurement, 56,* 197-208.

Thomsen, C. J., Borgida, E., & Lavine, H. (1995). The causes and consequences of personal involvement. In R. E. Petty & J. A. Krosnick (Eds.), *Attitude Strength: Antecedents and Consequences.* (pp. 191-214). Mahwah, NJ: Lawrence Erlbaum Associates.

Torabi, M. R. (1988). Factors affecting reliability coefficients of health attitude scales. *Journal of School Health, 58,* 186-189.

Turco, D. M. (1996). The effects of courtside advertising on product recognition and attitude change. *Sport Marketing Quarterly, 5,* 11-15.

Verplanken, B. (1991). Persuasive communication of risk information: A test of cue versus message processing effects in a field experiment. *Personality and Social Psychology Bulletin, 17,* 188-193.

Virnig, A. G., & McLeod, C. R. (1996). Attitudes toward eating and exercise: A comparison of runners and triathletes. *Journal of Sport Behavior, 19,* 82-90.

Wann, D. L., & Branscombe, N. R. (1990). Die Hard and fair weather fans: Effects of identification on BIRGing and CORFing tendencies. *Journal of Sport and Social Issues, 14,* 103-177.

Wegener, D. T., Downing, J., Krosnick, J. A., & Petty, R. E. (1995). Measures and manipulations of strength-related properties of attitudes: Current practice and future directions. In R. E. Petty & J. A. Krosnick (Eds.), *Attitude Strength: Antecedents and Consequences.* (pp. 455-487). Mahwah, NJ: Lawrence Erlbaum Associates.

Wood, W. (1982). Retrieval of attitude-relevant information from memory: Effects on susceptibility to persuasion and on intrinsic motivation. *Journal of Personality and Social Psychology, 42,* 798-810.

Zillman, D., Bryant, J., & Sapolsky, B. S. (1989). Enjoyment from sport spectatorship. In J. H. Goldstein (2nd Ed.), *Sport, Games and Play: Social & Psychology Viewpoints,* (p. 241-279). Hillsdale, N. J.: Lawrence Erlbaum Associates.

# CHAPTER 11

# Culture and Other Market Demand Variables:

# An Exploration With Professional Baseball in the USA and Taiwan

CHIA-YING (DORIS) LU
BRENDA G. PITTS

## Abstract

Even though the consumer of spectator sports in the United States has many choices, professional baseball is still one of the most popular sports. In Taiwan, however, the spectator has little choice-baseball is the only professional team sport. Unfortunately, there is very little

> In Taiwan the spectator has little choice—baseball is the only professional team sport.

research involving culture, other market demands, and baseball in America, and no research in Taiwan. Hence, the purpose of this study was to examine culture and other market demands in relation to factors that influence spectator attendance at professional baseball games in the Taiwan Major League (TML) and in minor league baseball (MiLB) in the United States. The findings revealed that fans in MiLB and TML have some different attendance factors. Especially, they have the most differences in the following factors: *offense of home team, offense on visiting team, defense of visiting team, official fan club member, special promotions, and going with family.*

## Introduction and Review of Literature

Baseball is one of the most popular sports in America. It has long occupied a special place in the cultural and social life of the United States (Land, Davis, & Blau, 1994). For example, in 2001, over 72 million spectators attended major league baseball (MLB) regular season games and the average attendance per game was 30,073 with 64.6% of seating capacity (percentage of seats occupied at home games; Thomas, 2001a, 2001b). Over 1.6 million people attended the playoffs and average attendance per game was 48,107 with almost 100% (96.2%) of seating capacity (Thomas, 2001c).

Although most public attention has been paid to major league baseball, minor league baseball (MiLB) has experienced resurgence in popularity in recent years, resulting in ever-increasing numbers of fans at the ballparks (Branvold, Pan, & Gabert, 1997). For example, attendance at MiLB games has grown from 11 million fans in 1975 (Morgenson, 1992) to 38.8 million in 2001 ("Attendance Hits 38.8 Million, Second Highest Ever," 2001). In the 2001 regular season alone, an average of 3,736 people attended per game in the MiLB games ("Attendance Hits 38.8 Million, Second Highest Ever," 2001). It has been found that historically the franchises that were virtually given away or sold for a low price, whereas today franchises are attracting offers of several hundred thousand dollars for Class A franchises to several million dollars for AAA franchises (Branvold et al., 1997; Johnson, 1993). In the same study, Branvold et al. also identified the two salient conjectural contentions that might explain this dramatic attendance increase: (1) the higher cost of attending major league games has made MiLB games an attractive economic alternative, and (2) the huge salaries and greater mobility enjoyed by major league players have reduced the fans' ability to relate to major league players. For the sport marketers, analyzing what factors account for this current booming phenomenon in MiLB would be beneficial.

**In Taiwan, baseball has become a major team sport partly because Taiwan teams have won consecutive Little League World Series Championships, Youth World Championships AA & AAA levels, as well as other amateur levels.**

In Taiwan, baseball has become a major team sport partly because Taiwan teams have won consecutive Little League World Series Championships, Youth World Championships AA & AAA levels, as well as other amateur levels. Professional baseball as a form of entertainment in Taiwan has been rapidly growing, beginning with the Chinese Professional Baseball League (CPBL) in 1990.

In its modest beginnings in 1990, the CPBL had only four teams-Elephants, Lions, Dragons, and Tigers. However, fan attendance has increased gradually, with a tremendous surge of interest after Chinese Taipei won a silver medal in baseball in the Barcelona Olympic Games in 1992. More and more enterprises wanted to join the CPBL. Being wary of overexpansion, the CPBL decided to allow only two more teams-Bulls and Eagles-to join the league. Being unable to join the league, two companies, Sampo and ERA together formed a second professional baseball league, the Taiwan Major League (TML), in 1997 (Chen, 2000).

The China Trust Whales joined the CPBL in 1998. However, three teams-Eagles, Tigers and Dragons-were terminated during 1998 and 1999. In 1999, the remaining four teams in the CPBL-Elephants, Lions, Bulls, and Whales-averaged 1,786 spectators per game for a total of 496,433 spectators. The TML had four teams with an average of 3,296 spectators per game and a total attendance of 553,659 spectators.

However, in 1996, there was a bribery scandal in the CPBL. This scandal influenced the whole Taiwan society dreadfully. Professional baseball was not perceived as a pure and clean game anymore. The role model function of professional baseball players was in question. In addition, the launching of the TML and the transference of star CPBL players to the TML in 1997 heavily affected attendance in the CPBL in 1997 (Liu, 1999). In Table 1, it is obvious that attendance in the CPBL has decreased significantly since the 1997 season. In addition, after six years of splitting the market, the two leagues finally decided to merge into one in the beginning of 2003. Two TML teams (Gida & Agan) joined CPBL, and there are six teams playing in the new CPBL this

**However, in 1996, there was a bribery scandal in the CPBL. Professional baseball was not perceived as a pure and clean game anymore.**

season. Although according to CPBL, the attendance has shown little comeback since last year, and strategies for attracting more people to games is an important issue for teams and the league.

Live games and televised games are the main products of professional sport teams. Indeed, professional sports exist for the purpose of entertaining spectators. Hence, game attendance is critical. It has been shown that gate receipts (sales of tickets and admission fees to games) can be a major source

Table 1 **Attendance of the Chinese Professional Baseball League and the Taiwan Major League**

| Year | CPBL Attendance | CPBL Per Game Average | TML Attendance | TML Per Game Average |
|------|-----------------|------------------------|----------------|----------------------|
| 1990 | 899,955 | 5,000 | ------ | ------ |
| 1991 | 1,238,063 | 6,878 | ------ | ------ |
| 1992 | 1,600,549 | 5,928 | ------ | ------ |
| 1993 | 1,607,677 | 5,954 | ------ | ------ |
| 1995 | 1,646,391 | 5,488 | ------ | ------ |
| 1996 | 1,364,424 | 4,548 | ------ | ------ |
| 1997 | 685,832 | 2,041 | 696,999 | 3,630 |
| 1998 | 690,089 | 2,191 | 695,936 | 3,222 |
| 1999 | 496,433 | 1,786 | 553,659 | 3,296 |
| 2000 (7/31/00) | 207,403 | 1,673 | 397,494 | 3,936 |

of revenue for major and minor professional sports teams and leagues. Other revenue sources include public funds, private sector investment, sponsorship funding, and media broadcasting rights fees. For some professional sports, revenue from ticket sales can account for as much as 60% of total revenue (Howard & Crompton, 1995; Howard & Crompton, 2004; Saudohar & Mangan, 1991; Zhang, Pease, & Smith, 1998). Green (1995) determined that attracting fans to games is the major avenue for professional sports franchises to distinguish themselves from the rest of their league. He also indicated that in order to increase their profits, home teams need to effectively utilize various marketing strategies to increase attendance.

## Consumer Behavior and Sport Business

The sport business industry has experienced phenomenal growth in a short period of time (Pitts & Stotlar, 2002). A successful marketing strategy can play a very important role in the sport business. Understanding sport event consumer behavior can help sport event managers and marketers to provided a more successful product. Therefore, consumer behavior theory is an important framework for study in sport event business.

Consumer behavior is an essential foundation for examining factors that might influence attendance at professional sports events. Consumer behavior literature shows that there are three categories of factors that affect consumer behavior: external influences, internal influences, and the consumer decision-making process (Louden & Della Brita, 1993; Miniard, Bhatla & Rose, 1990; Schiffman & Kanuk, 2000; Stahl, 1986).

## Culture Shapes Different Lifestyles

Consumers are surrounded by a host of external influences during their decision-making process. The external environmental influences are made up of five specific influences: *culture and subculture, social class, gender, race/ethnicity, and significant others.*

In society's broader framework, there are many cultures, subcultures, and countercultures that may nurture different lifestyles (Mullin, Hardy, & Sutton, 2000). Loudon and Della Bitta (1993) defined the concept of culture as "that complex whole that includes knowledge, belief, art, morals, law custom, and any other capabilities and habits acquired by man as a member of society. . . . the distinctive way of life of a group of people, their complete design for living. (p. 84)".

> **The external environmental influences are made up of five specific influences: culture and subculture, social class, gender, race/ethnicity, and significant others.**

*Culture* is one of the important components of consumer behavior. It can be seen as a characteristic of a society. Culture always changes because its dynamics interact with people who live within it and over time. Culture thus establishes its own vision of the world, with its own unique set of appropriate norms of beliefs and behavior (Schütte & Ciarlante, 1998). Therefore, Western culture is different from the Eastern culture; American culture is distinct from Hispanic culture, Asian culture, or European culture. Therefore, even on the same sport of baseball, the fan experience at the ball game and the reasons that people attending ball game differ from country to country.

*Subculture* can be referred to as a distinct cultural group that exists as an identifiable segment within a larger, more complex society (Schiffman & Kanuk, 2000). In the same country, people might be homogeneous in many ways because they are educated by the same culture, grow up in the same society, and possess with the similar values. However, members in the specific subculture tend to have unique beliefs, values, and customs that set them apart from other members of the same society (Schiffman & Kahuk, 2000). Thus, the behavior of baby boomers is different from Generation X-ers. For marketers, analyzing and identifying culture and subculture is a basic step so they can select and concentrate on their own particular consumer market segments.

> **Even on the same sport of baseball, the fan experience at the ball game and the reasons that people attending ball game differ from country to country.**

Sport marketing researchers (Green, 1995; Greenstein & Marcum, 1981; Hansen & Gauthier, 1989; Schofield, 1983; Zhang, Pease, Hui, & Michaud, 1995a; Zhang, Smith, Pease, & Jambor, 1997b; Zhang, Smith, Pease, & Lam, 1998) have generally concluded that the factors that affect spectator game attendance fall into the following four categories: (a) *game attractiveness* (e.g., individual skills, team records, league standing, record-breaking performance, closeness of competition, special events, and entertainment), (b) *economic* (e.g., ticket price, substitute forms of entertainment, television effect, and competition of other sport events), (c) *sociodemographic* (e.g., population, age, gender, ethnicity, occupation, education, and geography), and (d) *audience preference* (e.g., schedule, convenience, weather, stadium quality, and team history in a community). Figure 1 illustrates a model that we developed based on these categories and the many factors within each. Following is a brief description of each.

*Sociodemographic factors* include basic demographical and sociocultural characteristics including age, gender, ethnicity, occupation, education, income, and household status as well as geographical factors such as distance to the park and transportation type (Green, 1995; Hansen & Gauthier, 1989; Kasky, 1994). By collecting this type of information from spectators, the sport organizations should be able to develop a marketing plan and, ultimately, a product that is more customized to their consumers. For instance, driving distance and stadium location can influence an individual's intention to go to a game. It has been indicated that new stadiums located in the more densely populated areas have higher attendance (Hill, Madura, & Zuber, 1982). However, while population size has been found to have a positive effect on attendance (Hansen & Gauthier, 1989), the presence of ethnic groups has been identified as having a negative effect on game attendance (Schofield, 1983; Siegfried & Eisenberg, 1980; Zhang, Smith, Pease, & Mahar, 1996).

Figure 1 **The Lu & Pitts Model of Attendance Factors** (Developed From Previous Research)

| Sociodemographic Factors | Economic Factors | Game Attractiveness Factors | Audience Preferences Factors |
|---|---|---|---|
| 1. Gender<br>2. Age<br>3. Marital/household status<br>4. Highest education level<br>5. Numbers of children (18 years old and under)<br>6. Annual household income<br>7. Ethnicity<br>8. Occupation<br>9. Games attend each year<br>10. Season ticket holder<br>11. Transportation type<br>12. Distance to the ballpark | 1. Price of a ticket<br>2. Price of season ticket<br>3. Price of concessions<br>4. TV/Radio coverage of the home game in the local area<br>5. TV coverage of another sport event at time of the home game<br>6. Other sporting events in the area<br>7. Other activities taking place nearby<br>8. Other professional franchises in area | 1. Record (won-loss) of home team<br>2. Record (won-loss) of visitor team<br>3. Number of star players on home team<br>4. Number of star players on visitor's team<br>5. Offensive performance of the home team<br>6. Defensive performance of the home team<br>7. Offensive performance of the visitor's team<br>8. Defensive performance of the visitor's team<br>9. Closeness of competition<br>10. Games with rival teams<br>11. A chance to see a record breaking performance by a team or athlete<br>12. Special promotion (hat day, poster day, etc.)<br>13. Home team's place in the division standings<br>14. Home team's place in the league standings<br>15. Home team's involvement in race for a playoff spot<br>16. Media advertising (TV, Radio, Newspaper, Internet, etc.) | 1. Day games during the weekdays<br>2. Night games during the weekdays<br>3. Weekend day game<br>4. Weekend night game<br>5. Weather conditions<br>6. Cleanliness of the facility<br>7. Easy and/or multiple access to your facility<br>8. Availability of parking at or near facility<br>9. Size of the facility (seating capacity)<br>10. The crowd behavior at the game<br>11. New stadium or arena<br>12. Number of years the team has been in the area<br>13. The variety of concessions available<br>14. Violence in the game<br>15. The design and color of uniform<br>16. Going with family<br>17. Going with friends |

Age matters. It has been shown that young to middle-aged white males are most likely to attend professional sporting events (Greenstein & Marcum, 1981; Noll, 1974; Scully, 1974; Siegfried & Eisenberg, 1980; Simmons Market Research Bureau, 1990; Whitney, 1988; Zhang et al., 1996). While promotions are perceived as one of the most important strategies to attract people to games, promotion was found to have a negative relationship with age (Zhang, Pease, & Saffici, 1995b).

*Economic factors* include such factors as the costs of the tickets and other amenities, availability of substitute forms of

**The low cost of living and warm climate make Tampa an attractive area for leagues to place franchises. However, those same advantages have also become detrimental, as there is heavy competition within a crowded sports marketplace.**

entertainment or activities, television, and other sports events in the area. In general, most research reports show that these factors tend to have a more negative effect on sports event attendance (Hansen & Gauthier, 1989; Jones, 1984; Zhang et al., 1995a; Zhang et al., 1996). For instance, consumers may have a budget and, therefore, attending a sports event depends upon the many costs associated with the event (Green, 1995).

An area may contain several sport organizations that provide alternative sport entertainment choices for the consumer. For example, an article that examined the sport market in the Tampa Bay area reported that the low cost of living and warm climate make Tampa an attractive area for leagues to place franchises. However, those same advantages have also become detrimental, as there is heavy competition within a crowded sports marketplace. The sport marketers are not only competing with professional sports teams, they are also competing with such local attractions as Busch Gardens, Disney World, and the beach (Williams, 2001a, 2001b).

Zhang and Smith (1997a) indicated that "it is noteworthy that broadcasting of professional sports has become a central part of corporate planning of major league teams, broadcasters, and related organizations" (p. 23). However, studies related to professional sports found that televising a home game would negatively affect game attendance (Demmert, 1973; Noll, 1974; Zhang & Smith, 1997a). On the other hand, Zhang and Smith reported that "TV broadcasting of away games would increase attendance; cable TV access would not affect attendance; and radio broadcasting would increase attendance" (p. 23).

**However, since winning is not everything, only 25% of fans attended sporting events because of the team's winning record in another study.**

*Game attractiveness* includes such factors as player skills, team records, league standing, record-breaking performance, closeness of competition, special events, promotions, and entertainment. Game attractiveness factors have been found to be positively related to game attendance (Zhang et al., 1996). In one study, it was found that when the outcome of the game is predictably in favor of the winning team, attendance remains high (Demmert, 1973). However, since winning is not everything, only 25% of fans attended sporting events because of the team's winning record in another study (Greenstein & Marcum, 1981).

Game day promotions or other forms of promotions can affect attendance. Game day promotions are one of many marketing strategies used by sport organizations to attract more fans. Sales promotions have traditionally been in the form of price or nonprice promotions in professional sport (Mullin, Hardy, & Sutton, 2000; Pitts & Stotlar, 2002). Price promotions occur when an individual spectator or a selected group is admitted to the game at less than the regular price (e.g., 2-for-1 night, senior's night, kid's night). Nonprice promotions are those strategies where an individual fan or a selected group of fans receive merchandise or when value-added entertainment (e.g. firework displays, San Diego Chicken Night) is provided (McDonald & Rascher, 2000).

In general, promotions have been found to have a positive impact on attendance (Hill et al., 1982; Marcum & Greenstein, 1985; McDonald & Rascher, 2000; Zhang et al., 1995a; Zhang et al., 1996). Specifically, it has been found that promotion and income level are highly positive (Hill et al., 1982; Marcum & Greenstein, 1985; Zhang et al., 1995a; Zhang et al., 1996). In a study by McDonald and Rascher (2000), results showed that promotions have a discernible 14% impact on single game attendance among 19 MLB teams.

Some fans perceive themselves as "part of history" if they are able to see a record broken during a game. It has been found that the opportunity to see a record-breaking performance appears to be the most important factor influencing attendance at sporting events (Green, 1995). Many fans believe it is important to be associated with a winner

**It has been found that the opportunity to see a record-breaking performance appears to be the most important factor influencing attendance at sporting events.**

and are more likely to follow the team if they are winning or have a chance of getting in the playoffs (Schofield, 1983).

Fillingham (1977) reported several factors that could affect attendance: a strong rivalry between teams, the record-breaking performances of athletes, and the presence of outstanding athletes. While some baseball franchises are spending vast amounts of money to sign with star players, a study conducted by Noll (1974) showed that the number of star players on the team would attract fans to see the game. Specifically, Green (1995) reported that star players seem to be more important to basketball fans than to fans of other sports.

Lastly, it has been reported that the competitive level of the game attracts spectators (Hill et al., 1982) and that "spectators do prefer games featuring their favorite team, but they prefer games featuring the most disliked team only when that team is seen as a threat to the spectator's favorite team" (Mahony & Howard, 1998, p. 96).

*Audience preference factors* include such factors as game schedule, convenience, accommodation availability, weather, stadium quality, and team history in a community. Those factors were labeled as "environmental factors" by Green (1995) and "residual preference" by Hansen and Gauthier (1989).

Consumers have certain expectations about their comfort level when attending games (Green, 1995). Fans may want to attend a game in a relatively clean facility, sit with controlled crowds, and have readily available concessions, an easy parking area at available times as well as acceptable weather conditions.

Audience preference variables have been found to be positively related to game attendance (Zhang et al., 1996). Schedule and facility convenience (game period, day of week, weather, and accessibility to go to the game) have been found to have a significantly positive relationship with attendance and Fillingham (1977) reported that cleanliness and accessibility of the facility, and the scheduling of games are significant factors. In a study examining game-by-game attendance, it was found that one of the major factors is day of the week (Marcum & Greenstein, 1985). In another study involving MLB, accessibility to the game, games on weekends and doubleheader games positively affected fan attendance (Hill et al., 1982).

# Purpose of the Study

There is very little research involving culture, other market demands and baseball even though professional baseball is a popular spectator activity in the United States. In Taiwan, however, the spectator has little choice-baseball is the only professional team sport. Furthermore, we found no research involving consumer behavior and baseball in Taiwan. However, sport marketers need information that can help them with decisions to provide a more successful product. Information from sport marketing research can provide empirical

> **We found no research involving consumer behavior and baseball in Taiwan. However, sport marketers need information that can help them with decisions to provide a more successful product.**

support for marketing plans, management decisions, and marketing strategies to increase game attendance in both countries. Additionally, contributing to the small body of research involving consumer behavior in the sport marketing literature is needed. Furthering what we know about this area can greatly enhance our current understanding and add significantly to the current discourse in order to advance contemporary theory and research about culture and sport consumer behavior. Hence, the purpose of this study was to examine culture and other market demands in relation to factors that influence spectator attendance at professional baseball games in the TML and in minor league baseball in the United States. Based on the purpose of the study, we examined whether sociodemographic, economic, game attractiveness, and audience preferences factors as identified in previous research (refer to Figure 1) were influences on consumer behavior to attend games.

## Subjects

Rea and Parker (1997) state that populations of less than one hundred thousand could be considered small; therefore, the population of ball game attendance in this study was viewed as a small sample size. A 95% level of confidence in a population size of 5,000, with a ±5% margin of error, was applied in this study. In 2000, the average attendance per game of the TML was 3,381 and of the Southern League was 3,619. Therefore, according to Rea and Parker, "357" was considered to be the minimum sample size. Because the purpose of this study was to compare the spectators in two professional baseball leagues in two countries, a total minimum number of 714 surveys would be needed. Assuming that some surveys would not be useable for a variety of reasons, a larger number, 800 (400 from each league) would be collected.

**Data for this study were collected at four Southern League games and four TML games during the 2001 season. Minor league baseball was selected over major league baseball to compare to the TML because minor league baseball is much more comparable to TML baseball in most ways.**

Data for this study were collected at four Southern League games and four TML games during the 2001 season. Minor league baseball was selected over major league baseball to compare to the TML because minor league baseball is much more comparable to TML baseball in most ways. As a result, 460 spectators from the Southern League and 402 spectators (total of 862) voluntarily completed the survey (refer to Table 2).

One to three trained study assistants assisted at each game to collect data in the ballparks. To enhance random selection, a *mall approach* was used. Using this sampling method, the researchers and the assistants walked around the stadium grounds and inside the stadium, approached attendees in a random manner and asked them to participate in the survey. Additionally, a cross-section of attendees was sought by approaching attendees in various sections of the stadium: behind home plate, left field, center filed, and right field. This attempt was made based on the assumption that seats in those sections were priced at different levels, and therefore those attendees would represent different demographic groups. Fans were asked to participate in the survey 30 minutes prior to the game and throughout the game. Willing attendees then completed a survey and a consent form. A total of 862 people participated in the study by completing the survey.

Table 2  **Number of Surveys Collected From Eight Ballparks**

| Leagues | Ballparks | N | % |
|---|---|---|---|
| **U.S. Minor League** | Mobile | 92 | 20.0 |
| | Jacksonville | 115 | 25.0 |
| | Birmingham | 123 | 26.7 |
| | Greenville | 130 | 28.3 |
| | Total | 460 | 100.0 |
| **Taiwan Major League** | Taichung | 93 | 23.1 |
| | Chiayi | 53 | 13.2 |
| | Kaohsiung | 102 | 25.4 |
| | Taipei | 154 | 38.3 |
| **Total** | | 402 | 100.0 |

## Instrument

The questions in the survey used in this study were developed from those surveys used in the previous studies of Green (1995), Hansen and Gauthier (1989), Kasky (1994), Schofield (1983), and Zhang et al. (1995a). An English version for American fans and a Chinese version for Taiwanese fans were used. The first part of the survey examined 41 factors that affect attendance, while a second part of the questionnaire contained 13 questions concerning demographic data. A 5-point Likert Scale was used for scoring the survey instrument. The 5 points influencing rate were translated as follows: 1 = strongly disagree, 2 = disagree, 3 = neutral, 4 = agree, 5 = strongly agree.

## Reliability and Validity

Using Cronbach's alpha to test the reliability of the factors in the economic category, game attractiveness category, and audience preferences category and found reliability scores of .68, .87 and .71, respectively. The alpha coefficient for the total scale except the sociodemographic category was a .85 reliability coefficient. Because .85 is close to a perfect score, which is 1.00, overall, the instrument had an acceptable level reliability.

"The validity of a measurement instrument is the degree to which the instrument actually measures what it is supposed to measure" (Cicciarella, 1997, p. 79). Previous researchers all conducted studies relating to spectator attendance at sporting events (Green, 1995; Hansen & Gauthier, 1989; Kasky, 1994; Schofield, 1983; Zhang et al., 1995a). From the results of the previous studies, certain content areas are considered well represented. Although those researchers labeled attendance factors slightly differently, all researchers grouped factors according to a specific content area. The categorizations of factors indicate content validity for this study.

## Analysis of Data

First, descriptive statistics of the composite scores were calculated for each sociodemographic factor. Second, the data were analyzed by using univariate analysis of variance (ANOVA) to test for the differences between two leagues. Significance was set at .05. Procedure from the Statistical Package for Social Science (SPSS 10.0 version) was used to conduct the statistical analysis.

# Results, Conclusions, and Discussion

### Sociodemographic Factors

*Gender.* The results of this study indicated that both leagues had similar gender distribution in their attendances (refer to Tables 3a, 3b, 4, 5a, 5b, and 6). When examining female attendance to TML games, they composed 43.1% while males composed 56.9% of the total attendance. The percentage of female attendance in the 2001 season was 50.8%. In the MiLB, females composed 44.6% of the fans while males composed 55.4% of the total attendance. These finding are similar to previous studies of spectator attendance in which females composed at least 35% of the fans attending professional baseball games (Hansen & Gauthier, 1993; Liu, 1999; Green, 1995; Professional Baseball Promotion Corp., 2001).

*Age*

In regard to age as a factor affecting game attendance, the typical TML fan was 24.2 years old (± 8.5) while the average age in the MiLB was 40.1 years old (±13.6). Furthermore, TML fans in the 13-24 age group accounted for more than half of the total fans (58.5%), while this same age group attending MiLB accounted for only 13.0% of the fans. Composition of that age segment was found to be 47.8% students, and 81.5% singles in the TML, compared to the MiLB fans in which 9.0% were students and 21.9% were single.

*Highest Education Level*

Focusing on Americans aged 25 years or older, according to U.S. Census 2000, 82% were high school educated, 31% have an associate's degree or higher, 16% an undergraduate level degree or higher, and 9% a graduate or professional degree (U.S. Census Bureau, 2002a).

Table 3a **Descriptive Statistics for the Demographic Variables in U.S. ($n$=460)**

| Variables | Category | $n$ | % | Cumulative % |
|---|---|---|---|---|
| Gender | Female | 205 | 44.6 | 44.6 |
| | Male | 255 | 55.4 | 100.0 |
| Age | 13-18 | 31 | 7.1 | 7.1 |
| | 19-24 | 26 | 6.0 | 13.0 |
| | 25-29 | 34 | 7.7 | 20.8 |
| | 30-34 | 53 | 12.1 | 33.1 |
| | 35-39 | 60 | 13.7 | 46.8 |
| | 40-44 | 79 | 18.1 | 64.8 |
| | 45-49 | 50 | 11.4 | 76.3 |
| | 50-54 | 39 | 8.9 | 85.2 |
| | 55-59 | 29 | 6.7 | 91.8 |
| | 60-64 | 19 | 4.4 | 96.1 |
| | 65-69 | 7 | 1.6 | 97.7 |
| | 70-74 | 4 | 0.9 | 98.6 |
| | 75-79 | 4 | 0.8 | 99.8 |
| | 80-84 | 1 | 0.2 | 100.0 |
| Marital/ household Status | Single | 100 | 21.9 | 21.9 |
| | Married/Partner | 309 | 67.8 | 89.7 |
| | Divorced | 39 | 8.6 | 98.2 |
| | Widowed | 8 | 1.8 | 100.0 |
| Highest Education Level | Junior High | 8 | 1.8 | 1.8 |
| | High School | 139 | 31.1 | 32.9 |
| | Undergraduate | 196 | 43.8 | 76.7 |
| | Graduate school | 104 | 23.3 | 100.0 |

In comparison, 98.2% of MiLB fans have a high school diploma and above degree, 43.8% of fans received bachelor's degrees and 23.3% of fans have achieved a masters and above degree level. The education levels of minor league fans are higher than the average American.

In Taiwan, according to the 2000 Population and Housing Census, 68.4% of Taiwanese had at least graduated from high school, and 24.8% of Taiwanese received an associate degree or higher (Directorate General of Budget Accounting and Statistics Executive Yuan, R. O. C., 2002a).

**Table 3b  Descriptive Statistics for the Demographic Variables in U.S. (n=460)** (continued)

| Variables | Category | n | % | Cumulative % |
|---|---|---|---|---|
| Annual Household Income | >$19,999 | 15 | 3.9 | 3.9 |
| | $20,000-$29,999 | 23 | 6.0 | 9.9 |
| | $30,000-$39,999 | 44 | 11.4 | 21.3 |
| | $40,000-$49,999 | 37 | 9.6 | 30.9 |
| | $50,000-$59,999 | 55 | 14.3 | 45.2 |
| | $60,000-$69,999 | 36 | 9.4 | 54.5 |
| | $70,000-$79,999 | 34 | 8.8 | 63.4 |
| | $80,000-$89,999 | 41 | 10.6 | 74.0 |
| | $90,000-$99,999 | 21 | 5.5 | 79.5 |
| | $100,000-$109,999 | 21 | 5.5 | 84.9 |
| | $110,000-$119,999 | 9 | 2.3 | 87.3 |
| | $120,000+ | 49 | 12.7 | 100.0 |
| Ethnicity | American Indian | 2 | 0.4 | 0.4 |
| | African American | 11 | 2.4 | 2.8 |
| | Asian | 6 | 1.3 | 4.1 |
| | Caucasian | 417 | 92.7 | 96.8 |
| | Hispanic | 5 | 1.1 | 97.9 |
| | Multi | 4 | 0.9 | 98.8 |
| | Others | 5 | 1.1 | 100.0 |
| Occupation | Blue Collar | 29 | 6.5 | 6.5 |
| | Clerk | 14 | 3.2 | 9.7 |
| | Education | 43 | 9.7 | 19.4 |
| | Housewife/husband | 24 | 5.4 | 24.8 |
| | Management | 79 | 17.8 | 42.7 |
| | Military | 12 | 2.7 | 45.4 |
| | Professional | 120 | 27.1 | 72.5 |
| | Retired | 19 | 4.3 | 76.8 |
| | Sales | 21 | 4.7 | 81.5 |
| | Self-employed | 5 | 1.1 | 82.6 |
| | Student | 40 | 9.0 | 91.6 |
| | Technical | 19 | 4.3 | 95.9 |
| | Others | 19 | 4.9 | 100.0 |

In comparison, 86.3% of Taiwanese baseball fans have a high school diploma and above education level, and 43.0% have bachelor's degree. Results showed the TML spectators are more educated than Taiwan's average.

However, when university education is examined and compared between both countries, the percentage of people with an undergraduate degree is similar between the TML and the MiLB (43.0% and 43.8%, respectively). Furthermore, 23.3% of minor league spectators have a graduate degree and only 0.8% of TML spectators.

*Graduate Level Education*

Looking beyond the statistical data, there are two possible explanations for such a difference in the percentage of American and Taiwanese fans with graduate-level education.

First, in Taiwan, people need to pass a national high school entrance exam (this requirement was abolished two years ago, entrance is now based on academic grades and merit). In addition, a college entrance exam was required for individuals to obtain higher education. Furthermore, unlike the United States where there is compulsory K-12 education; mandatory education in Taiwan is 1-9 only. Naturally, therefore, the number of Taiwanese fans who are high school educated or above is lower

Table 4 **Descriptive Statistics for the Advanced Demographic Variables in U.S. ($n$=460)**

| Variables | Category | n | % | Cumulative% |
|---|---|---|---|---|
| **Season Ticket Holder** | Yes | 44 | 9.6 | 9.6 |
| | No | 410 | 89.9 | 100.0 |
| **Fan Club Member** | Yes | 6 | 1.3 | 1.3 |
| | No | 448 | 98.7 | 100.0 |
| **Games Attended Per Year** | 1-10 | 356 | 78.4 | 78.4 |
| | 11-20 | 50 | 11.0 | 89.4 |
| | 21-30 | 13 | 2.9 | 92.3 |
| | 31-40 | 11 | 2.4 | 94.7 |
| | 41-50 | 5 | 1.1 | 95.8 |
| | 51-60 | 4 | 0.9 | 96.7 |
| | 60+ | 15 | 3.3 | 100.0 |
| **Transportation** | Driving Cars | 446 | 97.8 | 97.8 |
| | Bus | 5 | 1.1 | 98.9 |
| | Subway | 2 | 0.4 | 99.3 |
| | Taxi | 1 | 0.2 | 99.6 |
| | Motorcycle | 2 | 0.4 | 100.0 |
| **Miles Traveled** | 0-10 | 140 | 30.8 | 30.8 |
| | 11-24 | 129 | 28.4 | 59.1 |
| | 25-49 | 95 | 20.9 | 80.0 |
| | 50-74 | 49 | 10.8 | 90.8 |
| | 75-100 | 18 | 4.0 | 94.7 |
| | 100+ | 24 | 5.3 | 100.0 |

than that of the United States Minor League, as there are 11.9% less graduates.

Secondly, a large portion of the fan base of Taiwanese baseball (30.6%) is composed of high school students aged 13 to 18 (Lu, 2001) who have yet to start their university education.

*Income Status*

According to the definition of The World Bank Group (2002), the gross national product (GNP) per capita is the dollar value of a country's final output of goods and services in a year divided by its population. It reflects the average income of a country's citizens. Knowing a country's GNP per capita is the first step toward understanding its economic strengths and needs. In 2001, according to Bureau of Economic Analysis (as cited in White House, 2002), the GNP per capita of U.S. was $23,639 compared to $12,941 in Taiwan (Directorate General of Budget Accounting and Statistics Executive Yuan, R. O. C., 2002b). In 2000, according to U.S. Bureau of the Census (as cited in White House, 2002), the average household income

> In comparing the average annual household incomes of fans in both countries we see substantial difference. In the Taiwan Major League, the mean of the annual household income was in the $50,000-$59,999 level while it was in the $60,000-$69,999 level in the Southern League.

Table 5a **Descriptive Statistics for Demographic Variables in Taiwan (*n*=402)**

| Variables | Category | n | % | Cumulative % |
|---|---|---|---|---|
| **Gender** | Female | 174 | 43.1 | 43.1 |
| | Male | 228 | 56.9 | 100.0 |
| | | | | |
| **Age** | 13-18 | 121 | 30.6 | 30.6 |
| | 19-24 | 110 | 27.9 | 58.5 |
| | 25-29 | 71 | 18.0 | 76.5 |
| | 30-34 | 41 | 10.3 | 86.8 |
| | 35-39 | 28 | 8.1 | 93.9 |
| | 40-44 | 15 | 3.8 | 97.7 |
| | 45-49 | 4 | 1.0 | 98.7 |
| | 50-54 | 3 | 0.8 | 99.5 |
| | 55-59 | 0 | 0.0 | 99.5 |
| | 60-64 | 2 | 0.5 | 100.0 |
| | | | | |
| **Marital/Household Status** | Single | 325 | 81.5 | 81.5 |
| | Married/Partner | 71 | 17.8 | 99.2 |
| | Divorced | 3 | 0.8 | 100.0 |
| | | | | |
| **Highest Education Level** | Elementary | 1 | 0.3 | 0.3 |
| | Junior High | 53 | 13.4 | 13.7 |
| | High School | 168 | 42.5 | 56.2 |
| | Undergraduate | 170 | 43.0 | 99.2 |
| | Graduate school | 3 | 0.8 | 100.0 |

of the U.S. was $42,148 compared to $22,601 in Taiwan (Directorate General of Budget Accounting and Statistics Executive Yuan, R. O.C., 2002c).

In comparing the average annual household incomes of fans in both countries we see substantial difference. In the Taiwan Major League, the mean of the annual household income was in the $50,000-$59,999 level while it was in the $60,000-$69,999 level in the Southern League.

### Ethnicity

For obvious reasons, the fans of Taiwanese baseball are Asian; however, several Caucasian students were observed attending the game in Taipei-students from America, Britain, and other countries who came to Taiwan to learn Chinese. For many it was their first time attending a game. TML may like to introduce international students to the game. They can have group ticket sales with those Chinese schools that offer classes to international students. Additionally, they can offer tickets give-a-way on local Chinese or English radio stations to promote the TML games.

Table 5b **Descriptive Statistics for Demographic Variables in Taiwan ($n$=402)** (continued)

| Variables | Category | n | % | Cumulative % |
|---|---|---|---|---|
| **Annual Household Income** | >$19,999 | 15 | 3.9 | 3.9 |
| | $20,000-$29,999 | 23 | 6.0 | 9.9 |
| | $30,000-$39,999 | 44 | 11.4 | 21.3 |
| | $40,000-$49,999 | 37 | 9.6 | 30.9 |
| | $50,000-$59,999 | 55 | 14.3 | 45.2 |
| | $60,000-$69,999 | 36 | 9.4 | 54.5 |
| | $70,000-$79,999 | 34 | 8.8 | 63.4 |
| | $80,000-$89,999 | 41 | 10.6 | 74.0 |
| | $90,000-$99,999 | 21 | 5.5 | 79.5 |
| | $100,000-$109,999 | 21 | 5.5 | 84.9 |
| | $110,000-$119,999 | 9 | 2.3 | 87.3 |
| | $120,000+ | 49 | 12.7 | 100.0 |
| **Ethnicity** | Asian | 402 | 100.0 | 100.0 |
| **Occupation** | Blue Collar | 34 | 8.7 | 8.7 |
| | Clerk | 12 | 3.1 | 11.8 |
| | Education | 6 | 1.5 | 13.3 |
| | Housewife/husband | 8 | 2.0 | 15.3 |
| | Management | 22 | 5.6 | 21.0 |
| | Military | 7 | 1.8 | 22.8 |
| | Professional | 64 | 16.4 | 39.1 |
| | Retired | 0 | 0.0 | 39.1 |
| | Sales | 27 | 6.9 | 46.0 |
| | Self-employed | 0 | 0.0 | 46.0 |
| | Student | 187 | 47.8 | 93.9 |
| | Technical | 5 | 1.3 | 95.1 |
| | Others | 19 | 4.9 | 100.0 |

According to the U.S. Census 2000 (U.S. Census Bureau, 2002b), 75.1% of the people in the U.S. were Caucasian, 12.5% were Hispanic or Latino, 12.3% were Black or African American, and 3.6% were Asian.

By averaging the racial percentage of counties within the 50-mile radius of four ballparks, 77.37% are Caucasians, 19.43% are African Americans, 2.25% are Hispanics, 0.68% are Asians. However, with data collection in ballparks, Caucasians (92.7%) composed the largest proportion in the fan base in the minor league baseball while only 2.4% of the fans were African American, 1.3% were Asian, and 1.1% were Hispanic.

Comparing the demographic results in this study to the Census 2000 data, there is a potential market in the local African-American residents and the Hispanic community as well. There is still great opportunity to increase the involvement of fans from Asian backgrounds.

The Street & Smith's *SportsBusiness Journal* reported that the Hispanic population increased by at least 100,000 in all but eight of the 24 U.S. baseball markets from 1990 to 2000. During that same 10-year span, the Asian population in seven MLB markets increased by 100,000 or more and by 45,000 or more in all but nine markets (King, 2002a).

Table 6  **Descriptive Statistics for Advanced Demographic Variables in Taiwan (*n*=402)**

| Variables | Category | *n* | % | Cumulative % |
|---|---|---|---|---|
| **Season Ticket Holder** | Yes | 77 | 19.7 | 19.7 |
| | No | 314 | 80.3 | 100.0 |
| **Fan Club Member** | Yes | 62 | 15.7 | 15.7 |
| | No | 333 | 84.3 | 100.0 |
| **Games Attended Per Year** | 1-10 | 186 | 47.2 | 47.2 |
| | 11-20 | 100 | 25.4 | 72.6 |
| | 21-30 | 55 | 14.0 | 86.5 |
| | 31-40 | 28 | 7.1 | 93.7 |
| | 41-50 | 25 | 6.3 | 100.0 |
| **Transportation** | Driving Cars | 128 | 32.1 | 32.1 |
| | Bus | 50 | 12.5 | 44.6 |
| | Subway | 6 | 1.5 | 46.1 |
| | Taxi | 18 | 4.5 | 50.6 |
| | Motorcycle | 180 | 45.1 | 95.7 |
| | Walk | 13 | 3.3 | 99.0 |
| | Others | 1 | 0.3 | 99.3 |
| | Bus & Subway | 3 | 0.8 | 100.0 |
| **Miles Traveled** | 0-10 | 217 | 55.4 | 55.4 |
| | 11-24 | 114 | 29.1 | 84.4 |
| | 25-49 | 47 | 12.0 | 96.4 |
| | 50-74 | 5 | 1.3 | 97.7 |
| | 75-100 | 3 | 0.8 | 98.5 |
| | 100+ | 6 | 1.5 | 100.0 |

With the American population more diverse than ever, this is evident in the composition of players in the professional baseball. In 2002, almost half of the players who are under contract with either MLB or MiLB were foreigners, and more than 80% of foreign-born major league players come from countries such as Japan, Korea, Puerto Rico, Mexico, Venezuela, and the Dominican Republic (King, 2002b). People like to see players from their own country. With more resources, MLB teams use different promotional methods to reach their fans and tailor specific marketing strategy to access different demographics. For example, due to a large Hispanic population in Houston, the Houston Astros have a Spanish version of the official team website, and Spanish-speaking channels carry the radio broadcasts. In addition, the Seattle Mariners and the LA Dodgers have a linkage on the website to MLB.com in Japanese because it features all the Japanese major leaguers.

> **However, there are still many marketing avenues open to a MiLB ball club to reach the African American and Hispanic communities.**

Executive VP and Chief Marketing Officer of the LA Dodgers, Kris Rone, declared that about one-third of MLB franchises will broadcast at least a portion of their schedule on Spanish-language radio this 2002 season. These special efforts to recognize and accommodate various ethnic groups will surely broaden the fan base of teams and leagues; sport websites and often sponsors are now demanding that the franchise have an ethnic component as part of their program to increase their share in these ethnic markets. However, regardless of the opportunities of the ethnic market, few baseball clubs, though aware, have found efficient ways to capitalize on them (Rone, 2002).

Due to the limited resources and budgets of minor league teams, they often cannot utilize the same promotional methods as their MLB counterparts. However, there are still many marketing avenues open to a MiLB ball club to reach the African American and Hispanic communities. Marketing practitioners can reach potential costumers/fans by placing advertisements in local African American, Hispanic, or Asian newspapers, radio, and television channels. Promoting through the school systems by rewarding game tickets to students or offering ticket sweepstakes to teams who play in local parks and recreation baseball or softball leagues is also an option. For instance, the Dodgers provide sponsorship packages to those sponsors who are looking for different ethnicity markets; the MiLB teams can also provide a vehicle to those local sponsors who want to seek ways to reach Hispanic or Asian markets.

### Available Transportation and Miles Traveled

When comparing the available modes of transportation available to fans in Taiwan and America (see Tables 4 and 6), the major difference appears to be that while 97.8% of Americans selected the automobile as their preferred method, fans in the TML used various transportation to get to the ballpark.

Parking availability is also a critical factor that will influenced how people travel to watch a game. Fans in both leagues all agree that if there were more available parking spaces, they would like to attend more games.

> **In Taiwan and Japan, fan clubs have a very special place in professional sports. Sports players, entertainers, and celebrities have fan clubs, and all professional baseball teams have them.**

While the researchers and assistants visited these four Southern League ballparks and found that the parking conditions were very good, ballparks charged people two to four dollars for parking and there was sufficient parking for all the fans. However, in Taiwan, two of the four TML ballparks (Chiayi and Kaohsiung) are located in suburbs, and people claim it is easy to find parking spaces. The Kaohsiung ballpark even has a huge underground parking lot. The problem exists with the other two ballparks, Taipei and Taichung, which are located in the urban area or downtown. Although people use mass transportation methods to attend the games, parking is still a serious problem, especially in Taipei. The Taipei ballpark is in an urban mixed area where many residents and businesses are located; therefore, parking in that area is very limited. Fans traveling to the Taipei ballpark complain that they need more parking spaces. If the TML can solve the parking problem or offer easier transferring to public transit, fans would be more willing to come to the game.

### Number of Games Attended

Although in both the American minor league and the TML the average number of games attended fell to 11-20 games per year. Overall, MiLB fans averaged 15.3 games per person, while the TML fans averaged 20.0 games.

### Fan Clubs

In Taiwan and Japan, fan clubs have a very special place in professional sports. Sports players, entertainers, and celebrities have fan clubs, and all professional baseball teams have them. Fan clubs are interactive organizations between fans and the ball clubs, and they are run voluntarily by enthusiastic and loyal fans. Cultural differences in Taiwan and the United States also translate into different consumer behavior; therefore, the type of fan clubs prevalent in both countries naturally exhibit some differences.

> **Fans may accumulate points and exchange them for coupons, free game tickets, discounts, or even entering a sweepstakes. Not many minor league baseball teams have developed fan clubs similar to the TML or MLB**

In the TML, one team or individual player may also have several fan clubs. These clubs have activities not only during the games but all year around, and people who join the fan clubs tend to attend more ballgames.

Members of TML fan clubs would attend more games if their fan club would have more activities on the game day. While MLB teams such as the Florida Marlins or the Anaheim Angels have official adult or kids' fan club where fans pay membership fees and receive a fan club-only T-shirt, photos, or other promotional products, several MLB teams now have another type of official fan club where fans sign up for free and are rewarded points by swiping membership card at the kiosk in ballparks. (e.g., Atlanta Braves' Bravo Club; San Diego Padres' Compadres Rewards Club).

Fans may accumulate points and exchange them for coupons, free game tickets, discounts, or even entering a sweepstakes. Not many minor league baseball teams have developed fan clubs similar to the TML or MLB, although the Mobile BayBears have a 'stadium club membership'. The membership costs $1600 for two people. Members receive access to the exclusive stadium club, beverage service at their seats, reserved VIP parking, nameplates on their seats, stadium club cards, and food and beverage specials (Mobile BayBears, 2002).

In MiLB, however, the popular booster club is the closest version to a fan club. Local business or individuals form booster clubs to raise finances and raise funds for the team. In return, booster club members have more access than normal fans to the players and because booster club members have better access to tickets it's easier for them to attend away games. The cost of booster membership can range from free to hundreds of dollars, either organized and voluntarily maintained by loyal and enthusiastic fans or by ball clubs as a revenue stream.

## Economic Factors

The results showed that the two leagues had significant differences on the following factors: price of tickets, season ticket price, home team's local television and radio broadcasting, other sport events in the area, other nearby activities and other nearby professional franchises (see tables 7 and 8).

> **In this study, results indicate that ticket price affects MiLB fans more than TML fans.**

### Table 7 ANOVA Examining the Different Factors Between Two Countries

| Category | Factors | F | $R^2/Eta^2$ | p |
|---|---|---|---|---|
| **Economic** | Price of tickets | 51.154 | .057 | .000* |
| | Season ticket price | 6.044 | .007 | .014* |
| | Price of concession | 1.497 | .002 | .222 |
| | TV/Radio at local | 6.518 | .008 | .011* |
| | Another game on TV at same time | .278 | .000 | .598 |
| | Other sport events in area | 6.860 | .008 | .009* |
| | Other activities taking place nearby | 9.117 | .011 | .003* |
| | Other Pro franchises | 5.685 | .007 | .017* |
| | | | | |
| **Game Attractiveness** | Record of home team | 57.800 | .065 | .000* |
| | Record of visiting team | 3.457 | .004 | .063 |
| | Star players of home team | 44.695 | .050 | .000* |
| | Star players of visiting team | 25.468 | .029 | .000* |
| | Offense of home team | 153.876 | .155 | .000* |
| | Defense of home team | 14.877 | .017 | .000* |
| | Offense on visiting team | 113.693 | .120 | .000* |
| | Defense of visiting team | 27.491 | .116 | .000* |
| | Closeness of competition | 41.567 | .047 | .000* |
| | Games with rival team | 15.120 | .018 | .000* |
| | A chance to see record-breaking performance | 33.543 | .039 | .000* |
| | Special promotional event | 14.021 | .016 | .000* |
| | Home team's division standing | ------ | ---- | ---- |
| | Home team's league standing | 79.340 | .086 | .000* |
| | Involvement in race for a playoff spot | 92.189 | .099 | .000* |
| | Media advertising | 1.356 | .002 | .245 |
| | | | | |
| **Audience Preferences** | Day games during weekdays | 58.700 | .067 | .000* |
| | Night games during weekdays | 29.789 | .034 | .000* |
| | Weekend day games | 1.918 | .002 | .166 |
| | Weekend night games | 3.211 | .004 | .074 |
| | Weather is comfortable | 1.934 | .002 | .165 |
| | Cleanliness of the facility | 1.004 | .001 | .317 |
| | Easy/multiple access to stadium | .258 | .000 | .612 |
| | Availability of parking | .004 | .000 | .951 |
| | Size of the facility | .666 | .001 | .415 |
| | Like the fan behavior | 3.535 | .004 | .060 |
| | New ballpark | 82.319 | .090 | .000* |
| | Many years in the area | 16.115 | .019 | .000* |
| | Variety concession | 3.289 | .004 | .070 |
| | Less violence in game | 5.717 | .007 | .017* |

## Table 8 Mean and Standard Deviation of the Differences Between Two Countries

| Factors | U.S. Minor League Mean | SD | TML Mean | SD |
|---|---|---|---|---|
| Economic Category | | | | |
| Price of tickets* | 4.294 | .812 | 3.863 | .941 |
| Season ticket price* | 3.693 | .947 | 3.850 | .897 |
| Price of concession | 3.509 | 1.174 | 3.409 | 1.191 |
| TV/Radio at local* | 2.796 | 1.032 | 2.593 | 1.259 |
| Another game on TV at same time | 2.951 | 1.735 | 3.005 | 1.130 |
| Other sport events in area* | 2.876 | 1.754 | 3.145 | 1.086 |
| Other activities taking place nearby* | 2.893 | 1.059 | 3.116 | 1.059 |
| Other Pro franchises* | 2.889 | 1.125 | 3.147 | 1.947 |
| Game Attractiveness Category | | | | |
| Record of home team* | 3.300 | 1.008 | 3.841 | 1.052 |
| Record of visiting team | 3.129 | .0867 | 3.252 | 1.071 |
| Star players of home team* | 3.497 | .940 | 3.923 | .904 |
| Star players of visiting team* | 3.279 | .880 | 3.604 | .989 |
| Offense of home team* | 3.413 | .875 | 4.153 | .846 |
| Defense of home team* | 3.360 | .836 | 3.613 | 1.062 |
| Offense on visiting team* | 3.212 | .789 | 4.172 | 1.702 |
| Defense of visiting team* | 3.213 | .775 | 3.620 | 1.045 |
| Closeness of competition* | 3.606 | .824 | 3.943 | .936 |
| Games with rivalry team* | 3.565 | .873 | 3.812 | .966 |
| A chance to see record-breaking Performance* | 3.609 | 1.735 | 4.173 | .880 |
| Special promotional event* | 4.081 | .872 | 3.844 | .971 |
| Home team's division standing** | 3.520 | .953 | ------ | ----- |
| Home team's league standing* | 3.527 | .932 | 4.095 | .912 |
| Involvement in race for a playoff spot* | 3.628 | .971 | 4.237 | .847 |
| Media advertising | 3.808 | 1.723 | 3.692 | .971 |
| Audience Preference Category | | | | |
| Day games during weekdays* | 2.623 | 1.185 | 3.234 | 1.090 |
| Night games during weekdays* | 3.610 | 1.082 | 3.202 | 1.083 |
| Weekend day games | 3.302 | 1.117 | 3.194 | 1.105 |
| Weekend night games | 3.867 | .988 | 3.987 | .929 |
| Weather is comfortable | 4.081 | .903 | 4.169 | .927 |
| Cleanliness of the facility | 4.289 | .748 | 4.198 | 1.736 |
| Easy/multiple access to stadium | 4.024 | .844 | 3.992 | .987 |
| Availability of parking | 4.220 | .741 | 4.211 | 2.776 |
| The ballpark is large | 4.134 | 1.576 | 4.207 | .865 |
| Like fan behavior | 4.072 | 2.554 | 4.326 | .830 |
| New ballpark* | 3.231 | 1.020 | 3.873 | 1.023 |
| Many years in the area* | 3.534 | .864 | 3.782 | .925 |
| Variety of concessions | 3.801 | .829 | 3.685 | 1.028 |
| Less violence in game* | 3.867 | .965 | 4.146 | 2.243 |
| Like design/color of uniform* | 3.290 | 1.076 | 3.715 | 1.002 |
| Fan club member* | 2.523 | .986 | 3.317 | 1.163 |
| Fan activity* | 2.875 | .963 | 3.662 | 1.818 |
| Go with friends* | 4.016 | .902 | 3.695 | 1.040 |
| Go with family* | 4.273 | .748 | 3.380 | 1.157 |

* Factors that have a significant $p$ value ($p < .05$)

** TML does not have divisions.

In this study, results indicate that ticket price affects MiLB fans more than TML fans. However, when comparing the season ticket price, the opposite was observed. In either scenario, however, the more affordable the price of the ticket, the more inclination to attend.

In Taiwan, the average TML single ticket price was $4.29 (New Taiwan Dollar $150) for inner field seats and while outfield seats were free. The average ticket price in four MiLB games was $6.62, above the national average of $4.50 (2000). However, in comparison to other professional sports tickets, the Southern League of the MiLB clubs claims their ticket prices are most affordable. [e.g., NBA ($51.02), NFL ($48.97) and NHL ($47.69; Professional Baseball Promotion Corp., 2001].

While previous studies found that the broadcasting home games had a negative impact on home game attendance (Demmert, 1973; Noll, 1974; Zhang et al., 1995; Zhang & Smith, 1997a), the MiLB fans tend to be more neutral while the TML fans tend to disagree with the response that they would be affected by television or radio broadcasting.

In addition, spectators with or without fan club membership and spectators with or without season tickets do not have differences on this broadcasting factor in both leagues ($p > .05$). The ballgame broadcasting is different in two countries. Most minor league games in America are carried on radio only. The four Southern League teams in this study have radio broadcast for 70 home games and 70 away games. Specifically, only the Mobile BayBears had eight live games telecast on Comcast Cable Port City Six. All eight games were televised on the Comcast Sports South (CSS), which is a regional sport channel and reaches 15 million homes throughout the south and southeastern United States (Nichols, 2001).

In Taiwan, however, most of the TML games are broadcast both on TV and radio. In this 2002 season, this is not only limited to Taiwan TV stations but will include ESPN Star Sports (ESPN in Asia). Since ESPN Star Sports covers several Asian countries, this is a huge step toward reaching an international market for TML (Huang, 2002).

Interestingly, however, while some American baseball spectators often have radios and listen to radio broadcast games while they are in ballparks, TML spectators do not. Often it is too loud in the park to listen to the radio, as fans supporting the home or visiting team bang drums and gongs, play trumpets, and use air horns to cheer or jeer.

TML and MiLB have significant differences in forms of entertainment available around the local area of their ball clubs. Compared to MiLB fans, results have shown that TML fans were influenced more by other sporting events, activities, and professional franchises in the local area. This finding in the TML is similar to those found in studies conducted by other researchers (Hansen & Gauthier, 1989; Jones, 1984; Zhang et al., 1995a; Zhang et al., 1996).

Inherent to professional baseball in Taiwan is that it is the only professional team sport in the country. With two professional baseball leagues (Taiwan major league and chinese professional baseball league) and significant overlap of ballparks (even the same ballpark), fan base, or potential fans, limited market and players, research has suggested that these two leagues should merge (Lin, Yeh, Yang, Lu, Chen, & Tzeng, 2000). However, both leagues are still attempting to find common ground and fighting for market share.

In Taiwan, however, most of the TML games are broadcast both on TV and radio. In this 2002 season, this is not only limited to Taiwan TV stations but will include ESPN Star Sports (ESPN in Asia).

While some American baseball spectators often have radios and listen to radio broadcast games while they are in ballparks, TML spectators do not. Often it is too loud in the park to listen to the radio, as fans supporting the home or visiting team bang drums and gongs, play trumpets, and use air horns to cheer or jeer.

In the United States, MiLB fans were less likely to be affected by other activities, as professional sports is prevalent in all of the cities although there are couple of other professional sport organizations in the local.

In the United States, these other professional sport franchises have different seasons. MiLB fans can support different sport teams and attend different sport games in the different times of the year. Taiwan has two professional baseball leagues and they both play in the same season.

## Game Attractiveness Factors

Differences were found in several of the factors in the category of game attractiveness factors, and many off these were significant (see Tables 7 and 8). TML fans more often made decisions to attend baseball games than MiLB fans based on the following factors: home team's winning record, involvement of star players (home and visitors), offensive and defensive plays, closeness of competition, rivalry, record-breaking performances, team's league standing and/or the race for the playoffs. In these results, it appears that TML fans care about the team and/or players' performance more than the MiLB fans. Especially, three out of five factors where the two countries have the most differences are in this category. They are offense of home team, offense of visiting team, and defense of visiting team. In contrast, MiLB fans react more to special promotional events.

> **In these results, it appears that TML fans care about the team and/or players' performance more than the MiLB fans.**

To attract more interest, MiLB franchises have developed many promotional events, and the results of this study revealed that MiLB fans reported that they would attend more games because of promotional events. MiLB teams have many special game day promotions, such as giveaway of hats, bats, towels, pizzas, and T-shirts. Between inning breaks, there are activities either on or off the field (e.g., OLD NAVY 7th-inning-scretch game and Bingo), or kids can have their birthday party during the game. Most teams have special theme nights during the season (e.g., 4th of July fireworks and San Diego Chicken night). Other promotional events might include ticket discounts or ticket packages and entertainment programs such as music, dance, light and sound. Many promotional events can be presented before, during, and after the games to draw and keep spectators at the park. The findings of this study agree with the findings of previous research that reported that promotions are attendance generators (Hill et al., 1982; Marcum & Greenstein, 1985; Siegfried & Eisenberg, 1980; Wall & Myers, 1989; Wells, Southall, & Peng, 2000; Zhang et al., 1995a; Zhang et al., 1995b).

> **When examining the results in relation to audience preference factors, it appears that the TML and the MiLB have few differences.**

Previous research has also found that the opportunity to see a record-breaking performance was an important influence on attendance at sporting events (Green, 1995). The findings in this study, however, are not in agreement with Green's study. For example, while the TML fans agreed that they would attend more games if there was a chance to see a record-breaking performance, the MiLB fans were neutral.

## Audience Preference Factors

When examining the results in relation to audience preference factors, it appears that the TML and the MiLB have few differences.

### Game Schedules

Previous studies have suggested that the convenience of the game schedule is one of the major factors that affect game attendance (Marcum & Greenstein, 1985; Zhang et al., 1995b). Generally, spectators favor attending weekend, holiday, and evening games. The MiLB schedules vary slightly from team to team, but most teams arrange games on weekday nights or weekends. The results of the current study are in line with previous studies. MiLB fans prefer not to attend during the week. They prefer night games on weekdays.

**However, unlike the stadium-building boom in America, it is hard to construct new stadiums in Taiwan because of limited land and budgets only a few stadiums are managed well enough to offer with quality professional baseball games facilities.**

In contrast, TML fans tend to be neutral regarding day games during the week. All TML regular games start at 6 pm from Wednesday to Sunday inclusive, with make-up games (rained-out) on Mondays and Tuesdays at 6 PM or Sunday afternoon at 1 PM. Though TML fans were neutral on the issue of scheduled day games, they believed that more games on weekend nights would likely translate into increased attendance. Indeed, attendance records showed that games on Saturday night had the largest crowds with an average of 2,832 people per game, followed by the second highest attendance of 2,620 people per game for games on Sunday, while games on Wednesday had the lowest attendance, 956 (Taiwan Major League, 2002).

*Stadium Building*

The TML fans agree that having a new ballpark would attract more fans. Kaohsiung ballpark is one of the newest in Taiwan, with nice seating and facilities; it also boasted the highest attendance numbers among the TML ball clubs (Taiwan Major League, 2002). However, unlike the stadium-building boom in America, it is hard to construct new stadiums in Taiwan because of limited land and budgets. Besides, because lack of budget and poor management, only a few stadiums are managed well enough to offer with quality professional baseball games facilities.

In comparison, the MiLB spectators do not feel the same need to build new stadiums. The four Southern league ballparks in this study average 22 years old, with Wolfson Park, home of the Jacksonville Suns, open since 1955. (The Suns have moved to play at the nearby baseball grounds at Jacksonville since the 2003 season). In contrast, however, the Mobile BayBears' Hank Aaron Stadium is the youngest, open since in 1997.

**This study's finding are in contrast to the minor league claims that new ballparks, new locations (or both) were key ingredients. Southern league fans' responses showed that cleanliness of the facility is far more important than having a new stadium.**

This study's finding are in contrast to the minor league claims that new ballparks, new locations (or both) were key ingredients for 4 leagues (International, Pacific Coast, Texas and Midwest) which exceeded their all-time records ("Minor League Attendance Hits 37.7 Million", 2000; "Building Boom Continues as New Season Opens", 2002). Southern League fans' responses showed that cleanliness of the facility is far more important than having a new stadium.

*Going with Friends and Family*

Ball games can be a social events for family, friends, or even businesses. "To be with friends" is a common reason that people give for any sport involvement. The MiLB fans stated they would go to more games if they go with friends or with family. TML fans were indifferent to going with family. Moreover, the effect size of going with family was one of the factors where the fans of the two leagues have the greatest difference (see Table 7).

# Summary and Recommendations

While some of the findings in this study agree with previous studies involving consumer behavior, culture, and other market demands in relation to factors that affect attendance at sports events, there were some contradictory findings. Overall, the results of this study contribute significantly to the current small body of research in this area. More research is needed to further our discourse and understandings of the behavior of sport event consumers.

> While some of the findings in this study agree with previous studies involving consumer behavior, culture, and other market demands in relation to factors that affect attendance at sports events, there were some contradictory findings.

The information from this study can be used by sport marketing educators in their courses to inform students who will be working in the sport business industry. With a constantly expanding and competitive sports entertainment industry in the United States, professional sport marketers have a need to understand consumer behavior: specifically, a need to know what consumers want and what will bring the consumer to the event. Research on culture as a consumer behavior factor, such as in this study and those cited in this paper, can help provide that information.

While differences were found between the fans attending the American games and the fans attending the Taiwan games, more research is needed to determine if these findings can be repeated. We would also recommend research in which sociocultural and sport consumer studies are involved in order to determine if baseball fans in Taiwan are different due to sociocultural differences or if these differences have more to do with the sports culture. Additionally, there should be studies involving categories of sports events other than baseball and other than professional sports to discern differences or similarities to the results of this study.

# References

Attendance Hits 38.8 million, second highest ever. (2001, end of season). *Baseball News, 17*(8), 1.

Branvold, S. E., Pan, D. W., & Gabert, T. E. (1997). Effects of winning percentage and market size on attendance in minor league baseball. *Sport Marketing Quarterly, 6*(4), 35-42.

Building boom continues as new season opens. (2002, opening day). *Baseball News, 18*(2), 1.

Chen, W. B. (2000). *An analysis of contract and system of professional baseball player.* Unpublished master's thesis, Fu-Jen University, Taipei, Taiwan.

Cicciarella, C. F. (1997). *Research in physical education, exercise science, and sport: An introduction.* Scottsdale, AZ: Gorsuch Scarisbrick.

Demmert, H. G. (1973). *The economics of professional team sports.* Lexington, MA: D.C. Health.

Directorate General of Budget Accounting and Statistics Executive Yuan, R.O.C. (2002a). 2000 *Population and housing census in Taiwan and Fu-kien Area.* Retrieved on April 3, 2002, from http://www.dgbas.gov.tw/census~n/Six/lue5/p89012_c.doc.

Directorate General of Budget Accounting and Statistics Executive Yuan, R.O.C. (2002b, February 22). *National income and economic forecasting.* Retrieved April 14, 2002, from http://www.dgbas.gov.tw/dgbas03/bs4/news/new09102.doc.

Directorate General of Budget Accounting and Statistics Executive Yuan, R.O.C. (2002c, March). *Household income and disposal income.* Retrieved April 14, 2002. Retrieved April 14, 2002, from http://www.dgbas.gov.tw/dgbas03/bs4/nis/p62.xls.

Fillingham, E. J. (1977). *Major league hockey:* An industry study. Master's thesis, University of Alberta, Alberta, Canada.

Green, F. E. (1995). *An examination of factors related to consumer behavior influencing attendance at professional sporting events.* Unpublished doctoral dissertation, Florida State University, Tallahassee.

Greenstein, T. N., & Marcum, J. P. (1981). Factors affecting attendance of major league baseball: Team performance. *Review of Sport and Leisure, 6*(2), 21-33.

Hansen, H., & Gauthier, R. (1989). Factors affecting attendance at professional sport event. *Journal of Sport Management, 3*(1), 15-32.

Hansen, H., & Gauthier, R. (1993). Spectators' views of LPGA golf events. *Sport Marketing Quarterly, 2*(1), 17-25.

Hill, J. R., Madura, J., & Zuber, R. A. (1982). The short run demand for major league baseball. *Atlantic Economic Journal, 10*(2), 31-35.

Howard, D. R., & Crompton, J. L. (1995). *Financing sport.* Morgantown, WV: Fitness Information Technology, Inc.

Howard, D. R., & Crompton, J. L. (2004). *Financing sport (2nd Edition).* Morgantown, WV: Fitness Information Technology, Inc.

Huang, T. (2002, March 12). Naluwan signed 2002 broadcasting contract with ESPN Start Sports. *Central New Agency.* Retrieved March 12, 2002, from http://news.yam.com/cna/sports/news/200203/200203122050414.html.

Johnson, A. (1993). *Minor league baseball and local economic development.* Champaign-Urbana, IL: University of Illinois Press.

Jones, J. C. H. (1984). Winners, losers and hosers: Demand and survival in the National Hockey League. *Atlantic Economic Journal, 12* (3), 54-63.

Kasky, J. (1994, October). Money's sports value rankings. *Money, 10,* 158-170.

King, B. (2002a). National pastime goes multinational: Booming Hispanic and Asian populations hold promise for all U.S. teams. *Street & Smith's SportsBusiness Journal, 4*(50), 23.

King, B. (2002b). Baseball: TV key to game's growth in Asia, Latin America. *Street & Smith's SportsBusiness Journal, 4*(50), 26.

Land, K. C., Davis, W. R., & Blau, J. R. (1994). Organizing the boys of summer: The evolution of U.S. minor league baseball, 1883-1990. *The American Journal of Sociology, 100*(3), 781-813.

Lin, H., Yeh, C., Yang, H., Lu, H., Chen, W., & Tzeng, W. (2000). *Professional baseball.* (NCPFS Publication No. Exc-089-003). Taipei, Taiwan: National Council on Physical Fitness and Sports, R.O.C.

Liu, M. Y. (1999). *Consumer behavior of the Taiwan's professional baseball.* Unpublished master's thesis, National Chen-chi University, Taipei, Taiwan.

Loudon, D. L., & Della Bitta, A. J. (1993). *Consumer behavior: Concepts and applications* (4th ed.). New York: McGraw-Hill.

Lu, D. (2001, May). *Factors affecting spectator attendance in professional baseball: A pilot study.* Paper presented at the 16th annual conference of the North America Society for Sport Management, Virginia Beach, VA.

Mahony, D. F., & Howard, D. R. (1998). The impact of attitudes on the behavioral intentions of sport spectators. *International Sports Journal, 2*(2), 96-110.

Marcum, J. P., & Greenstein, T. N. (1985). Factors affecting attendance of major league baseball: II. a within-season analysis. *Sociology of Sport Journal, 2*(4), 314-322.

McDonald, M., & Rascher, D. (2000). Does bat day make cents? The effect of promotions on the demand for major league baseball. *Journal of Sport Management, 14*(1), 8-27.

Miniard, P., Bhatla, S., & Rose, R. (1990). On the formation and relationship of ad and brand attitudes: An experimental and causal analysis. *Journal of Marketing Research, 27,* 290-303.

Minor league attendance hits 37.7 million. (2000, end of season). *Baseball News, 16*(8), 1.

Mobile BayBears. (n.d.). *Hank Arron Stadium: Stadium Club.* Retrieved April 15, 2002, from http://63.64.4.120/stadium-club.asp.

Morgenson, G. (1992). Where the fan still comes first. *Forbes, 149,* 40-42.

Mullin, B. J., Hardy, S., & Sutton, W. A. (2000). *Sport marketing* (2nd ed.). Champaign, IL: Human Kinetics.

Nichols, T. (2001). *BayBears 2001 souvenir yearbook.* (Brochure). Mobile, AL: Mobile BayBears Professional Baseball.

Noll, R. G. (1974). Attendance and price setting. In R. G. Noll (Ed.), *Government and the sports business* (pp. 115-157). Washington, DC: The Bookings Institute.

Pitts, B. G., & Stotlar, D. K. (2002). *Fundamentals of sport marketing* (2nd ed.). Morgantown, WV: Fitness Information Technology, Inc.

Professional Baseball Promotion Corp. (2001). *Minor league baseball: 100th anniversary* (Brochure). St. Petersburg, FL: Author.

Rea L. M., & Parker, R. A. (1997). *Designing and conducting survey research: A comprehensive guide* (2nd ed.). San Francisco: Jossey-Bass, Inc.

Rone, K. (2002). Marketing: Potential new fans waiting for pitch. *Street & Smith's SportsBusiness Journal, 4*(50), 31.

Saudohar, P. D., & Mangan, J. A. (Eds.). (1991). *The business of professional sports.* Urbana, Il: University of Illinois Press.

Schiffman, L. G., & Kanuk, L. L. (2000). *Consumer behavior* (7th ed.). Upper Saddle River, NJ: Prentice Hall.

Schofield, J. A. (1983). Performance and attendance at professional team sports. *Journal of Sport Behavior, 6*(4), 196-206.

Schütte, H., & Ciarlante, D. (1998). *Consumer behavior in Asia.* New York: New York University Press.

Scully, G. W. (1974). Pay and performance in major league baseball. *The American Economic Review, 64*(2), 915-930.

Siegfried, J. J., & Eisenberg, J. D. (1980). The demand for minor league baseball. *Atlantic Economic Journal, 8*(1), 59-71.

Simmons Market Research Bureau (1990). *Study of media & market: Sports & leisure.* New York: Simmons.

Stahl, M. J. (1986). *Managerial and technical motivation.* New York: Praeger.

Taiwan Major League (2002). *2001 Year Book.* Taipei, Taiwan: Taiwan Major League.

The World Bank Group. (n.d.) *Learning modules: GNP per capita.* Retrieved April 14, 2002, from http://www.worldbank.org/depweb/english/modules/economic/gnp/.

Thomas, G. S. (2001a). *Pro sports tracker. Street & Smith's SportsBusiness Journal, 4*(2), 35.

Thomas, G. S. (2001b). *Pro sports tracker. Street & Smith's SportsBusiness Journal, 4*(26), 39.

Thomas, G. S. (2001c). *Pro sports tracker. Street & Smith's SportsBusiness Journal, 4*(30), 47.

U.S. Census Bureau (2002a, September 4). Survey of income and program participation.

U.S. Census Bureau. (2002b, March 29) *Census 2000 Supplementary Survey.* Retrieve April 3, 2002, from http://www.census.gov/c2ss/www/products/profiles/2000/narrative/010/npo1000us.htm.

Wall, G. V., & Myers, K. (1989). Factors influencing attendance: Toronto Blue Jays game. *Sport Place International: An international Magazine of Sport, 3*(1/2), 29-33.

Wells, D. E., Southall, R. M., & Peng, H. H. (2000). An analysis of factors related to attendance at Division II football games. *Sport Marketing Quarterly, 9*(4), 203-210.

White House (2002). *Economic statistics briefing room.* Retrieved April 14, 2002, from http://www.whitehouse.gov/fsbr/income.html.

Whitney, J. D. (1988). Winning games versus winning championships: The economics of fan interest and team performance. *Economics Inquiry, 26,* 703-724.

Williams, P. (2001a). Minor leagues play major competitive role. *Street & Smith's SportsBusiness Journal, 3*(39), 40-41.

Williams, P. (2001b). Special report of minor league baseball: Small-time baseball, big-time success. *Street & Smith's SportsBusiness Journal, 4*(12), 21-27.

Zhang, J. J., & Smith, D. W. (1997a). Impact of broadcasting on the attendance of professional basketball games. *Sport Marketing Quarterly, 6*(1), 23-29.

Zhang, J. J., & Smith, D. W., Pease, D. G., & Jambor, E. A. (1997b). Negative influence of market competitors on the attendance of professional sport games: The case of a minor league hockey team. *Sport Marketing Quarterly, 6*(3), 31-40.

Zhang, J. J., Pease, D. G., & Saffici, C. L. (1995b, June). *Dimensions of spectators satisfaction toward the support programs of an NBA team.* Paper presented at the 10th Annual Conference of North American Society for Sport Management, Athens, GA.

Zhang, J. J., Pease, D. G., & Smith, D. W. (1998). Relationship between broadcasting media and minor league hockey game attendance. *Journal of Sport Management, 12*(2), 103-122.

Zhang, J. J., Pease, D. G., Hui, S. C., & Michaud, T. J. (1995a). Variables affecting the spectator decision to attend NBA games. *Sport Marketing Quarterly, 4*(4), 29-39.

Zhang, J. J., Smith, D. W., Pease, D. G., & Lam, E. T. C. (1998). Dimensions of spectator satisfaction toward support programs of professional hockey games. *International Sports Journal, 12*(2), 1-17.

Zhang, J. J., Smith, D. W., Pease, D. G., & Mahar, M. T. (1996). Spectator knowledge of hockey as a significant predictor of game attendance. *Sport Marketing Quarterly, 5*(3), 41-48.

# CHAPTER 12

# Sport Consumption: Exploring the Duality of Constructs in Experiential Research

MELISSA JOHNSON MORGAN
JANE SUMMERS

## Abstract

This paper explores the concepts of mood and involvement in experiential research. Sport spectating was chosen to represent leisure services in this investigation into the differences between traditional consumer decision-making constructs and experiential constructs. We propose that in leisure service encounters, both mood and involvement act as dynamic constructs operating on two levels. The first level is an *a priori* state: those brought to the experience by the consumer; the second level is an *experiential* state, where constructs actually change over the course of the consumption experience. Furthermore, we propose that the servicescape moderates the changes in mood and involvement during the experience. A review of the literature and a series of phenomenological focus groups facilitated the exploration of the propositions in this study. Our findings suggest that mood and involvement are in fact dual constructs, operating on both a priori and experiential levels. This study is truly exploratory in nature and suggestions for future research include the development of creative methodologies to quantify the operation of the mood and involvement constructs in the experiential consumption of leisure services.

## Introduction

Mood and involvement are staple constructs in the traditional decision-making literature and have been the focus of much consumer research in both goods and service applications. However, as consumer research seeks new explanations for hedonic consumption, emotive variables such as mood and involvement deserve to be re-evaluated under the experiential framework. The dynamic nature of experiential consumption calls for a re-evaluation of the nature and dimensions of many variables that have long

> **The dynamic nature of experiential consumption calls for a re-evaluation of the nature and dimensions of many variables that have long been considered rational and stable constructs under the decision-making model.**

been considered rational and stable constructs under the decision-making model.

In their seminal paper calling for more research into hedonic consumption, Hirschman and Holbrook (1982) point out that the variable nature of services and events poses many challenges for the researcher. They specifically highlight the threat to reliability of research into the leisure services such as concerts, theater, and sport, because they are all subject to variability across time and that the content and/or composition of the service offering also changes (Hirschman and Holbrook, 1982).

The fact that the service offering changes leads us to believe that the mood and level of involvement by consumers is in a continuous state of flux throughout the consumption experience. Retrospective or anticipatory a priori snapshots of mood and involvement are often used to predict satisfaction, emotional response, and even persuasion (Schultz, 1996) in service literature. Discovery that these constructs are variable during the service encounter could have a potentially dramatic impact on service and event research.

> **The fact that the service offering changes leads us to believe that the mood and level of involvement by consumers is in a continuous state of flux throughout the consumption experience.**

The purpose if this paper is to investigate the behavior of the mood and involvement constructs in a hedonic experiential-consumption setting. Current exploration of leisure services consumption suggests that customers are seeking excitement and stimulation (Wakefield & Blodgett, 1994), and the very nature of this anticipation supports the proposition that mood and involvement are likely to fluctuate during the consumption experience. Specifically, this research seeks to investigate whether there is evidence to support the premise that mood and involvement are not constant, static constructs in hedonic leisure service encounters.

In order to provide a more detailed rationale for our research questions, this paper begins with an overview of the current mindset and research findings in relation to mood and involvement in both the services marketing and experiential consumption literature. Following this, we will detail the study and present the findings. Theoretical implications and recommendations for ongoing descriptive research conclude the paper.

## Literature Review

The services marketing literature is rich with investigations into the role of both mood and involvement in service encounters (Knowles, Grove, & Pickett 1993), service quality (Csipak, Chebat, & Venkatesan, 1995), servicescapes (Ruyter & Bloemer, 1999; Wakefield & Blodgett 1994), and service relationships (McColl-Kennedy & Fetter, 2001). Most of this research has focused on customer's perceptions of service quality and/or service relationships, their resulting satisfaction with the service rendered, and the role of either mood and/or involvement in this subsequent evaluative process. The interaction of involvement and mood have further been shown to be important when considering leisure services such as restaurant experiences, theaters, resorts, amusement parks, and sporting events (Wakefield & Blodgett, 1994; Bitner, 1992).

In particular, it has been found that the positive servicescape attributes combined with high levels of emotion and involvement on the part of customers increases levels of satisfaction and ongoing interest in the consumption activity in leisure services (Wakefield & Blodgett 1994). In these studies, however, mood and involvement are considered stable or enduring constructs, and the methodologies used to investigate them only allow for single snapshot measures of positive or negative moods and high or low involvement states. Our proposition is that in leisure service encounters, both mood and involvement are actually dynamic constructs where an a priori state will change over the course of the consumption experience.

Sport spectating-more specifically, watching televised football-was chosen as an experiential consumption setting for this study as it offers a full scope of emotional response by respondents. The seeking of emotional arousal is a major motivation for the consumption of certain service and event classes such as plays and sporting events (Holbrook 1986). As such, a sport consumption setting should provide a rich context for the exploration of mood and involvement. A brief overview of the current literature in relation to both mood and involvement in sport consumption will provide support for our research proposition.

**Sport spectating-more specifically, watching televised football-was chosen as an experiential consumption setting for this study as it offers a full scope of emotional response by respondents. The seeking of emotional arousal is a major motivation for the consumption of certain service and event classes such as plays and sporting events.**

Mood is a concept closely aligned with emotion. In most definitions of mood, it is agreed that it is a state of emotional or affective arousal that is varying and transient (Peterson & Sauber 1983). Despite this affective commonality that mood and emotion share, researchers have seen cause to treat them as separate variables.

Chalip, Csikszentmihalyi, Kleiber, and Larson's (1984) study on variations of experience in sport was one of the first to consider mood as a dimension of experiential sport consumption where they noted that optimal experience is in part defined by mood. More specifically, they state that conditions conducive to optimal experience, or *flow,* are accompanied by states of high, positive moods. Mood states have also been shown to affect not only behavior, but also evaluation and recall in consumption experiences and are known to be significant in the progression of the experience itself (Gardiner, 1985). From these results we see that consumers may indeed regulate many factors of an experience, such as expectations, satisfaction, and verbalizations, depending on their mood before and even during the experience. Given the unpredictable nature of the sport experience, which is dependent on uncontrollable elements of competition, it is likely that mood will be a particularly dynamic factor over the course of the sport consumption experience.

**Consumers may indeed regulate many factors of an experience, such as expectations, satisfaction, and verbalizations, depending on their mood before and even during the experience.**

When considering involvement, traditional consumer research has focused on involvement as a measure of product relevance where the level of involvement is thought to reflect the inherent need fulfillment, value expression, or interest the consumer has in the product (Mittal & Lee, 1989; Zaichkowsky, 1985). Furthermore, involvement has also been shown to influence consumers' propensity to search externally for information to aid in their decision-making processes (McColl-Kennedy & Fetter, 2001). Involvement has also been shown to be important in experiential research, although its conceptualization focuses more on the consequences of heightened relevance rather than the relevance of a product or service itself.

Experiential consumption researchers have long advocated a shift in focus from the *degree of involvement* (low versus high) to the *type of involvement* (Holbrook & Hirschman, 1982), which will allow researchers to consider involvement in terms of the degree of activation or arousal during the experience. This approach would suggest that there is potential for involvement to change during an experience to moderate the effect of other factors, a phenomenon alluded to by Moneta and Csikszentmihalyi (1996), who hinted at this moderating and possibly even dynamic role of involvement with experience emotion and mood.

> **Thus, a gap exists in the literature on the nature of the role of both mood and involvement in experiential consumption, which this research aims to examine.**

Thus, a gap exists in the literature on the nature of the role of both mood and involvement in experiential consumption, which this research aims to examine. Consumer behavior and service literature have shown mood and involvement to be important predictive variables. However, if we consider the inherently variable nature of services and events, traditional measures of mood and involvement appear inadequate. If mood and involvement are indeed variable during the time of the consumption experience, marketers would have unique opportunities to influence this fluctuation or react to variations in the construction of the encounter.

We propose that consumers bring an existing mood state and level of involvement into any consumption experience, which we term, *a priori mood* and *a priori involvement*. We further propose that this mood state and level of involvement are likely to then vary constantly during the consumption experience, which we term to be *experiential mood* and *experiential involvement*. Therefore, we propose that in experiential leisure service settings, mood and involvement will be dynamic constructs operating both on a priori and experiential levels. Our research question then is, Is there evidence to support the dual and fluctuating nature of mood and involvement in an experiential sport consumption setting?

> **Is there evidence to support the dual and fluctuating nature of mood and involvement in an experiential sport consumption setting?**

## Method

In order to discover more about the operation of the mood and involvement constructs, three existential-phenomenology focus groups were conducted. Participants were encouraged to describe their experiences with sport consumption. There was an emphasis on letting the participants naturally describe only those factors of prior experiences that they considered relevant, avoiding the use of 'why?' questions at all times (Dale, 1996).

> **Two of the phenomenological focus groups were carried out before and during the televised broadcast of a live National Football League (NFL) game.**

Two of the phenomenological focus groups were carried out before and during the televised broadcast of a live National Football League (NFL) game. Conducting the focus groups during an actual experience of the type being investigated was required to conform to the phenomenological method of first-degree information collection.

Phenomenological focus groups are considered a particularly appropriate choice for those wishing to explore consumer experience (Calder, 1977) as they provide a systematic description in terms of first-degree constructs of the consumption-relevant intersubjectivity of the target segment. Phenomenological focus groups require the participants and the researcher to share participatively (Calder 1977). This means that researchers should immerse themselves in the experience, with the subjects, in order to collect data from the respondents about the experience. Another important reason for conducting the focus groups during an actual sport consumption experience was to document which characteristics of the game elicit responses, changes in mood, discussion among participants, emotion displayed, and so on.

Phenomenological focus groups require homogeneous participants in a natural setting (Calder, 1977). For this reason, participants were recruited using the snowball sampling technique. The groups were made up of friends and associates who normally watch football together, with the majority of participants being under thirty years of age; as expected, there were a significantly higher number of males included in the groups as this demographic fits the description of football fan most closely. The age and gender of participants in each focus group were as follows:

- Phenomenological Group 1: 6 males and 1 female, 24-32yrs.

- Phenomenological Group Two - 6 males, 22-29yrs.

- Phenomenological Group Three - 6 males and 2 females, 20-28yrs.

## Findings

This research provided evidence that sport spectators consider *involvement* and *mood* both a motivation to, and consequence of, watching football. We will begin the discussion of the findings with an investigation of mood.

*Mood.* Our research proposition was that in addition to an a priori mood state, mood may vary during the consumption experience. The *a priori mood* refers to the state of being of the individual as they begin the experience. For example, is the consumer in a good mood or a bad mood when they watch the football game? This mood may or may not be related to the experience or experiential phenomenon. The *experiential mood* however, refers to the state of being of the individual during the consumption experience. The difference between the two mood types is that the a priori mood seems to moderate the relationship between the events in the actual game and enjoyment of the game (possibly including variables such as emotion, satisfaction and involvement), whereas experiential mood depends on the actual game and other elements of the experience.

> **"Sometimes it is just as much fun to get together as it is to watch the game. It makes it much better too. The game was dismal last Monday but all the guys came round and we had a few beers and a BBQ. Everyone was in such a good mood the actual game didn't seem to matter much."**

The researchers observed several important characteristics of the consumption experiences during the phenomenological focus groups. One of the focus groups was a very happy, social occasion where the a priori mood of the individuals seemed to be more positive than those in the other groups. The researchers noted that the individuals seemed to take the game seriously but the negative aspects of the game did not upset them as much or for as long as those in other groups. This observation could be a function of many other factors but the moderating role of a priori mood appeared to be strong. In addition to the researcher's observations, the respondents actually described situations where a priori mood affected the football consumption experience. The following excerpt is typical of the comments regarding social interaction, a priori mood and the experience:

Respondent: "Sometimes it is just as much fun to get together as it is to watch the game. It makes it much better too. The game was dismal last Monday but all the guys came round and we had a few beers and a BBQ. Everyone was in such a good mood the actual game didn't seem to matter much."

Respondents spoke of times when positive football experiences put them in good moods and negative experiences that caused prolonged bad moods. There is evidence of this phenomenon in these separate excerpts.

> **"I get like ill, like a headache, and I feel so mad. Like if I come home from a game and it hasn't gone like I want it to then people know not to talk to me."**

Respondent: "I get like ill, like a headache, and I feel so mad. Like if I come home from a game and it hasn't gone like I want it to then people know not to talk to me."

> **"When you see a great game and your team wins, it can put you on the biggest high, but if they lose I can find myself thinking about it for days and I am always dragging my feet that day at least."**

Respondent: "Didn't they do a study or something about that once, like when the Saints lose, the production in the plants goes down in New Orleans that week. Anyway whether that's true or not, I know it gets me down. When you see a great game and your team wins, it can put you on the biggest high, but if they lose I can find myself thinking about it for days and I am always dragging my feet that day at least."

Mood states were also found to be dynamic, changing as a result of game characteristics. Respondents' testimonial evidence does give cause to acknowledge the potential dependent nature of experiential mood. Take the following statements, for example:

> **"I don't really consider myself to be very sporty. I'm not like a fanatic or anything. But it is weird how much football can affect you."**

Respondent: "I don't really consider myself to be very sporty. I'm not like a fanatic or anything. But it is weird how much football can affect you. When I go into the lunchroom on Monday or even Tuesday after the Monday night games, you can tell which teams won just by the mood. Even me, it puts me in a good mood if LSU or the Saints win. I mean that's probably true for everyone at the time of the game but I mean for days sometimes."

Respondent: "God damn it! I was in a really good mood today. Look's like that is set to change. I hate it when they just give the game away. Puts me in a bad mood all night."

Thus, from these preliminary findings it would appear that there is evidence to support the dual nature of the mood construct in experiential leisure service encounters, such as sport consumption, and further, that the experiential aspect of mood does appear to be moderated by the existence of others, the consumption setting (servicescape), and by the game performance (service delivery). We will now examine the results as they apply to the involvement construct.

*Involvement.* The very concept of having a favorite team or being not just a football fan but a Saints fan or a Dolphins fan is testimony to the traditional concept of involvement used in consumer research. The findings showed many examples of fans being highly involved with a particular team or game and how this moderated the relationship between the game characteristics and the outcome for the individual such as emotion, and satisfaction. Respondents also gave testimony of their loyalty to a particular team and how they were more involved in some games than others. It also shows how the level of involvement can change behavior and moderate emotion and satisfaction from the experience. For example:

> **"Sometimes football isn't a big deal at all. It just depends who's playing. If it's a team I'm really into, then the game is a big deal. If not, I might just catch the scores or something."**

Respondent: "You might follow all the teams in the league, but you have a favorite. Or maybe two or three teams that you just get more involved in."

Respondent: "Sometimes football isn't a big deal at all. It just depends who's playing. If it's a team I'm really into, then the game is a big deal. . . if not, I might just catch the scores or something."

Respondent: "Like if the Saints are playing and they don't win it will bother me. If it's the Saints and the 49ers I want the Saints to win and I really care if they win but if it's the 49ers and the Dolphins or something I mean. . . I'd watch it but when the game ends I don't care what happens."

Again, this comment suggests that a priori involvement appears to moderate a relationship between the events in the actual game (game characteristics) and the emotions experienced and/or the overall satisfaction with the game. The following comment also suggests that the degree to which a priori involvement exists, or can be created by the individual, affects the consumption experience:

Respondent: "Every team affects the team you care about. I really believe that. I really do. I can watch a game and it is like the worst game, the worst teams in the nation, and somehow I can rationalize that if this happens or that happens it will affect my team, you know. . . ."

Being a sport fan is in itself considered to be a form of involvement with a specific team, event, or person (McPherson 1972). Furthermore, the importance of sport to a particular person can be aligned to involvement as in Zaichkowsky's (1985) traditional product involvement construct. The following comments show evidence of this importance to both the game and with the experience.

> **"I guess it is more important to me than I realized. We dress in our purple and gold and it is a big deal to us. The tickets aren't cheap either. It costs us over $500 a year just for our tickets but it really is the biggest thing we do together."**

Respondent: "I guess it is more important to me than I realized. We have been going to LSU football games for as long as I can remember. My kids have been going since they were born. We dress in our purple and gold and it is a big deal to us. The tickets aren't cheap either. It costs us over $500 a year just for our tickets but it really is the biggest thing we do together."

Respondent: "I always enjoy watching my team more than just any game. I'll watch anything, but I always enjoy it better when it's LSU or the Saints. When it's more important to you it makes the win even better. Or in the case of the Saints it makes the loss even worse!"

The second type of involvement proposed by this research is unique to experiential consumption. Experiential involvement is believed to be a dynamic construct that depends on the servicescape (the presence of others and the consumption setting) and on service delivery (the game outcome). The concept is one best described by the respondents themselves when engaged in a conversation about previous games.

> **"Oh my God! It was the most pathetic beating I've seen. I honestly never watched the second half. It wasn't worth it. Sue couldn't believe it when she got home with the kids and the grass was cut. It just wasn't worth sitting and watching that. At least I achieved something cutting the grass."**

Respondent: "I was so pumped about that game. I had been thinking about it all week. I got rid of the kids, got a few beers, got all set up and then. . . oh my God! It was the most pathetic beating I've seen. I honestly never watched the second half. It wasn't worth it. Sue couldn't believe it when she got home with the kids and the grass was cut. It just wasn't worth sitting and watching that. At least I achieved something cutting the grass."

Respondent: "I will watch the whole game if my team is playing. Well, I say that and then this week I didn't even bother watching the whole thing. I was all psyched up to see them kill Tampa Bay, and they totally blew it. By the end of the second quarter, it wasn't even worth watching."

The respondent was initially "psyched up" or highly involved in the game (a priori involvement). However, as a result of the game characteristics his experiential involvement decreased. His a priori involvement moderated the relationship between the game and his expectations and satisfaction where as his experiential involvement was dependent upon the service delivery (the game outcome and characteristics).

The same phenomenon is evident as a result of extreme positive margins in the game itself. These responses explain how experiential involvement might work:

Respondent: "Depends on the game. . . you know if I was watching something that was just over at half time then I would get really pissed. Doesn't matter how much I like the team or how much I was into that game, I am going to get pissed at having to sit through a bunch of second stringers in the second half. That would make me mad, you know."

> **"No, I'm serious. Watching football is like sex."**

Respondent 1: "This game sucks."

Interviewer: "I thought you really like this team. You were excited about the game before, weren't you?"

Respondent 1: "Yeah, but it's over before half time. It's good they win but there is such a thing as winning too early."

Interviewer: "Winning too early?"

Respondent 1: "Yeah. . . it's like sex."

(much laughter from the group)

Respondent 2: "Everything is like sex to you." (female)

Respondent 3: "You know what they say about people who talk about it all the time. . . ." (male)

Respondent 1: "No, I'm serious. Watching football is like sex. You want to win, but if you win too early its boring!"

Respondent 2: "For her maybe. . ."(laughter)

Respondent 1: "That's what it's like. They've won now, there's not much point faking interest in the rest."

> **However, when the game became boring, his level of involvement changed. He didn't think any less of his team, just the experience itself. His *a priori* involvement (highly involved with that particular team) remained the same, but his experiential involvement decreased.**

The first respondent was initially very involved in the football game. He had an interest in the team and expressed positive anticipation and excitement about watching the game. However, when the game became boring, his level of involvement changed. He didn't think any less of his team, just the experience itself. His a priori involvement (highly involved with that particular team) remained the same, but his experiential involvement decreased. His sexual analogy is not dissimilar to the theory Hirschman and Holbrook (1982) used to explain the variation in emotions and fantasies over the course of consumption experience. They proposed that there is a preferred or most desirable pattern of emotional arousal for products experienced over a specific time frame.

Our findings, therefore, provide sufficient evidence to support our research proposition that in experiential leisure service encounters such as sport consumption, involvement will act as a dual construct consisting of both an a priori involvement level and an experiential involvement level.

## Implications and Conclusions

In conjunction with sport sociologist's beliefs that televised sport spectators try to increase their involvement (Eastman & Riggs, 1994) and want to experience heightened emotions (McPherson, 1975; Eastman & Riggs, 1994), the findings of this research are very important. The exploratory research described in this paper has found evidence to support previous findings (Gardner, 1985; George & Jones, 1996; Wakefield & Blodgett, 1994) that both mood and involvement are important constructs in understanding experiential leisure consumption and further that they are both dynamic constructs in these types of service encounters.

In relation to mood, we noted that an a priori mood, or the mood that the consumer enters or begins the experience with, is important in moderating satisfaction with the experience (George & Jones, 1996). We also found anecdotal evidence that this a priori state changes constantly during the consumption experience.

> **Marketers whose products are ritually linked to the sport consumption experience or who are trying to use sport consumption to position their products must understand the experience itself and the operation of the affective and behavioral variables in the experience.**

Marketers whose products are ritually linked to the sport consumption experience or who are trying to use sport consumption to position their products must understand the experience itself and the operation of the affective and behavioral variables in the experience. Perhaps marketers should find more predictable ways of helping consumers increase their own emotional output, and thus their mood, during sport consumption experiences.

This research established links between the characteristics of the game and the level of emotion of respondents. It is possible that marketers should spend more time examining the elements of the game that increase the level of excitement and, therefore, emotion for respondents. Isolating and replicating the elements of the experience that increase emotion, mood, and experiential involvement may be more important than trying to increase the consumer's level of a priori involvement with the experience as would be normal in traditional decision-based marketing.

Involvement has been widely considered in traditional consumer research (Zaichkowsky, 1985; Mittal & Lee, 1989). It has also been one of the foundation constructs examined by early experiential consumption researchers (Moneta & Csikszentmihalyi, 1996). While the focus of involvement has usually been as an a priori condition acting as an independent or moderating variable. Moneta and Csikszentmihalyi (1996) did allude to the experiential phenomena of involvement as a dynamic construct, and our research findings support this premise. The concept of a priori involvement in experiential consumption is closely aligned to the traditional continuum of involvement used in consumer research. Involvement is thought to reflect the inherent need fulfillment, value expression, or interest the consumer has in the product (Mittal & Lee, 1989; Zaichkowsky, 1985). In experiential research, the conceptualization focuses more on the consequences of heightened relevance for the individual in reaction to the experience.

Specifically, we found that events in a game could increase or decrease an individual's involvement with the experience, while the level of involvement with the team for example can stay the same. The dynamic nature of involvement was proposed by Hirschman and Holbrook (1982) to be a factor of the longitudinal nature of experiences such as football games, which are experienced over time and during which preferred patterns of arousal may be violated. Thus, sponsoring or aligning oneself with a team, an event, or a specific game as a marketer is an even riskier proposition if the consumer's emotion and satisfaction depend on the variable and unpredictable characteristics of the game.

> **Thus, sponsoring or aligning oneself with a team, an event, or a specific game as a marketer is an even riskier proposition if the consumer's emotion and satisfaction depend on the variable and unpredictable characteristics of the game.**

This research provides one step toward improving the level of understanding as to the nature of the person-experience interaction that most scholars agree influences marketing and other variables and that too few scholars explore thoroughly. In contrast to traditional product marketing, experiential leisure service consumption, such as sport spectating, forces marketers to examine the consumption experience from a different perspective than that offered by the traditional consumer decision-making approach (Hirschman & Holbrook, 1982). As Kates (1998) points out there has been little research to assist marketers in understanding the dynamics of experiential consumption.

> **In contrast to traditional product marketing, experiential leisure service consumption, such as sport spectating, forces marketers to examine the consumption experience from a different perspective than that offered by the traditional consumer decision-making approach.**

This study found evidence to support the proposition that mood and involvement are not static constructs in experiential leisure services such as sport consumption. While these results are truly exploratory in nature, this form of data collection, combined with some of the methods used by ethnographic researchers, would appear to be the logical choice for more robust and more generalizable results. There is now scope for future research to attempt to quantify these findings both in the sport consumption context and in the broader leisure service environment. The great challenge for future studies will be to develop methodologies that accommodate the dynamic and holistic nature of experiential consumption. The duality of the mood and involvement constructs suggests that future methodologies should include multiple measures of constructs during actual experience.

# References

Arnould, E. J., & Price, L. L. (1993). River magic: Extraordinary experience and the extended service encounter. *Journal of Consumer Research, 20*(June), 24-45.

Bitner, M. J. (1982). Servicescapes: The impact of physical surroundings on customers and employees. *Journal of Marketing, 56*(April), 57-71.

Burnett, J., Menon, A., & Smart, D. T. (1993). Sports marketing: A new ball game with new rules. *Journal of Advertising Research, 33*(September/October), 21-36.

Calder, B. J. (1977). Focus groups and the nature of qualitative marketing research. *Journal of Marketing Research, 14*, 353-364.

Celsi, R., Rose, R. L., & Leigh, T. W. (1993). An exploration of high-risk leisure consumption through skydiving. *Journal of Consumer Research, 20*(June), 1-23.

Chalip, L., Csikszentmihalyi, M., Kleiber, D., & Larson, R. (1984). Variation of experience in formal and informal sport. *Research Quarterly for Exercise and Sport, 55*(2), 109-116.

Csipak, J. J., Chebat, J. C. & Venkatesan, V. (1995). Channel structure, consumer involvement and perceived service quality: An empirical study of the distribution of services. *Journal of Marketing Management, 11*, 227-241.

Dale, G. (1996). Existential phenomenology: Emphasizing the experience of the athlete in sport psychology research. *The Sport Psychologist, 10*, 307-321.

Eastman, S. T., & Riggs, K. E. (1994). Televised sports and ritual: Fan experiences. *Sociology of Sport Journal, 11*, 249-274.

Gardner, M. P. (1985). Mood states and consumer behavior: A critical review. *Journal of Consumer Research, 12*(3), 281-301.

George, J. M., & Jones, G. R. (1996). The experience of work and turnover intentions: Interactive effects of value attainment, job satisfaction, and positive moods. *Journal of Applied Psychology, 81*(3), 318-326.

Hirschman, E. C., & Holbrook, M. B. (1982). Hedonic consumption: Emerging concepts, methods and propositions. *Journal of Marketing, 46*, 92-101.

Holbrook, M. B. (1986). Emotion in consumption experience: Toward a new model of the human consumer. In R. A. Peterson, W. Hoyer, & W. R. Wilson. (Eds.), *The Role of Affect in Consumer Behavior* (pp. 17-52). Lexington, MA: Heath.

Holbrook, M., & Hirschman, E. (1982). The experiential aspects of consumption: Consumer fantasies, feelings and fun. *Journal of Consumer Research, 9*(September), 132-140.

Kates, S. M. (1998). Consumer research and sport marketing: Starting the conversation between two different academic discourses. *Sports Marketing Quarterly, 7*(2), 24-31.

Knowles, P., Grove, S., & Pickett, G. (1993). Mood and the service encounter. *Journal of Health Care Marketing, 14*(3), 41 - 52.

McColl-Kennedy, J., & Fetter, R. E. (2001). An empirical examination of the involvement to external search relationship in services marketing. *Journal of Services Marketing, 15*(2), 82-98.

McPherson, B. (1972). Socialization into the role of sport consumer: A theory and causal model. (Doctoral dissertation, University of Wisconsin, 1990).

McPherson, B. (1975). Sport consumption and the economics of consumerism. In D. W. Ball & J. W. Loy (Eds.), *Sport and Social Order* (pp. 243-275). Reading, MA: Addison Wesley Publishing Company.

Mittal, B. & Lee, M. S. (1989). A causal model of consumer involvement. *Journal of Economic Psychology, 10*(November), 363-389.

Moneta, G. B., & Csikszentmihalyi, M. (1996). The effect of perceived challenges and skills on the quality of subjective experience. *Journal of Personality, 64*(2), 275-310.

Pavelchak, M. A., Antil, J. H., & Munch, J. M. (1988). The Super Bowl: An investigation into the relationship among program context, emotional experience, and ad recall. *Journal of Consumer Research, 15*, 360-367.

Peterson, R. A., & Sauber, M. (1983). A mood scale for survey research. *Proceedings of the American Marketing Association's Educators Conference* (pp. 409-414). Chicago, IL: The American Marketing Association.

Russell, J. A. and Pratt, G. (1980). A description of the affective quality attributed to environments. *Journal of Personality and Social Psychology, 38*(2), 311-322.

Ruyter, K., & Bloemer, J. (1999). Customer loyalty in extended service settings. *Journal of Service Industry Management, 10*(3), 320-336.

Schultz, R. J. (1996). The effects of mood states on service contract strategies. *Journal of Professional Services Marketing, 14*(1), 117.

Wakefield, K. L., Blodgett, J. G., & Jeffrey, G. (1994). The importance of servicescapes in leisure service settings. *The Journal of Services Marketing, 8*(3), 66.

Westbrook, R. A., & Oliver, R. L. (1991). The dimensionality of consumption emotion patterns and consumer satisfaction. *Journal of Consumer Research, 18*(June), 84-91.

Zaichkowsky, J. L. (1985). Measuring the involvement construct. *Journal of Consumer Research, 12*(December), 341-352.

# CHAPTER 13

# Membership Retention Within the Sporting Industry: Factors Affecting Relationship Dissolution

LARRY G. NEALE
TROY GEORGIU
SHARON PURCHASE

## Abstract

*Relationship dissolution* has been somewhat ignored in the study of the relationship marketing paradigm. While there has been an abundance of literature giving broad conceptualizations on how to master the intricacies of relationships, very little has discussed the concept of relationship dissolution. This is especially true of the sporting industry, which does not yet understand the factors that contribute to members relinquishing their membership and severing relationship ties with the club.

**The sporting industry does not yet understand the factors that contribute to members relinquishing their membership and severing relationship ties with the club.**

Team performance was found to be the most powerful predictor of relationship dissolution; however, both *satisfaction with the sportscape* and *emotional bonds* had a significant influence on the decision for a member not to renew their membership. Although team performance is mostly out of the hands of sport marketers, greater focus should be given to implementing strategies that enhance the emotional aspects of the club-member relationship while also improving aspects of the service facility.

**Greater focus should be given to implementing strategies that enhance the emotional aspects of the club-member relationship while also improving aspects of the service facility.**

# Introduction

The consumption of sport is becoming more congruent with the lifestyle of many Western people (Westerbeek, Shilbury, & Quick, 1998). Changes in the consumer way of life are forcing sporting organizations to be at the forefront of innovative, efficient, and effective marketing strategies that will generate long-term success within the sporting profession. Sport is no longer just a pastime. It is a fast-paced, competitive industry that requires ongoing profit to succeed and highly educated and experienced professionals willing to master its intricacies (Pitts & Stotlar, 1995). If professional sporting clubs are unable to produce that winning formula, their longevity within the industry may suffer.

> **Sport is no longer just a pastime. It is a fast-paced, competitive industry that requires ongoing profit to succeed and highly educated and experienced professionals willing to master its intricacies**

With decreasing amounts of leisure time, and discretionary income being judiciously allocated, sport now has to compete for the consumer dollar with a vast array of both sport and non-sport activities (Westerbeek et al., 1998 p. ix).

By incorporating the unique qualities of the sporting industry into the marketing mix, an organization has a greater chance of capturing that ever-elusive consumer dollar and enhancing the likelihood of off-field success.

The sporting industry is both dynamic and progressive. Its social impact on Australia's population and financial contribution to the economy clearly underlie the important role it currently plays in today's society. While there exists an extensive literature on sporting constructs such as *fan classification* (Hunt, Bristol, & Bashaw, 1999; Kolbe & James, 2000; Melnick, 1993; Murrell & Dietz, 1992) and fan attendance (Kahle, Kambara, & Rose, 1996; Macpherson, Garland, & Haughey, 2000; McDonald & Rasher, 2000; K. Wakefield, Blodgett, & Sloan, 1996), a definite lack of literature exists that examines the subject of *membership retention*. More specifically, the reasons why members of professional sporting teams decide not to renew their season membership and subsequently dissolve all relationship ties with the club needs more study.

> **The reasons why members of professional sporting teams decide not to renew their season membership and subsequently dissolve all relationship ties with the club needs more study.**

The data collected in this study came from members of the West Coast Eagles Football Club, which is an Australian Rules football team currently competing in the Australian Football League (AFL).

## West Coast Eagles Football Club

The West Coast Eagles Football Club (WCE) was formed in 1986 and became the first Western Australian football team to gain entry into the AFL. The team made their national debut in 1987 and finished the season with a credible 11 wins from 22 matches. The Eagles quickly achieved on-field success. During the 1990s they played in the finals series every year, winning two AFL championships.

> **Between 1990 and 1995, membership at the West Coast Eagles nearly tripled. There was not, however, a significant increase in membership the year after the Eagles won either of their premierships.**

The Eagles' proactive marketing department converted their on-field success into a large supporter and membership base. Between 1990 and 1995, membership at the West Coast Eagles nearly tripled, from just over 10,000 members in 1990 to nearly 28,000 by the start of the 1996 season. There was not, however, a significant increase in membership the year after the Eagles won either of their premierships. The 1993 season saw an increase of only 7.85% after winning their first championship in 1992 and an even smaller 2.15% the season after their second premiership win in 1994. These increases were in comparison to a 20% increase in membership in 1997 and nearly an 8% increase in 2000 (WCEagles, 2001). The membership figures for the past decade are illustrated in Figure 1.

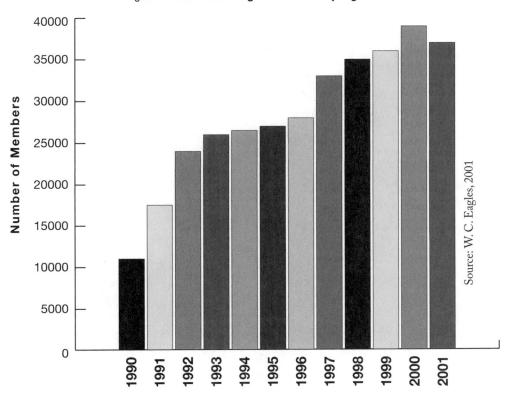

Figure 1 **West Coast Eagles Membership Figures**

Source: W. C. Eagles, 2001

At the start of season 2000, the West Coast Eagles had approximately 38,500 members, which was the second largest membership base in the AFL. At the conclusion of the 2000 AFL season, a record number of members decided not to renew their membership for the 2001 season. The club experienced a 15% reduction in the number of membership renewals. In addition, a membership waiting list that had the potential to create a further 4500 memberships produced only 400 (WCEagles, 2001). While the West Coast Eagles managed to gain some new members through various promotional campaigns prior to the start of the 2001 season, the membership retention rate of only 85% was a major concern for the club.

**The club experienced a 15% reduction in the number of membership renewals.**

Figure 2 illustrates the revenue sources of the West Coast Eagles. Thirty-eight percent of total revenue is generated through membership fees. Given the important role members play in relation to the financial success of the West Coast Eagles Football Club, this study investigates the factors that influence a member's decision to dissolve their financial relationship with the club.

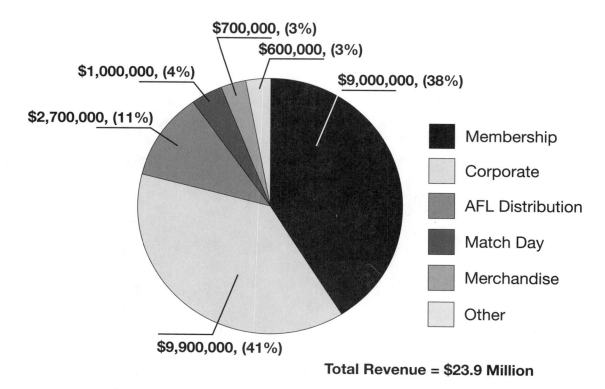

Figure 2 **Revenue Sources**

- $700,000, (3%)
- $600,000, (3%)
- $1,000,000, (4%)
- $2,700,000, (11%)
- $9,000,000, (38%)
- $9,900,000, (41%)

Legend:
- Membership
- Corporate
- AFL Distribution
- Match Day
- Merchandise
- Other

**Total Revenue = $23.9 Million**

# Literature Review

### Relationship Marketing

The direction of marketing is shifting from the activity of attracting customers to actions that keep and nurture customers (Gronroos & Ravald, 1996). Within the service industry in particular, there has been a significant shift away from the traditional four Ps of marketing to a new approach that involves the building and nurturing of relationships (Earp, Harrison, & Hunter, 1999; Fitchett & McDonagh, 1999; Gronroos, 1993; Gummesson, 1994; Lindgreen, 1999; Rich, 2000; Shani & Chalasani, 1992).

> **There has been a significant shift away from the traditional four Ps of marketing to a new approach that involves the building and nurturing of relationships**

Choosing a single definition of relationship marketing (RM) is difficult due to the varying importance given to the elements offered by marketing authors. The following definitions help to provide a basic comprehension of the important characteristics that are associated with RM in today's society.

Morgan and Hunt consider relationship marketing to be "[a]ctivities directed towards establishing, developing and maintaining successful relational exchanges" (1994, p. 22). Gronroos says that

> Relationship marketing is the process of identifying and establishing, maintaining, enhancing, and when necessary, terminating relationships with customers and other stakeholders, at a profit, so that the objectives of all parties are met, where this is done by a mutual giving and fulfillment of promises. (1990, p. 5)

Shani and Chalasari see relationship marketing as

> an integrated effort to identify, maintain and build up a network with individual consumers and to continuously strengthen the network for the mutual benefit of both sides, through interactive, individualized and value added contacts over a period of time. (1992, p. 34)

While each of these definitions sheds a different light on RM, the definition below will be used as the formal definition of RM for the purpose of the study.

> Relationship Marketing is an interactive process that involves all activities that help to identify, create, maintain, and enhance successful exchanges that consistently meet the objectives of both parties over an extended period of time. Relationship Marketing also includes any actions associated with the dissolution of relationships and the short and long term effects the relationship break-down has on each party.

Within the sporting industry, RM can play an integral part in achieving off-field success. With the large degree of variability of the core service offered by sporting organizations (team performance), it is essential to ensure that strong relationships exist between the members and the club. To achieve this, marketers must continually increase value-added interactions over a long period of time. The strength of the relationship needs to be maintained so that even when the core service (team performance) is not up to consumers' standard, there is still financial membership support shown for the club.

> **The strength of the relationship needs to be maintained so that even when the core service (team performance) is not up to consumers' standard, there is still financial membership support shown for the club.**

### Customer Satisfaction

The concept of *disconfirmation,* which measures performance against expectations (P-E), dominates satisfaction research. The basis of disconfirmation dates back to the mid-1960s and comes from adaptation-level theory that compares actual level with reference levels of satisfaction (Helson, 1964). Satisfaction is defined as ". . . a judgment that a product or service feature, or the product or service itself, provided (or is providing) a pleasurable level of consumption-related fulfillment, including levels of under- or over-fulfillment" (Oliver, 1997, p. 13).

Under disconfirmation theory, customer satisfaction can either be measured by comparing actual performance with expected performance (Cronin & Taylor, 1992; Oliver & Bearden, 1983; Oliver & Westbrook, 1982; Tse & Wilton, 1988) or by comparing actual performance with an ideal or norm (Tse & Wilton, 1988). These expectations and evaluations of the performance are made across a number of different attributes (Oliva, Oliver, & MacMillan, 1992; Zeithaml, Berry, & Parasuraman, 1993). These varied attributes have different levels of importance in the overall calculation of the level of satisfaction that customers experience with a service (Carmen, 1990).

A meta-analysis of customer satisfaction by Szymanski and Henard (2001) found that of the predictor variables investigated, the constructs of *functional value* and *disconfirmation* showed the strongest correlation with customer satisfaction.

> **Key areas such as *human resources, service facilities, communication,* and *price* were the four main areas indicated by respondents that contribute significantly to customer satisfaction.**

A study completed by Triand, Aparicio, and Rimbay (1999), suggested that other aspects of the service process within a sporting organization should be given sufficient attention. Key areas such as *human resources, service facilities, communication,* and *price* were the four main areas indicated by respondents that contribute significantly to customer satisfaction. These results indicate that developing and enhancing relationship ties between the club and their fans would influence the level of satisfaction experienced by the consumer.

## Customer Loyalty

Often confused with retention, the concept of loyalty has received considerable academic attention. The classical definition of brand loyalty given by Jacoby and Chestnut is

> "the (a) biased, (b) behavioral response, (c) expressed over time, (d) by some decision-making unit, (e) with respect to one or more alternative brands out of a set of such brands, and (f) is a function of psychological (decision making evaluative) processes." (Jacoby & Chestnut, 1978, p. 165)

Although there seems to be no universally accepted definition of retention (Aspinall, Nancarrow, & Stone, 2001), researchers distinguish retention from loyalty and contend that retention has no psychological processes, it is solely a behavioral phenomenon (East & Sinclair, 2000; Mellens, Dekimpe, & Steenkamp, 1996). East and Sinclair (2000) argue that retention is a construct measured by the length of duration the customer stays with the brand and, as distinct from loyalty, is behaviorally measured by share of category requirements and an attitudinal component. This is reinforced by Bass and Ehrenberg who argue that repeat-purchase theory can explain retention without reference to attitudinal aspects or marketers' actions (Bass, 1974; Ehrenberg, 1988).

## Relationship Commitment

*Relationship commitment* is central to relationship marketing (Gabrino & Johnson, 1999; Hocutt, 1998; Morgan & Hunt, 1994) and is based around the desire to continue relational exchanges with a partner (Dwyer, Schurr, & Oh, 1987; Hocutt, 1998; Morgan & Hunt, 1994). Within the sporting industry, the core characteristics of relationship commitment do not differ significantly (Carpenter, Keeler, Scanlan, Simons, & Schmidt, 1993).

**Their findings indicate that trust is an essential factor in the continuity of the relationship, which in turn is strongly influenced by the level of communication.**

Many authors have attempted to define the factors that determine relationship continuation. The Continuity of Relationship Model (Anderson & Weitz, 1989) investigated relationships within industrial companies. This model suggested that the continuity of a relationship is a function of the (1) trust between the parties, (2) imbalance of power, (3) communication between parties, (4) stakes in the relationship, (5) manufacturer's reputation, (6) age of relationship, and (7) past behavior (Anderson & Weitz, 1989). Their findings indicate that trust is an essential factor in the continuity of the relationship, which in turn is strongly influenced by the level of communication.

The commitment model (Carpenter et al., 1993) relates specifically to the sporting industry. Although looking at active participation, the model can also be interpreted at the spectator level to determine the commitment that a member demonstrates towards a sporting organization. The constructs that were examined included *sport enjoyment* (how much a person enjoys the game itself), *involvement alternatives* (other sporting club memberships or other general activities), *personal investments* (time, money, effort), *social constraints* (pressure from friends and family to continue member status) and *involvement opportunities* (opportunities or benefits that only exist by being a member-e.g., priority seating for finals). While this model can be applied to identify the level of commitment of a spectator, it does not discuss the likelihood of relationship dissolution that results from the level of commitment.

According to Alajoutsijärvi, Möller, and Tähtinen (1999), a relationship is dissolved when relationship activities are no longer carried out, relationship resources are not utilized, or the social bonds between the two parties are no longer active. A more simplified definition offered by Hocutt (1998, p. 193) defines relationship dissolution as "the permanent dismemberment of an existing relationship," whereby the dissolution is not so much an event, but more like an extended process that involves affective, behavioral, cognitive, and social components. In view of this, Hocutt developed a conceptual model (figure 3) of relationship dissolution concentrating primarily on three key constructs:

1. Satisfaction with service providers;

2. Quality of alternative providers; and

3. Investments in the relationship (Hocutt, 1998).

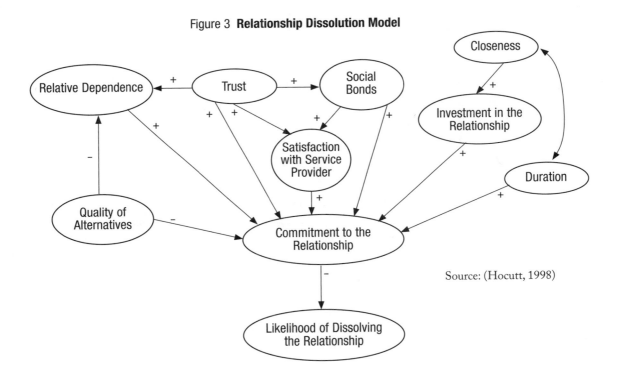

Figure 3 **Relationship Dissolution Model**

Source: (Hocutt, 1998)

Hocutt's relationship dissolution model provides a fundamental outline of the determinants of relationship commitment and relationship dissolution within a service industry.

This model has been chosen as the blueprint from which the conceptual model for this study is based. Importantly, the trust construct is not as prominent in this model, which is suitable because trust does not take on the same role within the sporting industry. Sport consumers are aware that the core product (team

**Sport consumers are aware that the core product (team performance) may not always result in a favorable outcome, unlike when a consumer purchases a television for example, and they trust that it will work every time that they turn it on.**

performance) may not always result in a favorable outcome, unlike when a consumer purchases a television for example, and they trust that it will work every time that they turn it on.

Although Hocutt's model provides a comprehensive outline of relationship commitment and relationship dissolution, there are unique characteristics to the sporting industry that must also be considered.

## Fan Attendance

"Sport has a special role in contemporary society that goes well beyond entertainment" (Kahle et al., 1996, p. 51). Fans often adopt a strong emotional attachment to their team and become highly involved in the team's level of success. A prime example of this is when fans bask in reflective glory when winning ("we" won) and become more subdued and maybe even disassociate themselves from the team when defeat is experienced ("they" lost) (Kahle et al., 1996; Wann & Branscombe, 1993). Pan, McGaugh, and Gabert (1997) believe that spectating behavior was not determined by a single motive or factor, but rather occurred for a wide variety of reasons including sportscape.

> **Sportscape refers to the environment in which the service is delivered, including any tangible or intangible commodities that facilitate performance or communication of the service.**

Sportscape refers to the environment in which the service is delivered, including any tangible or intangible commodities that facilitate performance or communication of the service (Lovelock, Patterson, & Walker, 1998). It refers to the sporting facility and other areas, food and beverage facilities, parking, public transportation, pricing, and game time that assist in making up the sporting experience for the consumer (Hill & Green, 2000; Morley & Wilson, 1986; Pan et al., 1997; K. Wakefield et al., 1996). A number of studies have grouped or labeled certain variables as the contributing motivational factors for sports fans to attend sporting events.

Pan, Mc Gaugh, and Gabert (1997) investigated the constructs of individual motives that constituted the decision process when purchasing a season membership for college basketball games. The results of the study indicated that *economic factors, athletic event,* and *team success* were the most important considerations for fans when deciding to purchase a season ticket. More specifically, fans under 40 years of age placed a greater importance on *social factors,* while respondents between 41 and 50 years of age displayed the strongest interest in *team's success.*

Hill and Green (2000) investigated *repeat attendance* as a function of the sportscape as well as a function of *involvement* and *loyalty.* The authors found that the sporting facility

> **The sporting facility should be regarded as the most important element in the marketing mix.**

should be regarded as the most important element in the marketing mix due to the sport placing a high dependence on the facility for its production and that most of the services are experienced within the stadium. They believed that in an increasingly competitive market, businesses are looking to maintain a competitive edge by offering high quality service at the point of sale, which for sport providers means the venue. More importantly, the results suggested that there was a need to build the spectators' "psychological involvement with the sport itself, and to build loyalty to the team" (Hill & Green, 2000).

## Fan Classification

Existing conceptualizations of spectator attendance have tended to concentrate more on aspects such as pricing, performance, and perception of sportscape, failing to identify the level of involvement and, more specifically, fan classification as prime motivators for repeat patronage or in this case, membership retention.

Hunt, Bristol, and Bashaw (1999) define a fan as an "enthusiastic devotee of some particular sports consumption object" (p. 40). The authors proposed that fans develop through a halo effect in a sequential motion over time. That is, a person may first become a fan of the sport itself, then migrate to a particular team before becoming increasingly motivated to engage in behavior relevant to prominent attitudes and feelings. This theory is somewhat supported through the introduction of the socialization theory developed by Kolbe and James (2000). The basis of the socialization theory involves "learning and internalizing the attitudes, values, knowledge and behaviors that are associated with fans of a team" (Kolbe & James, 2000 p.25). It suggests that factors such as personal characteristics, significant others and social settings, significantly contributes to the knowledge, values, dispositions and self-perceptions needed to be a sports fan.

Melnick's (1993) introduction of the sociability concept also follows the socialization theory framework in that it suggests that "sports spectating has emerged as a major urban structure where spectators come together not only to be entertained but to enrich their social psychological lives through the sociable, quasi-intimate relationships available"

**Melnick suggests that "sports spectating has emerged as a major urban structure where spectators come together not only to be entertained but to enrich their social psychological lives through the sociable, quasi-intimate relationships available."**

Murrell and Dietz (1992) provided a connection to fan identification that suggested that greater group identification can enhance group identity (fan support) independent of the outcome (result of game). For sports mangers this means that, the extent to which fans see themselves and their team as part of one group, the greater the possibility of continuing the relationship with the club (membership renewal) over a longer period of time.

Shank & Beazley (1998); Smith (1998) and Meir (2000) examined fan classification by concentrating on the level of involvement and emotional attachment and determining how this related to different types of sport behavior. The findings made a distinction between *serious* and *normal* sports fans. The major difference between the two, was that the serious fan had a deeper involvement in the actual process (game) to the extent of where the result of the game profoundly affected

**The findings made a distinction between *serious* and *normal* sports fans.**

the subsequent behavior of the spectator. Real and Mechikoff (1992) discussed the idea of a *deep fan*, which centralized around a profound self identification with the sporting object which develops into an expression and interpretation of social life.

## Team Performance

Many professional sporting organizations believe the only way to market their product is to win on the field (Bouvinet, 1999). In the past, clubs have resorted to employing short-term tactics such as firing a coach mid-season in an attempt to rejuvenate on-field success, believing that winning is the critical part of the consumer's experience (Gladden & Milne, 1999; Pan et al., 1997; K. Wakefield et al., 1996). Previous research discovered that only 25% of sports fans attended professional sporting events solely on based on a team's winning record (Pan et al., 1997). Similar findings by Hunt, Bristol & Bashaw (1999, p. 439) also supported this: "Fan motivation and subsequent behavior goes beyond the record of the teams and, at times, seems unrelated to performance."

**Previous research discovered that only 25% of sports fans attended professional sporting events solely on based on a team's winning record.**

Membership figures for the Australian Rules Football League (Beacham, 2001), suggested that the number of members for a club does not directly relate to the level of on-field success the club is experiencing. Essendon and St. Kilda were the only two teams to increase their membership numbers from the 2000 season; Essendon finished first and were crowned champions while St. Kilda finished last.

While there has been evidence to suggest that on-field performance may not be the sole determinant of commitment to a sporting club there is a need to consider the impact it has on membership. As team performance is the core product of a sporting organization (Gladden & Milne, 1999), it is imperative to identify the relationship between team performance and commitment to the relationship.

# Conceptual Development

### Research Model

The proposed model focuses on the different factors that may influence the likelihood of relationship dissolution with members of the West Coast Eagles Football Club. More specifically, the research studies the underlying factors that cause members to relinquish their season membership.

Figure 4 **Conceptual Model**

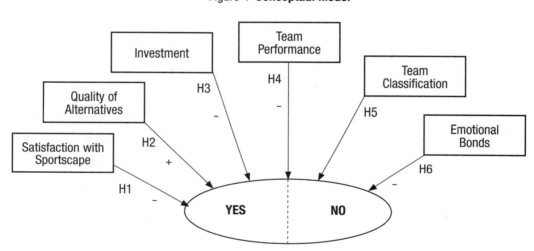

Figure 4 illustrates the proposed model for the study. It is similar to Hocutt's Dissolution Model, but has been modified to include the constructs that are unique to the sporting industry. In addition, some of the constructs that were presented in Hocutt's model (figure 3) were not included for similar reasons.

*Trust* was not included because there is no guarantee that the core service provided (the game itself) will result in what the customer expected. Trust between the spectator and the player consists of the members' reliance that the players will turn up at the required time to play.

There is also little *relative dependence* that exists within the relationship between the club and its members. Members do not require an abundance of information or guidance in order for the core service to be carried out.

*Duration of relationship* or length of membership is going to be included as part of *fan classification*, while 'closeness' will be examined as part of *social bonds*. The only other difference is that the outcome variable, *likelihood of relationship dissolution* will be a dichotomous variable.

# Hypotheses

From the proposed model (figure 4) and a review of the literature, four relevant hypotheses for the study have been developed. Our study could not measure the relationship between dissolution and either fan classification nor quality of alternatives due to survey instrument deficiencies, so these have been omitted.

### Satisfaction with Service Providers and Likelihood of Relationship Dissolution

Determining satisfaction levels of members in relation to all aspects within the control of the organization will provide sufficient evidence to indicate the likelihood of relationship continuation. Continually assessing customer satisfaction is important, especially in the service industry. Areas such as team performance and sportscape are directly linked to satisfaction (Macpherson et al., 2000; Robertson & Pope, 1999; K. Wakefield et al., 1996).

> H1: As *satisfaction with sportscape* increases, the likelihood of relationship dissolution will decrease.

> H4: As *satisfaction with team performance* increases, the likelihood of relationship dissolution will decrease.

### Investment and the Likelihood of Relationship Dissolution

Anderson and Weitz (1989) found evidence to suggest that the greater input of investments, the greater the level of commitment to the relationship. Time, money and effort are all factors of investment that will be tested to evaluate the level of commitment demonstrated by a member. The amount of time a member spends in association with the club (game day, members' functions) and their perception of costs will help determine the likelihood of the relationship dissolving.

> H3: As the *level of monetary investment* increases, the likelihood of relationship dissolution will decrease.

### Emotional Bonds and Likelihood of Relationship Dissolution

Hocutt (1998) suggested that people who develop close personal bonds will tend to hold on to the relationship longer. In addition, previous research in socialization theories (K. L. Wakefield, 1995) has indicated that social bonds affect not only satisfaction but also commitment.

> H6: As the *level of emotional bonds* increases the likelihood of relationship dissolution will decrease.

# Methodology

### Research Design

The research was conducted via a postal survey and targeted members who did not renew their membership for the 2001 AFL season. A mail-out was chosen to provide higher privacy for respondents, and the incentives included a game ball signed by the Eagles team members. A proportionate stratified random sampling method was used for the 800 nonrenewing members, and the 36% response rate yielded 293 completed surveys that were used as part of the data analysis.

## Data Analysis

Factor analysis of the variables yielded two factors that were labeled *emotional bonds* and *satisfaction with the sportscape*. The constructs *investment, quality of alternative,* and *fan classification* did not produce viable factors and were therefore eliminated from further analysis. The included variables and factor loadings are provided in the table below:

**Table 1**

| Factor Name | No. | Dissolution Variables | Factor Loading | % of variance | Cronbach Alpha |
|---|---|---|---|---|---|
| | 1 | I am a passionate supporter of the West Coast Eagles | 0.678 | 30.493 | 0.7145 |
| | 2 | My 2000 membership was a worthwhile purchase | 0.60. | | |
| Emotional Bonds | 3 | I do not feel a strong sense of belonging to the West Coast Eagles | 0.598 | | |
| | 4 | I am committed to supporting the West Coast Eagles | 0.548 | | |
| | 5 | Rate your satisfaction of the overall game day experience | 0.450 | | |
| | 1 | Rate your satisfaction of the parking facilities | 0.554 | 12.813 | 0.7157 |
| | 2 | Rate your satisfaction of the public transportation | 0.529 | | |
| Satisfaction with the Sportscape | 3 | Rate your satisfaction of the toilet facilities | 0.477 | | |
| | 4 | Rate your satisfaction of the scoreboard | 0.472 | | |
| | 5 | Rate your satisfaction of the entertainment | 0.430 | | |
| | 6 | Rate your satisfaction of the overall game day experience | 0.376 | | |

While *satisfaction with the sportscape* did not explain as much of the variance (12.813%) as *emotional bonds,* it is still considered a strong factor as it comprises six latent variables that all have factor loadings exceeding 0.03 (Hair, Anderson, Tatham, & Black, 1998).

The factor analysis produced three factors that had Eigenvalues greater than 1, yet after conducting reliability analyses on these factors, only *emotional bonds* and *satisfaction with the sportscape* produced satisfactory Cronbach Alpha levels above 0.7. The eliminated factor, relating to prices of food and beverage, had a Cronbach Alpha level of 0.65.

> While *satisfaction with the sportscape* did not explain as much of the variance (12.813%) as *emotional bonds,* it is still considered a strong factor.

A bivariate correlation matrix was developed to determine whether there were close correlations between the main factors. The results indicated that *satisfaction with the sportscape* and *emotional bonds* were significant and deemed convergent, while *emotional bonds* and *team performance* were also found convergent. Furthermore, each of the factors included items that were theoretically similar and meet the criteria for face validity.

**Table 2**

| | | Emotional Bonds | Satisfaction with the Sportscape | Team Performance |
|---|---|---|---|---|
| Pearson Correlation | Emotional Bonds | 1.000 | 0.182** | -0.239** |
| Pearson Correlation | Satisfaction with the Sportscape | 0.182** | 1.000 | -0.088 |
| Pearson Correlation | Team Performance | -0.239** | -0.088 | 1.000 |

** Correlation is significant at the 0.01 level (2 tailed)

## Results

Due to the dependent variable being binary and the non-normality of the data, logistic regression was chosen as the main analysis tool to test the hypotheses. The dependent variable was whether the respondent was a current member or a past member that has forgone membership for the 2001 AFL season. Forward stepwise logistics regression was used to determine the optimum model and included the three remaining constructs: *emotional bonds, satisfaction with the sportscape,* and *team performance.* This model explained 17.9% of the variance and correctly classified 68.6% of respondents (proportional chance = 36.4%). The Hosmer and Lemeshow Test was significant at the 0.01 level and indicated that logistic regression could be conducted.

**Table 3**

| Construct | Standardized Beta | S.E. | Wald Statistic | Exp (ß) | 95% CI for Exp (ß) | |
|---|---|---|---|---|---|---|
| | (ß) | | | | (ß) | |
| | | | | | Lower | Upper |
| Team Performance | -0.589** | 0.110 | 28.88 | 0.55 | 0.44 | 0.69 |
| Emotional Bonds | 0.458** | 0.151 | 9.15 | 1.58 | 1.17 | 2.13 |
| Satisfaction with Sportscape | 0.426** | .165 | 6.70 | 1.53 | 1.11 | 2.12 |
| Constant | 1.624 | 0.274 | 35.13 | 5.07 | | |

The Wald statistics suggest that *team performance* is a better predictor of the dependent variable than the other two factors due to its value being considerably higher. From these results, it can be concluded that H1, H4, and H6 are all supported.

*Satisfaction with the sportscape* (H1) is accepted. When *satisfaction with the sportscape* increased, there was a reduced likelihood of relationship dissolution. To retain membership, sports clubs should ensure that the facilities such as seating, food and beverages, and other facilities satisfy their current membership.

> **Sports clubs need to increase the emotional attachments of members to their team image to increase their percentage of membership retention between consecutive playing seasons.**

*Team performance* (H4) is accepted. The team's on-field performance does influence a member's decision to renew their membership for the following year. The relationship between team performance and membership is such that as team performance decreases then membership retention is likely to decrease.

*Emotional bonds* (H6) is accepted. When emotional bonds increase there is a reduced likelihood of relationship dissolution. This result indicates that sports clubs need to increase the emotional attachments of members to their team image to increase their percentage of membership retention between consecutive playing seasons.

## Discussion

The strength of team performance as a predictor in relationship dissolution supports past research by Pan, Mc Gaugh, and Bagert (1997) where team performance did stand out as an important factor when purchasing a membership. It should be noted that most past research on team performance considered the construct as a predictor of fan attendance. It is considered that a nonmember can still be a fan, and therefore, no inference can be made concerning team performance to fan attendance. Even though team performance is the strongest predictor of relationship dissolution, there is little sports management methods or personel can do concerning this variable. Therefore, sports management methods or personel should consider more carefully the results of the other two constructs: *satisfaction with the sportscape* and *emotional bonds.*

> **It is considered that a nonmember can still be a fan, and therefore, no inference can be made concerning team performance to fan attendance.**

The latent variables that represented sportscape in this particular study were parking, entertainment, toilets, overall game-day experience, public transport, and scoreboard. Past research (Macpherson et al., 2000; Robertson & Pope, 1999; K. Wakefield et al., 1996) has shown that these variables have an influence on ensuring high attendances. This research has taken this a step further and indicated a relationship between sportscape and membership retention.

Fans often adopt a strong emotional attachment to their team and become highly involved in the team's level of success (Kahle et al., 1996). The results from this study are supported in a nonsporting context by Morgan and Hunt (1994), Gabrino and Johnson (1999) and Hocutt (1998), such that emotional attachments and a feeling of commitment were crucial in maintaining and enhancing relationships.

There are two significant academic implications of this study. First, literature on relationship dissolution is applied to the sporting industry in a manner not done previously. Although Pan, Mc Gaugh, and Gabert (1997) examined factors that would influence the purchase of a season membership, there isn't much literature on the state of the relationship once it has already been established. By applying Hocutt's Dissolution model to sport, future researchers have an appropriate foundation to examine similar situations in the sporting industry.

> **Sports management should consider more carefully the results of the other two constructs: *satisfaction with the sportscape* and *emotional bonds.***

Second, key factors have emerged that should be included in future sport relationship studies. Satisfaction with the sportscape, emotional bonds, and team performance were found to be the key factors directly influencing likelihood of relationship dissolution.

This study also has managerial implications that are important for sports marketers and managers to consider. Although team performance is often out of the sports marketer's control, they can, to a greater extent, reinforce emotional attachments that currently exist between the club and its members, and improve the sporting facility.

> **Although team performance is often out of the sports marketer's control, they can, to a greater extent, reinforce emotional attachments that currently exist between the club and its members, and improve the sporting facility.**

## Limitations and Future Research

The data collection was undertaken mid-season for this study, which may have biased the responses somewhat. Future data collection on relationship dissolution should take place before, during, and after the regular season.

Our study could not measure the relationship between dissolution and either fan classification or monetary investment due to survey instrument deficiencies. Future researchers should consider the association of these two factors with relationship dissolution.

# References

Anderson, E., & Weitz, B. (1989). Determinants of continuity in conventional industrial channel dyads. *Journal of Marketing Science, 8*(4), 310-323.

Aspinall, E., Nancarrow, C., & Stone, M. (2001). The meaning and measurement of customer retention. *Journal of Targeting, Measurement and Analysis for Marketing, 10*(1), 79-87.

Bass, F. M. (1974). The theory of stochastic preference and brand switching. *Journal of Marketing Research, XI*(February), 1-20.

Beacham, D. (2001, April 22). Bomber bandwagon. *Sunday Times,* p. 93.

Bouvinet, J. W. (1999). Customer communication in selected professional sports (MLB, NFL, NHL, NBA): A test. *Sport Marketing Quarterly, 8*(3), 41-44.

Carmen, J. M. (1990). Consumer perceptions of service quality: An assessment of the SERVQUAL dimensions. *Journal of Retailing, 66*(Spring), 33-55.

Carpenter, P. J., Keeler, B., Scanlan, T. K., Simons, J. P., & Schmidt, G. W. (1993). An introduction to the sport commitment model. *Journal of Sport and Exercise Psychology, 15*(3), 1-15.

Cronin, J. J. J., & Taylor, S. A. (1992). Measuring service quality: A reexamination and extension. *Journal of Marketing, 56*(July), 55-68.

Dwyer, F. R., Schurr, P. H., & Oh, S. (1987). Developing buyer-seller relationship. *Journal of Marketing, 51,* 11-27.

Earp, S., Harrison, T., & Hunter, A. (1999). *Relationship marketing: Myth or reality?* Paper presented at the 15th Annual Industrial Marketing and Purchasing Conference, Dublin.

East, R., & Sinclair, J. (2000). *Loyalty: Definition and explanation.* Paper presented at the Australian and New Zealand Marketing Academy Conference 2000: Visionary Marketing for the 21st Century, Gold Coast.

Ehrenberg, A. S. C. (1988). *Repeat buying: Facts, theory and applications* (2nd ed.). Oxford: Oxford University Press.

Fitchett, J. A., & McDonagh, P. (1999). *A citizen's critique of relationship marketing in risk society.* Paper presented at the 15th Annual Industrial Marketing and Purchasing Conference, Dublin.

Gabrino, E., & Johnson, M. S. (1999). Examining the importance of brand equity in professional sport. *Sport Marketing Quarterly, 8*(1), 21-28.

Gladden, J. M., & Milne, G. R. (1999). Examining the importance of brand equity in professional sport. *Sport Marketing Quarterly, 8*(1), 21-28.

Gronroos, C. (1990). Relationship approach to marketing in a service context: The marketing and organizational behavior interface. *Journal Of Business Research, 20*(3), 38-46.

Gronroos, C. (1993). *From marketing mix to relationship marketing.* Paper presented at the Monash Colloquium in Relationship Marketing, Melbourne, Australia.

Gronroos, C., & Ravald, A. (1996). The value concept and relationship marketing. *European Journal of Marketing, 30*(2), 19-30.

Gummesson, E. (1994). *Broadening and specifying relationship marketing.* Paper presented at the Monash Colloquium in Relationship Marketing, Melbourne, Australia.

Hair, J. F., Anderson, R. E., Tatham, R. L., & Black, W. C. (1998). *Multivariate data analysis* (5th ed.). New Jersey: Prentice Hall.

Helson, H. (1964). *Adaptation level theory.* New York: Harper & Row.

Hill, B., & Green, C. (2000). Repeat attendances as a function of involvement, loyalty and the sportscape across three football contexts. *Sport Management Review, 3*(2), 145-162.

Hocutt, M. A. (1998). Relationship dissolution model: Antecedents of relationship commitment and the likelihood of dissolving a relationship. *International Journal of Service Industry Management, 9*(2), 189-200.

Hunt, K. A., Bristol, T., & Bashaw, R. E. (1999). A conceptual approach to classifying sports fans. *Journal of Services Marketing, 13*(6), 439-452.

Jacoby, J., & Chestnut, R. W. (1978). *Brand loyalty measurement and management.* New York: John Wiley and Sons.

Kahle, L. R., Kambara, K. M., & Rose, G. M. (1996). A functional model of fan attendance motivations for college football. *Sport Marketing Quarterly, 5*(4), 51-60.

Kolbe, R. H., & James, J. D. (2000). An identification and examination of influences that shape the creation of a professional team fan. *International Journal of Sports Marketing and Sponsorship, 2,* 23-37.

Lindgreen, A. (1999). *A proposal for the studying of relationship marketing dyads.* Paper presented at the 15th Annual Industrial Marketing and Purchasing Conference, Dublin.

Lovelock, C. H., Patterson, P. G., & Walker, R. H. (1998). *Services marketing.* Sydney: Prentice Hall.

Macpherson, T., Garland, R., & Haughey, K. (2000). *Attracting fans to the game.* Paper presented at the Australian and New Zealand Marketing Academy Conference 2000.

McDonald, M. A., & Rasher, D. (2000). Does bat day make cents? The effect of promotions on the demand for major league baseball. *Journal of Sport Management, 14*(2), 8-27.

Meir, R. (2000). Fan reaction to the match day experience: A case study in English professional rugby league football. *Sport Marketing Quarterly, 9*(1), 34-41.

Mellens, M., Dekimpe, M. G., & Steenkamp, J. B. E. M. (1996). A review of brand loyalty measures in marketing. *Tijdschrift voor Economie en Management, XLI*(4), 507-533.

Melnick, M. J. (1993). Searching for sociability in the stands: A theory of sports spectating. *Journal of Sport Management, 7*(4), 44-60.

Morgan, R. M., & Hunt, S. D. (1994). The commitment-trust theory of relationship marketing. *Journal of Marketing, 58*(3), 20-39.

Morley, C., & Wilson, K. G. (1986). Fluctuating VFL attendances: Some insights from an economic analysis. *The Journal of the Australian Society for Sports History, 3*(1), 69-80.

Murrell, A. D., & Dietz, B. (1992). Fan support of sport teams: The effect of a common group identity. *Journal of Sport and Exercise Psychology, 14*(1), 28-39.

Oliva, T. A., Oliver, R. L., & MacMillan, I. C. (1992). A catastrophe model for developing service satisfaction strategies. *Journal of Marketing, 56*(3), 83-95.

Oliver, R. L. (1997). *Satisfaction: A behavioral perspective on the consumer.* New York: McGraw-Hill.

Oliver, R. L., & Bearden, W. O. (1983). The role of involvement in satisfaction processes. *Advances in Consumer Research, 10,* 250-255.

Oliver, R. L., & Westbrook, R. A. (1982). The factor structure of satisfaction and related post purchase measures. In R. L. Day & K. H. Hunt (Eds.), *New Findings on Consumer Satisfaction and Complaining.* Bloomington, IN: Indiana University Press.

Pan, D. W., Gabert, T. E., & McGaugh, E. C. (1997). Factors and differential demographic effects on purchases of season tickets for intercollegiate basketball games. *Journal of Sport Behavior, 20*(4), 447-465.

Pitts, B. G., & Stotlar, D. K. (1996). *Fundamentals of sport marketing.* USA: Fitness Information Technology.

Real, M. R., & Mechikoff, R. A. (1992). Deep fan: Mythic identification, technology and advertising in spectator sports. *Sociology of Sport Journal, 9*(3), 280-285.

Rich, M. K. (2000). The direction of marketing relationship. *Journal of Business and Industrial Marketing, 15,* 170-179.

Robertson, D., & Pope, N. (1999). Product bundling and causes of attendance and non-attendance in live professional sport: A case study of the Brisbane Broncos and the Brisbane Lions. *The Cyber-Journal of Sport Marketing, 3*(1), 1-13.

Shani, D., & Chalasani, S. (1992). Exploiting niches using relationship marketing. *The Journal of Consumer Marketing, 9*(3), 33-43.

Shank, M. D., & Beasley, F. M. (1998). Fan or fanatic: Refining a measure of sports involvement. *Journal of Sport Behavior, 21*(4), 1998.

Smith, G. J. (1998). The noble sports fan. *Journal of Sport and Social Issues, 12,* 54-65.

Szymanski, D. M., & Henard, D. H. (2001). Customer satisfaction: A meta-analysis of the empirical evidence. *Journal of the Academy of Marketing Science, 29*(1), 16-35.

Triando, X. M., Aparicio, P., & Rimbau, E. (1999). Identification of factors of customer satisfaction in municipal sport centres in Barcelona. Some suggestions for satisfaction improvement. *The Cyber-Journal of Sport Marketing, 3*(4), 1-10.

Tse, D. K., & Wilton, P. C. (1988). Models of consumer satisfaction formation: An extension. *Journal of Marketing Research, 25*(May), 204-212.

Wakefield, K. L. (1995). The persuasive effects of social influence on sporting event attendance. *Journal of Sport and Social Issues, 19*(4), 335-351.

Wakefield, K., Blodgett, J. G., & Sloan, H. J. (1996). Measurement and management of the sportscape. *Journal of Sport Management, 10*(1), 15-31.

Wann, D. L., & Branscombe, N. R. (1993). Sports fans: Measuring degree of identification with their team. *International Journal of Sport Psychology, 24,* 1-17.

WCEagles. (2001). *Annual membership report.* Perth, Western Australia.

Westerbeek, H., Shilbury, D., & Quick, S. (1998). *Strategic sport marketing.* Sydney: Allen & Unwin.

Zeithaml, V. A., Berry, L. L., & Parasuraman, A. (1993). The nature and determinants of customer expectations of service. *Journal of the Academy of Marketing Science, 21*(Winter), 1-12.

# CHAPTER 14

# A Crossnational Analysis of Sport Consumption

JANE SUMMERS
MELISSA JOHNSON MORGAN

## Introduction

Sport consumption has received little attention in the consumer behavior discipline to date, with the field of sport marketing only recently receiving serious interest from academics. Most of the research conducted so far, however, has concentrated on sponsorship and promotion (Abratt et al., 1987; Abratt & Grobler, 1989; Crowley, 1991; Meenaghan, 1991; Pope & Voges, 1994).

**Sport-related research, which has focused on the motivations of sport consumers, has been mainly founded in the disciplines of sociology and psychology.**

Sport-related research, which has focused on the motivations of sport consumers, has been mainly founded in the disciplines of sociology and psychology. Yet even there, the focus has been more on either the social aspect of sport participation or on personality variables and their relationships to sport performance and motivation.

This paper will review the characteristics of sport consumption across three large national groups to explore the consistency of consumption behavior both nationally and demographically. In addition, the paper proposes that sport *enthusiasm*, a construct measured and developed in this research, will be a predictor of sport consumption regardless of national identity and demographic differences. Any model of sport consumption would be greatly strengthened if it was known to be internationally valid and the results of this study will provide this information for future researchers and sport marketers. These findings would also reassure sport-marketing practitioners in

**Sport enthusiasm, a construct measured and developed in this research, will be a predictor of sport consumption regardless of national identity and demographic differences.**

their use of such a model to assist them with their strategic decision-making on an international level.

In summary, this study will make three main contributions: (1) it will test the a priori assumption that sport consumption does vary by age and gender; (2) it will examine the national variability of sport consumption combining both direct and indirect consumption; and (3) the research will determine whether such a construct as sport enthusiasm is a valid predictor of sport consumption.

## Literature Review

Sport permeates all aspects of human life and has universal appeal. Sport speaks to all people of all ages across all cultural and national boundaries. Indeed, the role of the sport consumer is one of the most pervasive leisure roles in modern society. The global trends of increased personal wealth, higher sedentary lifestyles, and increased mechanization have resulted in an increased reliance and relevance of leisure activities in everyday lives of consumers (Arnaudon, 1993; Pitts & Stotlar, 1996; Shoham & Kahle, 1996).

For many individuals much of their everyday behavior involves the consumption of sporting (or leisure) goods and services (Kates, 1998). Sport can be classified as a type of consumption because in the simplest form, it involves the purchase (or rental), use, and disposition of a good or service.

**Sport speaks to all people of all ages across all cultural and national boundaries.**

People's choices of what sporting events to attend or what brand of sporting goods to purchase can, and have been explored with the traditional models of cognitive information processing used in consumer research (Bettman, 1979; Olson, 1980; Kates, 1998). The movement in consumer research to study the symbolic and experiential components of consumption (Holbrook, 1987; Holbrook & Hirschman, 1982) has allowed researchers to also examine the uses and meanings of sport and how consumers derive pleasure and enjoyment through their consumption of sport (Shoham & Kahle, 1996; Schouten & McAlexander, 1995; Mick, 1986; Kates, 1998).

**Sport consumption is a socially sanctioned mode of behavior where an individual can share something on an equal basis with others in the community.**

Sport consumption is clearly a high involvement phenomenon involving many cognitive and affective components. It has also been attributed with certain serious social functions. As early as 1929, Brill (1929) stated that vicarious spectator sports satisfied an important need in providing for the exercise of man's aggressive combative instincts. Gerth and Mills (1954) reported that the vicarious enjoyment derived by sport audiences serves, psychologically, the unintended function of channeling and releasing otherwise unplaceable emotions. It has also been suggested that sport consumption is a socially sanctioned mode of behavior where an individual can share something on an equal basis with others in the community (Beisser, 1967). Sport allows consumers to build a bridge to socially distant acquaintances by providing a common interest that can be free of social restrictions or stigmas (Voight, 1971; Dunning, 1969; Beisser, 1967; Boyle, 1963; Gross, 1961).

Sport consumption has been the focus of a number of researchers in the late 1970s and 1980s both directly and indirectly (Prensky & Wright-Isak, 1997; Kahle, 1983; Cialdini et al., 1976; Nielsen, 1971; Burnett et al., 1993; Kenyon & McPherson, 1973; Lowe & Harrold, 1972; McPherson, 1975; Voigt, 1971) and these early studies have shown that sport consumption does vary by age, gender, marital status, occupation, income levels, and opportunities provided by season length and type

**These early studies have shown that sport consumption does vary by age, gender, marital status, occupation, income levels, and opportunities provided by season length and type of sport.**

of sport. Indeed, some researchers have used traditional demographic bases to segment the consumption of specific sports (Summers & Johnson, 1999; Lascu, et al. 1995; Burnett et al., 1993) with some success.

These studies generally suggest that (a) males under 35 years are the highest direct consumers of sport (Nielsen, 1971; Burnett et al., 1993); (b) that those who have participated in sport are more likely to purchase season tickets

> Even though sport consumption was shown to vary based on demographic characteristics of respondents, we don't know why these differences in the levels of sport consumption occur.

(Lowe and Harrold, 1972); (c) that those from lower socioeconomic strata do not attend sport events as frequently as others (Kenyon & McPherson 1973); and (d) that women and older consumers prefer indirect consumption of sport (Summers & Johnson 1999). What is interesting about these results is that even though sport consumption was shown to vary based on demographic characteristics of respondents, we don't know why these differences in the levels of sport consumption occur.

This points to a general lack of exploration of consumption constructs within the sport domain (Shoham & Kahle, 1996; Prensky & Wright-Isak, 1997; Kahle, 1983; Cialdini et al., 1976). Results of such studies should provide sport marketers with highly valuable information relating to the segmentation, positioning, and product development variables of strategic marketing. These issues are becoming increasingly important for sport marketers due to the fierce competitiveness of the sport industry for consumers' time and money, and with the increasing investment in sport from the corporate sector. Some researchers have already attempted to gain an indication of sport enthusiasm through examination of sport activeness (Hawes & Lumpkin, 1984) and through investigation of the importance of sport to a particular individual (Dickerson & Gentry 1983). Though in both these cases, these measurements were for descriptive purposes only and were not linked to consumption.

> Sport enthusiasm will include not only the time spent physically engaging in sport, but also the use of sport as a social network, the relative importance of sport in respondents' lives, and an indication of the priority sport has in the decisions about time and monetary allocations.

*Sport enthusiasm* refers to the relative importance consumers place on sport consumption in relation to their everyday lives. The measure of sport enthusiasm will include not only the time spent physically engaging in sport, but also the use of sport as a social network, the relative importance of sport in respondents' lives, and an indication of the priority sport has in the decisions about time and monetary allocations.

Therefore, consumers who have high levels of sport enthusiasm might be expected to place a higher priority on sport consumption activities when considering how they spend their time and money. These individuals may also gain pleasure and enjoyment from the consequences of such decisions, such as enjoying conversations with others about sport, being knowledgeable about sport and being identified as a *sporting* person. Sport enthusiasm then, as a construct, should help researchers to better understand and predict how consumers make decisions about allocating the scarce resources of time and money when faced with a choice between sport consumption versus other pursuits both of the leisure and nonleisure variety.

Further, while it is known that sport consumption is related to a number of demographic bases, most specifically age and gender, the implications of these relationships need also to be explored for predictors of sport consumption as well as being examined for consistency across national boundaries. Thus, it is logical to investigate whether the demographic differences known to affect sport consumption also hold for sport enthusiasm. While it is reasonable to assume that this may be the case, the implications of such findings have significant strategic importance for practicing sport marketers.

For example, if it is found that sport enthusiasm does not vary by age and gender, then sport marketers need to look for other reasons for the differences in direct consumption levels for older people and for women. Perhaps the image of live sporting events as a masculine and unruly domain is off-putting to women and more mature people, maybe the style of seating is unattractive to older people, and so on. It could be some of these marketer-controlled issues that have resulted in lower levels of direct consumption and preferences for indirect consumption in these groups, and not their interest in, or enthusiasm for, consumption of sport in general.

If sport enthusiasm is shown to predict sport consumption, then how this relationship alters when the traditional demographic predictors (particularly age and gender) of sport consumption and sport preference are added to the model also needs consideration. If it is found that prediction of sport consumption and sport preference is enhanced by the addition of age and gender, then this means that although sport enthusiasm may add considerable depth and a richness of context to the understanding of sport consumption, age and gender could still be valid indicators of consumption and preference. They would have what is known as incremental validity. If, on the other hand, they are shown not to contribute, then this means that sport researchers and sport marketers alike would have a more powerful and useful predictor of sport consumption and preference-sport enthusiasm.

> **Researchers have collected data from their countries of origin, mainly the United States and Australia, but none have collected data across different countries, or if they have, they have not compared their results.**

Generally, in spite of a wide range of general sport consumption research conducted over the last 20 years or so, researchers have been reluctant to investigate the crossnational variability of sport consumption and, in turn, of its predictors. Researchers have collected data from their countries of origin, mainly the United States and Australia, but none have collected data across different countries, or if they have, they have not compared their results. This study will specifically address this deficiency by comparing three national samples of data collected using the same instrument.

## Method

The three countries chosen for this study were the United States of America (USA), Australia and Malaysia (specifically targeting Chinese-Malaysians). While these countries were initially chosen for convenience, they will provide interesting contrasts. Certainly, Australia and the USA are both known for their high levels of direct and indirect sport consumption per capita and one may propose that the consumption data should be reasonably consistent. The Chinese-Malaysian sample, however, provides information from a small Asian country with a strong sport consumption culture, though maybe less direct sport consumption opportunities than the other two countries. Similarly, it is not known whether the difference in the cultures of the three countries may result in differences in levels of sport enthusiasm and how this may affect sport consumption levels.

> **The Chinese-Malaysian sample, however, provides information from a small Asian country with maybe less direct sport consumption opportunities than the other two countries.**

The data for this study was collected via a self-completion questionnaire, which was delivered to potential respondents by university students. The questionnaire used in the study was divided into three sections over three pages and included 59 questions. The questionnaire took approximately 15 minutes to complete.

One of the main problems sport marketing researchers have when attempting to measure general sport consumption is in obtaining a sample that contains sufficient variability to allow inferences to the general population. Previous sport consumption researchers have contented themselves with samples taken at actual games or with using student-based samples, neither of which provide good samples from which to generalize to the population. The sampling methodology used here provided a low cost alternative to a random national survey exercise with large national samples and sufficient variability for analysis. This sampling design was tested here to determine its suitability for future sport consumption studies and is therefore discussed in some detail as follows.

The *population* of interest was defined as people over the age of 18 years in order to gain as wide a representation of people with as varied a potential range of sporting enthusiasm and consumption habits as possible.

The *sampling frame* that was determined to provide the most efficient, cost effective, and timely access to a representative sample of the population of interest was the personal networks of students from universities in all three countries (Australia, Malaysia, and the US). It was expected that these networks would include many nonstudents. This data collection technique has also been used successfully by many social science researchers, most recently Keaveney (1995) and Bitner, Booms, & Terreault (1990).

The *sampling method* then was for student researchers to deliver the questionnaire to ten people not necessarily known to them. Each person was to complete the questionnaire independently (self-completion) and then provide the student with a contact telephone number and name. The researcher later used these to ascertain that people other than the student had completed the questionnaire. If any contact person from a student's collection of ten questionnaires indicated that they did not complete the questionnaire, the entire ten questionnaires were discarded in an attempt to avoid the possibility that students had not collected the information from these third parties. While this method of sampling is convenient, as the selection of sampling units was left primarily to the student (Malhotra et al., 1996), it also had the following advantages:

a. low cost;

b. comparability with sampling methods employed by other researchers in the discipline;

c. no need for a list of the population; and

d. high expected response rate such that the resultant sample size would allow the multivariate analysis required.

The *sample size* was largely determined by the number of students completing the assigned task. (In this case, 234 Australian students meant that a sample of approximately 2,300 would be returned. Approximately 70 US students meant that a sample of approximately 700 would be returned.) In addition, approximately one third of the Australian student group were from South East Asia and therefore their data collection would be with people from that nationality (approximately 950 questionnaires were anticipated from Malaysia and other Asian countries).

# Results

The results of the study will be presented in two stages. First, the descriptive statistics will be reported, and second, the data analysis results will be presented.

The final sample of 2,980 responses comprises 1,359 Australians, 916 Malaysians, and 705 North Americans. Table 1 provides a summary of the main demographic characteristics of the three sample groups. The total sample of 2,980 respondents included slightly more males

**The total sample of 2,980 respondents included slightly more males (52% overall) than females (48% overall) with each sample group having approximately the same gender distribution.**

(52% overall) than females (48% overall) with each sample group having approximately the same gender distribution. Just over half, or 59% of the sample were single, 36% were married and the remaining 5% were divorced or separated.

A little over two-thirds of the total sample had no children (68%). This proportion was consistent in the Australian sample, with slightly more of the Malaysian sample indicating no children (80%) and slightly less in the American sample (57%). Almost half, or 49% of the total sample, were between 18 and 25 years old; over a third, or 42%, were aged 26-40 years; and the remaining 18% were over 41 years of age. This proportion was roughly consistent in each of the different country groupings, with the Malaysian group having the most in the 18-25 year age group (nearly 60%) and the least in the over 40 age grouping (9%).

### Table 1 - Demographic Characteristics of the Samples

|  | Aust. No. | (%) | Malaysian No. | (%) | USA No. | (%) | Total No. | (%) |
|---|---|---|---|---|---|---|---|---|
| **Gender** |  |  |  |  |  |  |  |  |
| **Female** | 667 | 49 | 437 | 48 | 337 | 43 | 1441 | 48 |
| **Male** | 691 | 51 | 479 | 52 | 368 | 57 | 1538 | 52 |
| **Age** |  |  |  |  |  |  |  |  |
| **18 – 21 yrs** | 384 | 28 | 271 | 30 | 141 | 20 | 796 | 27 |
| **22 – 25 yrs** | 249 | 18 | 256 | 28 | 167 | 24 | 672 | 22 |
| **26 – 30 yrs** | 197 | 14.5 | 182 | 20 | 92 | 13 | 471 | 16 |
| **31 – 40 yrs** | 230 | 17 | 116 | 12 | 198 | 17 | 544 | 18 |
| **41 – 50 yrs** | 191 | 14 | 70 | 7 | 127 | 18 | 316 | 10 |
| **51 – 60 yrs** | 68 | 5 | 19 | 2 | 47 | 7 | 134 | 4 |
| **over 60 yrs** | 38 | 2.5 | 2 | -- | 10 | 1 | 50 | 2 |
| **Marital Status** |  |  |  |  |  |  |  |  |
| **Married/de facto** | 577 | 42.5 | 211 | 23 | 279 | 39 | 1067 | 36 |
| **Single** | 712 | 52.5 | 694 | 76 | 361 | 51 | 1767 | 59 |
| **Other** | 68 | 5 | 11 | 1 | 65 | 10 | 144 | 5 |
| **Number of children** |  |  |  |  |  |  |  |  |
| **None** | 894 | 66 | 732 | 80 | 401 | 57 | 2027 | 68 |
| **One child** | 100 | 7.5 | 62 | 7 | 106 | 15 | 268 | 9 |
| **Two kids** | 193 | 14 | 52 | 6 | 123 | 17 | 368 | 12 |
| **Three or more kids** | 168 | 12.5 | 66 | 7 | 75 | 11 | 309 | 11 |
| **Occupation** |  |  |  |  |  |  |  |  |
| **White Collar/ Managerial** | 454 | 33.5 | 292 | 32 | 319 | 45 | 1065 | 36 |
| **Blue collar/ trades** | 107 | 8 | 25 | 3 | 60 | 8 | 192 | 6 |
| **Clerical/ Administrative** | 241 | 18 | 191 | 21 | 141 | 20 | 573 | 19 |
| **Student** | 396 | 29 | 333 | 36 | 123 | 17 | 852 | 29 |
| **Unemployed** | 70 | 5.5 | 46 | 5 | 34 | 5 | 150 | 5 |
| **Domestic** | 63 | 4.5 | 23 | 3 | 18 | 3 | 104 | 3 |
| **Retired** | 25 | 1.5 | 6 | 1 | 10 | 1 | 41 | 1 |

Source: Data collected for this study.

Approximately one-third, or 36% of the total sample, were employed in white collar/managerial professions, 29% were students, 19% were employed in clerical/administrative positions, 6% were employed in blue collar positions, and the remaining 9% were either retired, in domestic duties, or unemployed. While this general pattern was consistent across all three groups, the Malaysian group had the smallest proportion employed in blue collar professions (3%) and the most representation of students in their sample (36%).

## Variables in the Analysis

In this study, sport consumption was a composite measure incorporating indicators of both direct (how many sporting events attended and season ticket purchases) and indirect consumption (preferences for watching sport on television, purchase of merchandise). An initial principal components analysis (PCA) was conducted with the data to confirm the unidimensionality of the measure, with results indicatin g that one component was all that was needed to account for the relations among these items. This resulted in a measure of sport consumption that had a minimum score of 6 and a maximum score of 27, where a high score on this variable reflected high consumption of sport both directly and indirectly.

Sport enthusiasm was also measured using a multi-item scale consisting of six items shown in detail in table 2. The descriptive statistics (means and standard deviations) for the variables to be considered in the sport enthusiasm scale are reported in table 2 by national group. There are no major surprises in these results with most means being slightly less than three, suggesting that the majority of respondents had some interest in sport (a score of 1 indicated strong disagreement while a score or 5 indicated strong agreement with an item and a score of 3 indicated a neutral position).

Table 2 – Means and Standard Deviation of Sport Enthusiasm Items by Nationality

| | Australian group** | | Malaysian group** | | American group** | |
|---|---|---|---|---|---|---|
| | Mean* | Std Dvn | Mean* | Std Dvn | Mean* | Std Dvn |
| **Sport Enthusiasm** | | | | | | |
| I usually read the sports section in the paper | 3.00 | 1.57 | 3.45 | 1.36 | 3.21 | 1.49 |
| I Exercise regularly to stay fit | 3.37 | 1.27 | 3.52 | 1.16 | 3.49 | 1.18 |
| I would rather go to a sporting event than go shopping | 3.06 | 1.55 | 3.05 | 1.33 | 3.29 | 1.55 |
| Sports are a big part of my life | 2.98 | 1.38 | 3.08 | 1.21 | 3.14 | 1.26 |
| I would rather go to a sporting event than any other leisure activity | 2.50 | 1.30 | 2.79 | 1.17 | 2.73 | 1.23 |
| I am an active participant in one or more sports | 3.02 | 1.53 | 3.08 | 1.26 | 2.98 | 1.34 |
| I thoroughly enjoy conversations about sport | 3.17 | 1.31 | 3.28 | 1.14 | 3.38 | 1.19 |

** Australian group $n$ = 1359, Malaysian group $n$ = 916, American group $n$ = 705,

* Ratings from 1 = Strongly disagree to 5 = Strongly agree, 3 = neutral or no opinion

The factor solution of the exploratory factor analysis on the scale for each nationality showed little differences. In all cases, the scale was one-dimensional and the pattern of factor loadings between the three countries was also reasonably consistent. In addition to examination of the factor analysis results, Cronbach alpha can also be used to assess the internal consistency and reliability of a scale. The Cronbach alpha for all three countries was above 0.8, which is considered to be acceptable for reliable scales. These results are shown in table 3.

Sport consumption, age, gender, and nationality were then examined using a correlation analysis to further explore the pattern of relations between these variables. These results are shown in table 4. It can be noted that gender, age, nationality, and sport enthusiasm are all significantly correlated to sport consumption, but that sport enthusiasm has the strongest correlation (underlined values are significant).

Table 3 **Factor Solution–Sport Enthusiasm Scale (Item Deleted)**

|  | **Factor solution Australian data** <br> **($\alpha$ = 0.8810)** | **Factor solution Malaysian data** <br> **($\alpha$ = 0.8853)** | **Factor solution USA data** <br> **($\alpha$ = 0.8817)** |
|---|---|---|---|
| **Sports are a big part of my life** | 0.839 | 0.836 | 0.812 |
| **I thoroughly enjoy conversations about sport** | 0.803 | 0.776 | 0.837 |
| **I would rather go to a sporting event than any other leisure activity** | 0.744 | 0.744 | 0.765 |
| **I usually read the sports section in the paper** | 0.731 | 0.662 | 0.745 |
| **I would rather go to a sporting event than go shopping** | 0.711 | 0.733 | 0.725 |
| **I am an active participant in one or more sports** | 0.669 | 0.772 | 0.625 |
| **Variance explained** | **56.5%** | **57.1%** | **56.9%** |

* Gender is coded with 1 = female and 2 - male

** Nationality was coded 1 = Australia, 2 = Malaysia and 3 = USA.

Underlined correlations are significant at $p < 0.001$

Gender has a positive correlation with sport consumption, suggesting that males consume more sport generally than do females. Age has a negative correlation with sport consumption, indicating that as a person ages they are likely to consume less sport and this is also the same for sport enthusiasm. Nationality is significantly and positively correlated to both sport enthusiasm and sport consumption, suggesting that Americans may have higher levels of both than the other nationalities sampled, though the relationship appears to be weak. Closer examination of the relationship between nationality and sport consumption suggests that Americans have the highest levels of sport consumption ($\alpha2$ = 265.6, $df$ = 2, $p$ = 0.000) and that there is no difference between the consumption levels of the Australians and the Malaysians ($\alpha2$ = 1.48, $df$ = 1, $p$ = 0.223).

Further examination of the relationships between these variables and sport consumption was then warranted. Specifically, the measure of sport consumption could be decomposed into a measure of

> Nationality is significantly and positively correlated to both sport enthusiasm and sport consumption, suggesting that Americans may have higher levels of both than the other nationalities sampled, though the relationship appears to be weak.

Table 4 **Correlations of Items Related to Sport Consumption**

| | 1 | 2 | 3 | 4 |
|---|---|---|---|---|
| **1. Sport consumption** | | | | |
| **2. Gender*** | 0.170 | | | |
| **3. Age** | -0.055 | 0.019 | | |
| **4. Nationality**** | 0.206 | -0.022 | 0.020 | |
| **5. Sport Enthusiasm** | 0.533 | 0.196 | -0.093 | 0.070 |

* Gender is coded with 1 = female and 2 – male

** Nationality was coded 1 = Australia, 2 = Malaysia and 3 = USA.

Underlined correlations are significant at $p < 0.001$

direct consumption, a measure of indirect consumption, and a measure of how these variables might differ in relation particularly to nationality. It would seem that while the Americans in the sample still had the highest levels of both direct and indirect consumption of sport, ($\chi2$ = 557.73, $df$ = 1, $p$ = 0.000 - direct and $\chi2$ = 14.71, $df$ = 2, p = 0.000 - indirect) there was a significant difference between the Malaysian and Australian samples in this regard. Specifically, the Malaysians had the second highest levels of indirect sport consumption ($\chi2$ = 97.85, $df$ = 1, $p$ = 0.000) and the Australians had the second highest levels of direct consumption ($\chi2$ = 34.65, $df$ = 1, $p$ = 0.000).

These results appear to support the a priori assumptions that sport consumption should vary with age and gender and further that it also appears to vary with nationality. These assumptions will further be explored by way of a regression analysis. As the *a priori* assumptions of the relevance of age, gender, and nationality appear to hold true, these variables will be entered into the regression first as blocks 1 through 3 with sport enthusiasm then being entered as block 4.

*Discussion of regression analysis.* It can be seen in the first regression analysis that all four variables do predict sport consumption (see table 6), but that sport enthusiasm is the most powerful predictor. Furthermore, these results also show that when sport enthusiasm is added to the equation, that the effect of age on the prediction of sport consumption becomes non-significant. Thus it can be said that sport enthusiasm subsumes the effect of age in the prediction of sport consumption and therefore becomes a more useful and powerful predictor of sport consumption than age.

> These results appear to support the *a priori* assumptions that sport consumption should vary with age and gender and further that it also appears to vary with nationality.

> Sport enthusiasm subsumes the effect of age in the prediction of sport consumption and therefore becomes a more useful and powerful predictor of sport consumption than age.

Furthermore, the other variables in the equation, while significant in their contribution to the prediction of sport consumption, do not contribute much of note, as evidenced by the $R2$ values being very low. Therefore, it can be said that while the a priori assumption of sport consumption varying with age, gender, and nationality was confirmed in this analysis, when it comes to the prediction of sport consumption, sport enthusiasm is the most powerful and relevant predictor.

The positive values associated with sport enthusiasm suggest that increased levels of sport enthusiasm lead to an increase in sport consumption.

Table 6 **Regression Results for Sport Consumption**

| Block No. | Variable | Unstandardized B | Standard error | Standardised coefficient B | t-value | R2 | R2 change |
|---|---|---|---|---|---|---|---|
| | Constant | 11.655 | 0.150 | | 77.85 | 0.003 | 0.003 |
| | Age | 0.150 | 0.046 | -0.055 | -3.017 | | |
| 1 | Gender | | | | | | |
| | Nationality | | | | | | |
| | Sport Enthusiasm | | | | | | |
| | Constant | 9.596 | 0.262 | | 36.60 | 0.032 | 0.029 |
| | Age | -0.100 | 0.045 | -0.058 | -3.212 | | |
| 2 | Gender | 1.379 | 0.145 | 0.171 | 9.501 | | |
| | Nationality | | | | | | |
| | Sport Enthusiasm | | | | | | |
| | Constant | 7.661 | 0.302 | | 25.34 | 0.077 | 0.045 |
| | Age | -0.155 | 0.044 | -0.062 | -3.53 | | |
| 3 | Gender | 1.424 | 0.142 | 0.177 | 10.04 | | |
| | Nationality | 1.058 | 0.088 | 0.212 | 12.038 | | |
| | Sport Enthusiasm | | | | | | |
| | Constant | 3.178 | 0.294 | | 10.80 | 0.319 | 0.242 |
| | Age | -0.0028 | 0.038 | -0.011 | -0.748 | | |
| 4 | Gender | 0.606 | 0.124 | 0.075 | 4.870 | | |
| | Nationality | 0.863 | 0.076 | 0.176 | 11.39 | | |
| | Sport Enthusiasm | 0.312 | 0.010 | 0.506 | 32.46 | | |

Italicized values are significant at $p < 0.001$

# Discussion and Conclusion

This study was designed to satisfy three main objectives. The first was to confirm the a priori assumption that sport consumption does vary by age and gender. This was shown to be true with this large multinational sample, where sport consumption was shown to be positively and significantly correlated with gender, and negatively and significantly correlated with age. These findings suggested that males would have higher consumption levels than females and that as the sample aged, there would be less consumption of sport. The findings are consistent with prior research in this area; however, the interesting finding that females are just as enthusiastic about sport as males is an issue that sport marketers have not fully exploited to date. Also of interest was the finding that young females tended to be as highly involved with sport and as enthusiastic about sport as young males.

> The interesting finding that females are just as enthusiastic about sport as males is an issue that sport marketers have not fully exploited to date.

This declining level of sport participation by older females could possibly be explained by changes in life circumstances; however, this is a proposition that needs further investigation. What is known, however, is that as females age, their preferences for sport consumption change from direct consumption to more indirect consumption, a fact that sport media could capitalize on more thoroughly.

The second objective was to examine the national variability of sport consumption, combining both direct and indirect consumption. It was noted that the actual consumption of sport did vary with nationality, particularly when the type of consumption (direct versus indirect) was considered. When the measure of sport consumption was decomposed into direct and indirect consumption measures, it was found that while the Americans still significantly had the highest direct and indirect consumption of sport, the Malaysians had the second highest indirect consumption and Australians the second highest direct consumption.

Perhaps this finding can be explained by the bigger number of direct sporting opportunities found in both the American and Australian market, compared to the Malaysian market and the high value placed on sport participation and sport involvement in these cultures. The finding has implications for sport media, where it is likely that there would be high levels of support for telecast sporting events of a nature that appeals to the Malaysian market.

> **The finding has implications for sport media, where it is likely that there would be high levels of support for telecast sporting events of a nature that appeals to the Malaysian market.**

The third objective was to determine whether such a construct as sport enthusiasm is a valid predictor of sport consumption, and this was confirmed in the regression analysis where sport enthusiasm was shown to predict sport consumption more powerfully and with more accuracy than age, gender, or nationality. This suggests that sport enthusiasm may then be a more useful variable for sport marketers to use in their attempts to segment the sport market, particularly when it is also known that this construct is equally felt by both males and females. Given the dimensions of the construct, there are some valuable guidelines sport marketers could use to increase the level of interest and involvement in the consumption of sport either directly or indirectly.

> **Sport enthusiasm—a measure that both practitioners and academics alike can use easily—is a powerful predictor of sport consumption, and further that sport consumption itself varies with nationality.**

In conclusion, this study has provided valuable contributions to both sport marketing practitioners and sport marketing academics. It has found that sport enthusiasm-a measure that both practitioners and academics alike can use easily-is a powerful predictor of sport consumption, and further that sport consumption itself varies with nationality. Finally, this research has supported other findings that show that consumption of sport does vary with age and gender, but that sport enthusiasm does not, thus providing sport marketers with a useful tool to consider in design and delivery of strategic sport marketing activities.

# References

Abratt, R., Clayton, B., & Pitt, L. (1987). Corporate objectives in sports sponsorship. *International Journal of Advertising, 6,* 299 - 311.

Abratt, R., & Grobler, P. (1989). The evaluation of sports sponsorship. *International Journal of Advertising, 8,* 351-362.

Arnaudon, S. (1993). *Marketing Australian sport: The future.* Australian Council for Heath and Physical Education and Recreation Proceedings, Darwin, NT Australia, pp. 1-9.

Beisser, A. (1967) Membership in the tribe. In A. Beisser (Ed.), *The madness in sports* (pp. 124-141). New York: Meredith Publishing Company.

Bettman, J. R. (1979). *An information processing theory of consumer choice.* Reading: Massachusetts, Addison-Wesley.

Brill, A. A. (1929). The why of the fan. *North American Review, 228,* 429 - 434.

Boyle, R. (1963). *Sport: Mirror of American life.* Boston: Little, Brown.

Burnett, J., Menon, A., & Smart, D. T. (1993). Sports marketing: A new ball game with new rules. *Journal of Advertising Research,* (September/October), 21-36.

Cialdini, R. B., Borden, R.J., Thorne, A., & Sloan, L.R. (1976). Basking in reflected glory: Three (football) field studies. *Journal of Personality and Social Psychology, 34*(3), 366 - 375.

Crowley, M. (1991). Prioritizing the sponsorship audience. *European Journal of Marketing, 25*(11), 11-21.

Dickerson, M. D., & Gentry, J.W. (1983). Characteristics of adopters and non-adopters of home computers. *Journal of Consumer Research, 10*(September), 225-235.

Dunning, E. (1969, September). Some conceptual dilemmas in the sociology of sport. Paper presented at the International Workshop on Sociology of Sport, Macolin, Switzerland.

Gerth, H. H., & Mills, C. W. (1954). *Character and social structure.* London: Routledge and K. Paul.

Gross, E. (1961). A functional approach to leisure analysis. *Social Problems, 9*(Summer), 2-8.

Kahle, L. R. (1983). *Social values and social change: Adaptation to life in America.* New York: Praeger.

Kates, S. M. (1998). Consumer research and sport marketing: Starting the conversation between the two different academic discourses. *Sport Marketing Quarterly, 7*(2), 24-31.

Kenyon, G. S. & McPherson B D (1973). The significance of physical activity and sport: A process of socialization. In G. L. Rarick and H. Forrestt (Ed.), *Physical activity: Human growth and development* (pp. 303 - 332. New York: Academic Press.

Lascu, D., Giese, T., & Toolan, C. (1995). Sport involvement: A relevant individual difference factor in spectator sports. *Sport Marketing Quarterly, 4*(4), 41-46.

Lowe, B., & Harrold, R. D. (1972, January). *The student as sport consumer.* Paper presented at the 75th Annual Meeting of the National College of Physical Education for Men, New Orleans, LA.

McPherson, B. (1975). Sport consumption and the economics of consumerism. In D. W. Ball and J. W. Loy, (Eds.), *Sport and social order,* (pp. 243-275). Reading, Massachusetts: Addison Wesley Publishing Company

Meenaghan, T. (1991). The role of sponsorship in the marketing communications mix. *International Journal of Advertising, 10,* 35-47.

Nielsen, A.C. (1971). *A look at sports.* Chicago: A. C. Nielsen Company.

Olson, J. C. (1980). Encoding processes: Levels of processing and existing knowledge structures. In J. Olson (Ed.), *Advances in Consumer Research* (pp. 154-160). Ann Arbor, MI: Association for Consumer Research.

Mick, D. (1986). Consumer research and semiotics: Exploring the morphology of signs, symbols and significance. *Journal of Consumer Research, 13*(September), 196-213.

Pope, N. K., & Voges, K.E. (1994). Sponsorship evaluation: Does it match the motive and the mechanism? *Sport Marketing Quarterly, 3*(4), 37-45.

Pitts, B. G., & Stotlar, D. K. (1996, *Fundamentals of sport marketing.* Morgantown, WV: Fitness Information Technology, Inc.

Prensky, D.,& Wright-Isak, C. (1997). Advertising, values and the consumption community. In L. R. Kahle & L. Chiagouris (Eds.), *Advertising and Consumer Psychology: Values, Lifestyles and Psychographics.* Mahwah, NJ: L. Erlbaum and Associates conference proceedings, P415 - 423.

Schouten, J.W., & McAlexander, J. H. (1995). Subcultures of consumption: An ethnography of the new bikers. *Journal of Consumer Research, 22*(June), 43-61.

Shoham, A., & Kahle, L. R. (1996). Spectators, viewers, readers: Communication and consumption communities in sport marketing. *Sport Marketing Quarterly, 5*(1), 11-19.

Summers, J., & Johnson, M. (1999, June). Segmentation of the Australian sport market. In A. Manrai & H. L. Medows (Eds.), *World Marketing Congress on Global Perspectives in Marketing for the 21st Century, Volume IX.* Proceedings of the Academy of Marketing Science Conference, Academy of Marketing Science, Malta (pp. 237-288).

Voigt, D.Q. (1971). America's leisure revolution. In D. Q. Voigt (Ed.), *America's Leisure Revolution* (pp. 20-40). Reading, PA: Albright College Book Store.

# CHAPTER 15

# Spectator Satisfaction With the Support Programs of Professional Basketball Games

JAMES J. ZHANG
DALE G. PEASE
DENNIS W. SMITH
KENNETH A. WALL
CHRISTOPHER L. SAFFICI
LORI PENNINGTON-GRAY
DANIEL P. CONNAUGHTON

## Abstract

The purpose of this study was to evaluate spectator satisfaction with the support programs of an NBA team and its relationship to game attendance. This study involved the development and use of the Spectator Satisfaction Scale (SSS). The initial scale was formulated by identifying 27 organizational activities through observations, interviews, and a comprehensive review of literature. Five experts participated in the test of content validity. A random sample of NBA spectators ($N = 861$) was surveyed. Factor, multiple regression, and alpha analyses indicated good measurement characteristics for the SSS. The final version of the scale included 18 items under four factors: *satisfaction with ticket service, satisfaction with amenities of game, satisfaction with audiovisuals,* and *satisfaction with accessibility condition.* Except for *satisfaction with ticket service,* the remaining three factors were found to be positively ($p < .05$) predictive of game attendance and ticket consumption level. Regression and Kruskal-Wallis analyses revealed that the SSS factors were related to several sociodemographic variables (age, ethnicity, family size, economic status, and education). The findings imply that higher spectator *satisfaction with support programs* was associated with higher game attendance. An NBA team should take into consideration the sociodemographic backgrounds of spectators when formulating programs and services.

# Introduction

Professional sport teams are involved in the business of providing goods and services to meet sport consumers' needs. Ongoing analysis of consumer variables, such as customer service quality, is fundamental to marketing professional sports (Mullin, Hardy, & Sutton, 2000; Pitts & Stotlar, 2002; Stotlar, 1989; Yiannakis, 1989). To enhance the marketing of professional basketball teams, it is necessary to identify and study those customer service variables that affect game attendance. Previous studies have primarily been directed at variables related to the core function (i.e., the game itself). Limited investigations have focused on the game support programs that are related to the quality of game operations and their relationship to game attendance. Of the studies that considered game support programs, several investigators concluded that a part of spectator satisfaction came from support program offerings (Hansen & Gauthier, 1989; Noll, 1991; Schofield, 1983). Notably, there are a number of weaknesses associated with these former investigations. First, these studies were primarily descriptive in nature. Comments were made based upon professional insights rather than empirical evidence (Noll, 1991; Schofield, 1983). Second, of those quantitative investigations, a few items, typically one or two, related to support programs were included among many other game attendance-related variables (Hansen & Gauthier, 1989; Schofield, 1983; Wakefield & Sloan, 1995). Considering the fact that there are many types of game support programs, these studies were superficial and lacked specific usefulness in directing team management. To fill this void, a systematic research investigation appeared to be necessary. A systematic study would provide evidence and direction to the management and marketing practices of professional basketball teams.

> **Limited investigations have focused on the game support programs that are related to the quality of game operations and their relationship to game attendance.**

> **To fill this void, a systematic research investigation appeared to be necessary. [This] would provide evidence and direction to the management and marketing practices of professional basketball teams.**

The purpose of this study was to assess variables that affect spectator satisfaction with the support programs of professional basketball games. This involved the following three phases: (a) developing an instrument to measure spectator satisfaction with support programs; (b) examining the relationship of spectator satisfaction to game attendance and ticket consumption; and (c) differentiating spectator satisfaction with respect to sociodemographic variables.

# Review of Literature

National Basketball Association (NBA) teams have two primary product markets (i.e., ticket sales and broadcasting rights, accounting for an average of 41% and 40% of team revenue, respectively). Teams also have secondary revenue producers as well, such as parking, concessions, programs, endorsements, uses of team logos, and media productions. In fact, these secondary resources are an extension of ticket sales (Lachowetz, McDonald, Sutton, & Clark, 2001; Leonard, 1997; Noll, 1991). Therefore, in order to attract and retain spectators, it is necessary for an NBA team to evaluate those factors that may affect game attendance. Periodic evaluation should be conducted to determine target markets, analyze the current market situation and environment, develop marketing objectives and strategies, and provide feedback about the implementation of an overall marketing plan (Brooks, 1994; Mullin et al., 2000; Pitts & Stotlar, 2002; Stotlar, 1989; Yiannakis, 1989).

Researchers have studied the variables that affect game attendance mainly from the following four perspectives: (a) game attractiveness (e.g., individual skills, presence of star players, team records, league standing, record-breaking performance, and closeness of competition); (b) schedule convenience (e.g., game time, day of week, and weather); (c) economics and marketing (e.g., ticket price, marketing promotions, income, availability of substitute forms of entertainment, television effect, and competition caused by other sport events); and (d) sociodemographics (e.g., population, age, gender, ethnicity, occupation, education, and geography) (Greenstein & Marcum, 1981; Hansen & Gauthier, 1989; Schofield, 1983; Zhang, Pease, Hui, & Michaud, 1995). These variables collectively explain more than 50% of total game attendance variation (Baade & Tiehen, 1990; Marcum & Greenstein, 1985; Noll, 1991; Whitney, 1988). Game attractiveness as well as schedule convenience variables has generally been considered to be positively related to game attendance (Baade & Tiehen, 1990; Becker & Suls, 1983; Jones, 1984; Marcum & Greenstein, 1985; Noll, 1991; Whitney, 1988; Zhang et al., 1995; Zhang, Lam, & Connaughton, 2003). With respect to economic and marketing variables, income and marketing promotions have consistently been found to be positively related to game attendance, while ticket price, substitute forms of entertainment, television effect, and competition with other sport events have generally been found to be negatively related to game attendance (Baade & Tiehen, 1990; Bird, 1982; Hansen & Gauthier, 1989; Noll, 1991, Siegfried & Eisenberg, 1980; Zhang & Smith, 1997; Zhang, Smith, Pease, & Jambor, 1997).

**However, conflicting data exist with respect to the relationship of ethnicity to game attendance.**

In terms of sociodemographic variables, researchers have reported that community size (population) is positively related to game attendance. People most likely to attend professional men's sport events are young to middle-aged white males (Greenstein & Marcum, 1981; Noll, 1991; Siegfried & Eisenberg, 1980; Simmons Market Research Bureau, 2000; Whitney, 1988). However, conflicting data exist with respect to the relationship of ethnicity to game attendance. Some researchers considered that the presence of diverse ethnic groups has a negative effect on game attendance (Noll, 1991; Schofield, 1983; Siegfried & Eisenberg, 1980), while others disagreed (Baade & Tiehen, 1990; Schurr, Wittig, Ruble, & Ellen, 1988). Besides the data reported by Simmons Market Research Bureau (2000), few studies have examined the relationship of the educational and occupational backgrounds of spectators to game attendance. Furthermore, previous studies examining the relationships of sociodemographics and game attendance have usually calculated correlation coefficients (or compared the means) between sociodemographic variables and game attendance frequencies directly (e.g., Baade & Tiehen, 1990; Becker & Suls, 1983; Jones, 1984; Marcum & Greenstein, 1985; Noll, 1991; Whitney, 1988). While it is useful to identify the relationships that exist, vital information on where, why, and how relationships exist are unknown. Possibly, the relationships between sociodemographic

**Possibly, the relationships between sociodemographic variables and game attendance are due to some intermediary variables that are controllable**

variables and game attendance are due to some intermediary variables that are controllable (Zhang et al., 1995; Zhang, Smith, Pease, & Mahar, 1996). For instance, Zhang et al. (1995) found that home and opposing team qualities, game promotion, and scheduling convenience were mediators that affect the attendance decisions of spectators with different sociodemographic backgrounds. Hence, in order to improve game attendance, it is necessary to identify and study other mediating variables.

**The strategy should focus on the four interrelated elements of the marketing mix: product, price, promotion, and place. Of these four elements, product is essential.**

Gray (1996), Mullin et al. (2000), and Pitts and Stotlar (2002) explained that sport marketing is the performance of activities that direct the flow of goods and services from a sport organization to consumers in order to accomplish the organizational objectives and to satisfy the customer. The success of sports marketing requires the formulation of a strategy to attract and reach potential consumers. The strategy should focus on the four interrelated elements of the marketing mix: product, price, promotion, and place. Of these four elements, product is essential. According to Brooks (1994), Buell (1984), Mullin et al. (2000), Murray and Howat (2002), and Stotlar (1989), sport games are the core product function of a professional sport team. During a game, the coaching staff, players, and referees are primarily responsible for producing this core product, whereas a team's management usually has little involvement in this process. Instead, the team management primarily works on the other product functions of the game (i.e., game operations such as ticket service, physical and functional quality of the stadium, and intermission amenity activities). The quality of these support programs often affect the overall operational effectiveness of a sport event and may also affect the consumption levels of consumers.

In many ways, the support programs of a sport game are a form of customer service in a business activity. According to Bitran and Hoech (1990), Kotler and Armstrong (1997), and Sasser, Olsen, and Wyckoff (1978), customer service normally has four characteristics: intangible, inseparable, perishable, and variable. All customer services fall somewhere between the continuum of low contact on one end and high contact on the other end with the customers. Two extremes often exist simultaneously in different service areas/forms of an organization. Edvardsson, Gustavsson, and Riddle (1989) and Grönroos (1984) postulated two components of customer service quality: technical quality and functional quality. Technical quality is concerned with what the customer is actually receiving from the service, such as employee knowledge, facility, equipment, and program. Functional quality is concerned with the way in which the service is delivered and thus involves the interaction between the customer and the service deliver, such as courtesy and friendliness of the employee, and efficiency of service. These two dimensions together influence the corporate image of the organization.

> **Satisfied customers are more likely to become involved more frequently in larger volume, to take part in other services offered by the organization, to pay for the benefits that they receive, and to be more tolerant of price increases**

Stoner and Wankel (1989) pointed out that customer satisfaction, a pleasant feeling derived from fulfilled expectations or an unexpected positive surprise, is an important consequence of service quality. Numerous researchers have suggested that the provision of high service quality is critical to the profitability of an organization because it enhances customer satisfaction and in turn it earns customer loyalty (retention). Marketing resources are better spent by keeping existing customers than attracting new ones. In order to satisfy customers, service qualities have to meet or exceed their expectations. Satisfied customers are most often repeat customers. High customer satisfaction results in a better reputation of the organization, lower costs of attracting new customers, less resources devoted to handling and managing complaints, and more customer referrals. Satisfied customers are more likely to become involved more frequently in larger volume, to take part in other services offered by the organization, to pay for the benefits that they receive, and to be more tolerant of price increases (Anderson, Fornell, & Lehmann, 1994; Anderson & Sullivan, 1993; Fornell, 1992; Garvin, 1988; Reichheld & Sasser, 1990). Yiannakis (1989) remarked that one of the critical concerns in sport marketing is to "...monitor consumer satisfaction/dissatisfaction, needs, wants, expectations, and changes in preference over time" (p. 104) in an effort to efficiently identify contingent variables that may relate to the development of strategic marketing plans.

The impetus for research on service quality stemmed from trying to understand general consumer displeasure with services. Another reason for the interest in service quality was the mounting evidence showing that providing superior service produces a competitive advantage. Managers thus became increasingly interested in improving the quality of services provided to their customers. This trend has resulted in numerous studies related to service quality and satisfaction (Wright, Duray, & Goodale, 1992).

Oliver (1980) developed the 'expectancy disconfirmation theory' that suggests that feelings of satisfaction result when consumers compare their perceptions of a product's performance to their expectations. Petrick, Morias, and Norman (2000) explained that if the perceived performance is greater than the initial expectations, initial expectations should be satisfied. Conversely, if the perceived performance is less than expectations, then dissatisfaction should occur. Following the expectancy disconfirmation theory, Parasuraman, Zeithaml, and Berry (1988) developed the Service Quality Scale (SERVQUAL), claiming it as a generic scale for various industries. The SERVQUAL consists of 22 very general measurement questions in five dimensions: (a) tangibles, (b) reliability, (c) responsiveness, (d) assurance, and (e) empathy. The tangibles factor refers to the physical properties (technical) while the other factors refer to the intangible service aspects (functional).

**The SSI includes five factors: ticket service, game amenities, audiovisuals, arena staff, and arena accessibility.**

As Parasuraman et al. (1988) indicated, the SERVEQUAL requires modification and adaptation when applied to various organizational contexts, given that it was initially developed to be generic and adaptable across a broad spectrum of services. Murray and Howat (2002) supported this notion of industry-specific dimensions of service quality. One reason for the examination of industry-specific dimensions is the variability among industries in terms of the service environment. In the recreation and sports industry, services are more closely associated with intangibles. Additionally, the relational aspects of service in the recreation field appear to be related to personnel factors and peripheral factors. Adopting the content nature and factor structure of the SERVQUAL, McDonald, Sutton, and Milne (1995) developed the TEAMQUALTM scale, which includes 39 items under the same five dimensions of the SERVQUAL. This adaptation and modification took into consideration the congruence issue between customer expectation and customer perception (Zeithaml, Berry, & Parasuraman, 1988) and enhanced the measurement relevance to the operations of sport events.

The SERVQUAL model defined perceived service quality as the difference between consumer expectations and perceptions. It is operationalized by subtracting consumers' expectations scores from their perceptions of performance scores (Parasuraman et al., 1988). Although this approach of assessing consumer satisfaction has been widely adopted (Brown, Churchill, & Peter, 1993), a number of recent studies have found that performance-only measures are superior in terms of predictive validity and measurement reliability (Crompton & Love, 1995; Cronin & Taylor, 1992). Whipple and Thach (1988) stated, in explaining the superiority of performance measures, "there is evidence that pre-purchase choice criteria and post-purchase evaluation criteria are not the same" (p. 17). This supports the idea that customers may not be able to accurately indicate the importance of attributes on purchase evaluation and repurchase intentions; therefore, the exclusion of the importance construct may be more practical. Synthesizing the above theoretical concepts and indications, Zhang, Smith, Pease, and Lam (1998) developed the Spectator Satisfaction Inventory (SSI) by conducting an exploratory study that examined the service quality issues in a minor league hockey game setting. The SSI includes five factors: ticket service, game amenities, audiovisuals, arena staff, and arena accessibility.

Similar to marketing studies in other professional sports, professional basketball consumption has typically been investigated from the perspective of game core products (Hansen & Gauthier, 1989; Whitney, 1988; Zak, Huang, & Siegfried, 1979; Zhang et al., 1995). Little scientific evidence is available about the importance of the support programs of professional basketball games and their relevance to the level of game consumption. In this study, the following three research questions were investigated:

**What is the relationship of spectator satisfaction with the game support programs to the level of game consumption?**

1. What are the dimensions of spectator satisfaction with the support programs of professional basketball games?

2. What is the relationship of spectator satisfaction with the game support programs to the level of game consumption?

3. What is the relationship between the sociodemographic backgrounds of spectators and their satisfaction with the game support programs?

Spectators (*N* = 861) from six regular-season home games of a major NBA team in the Western Conference participated in the study.

# Method

## Participants

Spectators (*N* = 861) from six regular-season home games of a major NBA team in the Western Conference participated in the study. Random cluster sampling procedures were utilized to maintain sample representation of spectators with different seat sections, sociodemographic characteristics, and ticket types. This study was conducted during the second-half of a recent competition season, considering that the second-half of the season game would give spectators adequate time to become more familiar with the game support programs of the team.

## Measurements

The conceptual design of this study and selection of measurement variables required the development of a survey instrument that would be robust over time. A questionnaire was developed for this investigation and included two sections: the Spectator Satisfaction Scale and the Background Information Form.

*Spectator Satisfaction Scale (SSS).* Edvardsson et al. (1989) and Grönroos (1984) suggested two components of customer service quality: technical quality and functional quality. A review of literature also indicated that the support programs of an NBA team specifically included, but was not limited to, services, accommodations, arena accessibility, and amenity activities (Greenstein & Marcum, 1981; Hansen & Gauthier, 1989; Schofield, 1983). A number of recent studies have also indicated that performance-only measures are superior in terms of predictive-validity and measurement reliability (Crompton & Love, 1995; Cronin & Taylor, 1992; Whipple & Thach, 1988). Using these concepts as general theoretical guidelines, organizational activities were identified by (a) a review of literature, (b) observing organizational performance of the team during and off games, and (c) interviewing the administrators of the NBA team. In particular, research findings related to the SERVEQUAL (Parasuraman et al., 1988), the TEAMQUALTM (McDonald et al., 1995), the service quality attributes (Murray & Howat, 2002), and the SSI (Zhang et al., 1998) were taken into consideration. Consequently, 27 organizational activities that were related to both technical and functional components of game support programs were identified. These activities are general game operation efforts that are robust over time. To formulate the preliminary scale, each recognized activity was then phrased into a test item in Likert 5-scale (Very Satisfied, Satisfied, Somewhat Satisfied, Unsatisfied, Very Unsatisfied). Test items were arranged in a random order and directions were provided to the respondent.

The instruments were submitted to a panel of experts for content validity testing, which included three university professors in sport management and sport psychology, and two senior NBA team administrators.

*Background Information Form (BIF).* The BIF included three segments: (a) sociodemographic variables (age, family size, family annual income, gender, ethnicity, marital status, education, and occupation); (b) attendance frequencies (number of games having attended during the current season, number of games attended in the previous season, and number of seasons having attended to the NBA team home games); and (c) ticket information on present holding and future interest (full-season ticket, half-season ticket, 10-game ticket, 6-game ticket, and 1-game ticket).

## Procedures

Following the preliminary formulation of the questionnaire, the instruments were submitted to a panel of experts for content validity testing. The panel included three university professors in sport management and sport psychology, and two senior NBA team administrators. Each was asked to examine (a) the appropriateness of the format and the content, (b) the adequacy and representativeness of the identified organizational activities, and (c) the accuracy of a phrased statement. Based on a standard of 80% agreement in the panel, all 27 items were retained.

The arena had 75 seating sections. For each of the six games, 25 sections were randomly selected for the purpose of including subjects from various types of tickets, consumption levels, and sociodemographics. The questionnaire was passed out to the spectators before the start of a game and collected at game halftime. In the questionnaire, the purpose of the study, as well as instructions to the respondent, were presented. Twenty-five university students helped with the test administration of each game; that is, each student was in charge of one section. Data collection directions were provided to the students during a brief training session, which included (a) politely approaching spectators regardless their backgrounds (age, gender, race, etc.), (b) explaining to the spectators that participation in the survey was voluntary and there would be no penalty for failing to participate, (c) obtaining informed consent, (d) letting the spectator decide if he or she has adequate literacy, and (e) thanking the spectators. An average of 500 packets with the SSS and the BIF were delivered in each of the six games. Any spectator who came to more than one of the six games was asked to respond to the survey only once. An average of 144 completed packets were returned from each game (a return rate of 29%). A completed form was defined as one in which all SSS items had to be answered while allowing a couple of missing responses in the BIF variables.

## Data Analyses

Procedures from Version 10.0 of the SPSS for Windows (SPSS, 1999) were utilized to conduct statistical analyses. Construct validity of the SSS was examined through conducting a factor analysis with principal component extraction and varimax rotation. Alpha reliability was calculated for each retained factor. Utilizing the factor scores, regression analyses were conducted to evaluate the predictability of the SSS factors to game attendance. Regression and Kruskal-Wallis (nonparametric ANOVA) analyses were conducted to examine the relationship between ticket type and sociodemographic variables with SSS factors. The adoption of nonparametric statistics was due to considerably unequal sample sizes in the categories of the ticket consumption and sociodemographic variables (Thomas & Nelson, 2001). Since the factor scores were generated from an orthogonal rotation (i.e., the scores of the SSS factors have zero correlation), multiple applications of the Kruskal-Wallis test would not require additional alpha level correction.

# Results

Results are presented in the following sections: (a) characteristics of the subjects, (b) measurement properties of the SSS, (c) spectator satisfaction and ticket types, and (d) spectator satisfaction and sociodemographics.

## Characteristics of the Subjects

The age of the spectators ranged from 10 to 95 years (M = 33.32; SD = 14.08). The family size of the spectators ranged from having 1 person to having 11 persons in a household (M = 3.17; SD = 1.56). The mean annual income of a household was $77,307.69 (SD = $54,012.13). An index for individual economic status was calculated by computing the ratio between family annual income and family size of the household. The mean economic status of the subjects was $29,402.92 (SD = $24,314.38). Frequency distributions of the categorical sociodemographic variables are summarized in Table 1. In general, the characteristics of the subjects were consistent with the profiles of professional basketball game attendants. Yet, the sample had a higher portion (55.6%) of spectators with a household income of $60,000 or more as compared to 20.9% reported by Simmons Market Research Bureau (2000).

The number of season home games spectators attended during the previous season ranged from 0 to 42 (M = 5.42; SD = 9.88). The number of games spectators had attended during the current season ranged from 1 to 41 (M = 6.3; SD = 10.56). The number of seasons spectators had attended the home games of the team ranged from 1 to 23 (M = 4.08; SD = 4.84). With respect to the current ticket holding of the spectators, 99 (11.50%) had full-season tickets, 80 (9.25%) had half-season tickets, 55 (6.39%) had 10-game tickets, 34 (3.95%) had 6-game tickets, and 593 (68.87%) had 1-game tickets at a time. With respect to future ticket interests of the spectators, 203 (23.58%) would like to purchase full-season ticket, 118 (13.70%) would like to purchase half-season ticket, 128 (14.87%) would like to purchase 10-game ticket, 147 (17.07%) would like to purchase 6-game ticket, and 265 (30.78%) would like to purchase 1-game ticket at a time. Spectators generally showed interest in upgrading ticket consumption level in the future.

## Measurement Properties of the SSS

Construct validity of the SSS was tested by a factor analysis. The Kaiser-Meyer-Olkin measure of sampling adequacy (Kaiser, 1974) was .93, indicating that the sample was adequate for conducting a factor analysis. The Bartlett Test of Sphericity was 5812.81 ($p$ = .000), indicating that the hypothesis of the variance and covariance matrix of the variables as an identity matrix was rejected; therefore, a factor analysis was appropriate. From a principal component extraction, 4 factors had an eigenvalue equal to or greater than 1.0, with a total of 57.9% variance explained. The extracted factor matrix was rotated through varimax rotation. Final decisions on the factors and the items were based upon the following criteria: (a) a factor had an eigenvalue equal to or greater than 1; (b) an item had a factor loading equal to or greater than .40 without double loading; (c) a factor was interpretable in terms of its items; (d) a loaded item on a factor was interpretable in terms of remaining items; and (e) a factor had at least two items (Disch, 1989; Nunnally, 1978; Nunnally & Bernstein, 1994; Tabachnick & Fidell, 1996). Consequently, all four extracted factors were determined as the clusters of spectator satisfaction variables toward professional basketball game support programs, with a total of 18 items retained: *satisfaction with ticket service* (STS - 8 items), *satisfaction with amenities of game* (SAG - 4 items), *satisfaction with audiovisuals* (SAV - 3 items), and *satisfaction with accessibility condition* (SAC - 3 items). The re-calculated factor structure for the 18 items is presented in Table 2.

Utilizing the factor scores, relationships between the SSS factors and attendance variables were tested to examine the predictive validity of the scale. Stepwise multiple regression analyses revealed that two factors of SAG and SAV were significantly (p < .05) related to the number of games attended in the previous season, with a total of 6.9% variance explanation. Three factors of SAG, SAC, and SAV were found to be

**Three factors of SAG, SAC, and SAV were found to be significantly (*p* < .05) related to the number of games having attended during the current season, with a total of 7.5% variance explanation.**

## Table 1 Descriptive Statistics for the Sociodemographic Variables (N = 861)

| Variables | Category | N | % | Cumulative % |
|---|---|---|---|---|
| Gender | Male | 533 | 61.9 | 61.9 |
| | Female | 328 | 37.1 | 100.0 |
| Ethnicity | Caucasian | 617 | 71.7 | 71.7 |
| | Hispanic | 103 | 12.0 | 83.7 |
| | African American | 62 | 7.2 | 90.9 |
| | Asian | 23 | 2.7 | 93.6 |
| | Others | 46 | 6.4 | 100.0 |
| Marital Status | Married | 460 | 53.5 | 53.5 |
| | Single | 291 | 33.8 | 87.3 |
| | Divorced | 46 | 5.3 | 92.6 |
| | Widowed | 14 | 1.6 | 94.2 |
| | Others | 50 | 5.8 | 100.0 |
| Income | Below $20,000 | 57 | 7.5 | 7.5 |
| | $20,000 - $39,999 | 134 | 17.7 | 25.2 |
| | $40,000 - $59,999 | 154 | 20.3 | 45.5 |
| | $60,000 - $79,999 | 135 | 17.8 | 63.3 |
| | $80,000 - $99,999 | 116 | 15.3 | 78.6 |
| | $100,000 - $149,999 | 87 | 11.5 | 90.1 |
| | $150,000 - $199,999 | 49 | 6.5 | 96.7 |
| | $200,000 or Above | 25 | 3.3 | 100.0 |
| Education | College Graduate | 270 | 31.4 | 31.4 |
| | High School Graduate | 189 | 22.0 | 53.4 |
| | Advanced Degree | 129 | 15.0 | 68.4 |
| | School Student | 114 | 13.2 | 81.6 |
| | College Student | 73 | 8.5 | 90.0 |
| | Other | 86 | 10.0 | 100.0 |
| Occupation | Professional | 207 | 24.0 | 24.0 |
| | Management | 141 | 16.4 | 40.4 |
| | Sales | 75 | 8.7 | 49.1 |
| | Technical | 59 | 6.9 | 56.0 |
| | Education | 59 | 6.9 | 62.9 |
| | Skilled Worker | 39 | 4.5 | 67.4 |
| | Clerical | 24 | 2.8 | 70.2 |
| | Non-skilled Worker | 13 | 1.5 | 71.7 |
| | Other | 244 | 28.3 | 100.0 |

Table 2 **Solution of Factor Analysis by Principal Component Extraction and Varimax Rotation**

| Factor/Items | Factor Loading | | | |
|---|---|---|---|---|
| | F1 | F2 | F3 | F4 |
| Satisfaction with Ticket Service (8 items) | | | | |
| 1. phone order service | .73 | .17 | .22 | .04 |
| 2. game calendar and schedule | .72 | .04 | .23 | .07 |
| 3. ticket personnel appearance | .71 | .07 | .05 | .36 |
| 4. mail order | .71 | .14 | .16 | .21 |
| 5. availability of ticket sale locations | .69 | .27 | .06 | .05 |
| 6. box office locations | .67 | .10 | .06 | .33 |
| 7. personnel friendliness | .55 | .17 | .31 | .22 |
| 8. ticket price | .50 | .18 | .04 | .14 |
| Satisfaction with Amenities of Game (4 items) | | | | |
| 9. half-time activities | .16 | .78 | .23 | .22 |
| 10. time-out entertainment | .16 | .70 | .25 | .29 |
| 11. dance team (cheer leaders) | .16 | .70 | .17 | .15 |
| 12. food and drink | .19 | .68 | .11 | .19 |
| Satisfaction with Audiovisuals (3 items) | | | | |
| 13. scoreboards | .16 | .09 | .68 | .20 |
| 14. music | .06 | .15 | .61 | .25 |
| 15. public address system | .18 | .26 | .44 | .33 |
| Satisfaction with Accessibility Condition (3 items) | | | | |
| 16. arena access | .14 | .14 | .30 | .71 |
| 17. parking | .06 | .30 | .16 | .68 |
| 18. cleanliness | .24 | .35 | .25 | .55 |

significantly ($p < .05$) related to the number of games having attended during the current season, with a total of 7.5% variance explanation. SAG was also found to be significantly ($p < .05$) related to the number of seasons having attended, with 1.5% variance explanation (Table 3). Alpha coefficients for the factors of STS, SAG, SAV, and SAC were .86, .76, .57, and .71, respectively, indicating that the factors had acceptable internal consistence level (Cronbach, 1951). Overall, the scale displayed good measurement characteristics.

## Spectator Satisfaction and Ticket Types

To further examine the relationship between spectator satisfaction with support programs and game consumption level, the SSS factors were examined in terms of ticket types: presently holding and future interest, respectively. Kruskal-Wallis H tests were conducted to compare mean rank SSS factor scores. For current ticket types, the mean rank SAG and SAV scores, but not STS and SAC scores, were found to be significantly ($p < .05$) different. Compared to season ticket holders (i.e., full season and half season), ticket holders of lower consumption levels (i.e., 10-game, 6-game, and 1-game) were more satisfied with SAG. Season ticket holders were more satisfied with SAV. Tests of Spearman Rank Order Rho correlation coefficients confirmed these findings. For future ticket interest, the mean rank SAV and SAC, but not STS and SAG, were significantly ($p < .05$) different. Season ticket holders were

**Table 3 Stepwise Regression Analysis Examining the Predictability of the SSS Factors to Game Attendance Variables**

| Step | Variable | R | R2 | ΔR2 | B | SE B | ß | F |
|------|----------|------|------|------|-------|------|------|--------|
| **Attendance** of Last Season | | | | | | | | |
| 1 | SAG | .224 | .050 | .050 | 2.190 | .453 | .222 | 23.330 |
| 2 | SAV | .262 | .069 | .019 | 1.269 | .429 | .136 | 8.742 |
| **Attendance of Current Season** | | | | | | | | |
| 1 | SAG | .223 | .050 | .050 | 2.456 | .507 | .223 | 23.496 |
| 2 | SAC | .250 | .063 | .013 | 1.314 | .497 | .122 | 6.998 |
| 3 | SAV | .274 | .075 | .012 | 1.181 | .492 | .110 | 5.750 |
| **Attendance of Seasons** | | | | | | | | |
| 1 | SAG | .122 | .015 | .015 | 0.573 | .226 | .122 | 6.399 |

**Table 4 Kruskal-Wallis H Tests and Spearman Rank Order Rho Correlation Coefficients Examining the Relationship of the SSS Factors to Ticket Consumption**

| Ticket Type | N | Mean Rank | | | |
|-------------|-----|--------|--------|--------|--------|
| | | STS | SAG | SAV | SAC |
| **Kruskal-Wallis H Tests: Present Holding** | | | | | |
| **Full Season** | 99 | 217.89 | 174.39 | 262.83 | 253.79 |
| **Half Season** | 80 | 249.21 | 167.97 | 233.82 | 203.86 |
| **10-Game** | 55 | 235.41 | 207.89 | 187.19 | 215.85 |
| **6-Game** | 34 | 239.25 | 255.61 | 237.46 | 207.25 |
| **1-Game** | 593 | 208.29 | 230.52 | 207.26 | 212.37 |
| | *H Test* | 5.51 | 18.06 | 11.53 | 5.51 |
| | *p value* | .24 | .00 | .02 | .24 |
| | *Spearman Rho* | .09 | -.18 | .13 | .06 |
| | *p value* | .08 | .00 | .01 | .18 |
| **Kruskal-Wallis H Tests: Future Interest** | | | | | |
| **Full Season** | 203 | 227.01 | 209.86 | 250.69 | 218.44 |
| **Half Season** | 118 | 212.78 | 153.85 | 222.55 | 163.95 |
| **10 Game** | 128 | 209.63 | 204.49 | 163.97 | 219.78 |
| **6 Game** | 147 | 197.78 | 211.10 | 185.32 | 174.36 |
| **1 Game** | 265 | 187.15 | 215.96 | 184.51 | 212.86 |
| | *H Test* | 7.96 | 8.95 | 31.32 | 11.12 |
| | *p value* | .09 | .07 | .00 | .03 |
| | *Spearman Rho* | .14 | -.05 | .23 | .01 |
| | *p value* | .01 | .35 | .00 | .83 |

more satisfied with SAV. Full season ticket, 10-game, and 1-game ticket holders were more satisfied with SAC. Tests of Spearman Rank Order Rho correlation coefficients confirmed the findings related to SAV, yet not SAC. Tests of Spearman Rank Order Rho correlation coefficients also revealed that STS was positively ($p < .05$) related to future ticket consumption level (Table 4).

Table 5 **Regression Analyses Examining the Relationship Between the Continuous Sociodemographic Variables With the SSS Factors**

| Predicting Variable | Criterion Variable | R | R² | B | SE B | β | t | p |
|---|---|---|---|---|---|---|---|---|
| Age | STS | -.117 | .014 | -.009 | .004 | -.117 | 2.472 | .014 |
| | SAG | -.259 | .067 | -.019 | .003 | -.259 | 5.622 | .000 |
| | SAV | .019 | .000 | .001 | .004 | .019 | 0.398 | .691 |
| | SAC | .156 | .024 | .012 | .004 | .156 | 3.315 | .001 |
| Family Size | STS | .075 | .006 | .044 | .029 | .075 | 1.523 | .128 |
| | SAG | .110 | .012 | .062 | .028 | .110 | 2.240 | .026 |
| | SAV | .046 | .002 | .027 | .029 | .046 | 0.937 | .349 |
| | SAC | -.008 | .000 | -.004 | .028 | -.008 | 0.156 | .876 |
| Economic Status | STS | .021 | .000 | .001 | .002 | .021 | 0.393 | .695 |
| | SAG | -.105 | .011 | -.005 | .002 | -.105 | 2.016 | .045 |
| | SAV | -.101 | .010 | -.005 | .002 | -.101 | 1.953 | .050 |
| | SAC | .022 | .000 | .001 | .002 | .022 | 0.431 | .681 |

## Spectator Satisfaction and Sociodemographics

Utilizing the factor scores, regression analyses revealed that spectator age was negatively ($p < .05$) related to STS and SAG, while positively ($p < .05$) related to SAC. Family size was found to be positively ($p < .05$) related to SAG. Individual economic status was negatively ($p < .05$) related to SAG and SAV. Yet, these relationships generally explained a very small portion of variance of the SSS factors (Table 5). Kruskal-Wallis H tests were conducted to compare mean rank SSS factor scores in terms of gender, ethnicity, income, marital status, education, and occupation. There were no significant ($p > .05$) difference between male and female spectators toward the SSS factors, except for that female spectators were significantly ($p < .05$) more satisfied with SAV than male spectators. Spectators of different ethnicities had similar satisfaction with the SSS factors, except that Hispanic and African American spectators were significantly ($p < .05$) more satisfied with SAC than Caucasian and Asian spectators. College and school students were more satisfied with SAG, while education was not related to other factors. Family income, marital status, and occupation were not found to be significantly ($p > .05$) related to the SSS factors (Table 6).

**Family income, marital status, and occupation were not found to be significantly ($p > .05$) related to the SSS factors.**

## Discussion

Besides those who are directly involved in the core product of a game (e.g., athletes, coaches, referees, and trainers), many individuals in a professional sport franchise serve as support staff members working in a variety of areas related to administration, marketing, and particularly operations (e.g., ticket sales, electronics, parking, security, cleaning, and amenity activities). The primary functions of these staff members are to provide quality support programs and services to meet customer needs. Consequently, efficiently identifying the needs and wants of spectators and formulating strategies to satisfy

**Table 6  Kruskal-Wallis H Tests Examining the Relationship Between the Categorical Sociodemographic Variables and the SSS Factors**

| Variable | N | | Mean Rank | | | |
|---|---|---|---|---|---|---|
| | | | STS | SAG | SAV | SAC |
| **Gender** | | | | | | |
| Male | | 533 | 208.08 | 216.40 | 196.80 | 212.96 |
| Female | | 328 | 227.97 | 208.33 | 254.63 | 216.47 |
| | *H Test* | | 1.52 | 0.62 | 4.43 | 0.27 |
| | *p value* | | .13 | .54 | .00 | .79 |
| **Ethnicity** | | | | | | |
| Caucasian | | 617 | 215.96 | 221.50 | 220.74 | 215.98 |
| Hispanic | | 103 | 250.19 | 224.86 | 236.24 | 254.43 |
| Afro-American | | 62 | 240.59 | 221.24 | 228.85 | 264.47 |
| Asian | | 23 | 215.94 | 225.63 | 205.75 | 181.06 |
| Other | | 46 | 186.40 | 215.60 | 145.60 | 185.40 |
| | *H Test* | | 4.69 | 0.61 | 2.89 | 15.52 |
| | *p value* | | .32 | .99 | .58 | .00 |
| **Marital Status** | | | | | | |
| Married | | 460 | 206.62 | 209.47 | 221.63 | 217.48 |
| Single | | 291 | 230.35 | 231.56 | 211.43 | 212.24 |
| Divorced | | 46 | 238.18 | 192.78 | 232.18 | 271.34 |
| Widowed | | 14 | 252.43 | 213.86 | 257.57 | 228.43 |
| Other | | 50 | 172.50 | 244.50 | 220.00 | 215.13 |
| | *H Test* | | 5.70 | 4.45 | 1.68 | 4.91 |
| | *p value* | | .22 | .35 | .80 | .30 |
| **Income** | | | | | | |
| Below $20,000 | | 57 | 202.77 | 246.67 | 240.02 | 207.17 |
| $20,000-39,999 | | 134 | 200.43 | 205.47 | 204.10 | 188.84 |
| $40,000-59,999 | | 154 | 217.23 | 200.05 | 210.32 | 213.62 |
| $60,000-79,999 | | 135 | 191.62 | 207.86 | 191.33 | 189.49 |
| $80,000-99,999 | | 116 | 194.91 | 197.93 | 213.65 | 231.23 |
| $100,000-149,999 | | 87 | 182.01 | 175.35 | 181.63 | 176.96 |
| $150,000-199,999 | | 49 | 225.22 | 240.11 | 157.78 | 225.56 |
| $200,000 or Above | | 25 | 243.66 | 185.50 | 194.30 | 216.94 |
| | *H Test* | | 6.98 | 8.38 | 7.55 | 8.71 |
| | *p value* | | .43 | .30 | .37 | 27 |

these needs and wants are substantial in helping support staff members to improve their work quality/productivity (Brooks, 1994; Buell, 1984; Mullin et al., 2000; Pitts & Stotlar, 2002; Stotlar, 1989). Stotlar (1989) stated, "marketing's cornerstone is to provide goods and services to meet customer needs" (p. 23).

> A careful consideration was made to include only those variables that are robust over time for NBA game operations.

Table 6 **(continued)**

| Variable | N | Mean Rank | | | |
|---|---|---|---|---|---|
| | | STS | SAG | SAV | SAC |
| **Education** | | | | | |
| College Graduate | 270 | 219.28 | 188.51 | 202.11 | 228.73 |
| H-School Graduate | 189 | 195.28 | 210.92 | 231.10 | 219.69 |
| Advanced Degree | 129 | 207.58 | 200.53 | 190.18 | 203.53 |
| School Student | 114 | 223.15 | 261.85 | 222.29 | 174.50 |
| College Student | 73 | 226.96 | 251.28 | 237.90 | 229.82 |
| Other | *86* | 280.00 | 167.20 | 156.50 | 221.80 |
| | *H Test* | 6.71 | 22.60 | 9.75 | 10.32 |
| | *p value* | .24 | .00 | .08 | .07 |
| **Occupation** | | | | | |
| Professional | 207 | 204.45 | 187.50 | 202.20 | 194.94 |
| Management | 141 | 171.36 | 183.84 | 185.50 | 208.87 |
| Sales | 75 | 212.39 | 184.06 | 194.42 | 197.56 |
| Technical | 59 | 202.41 | 176.96 | 151.96 | 226.26 |
| Education | 59 | 224.67 | 214.81 | 223.25 | 205.44 |
| Skilled Worker | 39 | 203.32 | 214.74 | 220.23 | 219.36 |
| Clerical | 24 | 192.00 | 199.83 | 116.17 | 191.33 |
| Non-skilled Worker | 13 | 198.93 | 257.79 | 196.07 | 184.93 |
| Others | 244 | 200.22 | 233.92 | 223.30 | 179.06 |
| | H Test | 6.67 | 13.78 | 15.50 | 5.82 |
| | *p* value | .57 | .09 | .05 | .67 |

Through systematically assessing the quality of service and support programs of an NBA team, this study has addressed the importance of satisfying spectator needs through game support programs. This study focused on those support programs (particularly operational practices) that are directly observable and relevant to consumer satisfaction. Because the quality of game management and marketing activities are less relevant to spectator enjoyment of a game, they were excluded in the research design. As part of the study, the Spectator Satisfaction Scale (SSS) was developed. Particularly, a careful consideration was made to include only those variables that are robust over time for NBA game operations. The scale was tested and found to be valid with respect to its content, construct, predictability, and reliability. The relationship of the SSS factors to game attendance, ticket consumption, and sociodemographic variables were then examined using factor scores. It was concluded that to a certain extent the SSS factors were related to game attendance and ticket consumption level, as well as several sociodemographic variables (age, ethnicity, family size, economic status, and education). Unlike other studies that are related to professional basketball attendance (Hansen & Gauthier, 1989; Noll, 1991; Zak et al., 1979; Whitney, 1988), this study was unique in that it systematically evaluated the quality of support programs of an NBA team. Results imply that an NBA team should focus on the identified support program areas so as to satisfy spectator needs through game-extensions.

Out of the 27 game support activities that were identified to be possibly related to spectator satisfaction, 18 were retained in the factor analysis and fell into four factors: satisfaction with ticket service (STS), satisfaction with amenities of game (SAG), satisfaction with audiovisuals (SAV), and satisfaction with accessibility condition (SAC). Three factors (SAG, SAC, and SAV) were found to be predictive of game attendance. Overall, the SSS was found to have good measurement qualities. According to the criteria outlined by Thurstone (1947), simple factor structure was achieved by having a variable loaded highly on one factor (i.e., a factor loading equal to or greater than .40 without double loading). The factors displayed acceptable internal consistency, and they together explained close to 60% variance. These constructs are primarily related to game operation activities, and they were consistent with the two components of customer service quality conceptualized by Edvardsson et al. (1989) and Grönroos (1984): technical quality and functional quality. The SAV and the SAC factors were reflection of the technical component while the STS and the SAG factors were reflection of functional component. The resolved factors were also coherent with the indications related to game attendance by numerous researchers (Greenstein & Marcum, 1981; Hansen & Gauthier, 1989; Schofield, 1983; Zhang et al., 1998). The factor constructs have provided professional basketball teams with fundamental directions to the planning and organization of game support services and programs. The team management would dictate the extent to which staff members actualize these constructs. A professional basketball team administration should focus on the four areas and work with staff members to enhance the role performance in these areas so as to ultimately satisfy spectator needs. As mentioned, this study has focused on support programs primarily related to game operations. There are support staff members at other administrative hierarchy, such as senior team management and marketing. It is unknown whether their performances would be directly related to spectator satisfaction. Hence, additional areas may be identified over time for exploration. Because an orthogonal rotation was used in the factor analysis, the resolved scale may be considered as a multidimensional scale; therefore, each factor may later be adopted individually for different research purposes in a professional basketball setting. If the scale is used to evaluate spectator satisfaction in any other sport, it should be modified and validated.

The finding that SAG, SAC, and SAV were positively related to game attendance with up to 7.5% variance explanation indicates that in general the more satisfied a spectator is toward the quality of amenity programs, arena accessibility, and audiovisuals, the more games he/she attends. That SAG was positively related to season attendance with 1.5% variance explanation indicates that the quality of amenity was predictive of game attendance over seasons. The findings confirmed the general belief in business management that satisfied customers are more likely to become involved more frequently in larger volume (Anderson et al., 1994; Anderson & Sullivan, 1993; Fornell, 1992; Garvin, 1988; Reichheld & Sasser, 1990). They are also consistent with the beliefs of several sport marketing researchers: the quality of support programs affect the overall operational effectiveness of a team and promote the consumption levels of consumers (Brooks, 1994; Buell, 1984; Mullin et al., 2000; Stotlar, 1989; Yiannakis, 1989).

> **Out of the 27 game support activities that were identified to be possibly related to spectator satisfaction, 18 were retained in the factor analysis and fell into four factors:** *satisfaction with ticket service (STS), satisfaction with amenities of game (SAG), satisfaction with audiovisuals (SAV),* **and** *satisfaction with accessibility condition (SAC).* **Three factors (SAG, SAC, and SAV) were found to be predictive of game attendance.**

> **The quality of support programs affect the overall operational effectiveness of a team and promote the consumption levels of consumers.**

> **7.5% variance explanation could mean a difference of three games in attendance. Three games could mean a revenue of $1,620,000.**

Total variance explained in the regression models was less than 10%. While this may not seem to be substantial, this study only focused on one aspect (i.e., spectator satisfaction of support programs) out of many potential variables affecting game attendance. Therefore, the actual variance explained (7.5%) is a considerable portion. An NBA team currently has 42 season home games, not including playoff games. Assuming that service quality of support programs was independent to other game-attendance-related variables not included in the study (e.g., decision making variables), 7.5% variance explanation could mean a difference of three games in attendance. Further assuming that a basketball arena has a capacity of 18,000 and an average ticket costs $30, three games could mean a revenue of $1,620,000. Considering that the mean number of season home games spectators attended during the previous season was 5.4 and the mean number of games spectators had attended during the current season was 6.3, there is no doubt that three games are substantial to marketing strategies of a professional basketball team.

Gray (1996), Mullin et al. (2000), Pitts and Stotlar (2002), and Stotlar (1989) indicated that the competition for the entertainment dollar has increased in recent years. Organizations of all types compete for the customer's discretionary time and money. To counter the competition effectively, professional sport teams need to formulate effective marketing strategies. The management of a sport team generally has little control over the core product (i.e., the game itself). Professional basketball teams should pay attention to the event amenity programs, such as activities before and during games, in order to increase the entertainment value of the game package. Zhang et al. (1995) remarked that various event amenities (e.g., singing, music, dance, mascot, and shooting contest) may be used as a way to promote games by amplifying the fun and exciting atmosphere. Events such as theme nights (e.g., Valentine's night, Mother's Day night, family night) and tie-ins with popular events may be adopted to heighten the entertainment value of the game. Having selected spectator(s) involved in half-time activities is another example

> **Events such as theme nights (e.g., Valentine's night, Mother's Day night, family night) and tie-ins with popular events may be adopted to heighten the entertainment value of the game.**

to increase the participation level of the whole audience. It is necessary to emphasize that event amenities should take into consideration the sociodemographic variables, particularly age, gender, and ethnicity, of the spectators. It is interesting to note that spectators considered food and drink as a part of amenity activities, suggesting that purchasing and consuming food and drink not only provide individual or group activities during the game but may also add excitement to the game contemplation experience. Gantz and Wenner (1995) asserted that having a drink (usually beer) is a typical

> **Spectators considered food and drink as a part of amenity activities, suggesting that these not only provide individual or group activities during the game but may also add excitement to the game contemplation experience.**

group socialization behavior when watching sport events. Frost (1990) asserted that food and drink are an important source of revenue and they should be enjoyable. Wakefield and Sloan (1995) remarked that the quality of food and drink service is a function of variety, taste, and price. Many sport arenas have expanded choices from typical snacks and fast food fare to more formal dinner options such as barbecue. Contracting with established local restaurants to provide better food and choices is a good way for quality control. "In keeping with current societal concerns, stadium (arena) food service might offer some healthier food alternatives and no-alcohol beers" (p. 165). Food prices should be more competitive with restaurants/bars outside the arena.

Arena accessibility generally refers to facility location, design, and management. The finding that spectator satisfaction with accessibility was related to game attendance is consistent with previous beliefs or research conclusions of numerous researchers (Hansen & Gauthier, 1989; Mullin et al., 2000; Mulrooney & Farmer, 1996; Schofield, 1983; Wakefield & Sloan, 1995). Mullin et al. (2000) indicated that "a consumer's

**In keeping with current societal concerns, stadium (arena) food service might offer some healthier food alternatives and no-alcohol beers.**

first impression of her (his) sport experience and critical to her (his) satisfaction and desire to repeat the experience is her (his) journey to and arrival at the facility" (p. 229). Therefore, the arena should be of a location readily accessible from major highways and mass transit. As long as the increased costs are justified by the potential revenue return, a high traffic location is usually necessary to warrant a high level of visibility/exposure. Melnick (1993) suggested that arena accessibility also include the width of aisles and concourse, the space and arrangements of seats, the amount of room afforded for concessions and restroom facilities, and the size of the crowd. The interior design of the arena should have spectators' needs in mind, including comfort, convenience, enjoyment, and social interactions. Mullin et al. (2000) summarized the following three key points related to facility layout: (a) ease of access and exit to minimize length of lines, (b) convenient location and sufficient number of food services, concession stands, and restrooms to reduce lines, and (c) provisions for crowd management and control. Jewel (1992) and Mulrooney and Farmer (1996) added that ticket window location should be of easy accessibility and convenience. The size and number of the box office windows, as well as the waiting area, should be large enough to handle an unexpected number of walk-up sales. Sales windows should be located on all sides of the facility. According to Mullin et al. (2000), Mulrooney and Farmer (1996), and Wakefield and Sloan (1995), there should be ample parking spaces. A general rule for an arena is at least one parking space for every four seats. The arena operator should also own or operate the parking facility in order to control personnel quality, price, safety, and of course, parking revenue, if any. Excessive time spent searching for parking or walking to the arena may add frustration for some low-tolerant or task-oriented individuals. Expected difficulty in leaving the game may cause spectators to leave the game early to avoid long waits in traffic. Both situations may lead to spectator dissatisfaction. Several researchers have indicated that arena cleanliness affects game enjoyment of spectators (Hansen & Gauthier, 1989; Mulrooney & Farmer, 1996; Wakefield & Sloan, 1995). Although arena cleanliness may be affected by its architectural design and age, other aspects of cleanliness are controllable by arena management. Restrooms and concession areas are very easily overflowed with trash and spilled drinks and food by half-time and later part of a game. Hence, there should be a cleanliness monitoring plan that is beyond the pregame preparation by the arena personnel.

Using auditory and visuals as primary channels, the media department of a professional sport team plays a very important role in the presentation, coordination, and facilitation of a game. An electronic score board extends the core product of the game and adds game excitement by displaying update information (e.g., scores, time, foul, and players in game) to the audience (Mullin et al., 2000). Currently, there is a technological trend to build a giant screen adjacent to the scoreboard, which may be used for replay, slow motions, promotions, and even advertisements. In a sense, the television screen serves as a visual procedure for public address. Having a scoreboard of four sides hanging over the center of the court makes it convenient for spectators to look at it without turning their heads, although end-court score boards are still necessary. Today, new basketball arenas are getting bigger, with more suites and club seats, while many older arenas have gone through or planned for similar renovations and expansions. Having television screens for seats that are further away and higher up gradually becomes necessary in order to improve game viewing clarity (Mulrooney & Farmer, 1996). As an integral segment of the media department, the public address broadcasting has been primarily used to announce present activities, future games, or promotions and recognize groups in attendance. Yet, it may be utilized for extended purposes, such as motivating/cheering the fans, educating spectators, controlling the crowd, and tying in with sponsors. Good public address conduct can add game excitement to the spectators (Mullin et al., 2000). Furthermore, it is interesting to note that the quality of music was clustered by the spectators to be under the audiovisuals factor, instead of game amenity activities. This may be because music is played through radio broadcast, and there is commonality between

**Music is a key entertainment element for professional basketball games. It could provide spectators a sensational feeling from the moment when one enters into the arena.**

the quality of music broadcast and other audiovisual variables. Regardless, music is a key entertainment element for professional basketball games. With appropriate selection and broadcasting, music could provide spectators a sensational feeling from the moment when one enters into the arena. Selection of music should take into consideration the sociodemographic characteristics of spectators, such as age. This point will be further emphasized later on when discussing the relationship between the SSS factors and sociodemographic variables.

Mulrooney and Farmer (1996) indicated that the ticket service is usually the first contact of spectators with a sport team and it serves as a financial entity collecting the majority of revenue. Maintaining effective and efficient ticket service would enhance the interests, loyalty, and attendance of sport fans. Yet the findings of this study did not strongly confirm this belief. Although ticket service was extracted as the first factor in the factor analysis and it was found to be of significant zero-order correlation with the total number of games attended in the previous season, it did not resolve as a significant factor in the multiple regression model. There may be three explanations. First of all, unlike previous presumptions, findings of this study were from a data-based investigation. It may be true that in reality ticket service is not related to the attendance of professional basketball games. Secondly, most of the professional sport teams contract their ticket sales with local and/or national ticketing companies. Many spectators purchase their tickets through these companies; therefore, they do not directly deal with the arena ticket sales. Finally, the subjects of this study included spectators of different ticket consumption levels. To some extent, spectators of different ticket types may have received somewhat different services. Thus, variations within one ticket type may have canceled out the variations of other ticket types. Nonetheless, these speculations deserve future investigation.

**Maintaining effective and efficient ticket service would enhance the interests, loyalty, and attendance of sport fans. Yet the findings of this study did not strongly confirm this belief.**

It would be reasonable to assume that ticket consumption level and game attendance level are highly correlated, but they are not identical because a season ticket holder may attend only some of the home games while a single ticket holder may attend multiple games. For example, Zhang and Houston (1995) found that 75% season ticket holders of an NBA team attended 25 or fewer games. The findings of this study revealed that for current ticket holding, ticket holders of lower consumption ticket holders were more satisfied with game amenity activities while higher consumption ticket holders were more satisfied with audiovisuals. This may be due to a variety of reasons, such as interest, familiarity, expectation, and seat section. Higher consumption ticket holders, who generally attend more games, are more familiar with the amenity activities that a team provides. Findings by McDonald (1996) supported this assumption. Providing varying and surprising activities may be a way to generate interest and satisfy needs. On the other hand, lower consumption ticket holders may have lower expectations that may be easier to satisfy. Since audiovisuals are related to the design of the basketball arena, they may have been more effective to those seat sections generally arranged for higher ticket consumption. Location of seat may place one closer to action; so audiovisuals may be unnecessary for better seats. When possible, arenas need to improve the quality of audiovisuals to seat sections generally used for lower ticket consumption. It is necessary to note here that the variable of seat section price was not investigated in this study. The findings that spectator satisfactions toward audiovisuals, accessibility condition, and ticket services were related to future ticket interests have simply confirmed the preceding discussions that better support programs are associated with high consumption. It should be noted that this study was correlational in nature, that is, correlated variables may not have cause-effect relationship. Whether spectator satisfaction with support programs causes change in ticket consumption level deserves further investigation. In order to establish cause-effect relationship, an experimental or longitudinal study is necessary.

**Older spectators tend to be less satisfied with amenity activities and ticket services while younger spectators tend to be more satisfied.**

The fact that age was negatively related to SAG and STS indicated that older spectators tend to be less satisfied with amenity activities and ticket services while younger spectators tend to be more satisfied. These findings imply that formulation of amenity activities should take into considerations the various needs of different age groups. Entertaining programs geared toward young people would not meet the taste of older spectators. Quality ticket service is necessary for older people, particularly in the areas of personnel friendliness and appearance, convenience of ticket sale location, box office, phone order, mail order, and game calendar. Because the ultimate goal of ticket service is to secure service request and provide efficient operation, sales personnel should dress professionally (uniform preferable) and should be trained in professional characteristics: enthusiasm, courtesy, knowledge, ability, and efficiency. Ticket sale locations should be easy accessible and convenient, particularly for senior citizens. Availability of phone and mail order services should be convenient for spectators of all ages. Adequate information should be provided to the patrons about the payment, regulations, restrictions, and ticket pick-up. A convenient will-call service would help to facilitate the phone and mail orders. Mail orders also help the team management build a mailing list for future events. Game calendars should be

**Sales personnel should dress professionally (uniform preferable) and should be trained in professional characteristics: enthusiasm, courtesy, knowledge, ability, and efficiency.**

clear and straight-forward, which should include adequate information on schedule, ticket type (e.g., season, mini-season, or group tickets), seating, price, ordering procedures, and broadcasting schedule. Because previous studies revealed that ticket price was negatively related to game attendance (e.g., Baade & Tiehen, 1990; Hansen & Gauthier, 1989; Zhang et al., 1997), satisfaction with ticket price may suggest lower cost, coupons, and/or discounts. That age was positively related to SAC indicates that older spectators tend to be more satisfied with accessibility conditions while younger spectators

**Generally speaking, the relationships of family size, family income, and individual economic status to spectator satisfaction with game support programs are minimal.**

are less satisfied. This may be due to the greater mobility of younger spectators. Special parking arrangements (e.g., VIP parking), adequate concourse space, mobilized entrance and exit, and educational message requesting to follow regulations (e.g., broadcasting message and printed materials) are a few possibilities to address this issue so as to satisfy the needs of different age groups. Effective traffic safety, crowd control, and risk management procedures need to be highlighted in the overall marketing plan (Mulrooney & Farmer, 1996).

Generally speaking, the relationships of family size, family income, and individual economic status to spectator satisfaction with game support programs are minimal. The finding that family size was positively related to SAG indicated that spectators of larger family tend to be more satisfied with game amenity activities. Data of this study could not provide specific explanations. Yet a couple of possible speculations may be that spectators of larger family size are more likely to have more people attend game together (i.e., socializing and cheering together), and they are more likely to own a lower level of tickets (e.g., season ticket) and hence have lower expectations. A family theme night with appropriate amenity selections could be a good promotional experiment. These speculations need further investigation. That individual economic status was negatively related to SAG and SAV indicated that spectators of higher economic status were less satisfied with game amenities and audiovisuals. Assuming economic status and ticket types are positively correlated, these findings are consistent with those related to ticket consumption levels. Spectators of different economic status may also have different needs and expectations regarding the amenities and audiovisuals. Their needs should be further studied in order to provide more specific evidence to game operations.

**Audiovisuals may be a way to promote female spectators because they are of great market potential for sport events.**

Varying relationships were found between the SSS factors with gender, ethnicity, and education level. Data of this study could not explain why female spectators were more satisfied with audiovisuals than male spectators. A couple of speculations may be (a) male and female spectators have different attention styles and (b) male spectators have higher expectations for audiovisual quality since they usually attend more sport events according to Simmons Market Research Bureau (2000). Regardless, to some extent, audiovisuals may be a way to promote female spectators because they are of great market potential for sport events. That Hispanic and African American spectators were more satisfied with accessibility conditions than Caucasian and Asian spectators may have been due to the higher expectation level of Caucasians spectators who generally attend more sport events (Simmons Market Research Bureau, 2000). Asians may have different cultural habits, but they accounted for a very small portion of the sample. Anyhow, the service quality of accessibility should be addressed to spectators of all ethnic backgrounds. Overall, minority spectators are great market potential to professional basketball teams and their different needs should be addressed in formulating support programs of games. College and school students were more satisfied with amenity activities and that may be because they are generally younger in age and lower in economic status, game attendance level, involvement level, and hence, expectations. Students represent the future market and therefore professional basketball teams should continue

**A 'Student Theme Night,' along with promotional activities at colleges/schools, may be a good way to enhance student attendance.**

to meet their needs and preference for amenity programs whenever possible. A 'Student Theme Night', along with promotional activities at colleges/schools, may be a good way to enhance student attendance. Furthermore, the fact that the mean factor scores of the SSS factors were not found to be different with respect to marital status and occupation indicated that spectators of different marital status and professions may have similar needs and expectations toward game support programs. It is also possible that the team involved in this study has done well in addressing the needs of spectators of these two sociodemographic variables.

**It is suggested that the findings of this study are generalized to professional basketball teams in the same or similar competition level and environment.**

In summary, through this investigation a valid instrument was made available to analyze demand trends from the perspective of spectator satisfaction with support programs of a professional sport event. This research also revealed the importance of providing quality programs and services and the necessity of developing diversified programs and services. Future studies should continue to examine the relationship of spectator satisfaction with other sport attendance related variables (such as team winning records, game attractiveness, team identification, team knowledge, attendance motivation, and decision making) and how the variables function together and lead to increased attendance at professional basketball games. Finally, this study was limited to a sample of spectators attending home games of one NBA team in a major southern city of the United States. The city has a population of over three million with a greater portion of minority groups (i.e., African American, Hispanics, and Asian) compared to the national norm. Although many similarities exist among NBA teams and their market environment, differences may exist. Hence, it is suggested that the findings of this study are generalized to professional basketball teams in the same or similar competition level and environment. Similar studies are suggested for other professional basketball teams, as well as for teams of other sports.

# References

Anderson, E. W., & Sullivan, M. (1993). The antecedents and consequences of customer satisfaction for firms. *Marketing Science, 12,* 125-143.

Anderson, E. W., Fornell, C., & Lehmann, D. R. (1994). Customer satisfaction, market share, and profitability: Findings from Sweden. *Journal of Marketing, 58*(3), 53-66.

Baade, R. A., & Tiehen, L. J. (1990). An analysis of major league baseball attendance, 1969 - 1987. *Journal of Sport and Social Issues, 14,* 14-32.

Becker, M. A., & Suls, J. (1983). Take me out to the ball game: The effect of objective, social, and temporal performance information on attendance at major league baseball games. *Journal of Sport Psychology, 5,* 302-313.

Bird, P. J. (1982). The demand for league football. *Applied Economics, 14,* 637-649.

Bitran, G. R., & Hoech, J. (1990). The humanization of service: Respect at the moment of truth. *Sloan Management Review, 31,* 89-96.

Brooks, C. M. (1994). *Sport marketing: Competitive business strategies for sport.* Englewood Cliffs, NJ: Prentice-Hall.

Brown, T. J., Churchill, G. A., & Peter, J. P. (1993). Improving the measurement of service quality. *Journal of Retailing, 69,* 127-139.

Buell, V. P. (1984). *Marketing management: A strategic planning approach.* New York: McGraw-Hill.

Crompton, J. L., & Love, L. L. (1995). The predictive validity of alternative approaches to evaluation quality of a festival. *Journal of Travel Research, 34*(1), 11-24.

Cronbach, L. J. (1951). Coefficient alpha and the internal structure of tests. *Psychometrika, 16,* 297-334.

Cronin, J. J., & Taylor, S. A. (1992). Measuring service quality: A re-examination and extension. *Journal of Marketing, 56(3),* 55-68.

Disch, J. (1989). Selected multivariate statistical techniques. In M. J. Safrit & T. M. Wood (Eds.), *Measurement concepts in physical education and exercise science* (pp. 155 - 179). Champaign, IL: Human Kinetics.

Doyle, R. C., Lewis, J. M., & Malmisur, M. (1980). A sociological application of Rooney's fan region theory. *Journal of Sport Behavior, 3*(2), 51-60.

Edvardsson, B., Gustavsson, B. O., & Riddle, D. J. (1989). *An expanded model of the service encounter, with emphasis on cultural context* (Research Report No. 89-4). Sweden: University of Karlstad, Services Research Center.

Fornell, C. (1992). A national customer satisfaction barometer: The Swedish experience. *Journal of Marketing, 56,* 6-21.

Frost, D. (1990). Stadium marketers go soft. *American Demographics, 12,* 22-23.

Gantz, W., & Wenner, L. A. (1995). Fanship and the television sports viewing experience. *Sociology of Sport Journal, 12,* 56-74.

Garvin, D. A. (1988). *Managing quality: The strategic and competitive edge.* New York: Free.

Gauthier, R., & Hansen, H. (1993). Female spectators: Marketing implications for professional golf events. *Sport Marketing Quarterly, 2*(4), 21-28.

Godbey, G., & Robinson, J. (1979). The American sports fan: "Spectatoritis" revisited. *Review of Sport & Leisure, 4*(1), 1-11.

Gray, D. P. (1996). Sport marketing: A strategic approach. In B. L. Parkhouse (Ed.), *The management of sport: Its foundation and application* (2nd ed.) (pp. 249-289). St. Louis, MO: Mosby.

Greenstein, T. N., & Marcum, J. P. (1981). Factors affecting attendance of major league baseball: I. Team performance. *Review of Sport & Leisure, 6*(2), 21-34.

Grönroos, C. (1984). A service quality model and its marketing implications. *European Journal of Marketing, 18*(4), 36-44.

Hansen, H., & Gauthier, R. (1989). Factors affecting attendance at professional sport events. *Journal of Sport Management, 3,* 15-32.

Hart, R. A., Hutton, J., & Sharot, T. (1975). A statistical analysis of association football attendance. *Applied Statistics, 24,* 17-27.

Hill, J. R., Madura, J., & Zuber, R. A. (1982). The short run demand for major league baseball. *Atlantic Economic Journal, 10*(2), 31-35.

Hunt, J. W., & Lewis, K. A. (1976). Dominance, recontracting, and the reverse clause: Major league baseball. *The American Economic Review, 66,* 936-943.

Jewel, D. (1992). *Public assembly facilities.* Malabar, FL: Krieger.

Jones, J. C. H. (1969). The economics of the National Hockey League. *Canadian Journal of Economics, 2,* 1-20.

Jones, J. C. H. (1984). Winners, losers and hosers: Demand and survival in the National Hockey League. *Atlantic Economic Journal, 12*(3), 54-63.

Kaiser, H. F. (1974). An index of factorial simplicity. *Psychometrika, 39,* 31-36.

Kotler, P., & Armstrong, G. (1997). *Marketing* (4th ed.). Englewood Cliffs, NJ: Prentice-Hall.

Lachowetz, T., McDonald, M., Sutton, W., & Clark, J. (2001). The national basketball association: Application of customer lifetime value. *Sports Marketing Quarterly, 10*(3), 181-184.

Lee, B. A., & Zeiss, C. A. (1980). Behavioral commitment to the role of sport consumer: An exploratory analysis. *Sociology and Social Research, 64,* 405-419.

Leonard, W. M. (1997). Some economic considerations of professional sports. *Journal of Sport Behavior, 20,* 338-346.

Marcum, J. P., & Greenstein, T. N. (1985). Factors affecting attendance of major league baseball: II. Within-season analysis. *Sociology of Sport Journal, 2,* 314-322.

McDonald, M. A. (1996). *Service quality and customer lifetime value in professional sport franchises.* Unpublished doctoral dissertation, University of Massachusetts, Amherst.

McDonald, M. A., Sutton, W. A., & Milne, G. R. (1995). TEAMQUALTM: Measuring service quality in professional team sports. *Sport Marketing Quarterly, 4*(2), 9-15.

Melnick, M. J. (1993). Searching for sociability in the stands: A theory of sports spectating. *Journal of Sport Management, 7,* 44-60.

Mullin, B. J., Hardy, S., & Sutton, W. A. (2000). *Sport marketing* (2nd ed.). Champaign, IL: Human Kinetics.

Mulrooney A., & Farmer, P. (1996). Managing the facility. In B. L. Parkhouse (Ed.), *The management of sport: Its foundation and application* (2nd ed.) (pp. 223-248). St. Louis, MO: Mosby.

Murray, D., & Howat, G. (2002). The relationships among service quality, value, satisfaction, and future intentions of customers at an Australian Sports and Leisure Center. *Sport Management Review, 5,* 25-43.

Noll, R. G. (1991). Professional basketball: Economic and business perspectives. In P. D. Staudohar & J. A. Mangan (Eds.), *The business of professional sports* (pp. 18-47). Urbana, IL: University of Illinois.

Nunnally, J. C. (1978). *Psychometric theory* (2nd ed.). New York: McGraw-Hill.

Nunnally, J. C., & Bernstein, I. H. (1994). *Psychometric theory* (3rd ed.). New York: McGraw-Hill.

Oliver, R. L. (1980). A cognitive model of the antecedents and consequences of satisfaction decisions. *Journal of Marketing Research, 42,* 460-469.

Parasuraman, A., Zeithaml, V. A., & Berry, L. L. (1988). SERVQUAL: A multiple-item scale for measuring customer perceptions of service quality. *Journal of Retailing, 64*(1), 12-40.

Petrick, J. F., Morais, D. D., & Norman, W. C. (2000). An examination of the determinants of entertainment vacationers intentions to revisit. Proceedings of *2000 TTRA Annual Conference Proceedings,* 117- 125.

Pitts, B. G., & Stotlar, D. K. (2002). *Fundamentals of sport marketing* (2nd ed). Morgantown, WV: Fitness Information Technology.

Reichheld, F. F., & Sasser, E. W. (1990). Zero defections: Quality comes to services. *Harvard Business Review, 68,* 105-111.

Sasser, W. E., Olsen, R. P., & Wyckoff, D. D. (1978). *Management of service operations: Text and cases.* Boston, MA: Allyn & Bacon.

Schofield, J. A. (1983). Performance and attendance at professional team sports. *Journal of Sport Behavior, 6*(4), 196-206.

Schurr, K. T., Wittig, A. F., Ruble, V. E., & Ellen, A. S. (1988). Demographic and personality characteristics associated with persistent, occasional, and non-attendance of university male basketball games by college students. *Journal of Sport Behavior, 11*(1), 3-17.

Siegfried, J. J., & Eisenberg, J. D. (1980). The demand for minor league baseball. *Atlantic Economic Journal, 8*(1), 59-71.

Siegfried, J. J., & Hinshaw, C. E. (1977). Professional football and the anti-blackout law. *Journal of Communication, 17,* 169-174.

Simmons Market Research Bureau. (2000). *Study of media & markets: Sports & leisure.* New York: Simmons.

SPSS. (1999). *SPSS 10.0: Guide to data analysis.* Upper Saddle River, NY: Prentice Hall.

Stoner, J. A. F.; & Wankel, C. (1989). *Management* (3rd ed.). Englewood Cliffs, NJ: Prentice-Hall.

Stotlar, D. K. (1989). *Successful sport marketing.* Dubuque, IA: W. C. Brown.

Tabachnick, B. G., & Fidell, L. S. (1996). *Using multivariate statistics* (3rd ed.). New York: Harper & Row.

Thomas, J. R., & Nelson, J. K. (2001). *Research methods in physical activity* (4th ed.). Champaign, IL: Human Kinetics.

Thurstone, L. L. (1947). Multiple-factor analysis. Chicago: University of Chicago.

Wakefield, K. L., & Sloan, H. J. (1995). The effects of team loyalty and selected stadium factors on spectator attendance. *Journal of Sport Management, 9,* 153-172.

Whipple, T. W., & Thatch, S. V. (1988). Group tour management: Does good service produce satisfied customers? *Journal of Travel Research, 27*(2), 16-21.

Whitney, J. D. (1988). Winning games versus winning championships: The economics of fan interest and team performance. *Economic Inquiry, 26,* 703-724.

Wright, B. A., Duray, N., & Goodale, T. L. (1992). Assessing perceptions of recreation center service quality: An application of recent advancements in service quality research. *Journal of Parks and Recreation Administration, 10*(3), 33-47.

Yiannakis, A. (1989). Some contributions of sport sociology to the marketing of sport and leisure organizations. *Journal of Sport Management, 3,* 103-115.

Zak, T. H., Huang, C. F., & Siegfried, J. J. (1979). Production efficiency: The case of professional basketball. Journal of Business, 52(3), 19-23.

Zeithaml, V. A., Berry, L. L., & Parasuraman, A. (1988). Communication and control process in the delivery of service quality. Journal of Marketing, 52, 35-48.

Zhang, J. J., & Houston, L. (1995). *Survey report on the Houston Rockets season ticket holders.* Unpublished research report, the Houston Rockets, Houston, TX.

Zhang, J. J., & Smith, D. W. (1997). Impact of broadcasting on the attendance of professional basketball games. *Sport Marketing Quarterly, 6*(1), 23-29.

Zhang, J. J., Lam, E. T. C., & Connaughton, D. P. (2003). General market demand variables associated with professional sport consumption. *International Journal of Sports Marketing & Sponsorship, 5,* 33-55.

Zhang, J. J., Pease, D. G., Hui, S. C., & Michaud, T. J. (1995). Variables affecting the spectator decision to attend NBA games. *Sports Marketing Quarterly, 4*(4), 29-39.

Zhang, J. J., Smith, D. W., Pease, D. G., & Jambor, E. A. (1997). Negative influence of market competitors on the attendance of professional sport games: The case of a minor league hockey team. *Sport Marketing Quarterly, 6*(3), 31-40.

Zhang, J. J., Smith, D. W., Pease, D. G., & Lam, E. T. C. (1998). Dimensions of spectator satisfaction with support programs of professional hockey games. *International Sports Journal, 2*(2), 1-17.

Zhang, J. J., Smith, D. W., Pease, D. G., & Mahar, M. T. (1996). Spectator knowledge of hockey as a significant predictor of game attendance. *Sport Marketing Quarterly, 5*(3), 41-48.

# Editor Bio

**Dr. Brenda G. Pitts** is currently a professor and the Director of Sport Management and the Director of the Sport Business Research Center at Georgia State University in Atlanta, Georgia. She is distinguished as the Dr. Earle F. Zeigler Scholar of 2000, one of the first Research Fellows of the North American Society for Sport Management in 2001, and the 2004 Dr. Garth Paton Distinguished Service Award. Dr. Pitts is author or coauthor of four sport marketing textbooks and numerous publications and presentations, and is published in scholarly journals such as the *Journal of Sport Management*, *Sport Marketing Quarterly*, *Journal of Vacation Marketing*, *International Journal of Sports Marketing and Sponsorship*, and *International Journal of Sport Management*.

# Author Bios

**Daniel P. Connaughton** is an assistant professor at the University of Florida, Gainesville, FL. His research interests center on legal issues and risk management in exercise and sport sciences.

**Dr. Vassilis Dalakas** is an assistant professor of marketing at the Campbell School of Business at Berry College. He earned his Ph.D. in marketing from the University of Oregon in 1999. His research interests include consumer behavior, sponsorship, sports marketing, consumer socialization, and cross-cultural marketing. His research has been published in the *Journal of Business Research*, the *Journal of Consumer Psychology*, the *Journal of Consumer Marketing*, *Sport Marketing Quarterly*, the *Journal of Euro-Marketing*, and several conference proceedings.

**Angela Elizabeth Dunnam** has been published in both fiction and non-fiction, short and novel length. She holds a master's degree from the University of Texas in Advertising and is the Senior Editor for the VIP Guide in Austin, Texas.

**Dr. John A. Fortunato** is an assistant professor in the department of advertising at the University of Texas at Austin. Dr. Fortunato is the author of "The Ultimate Assist: The Relationship and Broadcast Strategies of the NBA and Television Networks. He received his Ph. D. from Rutgers University.

**Dr. Daniel C. Funk** is an Assistant Professor in the Sport Management program at the University of Texas at Austin. Dr. Funk earned a Ph.D. in Sport Management at The Ohio State University with an emphasis in Consumer Behavior. His primary research interests include understanding the psychology behind sport consumption in the sport market place. Dr. Funk has published scholarly work in scientific journals including *Leisure Sciences, Sport Marketing Quarterly, Sport Management Review, Journal of Sport Management, International Journal of Sports Marketing and Sponsorship, and International Journal of Sport Management*. He has worked on various national and international projects examining consumer involvement with professional sport teams and leisure activities.

**Dr. Robin Hardin** is an assistant professor in the Department of Sport & Leisure Studies at the University of Tennessee. His research interests include issues related to collegiate sports information and the role media play in the perception of athletes.

**Dr. Chia-ying (Doris) Lu** is an assistant professor in sport management department at National Taiwan College of Physical Education. After she earned doctoral degree from Flordia State, she went back to Taiwan to work in an academic environment and help prepare individuals to work in the sport industry. Her primary areas of research interest are sport marketing, sport management and consumer behavior.

**Dr. Steven McClung** is assistant professor in the Department of Interactive Media at Florida State University. His research interests include traditional media use of the Internet, collegiate athletics use of the Internet and college radio.

**Dr. Michael Mondello** is an assistant professor in the Department of Sport Management, Recreation Management and Physical Education at Florida State University. His research interests include issues related to sport finance and economics, ethics, and the development of the academic field of sport management.

**Dr. Melissa Johnson Morgan** is a Senior Lecturer in the Marketing and Tourism Department of the University of Southern Queensland's Faculty of Business in Australia. Up until December of 2002 she was an Assistant Professor of Marketing at the A.B. Freeman School of Business at Tulane University in New Orleans, USA. Her research focuses on the experiential consumption of sport and she has developed a unique phenomenon sampling methodology. Her other research interests include extreme sport consumption communities, sport tourism and sport governance effectiveness.

**Dr. Dale G. Pease** is a professor at the University of Houston, Houston, TX. His research interests center on sport fan psychology and informal leadership in sport.

**Dr. Lori Pennington-Gray** is an assistant professor at the University of Florida, Gainesville, FL. Her research interests center on marketing issues in leisure and tourism.

**André Richelieu** is a marketing professor at Université Laval, Québec, Canada. In 2002, he completed his PhD at the joint doctoral program in administration in Montréal. His research interests focus on i) the development of brand equity by professional sports teams and how they leverage their brand; ii) the internationalization of the firm and the institutional levers that firms can use in order to enter foreign markets.

Prior to his academic career, André Richelieu worked in the business industry, spending, among others, over two years in Romania. He has lived in or visited 40 countries.

**Dr. Gregory Rose** is an associate professor of marketing at the Milgard School of Business at the University of Washington - Tacoma. He earned his Ph.D. in marketing from the University of Oregon in 1995. His research interests include consumer socialization, sports marketing, and cross-cultural consumer behavior. He has published articles in the *Journal of Consumer Research, Journal of Consumer Psychology, Journal of Business Research, Journal of Advertising, Journal of the Academy of Marketing Science, Journal of Marketing, Sport Marketing Quarterly*, and other journals and conference proceedings.

**Dr. Christopher L. Saffici** is an assistant professor at East Stroudsburg University, East Stroudsburg, PA. His research interests center on management issues in exercise and sport sciences.

**Dr. Dennis W. Smith** is a professor at the University of Houston, Houston, TX. His research interests center on promotional issues related to health and human performance.

**Dr. Jane Summers** is the Head of the Marketing and Tourism Department in the Faculty of Business at the University of Southern Queensland in Australia. Her teaching and research interests are in the areas of consumer behaviour, e-marketing and sport marketing. Her specific interest in sport marketing has evolved due to the call from both practioners and academics for more research in this area and for a greater understanding particularly of consumer behaviour and attitudes in relation to sport consumption. She is also currently researching the international applicability of some of these consumption related issues.

**Dr. Kenneth A. Wall** is an associate professor at Springfield College, Springfield, MA. His research interests center on comparative issues in physical education and sport.

**Daryl Wirakartakusumah** received his B.S. degree in Computer Science from the University of Indonesia. He then established himself in the sport community by earning his M.S. degree in Sport Administration from the University of Wisconsin-La Crosse. During his collegiate years, he has been directly involved with various interscholastic sport activities, either as an athlete, coach, or administrator. Daryl is currently a Graduate Assistant at the United States Sports Academy where he is expected to obtain his Doctoral Degree in August 2005. Daryl has an ultimate goal to help his country, Indonesia, develop a reputable sport industry. In the meantime, he would like to enhance his knowledge and skills in sport management and establish as much connections as possible before he returns to his home country.

**Dr. James J. Zhang** is an associate professor at the University of Florida, Gainesville, FL. His research interests center on sport consumer behavior studies.